Thus Spake David E.

Mr Hinson, Sir ————
Your family looms large
in my history, but I've
now known you far longer
than my classmate, Jack.
Cogito ergo zoom!
David E Davis

Thus Spake David E.

The collected wit and wisdom
of the most influential
automotive journalist of our time.

David E. Davis, Jr.

Momentum Books, Ltd.
Troy, Michigan

Manufactured in the United States of America

All articles in "The *Car and Driver* Years" are reprinted with the permission of *Car and Driver* Magazine, copyright of Hachette Filipacchi Magazines, Inc.

Car and Driver® is a registered trademark of Hachette Filipacchi Magazines, Inc.

All articles in "The *Automobile Magazine* Years" are reprinted with permission of *Automobile Magazine,* copyright of K-III Magazine Corporation.

Published by Momentum Books, Ltd.
1174 E. Big Beaver Road
Troy, Michigan 48083

Library of Congress Cataloging-in-Publication Data

Davis, David E., 1930–
    Thus spake David E. : the collected wit and wisdom of the most
influential automotive journalist of our time / David E. Davis, Jr.
        p.   cm.
    Includes index.
    Articles collected from Car and driver; Automobile magazine.
    ISBN 1-879094-55-X (alk. paper)
    1. Automobiles--Anecdotes. 2. Automobile industry and trade-
-Anecdotes. 3. Davis, David E., 1930– --Anecdotes. I. Title.
TL8.D38   1999
388.3'42--dc21   98-54772
                                                                       CIP

In the broadest sense, this book is dedicated to the hundreds of thousands of car enthusiasts who've supported me since I joined *Car and Driver* magazine in 1962, and since I launched *Automobile Magazine* in 1986. In a narrower sense, it is dedicated to Elmore Leonard, who helped me make the transition from storyteller to writer when we worked together at the beginning of the Sixties. In the most personal sense it is dedicated to my wife, Jeannie L. K. Davis—the woman who changed my life—the one who all too frequently has to stop what she's doing and listen to whatever I've written that day, because Elmore Leonard taught me to test my work by reading it aloud.

Cogito ergo zoom

Contents

The *Car and Driver* Years

The *Automobile Magazine* Years

Foreword

This book is a friendship, in print, with David E. Davis, Jr. Of course, if you're a reader of *Automobile Magazine* or were a reader of *Car and Driver* in its salad days (1962-1967) or prime rib years (1976-1985), you're already friends with David E. In all likelihood I mean that literally. The man's range of acquaintance is immense. He seems to know everyone involved with motor vehicles. And everyone is. The most important thing in this century is the car. If you think otherwise, try going out on the back roads at midnight and really putting the boot to a microchip, or try impressing your date with penicillin, or getting the kids to Disney World by means of an atomic bomb (although it depends on the kids). Thus, there are 5.7 billion people in the automotive world, whether they know it or not. David E. will meet us all in the Oak Bar at the Plaza Hotel, 59th and 5th, Thursday—say 6-ish?

No. There are certain practical difficulties with having 5.7 billion pals in the flesh. Plus David is only human and has occasional fallings-out. I know for a fact that, at the moment, he'd like to send Al Gore around Talladega at 150 mph sans Chevrolet. And he still hasn't forgiven Jimmy Carter for the Billy Carter IQ speed limit or for responding to OPEC by swatting it with Rosalyn's purse. So there's the offhand chance that you, the reader, do not physically bend an elbow with David E. Davis or swap MacPherson-strut anecdotes in real time. Alas. But, herewith, the next best thing.

This is not a collection of what David E. has written about cars. That would make a book which, placed on Madeleine Albright's chair, would let her eat dinner with the grown-ups in NATO. A few feature articles are included, but most of what you hold is culled from monthly editorial columns. And, having said that, I wince. Editors' columns in non-Davis car magazines tend to the shameless product puff ("Dodge Aspen—Quattroporte for the Masses?") or ramblings about how it's more fun to be employed at a car magazine than to be in a dentist's office reading one or—most usually—twaddle to create gray space. That way the ad salesman can promise every brand of chrome brightener or vinyl spray a "front-of-the-book position opposite editorial." Such is not the David E. Davis, Jr. method.

"People invite me into their homes once a month," says David E. "And I'd better be a good guest." Since he can't bring flowers (which would get squashed in the mail and make a mess at the newsstand) he brings great conversation—about cars, naturally, but also about cabbages and kings and places where they cook the sauerbraten perfectly and treated Juan Manuel Fangio like a prince. The wonderful, the awful, the sad, and the hilarious are mixed, as they should be in well-seasoned chat. The mystery is how David keeps this from being one-sided. You can't talk back to a magazine. Well, you can, but the stewardess will stop serving drinks.

Part of the secret is good writing. You'd have David E. over to dinner a dozen times a year just to hear him call the *Wall Street Journal*'s automotive reporter "your winsome, high-school-graduate correspondent" or describe someone's "noisy after-shave lotion," or opine that a certain contributor to the *Automobile Magazine* letters column "demonstrates sensitivity worthy of a career in TV journalism." Then there's David on what a wild duck designed to withstand a 30-mile-per-hour barrier impact would look like, and David on the subject of the American cultural elite's long-standing "discrimination against winners." But you can read a lot of good writers without feeling that you know them, or want to. In fact, there are a number of good writers—Hemingway, Fitzgerald, and Faulkner come to mind—that you thank heaven they're dead so there's no chance they'll want to hang out. Nor is David's mastery of the direct, personal, spoken-English tone the reason for his success. Kerouac had that and we come away from *On the Road* driven crazy by the desire to find a beatnik and stuff a used oil filter in his pie hole.

David E.'s ability to give us a conversation without monopolizing same is based upon inclusiveness. David knows that the automobile is a compendious topic; the motor vehicle embraces the modern universe, and the passion for cars is a promiscuous love. Car magazines are not "buff books" or "fanzines" any more than the Kama Sutra is. In the automotive world there is no division between audience and star, spectator and player, amateur and professional. Every free and able-bodied person of voting age in America (except for a few individuals convicted of motor vehicle felonies or being intellectuals in New York) is a licensed pro behind the wheel.

You don't have to know much about cars to read David E. and the magazines he has put together. In fact, you don't even have to know very much about cars to write for those magazines. I'm proof of that. I've been writing for David for more than twenty years, as a kind of ambassador of car-love to those readers who know practically as little about cars as I do. I mean, I'm sure overhead valves are a very good thing and much more comfortable than up-the-nose valves would be.

Or maybe you think valves—and pistons and rods and crankshafts—should all get stuffed. Maybe you hate cars. You can still enjoy David E. Davis, even though you're completely wrong. You just think you hate cars. But you haven't thought hard enough. Our nation's vice-president probably thinks he hates cars—the pollution, the urban sprawl, the honking while he's trying to sleep through some foreign dignitary's funeral. But the vice-president travels everywhere in a motorcade of armored Suburbans. Let him carry all those Kevlar body panels and bulletproof windows around on his back for an afternoon and let's see what he thinks.

Compared to the invention of the automobile the domestication of the horse was a mere bringing home a pet gerbil for the kids. The horse has not, as the car has, stimulated mankind intellectually, economically, or even romantically. The horse is a fine romantic symbol, which is why a Ferrari has one on the hood. But, as for any actual romance in a horse-drawn vehicle, this is severely curtailed by the close-up view of horse butt from the buggy seat. Economically, vast wealth has been created by cars, and remarkable inventions have been made in order to produce better cars. The horse and how it's produced remain much as they have been these 3000 years. As for intellect, let me only mention that the stirrup wasn't thought of until 500 AD. If cars led to that kind of brain work, we'd be pedal-less and dragging our feet on the pavement until the year 3400. Although it could be argued that the car has led to too much thinking. What if the eggheads, three millennia ago, had applied to the horse the bright ideas that they want to apply to the automobile today: low emissions, safe speeds, total occupant protection, alternative energy source. The result would be a starved turtle on its way to the electric chair.

Imagine a world without automobiles. Thanks in large part to David E. Davis, I can't. But I visited the old Soviet Union during the Brezhnev era. Nice place. And I don't want to hear evil spoken of fossil fuels. I've been in a rickshaw jam in Bangladesh when the temperature was 100 degrees. Me for the warm, reassuring scent of greenhouse gassing that emanates from "Cogito Ergo Zoom." There are worse things you can do with a nation than pave it, as the Serbs are proving in Kosovo.

"We drive our cars because they make us free," says David E. Davis. "With cars we need not wait in airline terminals, or travel only where the railway tracks go. Governments detest our cars: They give us too much freedom. How do you control people who can climb into a car at any hour of the day or night and drive to who knows where?"

David E. has been able to turn his editorials into a gabfest among friends because we're all in that car going who-knows-where together. With David in the driver's seat. He is a car man born and raised. He owes his livelihood to cars. He owes his physiognomy to a car wreck. He owes his family's escape from the hills of Kentucky to the car industry in Detroit. And David knows what every sixteen-year-old knows, but what no elected official, self-appointed quality-of-life advocate, or double-domed social visionary seems to—that cars confer upon us the ultimate and most important of human freedoms. We can leave.

If it weren't for cars, we'd all be sitting in a ditch somewhere. But at least David E. would be sitting with us, probably talking about an idea for a new magazine, a revolutionary magazine, a magazine "That's not just about feet." And that, too, would be a great conversation.

P.J. O'Rourke
March Hare Farm
New Hampshire
May 1999

Introduction

I n which the author is interviewed by someone who's known him all his life: Himself.

Interviewer: *Who are you, anyway?*
DED, Jr.: I am the editor and founder of *Automobile Magazine;* the former editor and publisher of *Car and Driver.* I write about automobiles and the automotive experience.

Interviewer: *Why have you done this book?*
DED, Jr.: I wanted to see my best stuff from *Car and Driver* and my best stuff from *Automobile Magazine* all together in one handy volume. I did it for love. For art. For literature. For posterity. And because if I make enough money on it I can buy the Lancia Aurelia coupe of my dreams.

Interviewer: *Does this make you an automotive journalist?*
DED, Jr.: Probably not. "Journalist" implies some lust for objectivity, some preoccupation with mayhem and malfeasance. I'm just a car enthusiast, a storyteller. I'm obsessed with cars and magazines, and I get to obsess about cars in my magazine every month. It's a nice arrangement.

Interviewer: *You're a grown man. How can you spend all your time mooning about cars?*
DED, Jr.: Back off, pal. I only spend most of my time mooning about cars. It's worth remembering that it was the automobile, more than the jet plane or the atomic bomb, that shaped this century. The automobile is one of this era's great art forms, and it probably represents better and more interesting industrial design than average consumers can find anywhere else in their lives.

I also spend time mooning about double-barreled shotguns, single-shot rifles, farm tractors, old houses, old movies, old records, and old friends, male and female.

Interviewer: *You like women?*

DED, Jr.: Are you kidding? I love women! Women and automobiles were my drugs of choice, the only stimulants I ever needed. Women have played an altogether disproportionate role in the success I've enjoyed. They've been my mentors, my colleagues, my sounding boards, my drinking pals, and my lovers. My mother, her mother, and my mother's remarkable sisters plied me with books and shared with me their encyclopedic store of information about everything from human nature to herbal medicine. Elaine Bond, at *Road & Track*, who taught me how to run a magazine.

Interviewer: *Do women like you?*

DED, Jr.: I think so. I certainly hope so. There are exceptions, of course. My first wife will go to her grave believing that I am a perpetual adolescent, a boy/man propelled through life by daydreams and fantasies. She also thought I was sexually deviant. From her standpoint, she was probably right on all counts.

Interviewer: *Do you have erotic fantasies?*

DED, Jr.: No. I have erotic memories. When I fantasize, it generally involves cars. For example, there's a section of road near my late mother's home in Ohio—a series of turns down into a shallow ravine, across a bridge, then winding uphill to a junction with another road. For more than twenty years, every time I approached that stretch I imagined myself driving a Maserati 300S sports-racing car.

When I can't sleep at three in the morning, I close my eyes and run movies on the insides of my eyelids, movies of me driving various cars. Lately, I imagine myself driving my own ex-Fangio 1939 Chevy Turismo de Carretera racing car through the Andes on a narrow twisty road at warp speed. The Juan Manuel Fangio Museum in Argentina gave me the old racer when Fangio died.

Interviewer: *Okay, we're back to automobiles. Do you have a favorite car?*

DED, Jr.: Actually I have about thirty, but perhaps I can narrow it down. I was originally seduced by the Frank Kurtis Offenhauser-powered midget racing cars of the late Forties. Then, in 1950, I saw my first Jaguar XK120 roadster. That Jag and the little Kurtis-Offies will always be with me. Stealing a line from George Harrison, the BMW 2002 looms large in my legend. The king of all cars is the Chevrolet (or GMC) Suburban. I just got my sixth one, a diesel-powered 4x4. I am mad about Subarus, especially the current Forester model. I love all V-12 Ferraris, but I particularly admire the 250GT Tour de France from the Fifties and the Short Wheelbase Berlinetta (SWB) of the early Sixties. The Porsche 911 continues to be a paragon of usefulness combined with heart-stopping performance. I prize usefulness in automobiles.

Interviewer: *Where do you come from?*

DED, Jr.: I was born in a house without running water or electricity near Burnside, Kentucky. I come from the Celtic fringes of the Anglo-Saxon world. My people were Welsh and Scots-Irish immigrants who settled in the American south. Farmers, teachers, preachers, storekeepers, a writer or two; soldiers when they had to be. They were part of a great storytelling tradition—they didn't talk in one-liners. They were people who knew the constellations, who could chat knowledgeably about the Bible as literature. People who got their drinking water from springs and their light from kerosene lamps. They traveled on muleback and by horse-drawn wagon. I came by car.

Interviewer: *You look kind of strange. You seem to have one bedroom eye and one bathroom eye. Is that hereditary?*

DED, Jr.: The right side of my face is all original equipment. The left side is the result of a lot of structural and cosmetic reconstruction. I wrecked a racing car in 1955 and lost the left side of my face. As a result, my left eye has always looked sort of surprised. Also, for the same reason, I'm unable to show my teeth when I smile—there's just this black hole where my radiant smile should be—so I tend to look like a startled Kris Kringle who's just run up several flights of stairs. My doctors told me that I should be grateful for the Korean War, during which a number of significant advances were made in the field of reconstructive surgery. I may be the only man of my age in the United States or the two Koreas who feels that way.

My mother was worried about her mother's reaction to the news that I'd lost what was actually a pretty nice face. She waited a long time to write the letter. When she finally delivered the bad news, my grandmother didn't seem too concerned. In her answering letter, she went on about the weather and the agricultural prospects for Pulaski County, Kentucky, and only as a sort of afterthought did she write: "Your mention of David's face puts me in mind of one of the Foster boys, who was in a hardware store when a keg of black powder blew up. His face was always sort of blue after that."

My face is one of God's jokes.

Interviewer: *Do you believe in God?*

DED, Jr.: Of course I believe in God. God is the CEO/COO of the entire universe. He's a little old, and His inability or unwillingness to del-egate authority has resulted in some dreadful screwups, but it's His bat and ball and we play by His rules.

Interviewer: *Are you suggesting that He doesn't do a very good job?*

DED, Jr.: Well, He has given us war, famine, disease, racial and religious intolerance, and women who wear those marsupial zipper bags across their abdomens when they go on vacation. On the other hand, the world is a pretty nice place, and He gives us a hero every once in a while, so that we can know how we'd behave if we had any character.

Interviewer: *Do you have any heroes?*

DED, Jr.: Hundreds! Juan Manuel Fangio, Dan Gurney, Phil Hill, Stirling Moss, Carroll Shelby, Jackie Stewart, Masten Gregory, René Dreyfus, Luigi Chinetti, Froilan Gonzalez, Tazio Nuvolari....

Interviewer (interrupting): *Your heroes have always been racing drivers?*

DED, Jr.: No. I should also mention Django Reinhardt, Stéphane Grappelli, Antonio Vivaldi, Bix Beiderbecke, Ray Charles, Bunny Berrigan, Duke Ellington, Alicia de la Roccha, Fats Waller, Lee Wiley, and Gioacchino Rossini. I'd include Jess Stacy for his piano solo in the middle of Benny Goodman's rendition of "Sing Sing Sing" at Carnegie Hall in 1938. And I dream of being able to stand up in a crowded, smoky club and play Coleman Hawkins's version of "Body and Soul" on the tenor. I'd also like to play the Roy Eldridge trumpet passage that starts Gene Krupa's "After You've Gone."

Interviewer: *So it's racing drivers and musicians?*

DED, Jr.: Not exactly. I have to list my mother's ancestors, who walked from North Carolina to Kentucky to claim land grants they'd received in lieu of back pay for their service in the Revolutionary War. There's also Abraham Lincoln, Ronald Reagan, Margaret Thatcher, William Tecumseh Sherman, Teddy Roosevelt, Sam Houston, the Duke of Wel-lington, each of the Welsh soldiers who fought in the Battle of Rorke's Drift, and my former boss, Tom Adams, who is a great war hero, a great athlete, and a great pal. That's a smattering.

Interviewer: *You read a lot?*

DED, Jr.: I try to read a book a week—mainly biographies, military his-tory, mysteries, and, of course, tons of automotive stuff. One of several reasons that my father was disappointed in me had to do with my face being stuck in books when he thought I should be out boxing, or play-ing baseball.

Interviewer: *Do you have any writer heroes?*

DED, Jr.: You bet! Whoever it was who wrote *Ecclesiastes*, for a start. My friends P.J. O'Rourke and Brock Yates. Elmore Leonard, who—when we worked together as advertising copywriters—helped me turn my inherited knack for storytelling into a useful writing skill. Bruce McCall, who I induced to come to the United States, and whose writings are a constant pleasure to me. Plus Jim Harrison, David Halberstam, John Weitz, Mari Sandoz, Shelby Foote, A.J. Liebling, Janet Flanner, Joseph Mitchell, James Thurber, Tom Wolfe, Patrick O'Brian, and especially Thorne Smith.

Interviewer: *Thorne Smith?*

DED, Jr.: Yes. I read every one of Thorne Smith's books when I was a kid. They all involved gorgeous girls dashing down hotel corridors in their underwear, pursued by men in white tie and tails carrying pitchers of martinis. His novels provided me with a road map for my life, not unlike the way in which some guys were deeply influenced by the Boy Scout Manual.

Interviewer: *You wanted to be the guy in the tail coat?*

DED, Jr.: No, stupid, I wanted to be the girl. I bought the *New Yorker* and *Esquire* with money from my paper route, so that I might become more sophisticated. I even tried to affect a sort of sophisticated Jewish accent. When I was kicked out of Olivet College at Christmas, 1949, I went to work as a sales trainee with a firm that sold mail-order custom-tailored men's clothing. The senior salesmen there were the most sophisticated men I'd ever been around. They ordered me my first two bespoke suits and a gorgeous, navy blue Chesterfield topcoat. They taught me how to act like an adult, how to wear a hat, how to behave in bars, how to qualify a prospect, how to close a deal. But the most important thing they taught me was "Dress British, think Yiddish." I owe them a lot. I wish they were still around to read this book. Maybe they'd feel that their efforts on my behalf weren't wasted.

The Car and Driver *Years*

A survivor of the imported-car revolution recalls what it was like to be a wild-eyed enthusiast the year *Car and Driver* was born.

◦◦◦

Nineteen fifty-five was the year of the new small-block Chevy, and we all wondered what might happen if they ever got around to mating that wonderful little V-8 to a four-speed gearbox and installing it in the silly Corvette they were building. It was the year when Jaguar replaced the XK120 with the XK140. We hated the XK140 in direct ratio to our love for the XK120. It was garish, tasteless, and chrome-laden. Whatever improvements they might have made in its drivability were simply not worth the aesthetic cost. The long-awaited Mercedes-Benz 190SL arrived at last, and landed with a dull thud. The mindbending Mercedes 300SL gull-wing coupe could be bought for less than $7500 in 1955, and it had led us to believe that the 190SL would be the same wonderful thing, only cheaper, and with a top that went down. How wrong we were. Later in the year the new MGA came out, and I almost traded my TF 1500 for one, but was put off by the waiting time. Had I done so, I wouldn't have altered my physiognomy as I did the day before Halloween.

It's interesting to me that *Car and Driver* was launched that year—as *Sports Cars Illustrated*—because it's the year I remember most vividly from the entire decade of the Fifties.

The first Mrs. Davis and I arrived in California by the Fourth of July. I was stunned by the palm trees and the gas stations with the open-air service bays. My car was an MG TF 1500 with an inch-and-three-quarter straight pipe (copper). We'd driven all the way out with the top down and the side curtains in, and we were seriously tanned. I was under the impression I'd died and gone to heaven. I went to a California Sports Car Club race at Santa Barbara. The big time! I went to a ghastly affair at Torrey Pines, where a spectator scragged himself charging around the course the night before the race, and a lady competitor was killed in the (you won't believe this) Powder Puff Derby. The main event at Torrey was won by Carroll Shelby in a 4.5-liter Ferrari. Legend! Not only that,

John von Neumann (more legend!) handed his Ferrari Monza over to Phil Hill (PHIL HILL, folks), who finished second. We went to the Lighthouse in Hermosa Beach, where we ate Chinese food, listened to jazz, and talked about sports cars to Bud Shank, Bob Cooper (June Christy's husband, ferchrissake), Frank Rossellino, and Stan Levey (the very same Lighthouse All-Stars whose every record I had). My wife worked second-shift at American Airlines reservations on Pershing Square in downtown Los Angeles and I got to roar through the streets of L.A. at one in the morning night after night, tearing down to pick her up when she got out of work. It was the Promised Land. I met a guy named Gordon Jennings at Newcastle Imported Cars in Hermosa Beach and he showed me their MG TC Special, a low, rakish, cycle-fendered race car with a 1466cc Laystall-Lucas engine. Next he showed me a DOHC cylinder head, built in some local machine shop, that they were about to install on this mean blue knee-high racer. So much wonderfulness was hard to index in my scrambled brain. Every day, it seemed, I saw some car or driver or mechanical component that I'd only read about back home.

On October 30, I ran my MG in a race at Sacramento, California. I'd decided to run at the last minute, and had burned a lot of midnight oil getting the race car ready. One night it fell off the jacks while I was relining the brakes, and en route to the race our town car overheated on the infamous Grapevine, north of L.A. Obviously, something was telling me not to go. During practice, Ken Miles helped me correct some minor handling problems and gave me invaluable tips on the fastest way around the old fairgrounds. Ken Miles, and me a total stranger. In the fourth lap of the first race I was leading all the MGs by a substantial margin, thanks to Miles' advice and a certain banzai motivation all my own, when I hit the hay bales in the first turn and rolled, catching my head between the back of the seat and the pavement—roll bars would not become mandatory until 1956. The car slid across the track upside down, then hit the bales on the other side and flipped onto its wheels. I hadn't lost consciousness, and I pulled off my gloves and reached up toward my visor, finding it torn and hanging on my right shoulder. I then put my hands over my face and felt that my nose was gone and everything seemed to be a sticky mess. As it turned out, I'd also lost both eyelids on the left side, knocked out all but a dozen teeth, suffered over a hundred compound fractures on my upper and lower jaws, and wedged the roof of my mouth into my throat. The car had only sustained about 250 bucks' worth of damage, but the fun was over for a while.

Recuperating at home in Manhattan Beach, I couldn't go out, because people kept running away, or calling the cops, whenever they saw me coming down the street. After I caused a traffic accident one day at the corner of Rosecrans and Highland, I decided simply to stay in the apartment and listen to the radio until I looked better. The grimness of that prospect was saved by one person, beyond my wife and my bird dog. Gordon Jennings, the guy I'd met at Newcastle Imported Cars, lived three doors down the street from our new apartment. He came to see me regularly, and kept me supplied with car magazines, motorcycle magazines, and hope. We talked about cars and bikes for months. I read his entire collection of automotive books, and discussed them with him avidly. During that time I began to educate myself about cars, drivers, and the history of both. Even though I'd probably never drive a race car again, I still wanted to be involved with the sport and the cars. I decided to write about them, and two years later, when I was working at *Road & Track,* I convinced John R. Bond that he ought to hire Gordon Jennings as his technical assistant. And eight years after that, when I became publisher of *Cycle* magazine—in addition to being editor and publisher of *Car and Driver*—I hired Gordon to be its new editor. Eventually, he followed me as editor of this magazine, but now he's back in California writing about motorcycles and abrading the bad guys. Kismet.

I Drove a Ferrari 275/LM
from Philadelphia to New York
and Found Truth (Graunch!)

W|ell, there it is. Boy, it's tiny! Boy, it's mean-looking! Do you suppose they really mean for me to drive that mother back to New York? They said they did, so I guess it's on the level. A Ferrari 275/LM is pretty heady stuff for a simple kid from the Midwest.

"I'm sure glad we got a break in the weather, can you imagine driving that little icebox all the way from Philadelphia to New York if the temperature was still down in the teens? I shudder to think of it. I guess Al Garthwaite and Coco Chinetti like to froze to death when they brought it over here—they were absolutely blue when they climbed out!

"Where did Al go, anyway? I'd kinda like to get going. I hope he's not too nervous about letting me drive the thing, although I wouldn't really blame him too much if he was—you know, some nut comes wandering in to drive your 20,000-dollar race car back to New York, and you're entitled to a few niggling doubts, I guess.

"Hey Steve, did you see that lady? She's on the other side of the pillar—you can see her if you edge over just about two feet. Oops, I guess that's Mrs. Garthwaite. Well if he didn't think we were nuts before, he will now.

"All set? I guess I'm ready if you are." Wrestle that flimsy little door open... Wrestle your non-flimsy 210-pound frame into the seat. Hell, except for that complicated-looking five-speed shift gate, it's just like a Ferrari street machine. "Turn the key and push in, right?"

Clank-a-clank-a-clank-a... Nothing, give it some throttle. Clank-a-clank-a-clank-a-clank-a-WHOOOOM! IT DOESN'T HAVE STREET MUFFLERS! How in hell am I supposed to drive through Philadelphia, across the cop-laden Jersey Turnpike, and all over New York City in THIS? Ain't that some nice noise though!

Okay, find first—all the way to the left and back. Graunch. Nice work, idiot, any minute now he's going to suggest that maybe he should drive after all. Now let the clutch out a bit. Nothing. Let it out a bit more. Nice work, idiot, you killed the engine. Okay, cool it. It's only a Ferrari, right? It's not going to bite you, right? Back to neutral. Turn the key and push. WHOOOM! First gear, slip the clutch in. Damn, that throttle has a lot of travel, hey, it's moving! Here we go, 3000 in first, clutch, across the gate and up to second, graunch, graunch, shift faster, idiot—now that wasn't too bad. Son of a gun, I think you just might be able to drive this kid after all. Even Garthwaite looks a little less concerned.

Careful, don't lose Steve and Mrs. Garthwaite in the traffic. After all, they're only driving a puny 2+2 Ferrari—ah, there they are. Okay, on to the expressway, second, third, fourth, cruise in fourth for a while, now fifth. How about that! I'm in fifth and I'm only turning 2100 and it feels like a Cadillac. Amazing. I wonder if I look like I own it? Boy, would I like to see somebody I know right now. I was meant for this.

It's really remarkable how comfortable it is. And the ride! It rides better than the 2+2! If it wasn't for all the exhaust noise and the banging and crashing in the suspension, it could be a touring car. Poor old Al doesn't look too comfortable though—I wonder if he could get electrocuted with his knees against that fuse panel that way. I guess not, it would have happened by now, if it was going to happen at all.

Fantastic visibility. That nose is so short, and it drops off so sharply that you can see everything—even the view out the back is pretty good. How about this! Me, the kid that rode the bus all the way across Detroit to watch Sam Hanks drive midgets, yowling along in a Ferrari 275/LM. This is the life!

It's Thrill Time! There's no traffic, and this looks like a poor place to hide a radar trap, so down to fourth, then down to third, a little graunch, but not too bad. Now stand on it. HOO BOY! 4000, 5000, 6000, shift fast, no graunch, 6000 in fourth, shift again, no graunch, 5000 in fifth, man, are those ratios ever close. I must be doing a hundred-thirty. Oops, traffic, on the brakes, boy, do those trucks get big fast. This thing really has a bunch of pedal pressure.

There, seventy again, no cops. You idiot, Davis, you're lucky you're not in jail.

Toll booth. Incredulous toll-taker peers down from his perch and wonders what manner of beast is this. Al squirms around and slides the plastic window back and reaches up with the money. There's one toll-taker who'll have a story for the wife and kiddies tonight. First gear. Some throttle. Lurch forward with a real, honest-to-goodness "Sounds of Sebring" exhaust noise. "Take that, toll-taker!"

Howl along at seventy and enjoy the sensations. The reclining seat position is really very nice. Once you learn to throw the shift lever fast enough, it's very nice too, with minimum graunching. The pedals are offset rather sharply toward the center of the car, which takes some getting used to, but you get used to it. The pedal travel is almost directly horizontal, so that you have to sort of point your toe like a ballet dancer to get the full travel, then you catch the heel of your loafer on the floor when you let the clutch out, and that doesn't make for the world's smoothest shifts.

The steering is super-accurate and right-now quick. The brakes require all the strength you can muster, but they stop the thing like it ran into something. There's a dead-pedal to the left of the clutch that would make a fine footrest in a race, but tends to be where the passenger's feet are, when you have a passenger. The ride is the greatest thing of all. It rides like an American car. Really! There's some harshness, and there's quite a lot of panel noise that seems related to the movements of the suspension, but the ride is dead smooth.

"What the hell does Steve want? Come on, come on, what is it with the face-making and the obscure hand-signals?" Oh, he wants to pull in at the next Howard Johnson's—I don't know what for, I'm happy as a clam and we have lots of gas.

"A change of co-drivers? Al goes with you and I get Mrs. Garthwaite? Why Steve, how thoughtful of you—you keep this up and I'll have to give you a raise. Don't worry, Al, I won't kill her, and I won't do anything dumb to the Ferrari." I don't think he believes me. "How do you get in? Easy, Ann, just dive in head first, like you were going to go clear across to the other side—now drop your, uh, sit down and swing your feet in, heels together, all at the same time. No that's not the clutch pedal, you can rest your feet on it if you want to. Oh. Better keep your knees off of that fuse panel—it probably won't electrocute you, but it could snag your hose."

Now the pressure's really on—it was bad enough with Al in the bloody car, but he's a man and he's naturally more tolerant of your ham-fisted gaffes with the gearbox—this is a very handsome lady, with breeding, and she isn't going to understand at all if the transmission falls out in the middle of the Jersey Turnpike.

Over and back to first—try to look like an expert—gently, gently, with the clutch and the throttle. Beautiful, here we go. Second, third, ease out onto the Turnpike, give it a blast in third, just for fun. Pretty good idea, Davis, the lady thinks it's fun. SHE thinks it's fun, she should know what YOU think.

"Yeah, I guess it is kind of a funny position to sit in, but after you get used to it, you'll find that it's very pleasant—like, uh, hanging, ha ha, unpleasant at first, but then you become accustomed to it. Better keep our knees away from the fuse panel, Ann. Go fast again? We'd better not. I don't think your husband would be exactly enthralled if we disappeared down the road in a great cloud of smoke and noise, and besides, this is New Jersey, and the police have virtually no sense of humor at all. Now if we were in Italy..."

Watch it Davis, keep this up and you'll be quoting the poets and talking about truth and death and meaningful relationships. "Boy, it's hot in here, I'm glad we tore the masking tape off all the fresh air holes— you'd be roasting in that suit, otherwise." God, I hope she doesn't mind all that crud that's blowing in through those cotton-picking vents—she's going to be covered.

The most interesting thing about racing cars today is that the all-out racers—like the Ferrari—are infinitely more civilized than the so-called production cars that are being raced in the United States. Price is obviously the biggest part of that difference, but purpose has something to do with it too. The production sports car is designed to be all things to all men. It has to be so multi-purpose that anybody—regardless of his transportation needs—can rationalize and justify the purchase of one. It winds up being a little bit of everything, but not enough of anything. To be raced, it has to be turned into a NASCAR stocker. The Ferrari may not be much of a station wagon or an economy car, but it goes faster, in greater comfort relative to its peers, than anything else in the world. It's a case of the designer making up his mind about the one thing that his machine must do, then setting out to do it without compromises of any kind. The twenty-grand it costs doesn't hurt either.

Leave the Turnpike. Go down through the gears. You have to take them in order because the lock-out on the gate is progressive—second can't be engaged without going through third, et cetera. Another toll guy—this one's a lady—she thinks the Ferrari is some kind of a practical joke and seems reluctant to take the money, lest she fall for whatever gag is being perpetrated.

This is the last chance for any fun before the tunnel and New York City traffic. Mash the throttle in first! Screech away from the other traffic, not to mention reality. 6000 in first, hit second, no graunch, just like you'd been doing it all your life, hit a puddle just as the clutch bites and the exhaust note does its ear-splitting impersonation of a salvo from an automatic 3-inch battery. The tail comes out, stays out, and you fly through a long, sweeping right-hander that feeds you up onto another super-highway. The V-12 winds out just before the corner starts to open.

Slam the lever from second straight back to third, mash it again, another jarring salvo from the four exhaust pipes and then it's time to shut off for the upcoming merge.

"Hey, how about THAT, Ann! Did you feel the way this thing bit into the pavement coming around that corner? Son of a Gun! It felt like it might oversteer, but it's actually somewhere between neutral and a little under! Wasn't that great! Ann? Ann, there's no need to apologize. No, I didn't mind that you grabbed my arm, hell, I didn't even know it! Oh come on, don't be silly, lots of people get shook up the first time they have an experience like that. No, it's my fault, I shouldn't have subjected you to that without warning you—but you did say you wanted to go fast." Nice work, idiot, you're lucky she didn't faint or something, imagine yourself trying to explain THAT to old Al ("Uh, listen, Al, it's about your wife, uh, what happened was I was going around this corner, and she fainted—Like, uh, passed out, you know?")

Dive into the Lincoln Tunnel, winding in first. Then lift your foot and let the over-run scream a jillion-decibel scream at all those poor guys that are just driving along minding their own business. With any luck at all the noise will split that tiled tunnel wide open and the old Hudson River will come rushing in and you won't ever have to give the Ferrari back, or return to the office.

Pull up in front of the Casa Rex on West Fiftieth Street, blip the throttle and clear the engine with a great whooping $20,000 burst of noise. Bring mobs of school kids and housewives and bartenders and cops out to see what all the commotion is. Then go inside and have a beer and some pasta and try to look like nothing had happened. But do it in such a way that everybody in the place will recognize you as the adventurous young multi-millionaire who drove up in that wild looking blue Ferrari 275/LM with that glamorous lady.

You've made it. You are a composite of all the heroes since Beowulf. You drove all the way from Philadelphia to New York in a real, honest-to-goodness Ferrari 275/LM. Son of a Gun!

Mercedes W196
A Dream, Made from Equal Parts
of Fear and Joy

❧

"I must have gone to sleep the minute the plane left Copenhagen." It's probably just as well that stewardess is going on to Lisbon, baby, you blew it. Sprawled in the damn seat with your mouth open, wheezing away like an unwell steam calliope, some lady's man! Ah well, her warm smile was simply good SAS manners and Stockholm tradition anyway, so forget it.

Stuttgart is sure nice from the air. It's so green and the roofs are so red that it all looks kinda phony. There's the autobahn, how about that, it looks just like an autobahn. Land. Or crash gently, depending on your viewpoint. Sail past herds of sheep grazing by the runway.

Hey, lovely, there's Artur Keser at the foot of the ramp, that's great, Daimler-Benz didn't forget me. Exchange greetings, shake hands, lie about amorous activities in Sweden, jam into keen little Mercedes bus that goes from plane to airport, meet newest man in Daimler-Benz PR Department. Herr Strassl, handsome young guy, speaks English like an American.

Get instructions about schedule from Artur. "Uh-huh, uh-huh, Strassl takes me to hotel, shows me where to park 220-SE, uh-huh, meet Strassl at press department at 8:30 in the morning, uh-huh, interview with Uhlenhaut, uh-huh, meet you in Mannheim at truck plant after I drive W196 Grand Prix car at test track, uh-huh... wait a minute, AFTER I DO WHAT? You're putting me on. You mean to tell me that Uhlenhaut will LET ME DRIVE THE W196?"

Never mind Davis, it'll rain or something. Something'll happen. It looks like rain. You won't get to drive it. Forget it.

Next day, 8:30 AM, coffee in the press department at Untertürkheim. 9:15, walk over to Dr. Uhlenhaut's office. It's pouring rain, you'll never get to drive the thing in this kind of weather—they're not crazy. Uhlenhaut cordial, full of information, opinions, charm, ideas, authority. Sitting and talking in these surroundings, you expect him to be interrupted by a phone call from Rudi Caracciola, or to have a development engineer come in and ask him some question about a small problem on the new car for the 1939 formula. Although nothing terribly important gets discussed, you feel like you're sitting where it's happening, man, like this is where they keep all the truth.

Didn't they say I'd drive the car at ten o'clock? Hell, it's ten-fifteen and still raining, so I guess we can forget it. Guess again, Uhlenhaut looks out the window, utters a very un-German "Crikey, look at that rain," says he'll meet us at the track, disappears. We motor over in a metallic-blue Mercedes 600 with blue velour interior that is designed to be Juan Fangio's personal car. Nice twist—riding to the track in Fangio's next car to drive one of his most famous old ones.

Go to the track and find four or five mechanics huddled under a big striped umbrella next to what looks like a pile of canvas with knock-off wire wheels. The W196, one of history's most significant racing automobiles, is apparently no happier about this little adventure than the mechanics, who seem quite confident that the Ami with the bushy moustache has come to destroy their pride and joy, this beautiful eight-cylinder, 2.5-liter Grand Prix car, retired in 1955 at the peak of its prowess with no dangerous competition in sight.

It's the car that Karl Ludvigsen drove and described in the December '61 issue of Car and Driver. Dry weight is around 1480 lbs and the engine produced something like 290 bhp at 8500 rpm in racing tune. The chassis is a very stiff—for its time—space frame that weighs 79 lbs. The engine, a straight eight, is actually two four-cylinder blocks tied together with the drive taken off the middle via a short drive shaft to the five-speed transmission. Its most outstanding feature is its nearly unbreakable desmodromic valve gear. Suspension is traditional Mercedes low-pivot swing axles at the rear and independent front.

Funny. The W196 has a number of classic racing car features like big, finned drum brakes, bolt-upright driving position, front engine, and skinny little tires on narrow-rim wire wheels, but it still looks tough and up-to-date. Let's face it, kids, compared to an Indy roadster, it's still something out of science fiction—maybe that's why it doesn't look very old or out-classed.

The canvas cover is off. God. Ten years ago I'd have given an arm to hear this thing run, and here I am about to drive it. With none other than Rudolph Uhlenhaut himself explaining the controls to me. We take his 200-SE sedan around once or twice and he shows me all the bumps and puddles and slippery spots and we return to the mechanics, waiting around under their drooping umbrella.

Suit jacket off, white Mercedes coveralls on, rain jacket pulled over the rest, biggest available helmet chosen from six possible candidates, rain-shield rather than goggles. Too-small helmet pulled on with some effort, aided by Herr Bunz, the last of the technicians from the great Mercedes racing organization. Herr Bunz may not know it, apprehensive though he may be, but he's about to have a couple of bad days.

He removes the steering wheel. The seat is covered with some sturdy plaid material, which is in turn protected by a large wiping cloth. It's like being a kid and opening the back door only to find that your mother has just scrubbed the floor, and—short of flying—there's absolutely no way to get in without messing it up. Boy, is that a big cockpit! Compared to a contemporary GP car, it looks like it should have two seats. Aha! That's where my legs go—astride the engine, between the frame rails and the clutch housing. Hold yourself up with your arms, and feed your feet down into their respective hollows. There, drop into the seat (just before you hit the bottom, Herr Bunz snatches the rag out from under you—it's evidently all right now, your body will keep the rain off the seat).

Wiggle around. Can I actually use the clutch with my legs so far apart? I'd damn well better. Bunz replaces the steering wheel. Oh I wish I was a Catholic so I'd have some beads to hang onto. Uhlenhaut, watching from under the umbrella till now, comes over and gives me the drill. "Yessir, uh-huh, don't use first, starting gear only, right. Start in second, which is where it's supposed to be, okay, third is straight forward. Straight forward? Oh man, the shift pattern is backwards—instead of pulling straight back for upshifts, you push straight ahead. Fourth is across the gate and back, and fifth is straight ahead again. I didn't have enough problems, now a strange shift pattern. Goody.

Is that all they're going to tell me? They're pushing me off already! Switch on, Bunz saw to that, get second gear, clutch depressed, hold the starting knob out, "NOW," Bunz grunts, and it's running. Is it running! Man, what a lovely racket. The throttle travel is long, but the response is instantaneous. Blip the throttle, R-A-A-A-CK, R-A-A-A-CK, R-A-A-A-CK, feel everything out. Where is everybody? Well, you're all alone now, hot dog. Your face shield is already covered with rain, all you can see is featureless concrete in every direction, and you never sat in one of these things before in your life. With any luck at all, you may not make a complete fool of yourself.

Naturally, you're not that lucky. Ease the clutch in. I'll be darned, it's easy! It just moves off like any old production car. Well, this won't be so bad, you're gonna be all right, old friend. WHAT THE HELL! I'm going the wrong way on the test track! Oh nice. Stop. Try a U-turn.

Track's too narrow. Try to find reverse. Ah, that's how the lock-out works. Reverse. Don't kill the engine. Second. Nobody coming? Good. Go. Accelerate away at half-throttle, shift to third at 3500. Go past the mechanics. What's that signal? NOW he tells me which way to go. Thanks a lot, fella.

Two very slow laps, try to remember everything Uhlenhaut said. Now it's easier, a couple of botched shifts because of the funny linkage, but so far so good. Faster. 6000 in second up the little straight, hit third, go to about 5000 and back off for the nasty little button-hook at the end. Back to second, around the turn on trailing throttle, HIT IT! Just as you exit the turn the tail snaps loose in the wet, but you're not going fast enough to be in any trouble, and you catch it. No sweat. Third gear, throttle cracked wide open, hit the bump that precedes the left-hand bend around the U.S. Seventh Army laundry building, slither through the puddles around that bend and on to the banked 180 on trailing throttle. Open it up gently as you traverse the banked turn, and come out strong. Up the straight again, second, third, fourth for an instant, bang on the brakes. Did I wait too long? No, hell, it's stopping all right. Around the slow one again, faster this time.

It doesn't feel too bad at all now. The tail is a little erratic on the soaked pavement, what with no rain tires and all, but it sure feels nice. Even with the water pouring into your cuffs and over the knot in your tie, it feels great. Keep going, run all day, why not? This is once in a life-time. People have parked their cars outside the fence down by the but-tonhook, and they're standing there in the downpour, watching YOU, hero, they think you're the real McCoy, or whatever that is in the Swabian dialect. Don't let them know the truth.

Finally, after about ten laps, none of them good, but each one a never-to-be-forgotten experience, you come in. Herr Bunz reaches in and switches it off, then removes the steering wheel. One last loving look, water normal, oil normal, tachometer tell-tale stuck at about 6300, metabolism out of sight. Try to apologize to Bunz for going the wrong way, but with the language barrier and his controlled good manners, he's unreachable. Just a half-smile, some muttered reassurance, and a search-ing scrutiny of the car. His reason is more than father love, it turns out, because he has just painstakingly prepared this car for Fangio to drive in an exhibition at Monaco. I'm glad I didn't know that before.

Ten o'clock the next morning. A hurried tour of the fabulous works museum is just finished. "What now, Herr von Urach? The test track? What for? Why no, I'd be delighted to do it again for the photog-rapher."

Back to the test track, this time in another big 600. Same mechanics, same apprehensive looks, same pouring rain, same eternally cheerful Strassl representing the unquenchable enthusiasm of PR men everywhere. White suit, rain jacket, painfully cramped helmet, steering wheel off, Davis in, photographer bustling about, push off, drop the clutch in, ROAR!

Idle out onto the track—the right way this time—build up to speed more quickly today, it's beginning to feel like old stuff. Now you know the line, and you know all the puddles and slippery places, and you try a little harder. Rooster tails spire straight up from all four wheels, and you know where the power comes in, and where the wheels spin, and how much juice you can give it coming off which corner and it's too beautiful for words. You don't even notice the water running down your sleeves and over your Adam's apple. Once, you deliberately charge through a puddle coming out of a slow turn, just to give yourself a great, hilarious shower. You run five laps like that, and the world is yours for the asking, you think.

At the end of the short straight, where the Seventh Army laundry marks the bend with the bumps, you have to take a bus on the inside. It's easy, you just cut the corner a little finer than you normally would, planning to adjust your line coming out. Easy, right? You get past the bus and back on the throttle and you're heading for the next bend on the wrong line. You stay on it and twitch the wheel slightly to the left, to get the big silver racing car aimed where it belongs. You're going how fast? Fifty? Fifty-five? Maybe even seventy or seventy-five—who's counting? The tail breaks loose. Not a smartalecky little jerk to the outside like before, but GONE, spinning, coming around a full hundred-eighty degrees. Oh Mother look at that wall coming. I can't possibly miss it. I'm going to hit it at about fifty, tail first, and I'm going to destroy a museum piece, a car that was probably worth hundreds of thousands of Deutschmarks new, and worth ten times today. Steer. Do something with your feet. Steer some more. Oh Mother look at that wall come. Why brace yourself, or duck? With luck, maybe you can get killed in the accident and you won't have to face Uhlenhaut, or worse than that, Technician Bunz.

Silence. It stopped. I didn't hit the wall. I've killed the engine. I'm an idiot. They'll never allow me to drive another Mercedes as long as I live. Bunz will have my head bronze-plated and he'll hang it from his rear-view mirror. Disgrace. Suddenly my elbows feel very wet and cold from the water in my sleeves.

There's Strassl, still smiling. How can he do that? There's Bunz, not smiling; God, am I glad I didn't tear up his race car. Just some paint scraped off by the right front wheel when I went to full lock trying to catch the slide. Believe me, Bunz, I'm sorry.

"Strassl, old friend, let's go get a drink."

Nice guys
and where I'd like to see them finish.

⁓⊱⊰⁓

Roy Chapin and I have a lot in common. He runs American Motors Corporation, and I like cars. He's pursued a daring and innovative policy there, and I've cheered from the sidelines. He is exactly the sort of man you'd like to have running any major corporation in which you were a controlling shareholder: handsome, sincere, nice healthy color, properly educated and to the manner born—just like me. He's outdoorsy. I'm outdoorsy. He supports Ducks Unlimited; heck, ducks name their children after me. He is on the national board of Trout Unlimited, and I have personally broken the tip off of one pretty good flyrod by closing a door on it. He wouldn't be seen in the Detroit standard-issue cranberry double-knit slacks with wide white vinyl belt, and I would sooner die. Furthermore, Preston Mann, dog trainer to the stars, raconteur and frequent humbler of auto-industry biggies, has taken both of us for sums of money far greater than we'd ever admit to and treats each of us with the kind of good-humored contempt that every great con man from Lord Duveen to Rasputin has felt for his gullible clients—though the bird dogs we have purchased from Preston love us totally and without reservation. As you can see, Roy Chapin and I are practically blood brothers, despite the fact that we only met once, at a DU dinner, and he didn't get my name.

Anyway, here's Roy Chapin, a near-perfect person blessed with every attribute required for the Compleat Tycoon's Tool Kit, yet he and his corporation have been fighting an apparently losing battle with consumer perversity ever since the end of the energy crisis. Why? America is supposed to love the underdog, but I get the feeling that America is enjoying some sadistic gratification from AMC's pain and suffering. Granted, AMC may not have authorized any automotive breakthroughs beyond its innovative warranty program, but it has consistently provided us with designs that reflected real imagination and discrimination in a homogenized world.

Look at the Hornet, the Gremlin, the Pacer. Each represents an interesting and stimulating approach to some market-segment's specific automotive need. They stand clearly apart from the common herd, possibly because they're designed by Dick Teague, a genuine card-carrying enthusiast with good taste in cars—even though he does show up in cerise trousers at times—and a lot of vehicular *chutzpah*. He's articulate, a pretty fair automotive scholar and an altogether appropriate chief designer for Chapin and AMC.

Some critics might say that AMC needs new engines and more innovative chassis layouts, that AMC's singular "hit it where they ain't" styling can't offset mundane underpinnings. But the success of everybody else in the domestic auto industry, usually with equally mundane underpinnings, would seem to belie that. Conservatives say that the controversial styling itself is a weakness, but we don't believe it.

Chapin, Teague and their fellow AMC believers have their work cut out for them. It's the hardest, meanest work there is, making a comeback in the automobile business. Dealers, the daily press, bureaucrats and consumer advocates all know better than the people that run the company, and the average citizen cannot comprehend the huge amounts of real money that ride on every decision. The people at AMC haven't let any of that cow them yet, and we fervently wish them every success. Nice guys *do* win occasionally, and these guys certainly deserve a victory.

In BMW, Veritas.

I sat around trying to conjure up a proper subject for this month's column, and our cover caught my eye. We have a big test on the new BMW 630CSi coupe in this issue, and we went out to BMW's palatial headquarters in Montvale, New Jersey to photograph the car en situ. I have lots of great BMW memories, and the photographic expedition brought them flooding back.

The first BMW I ever got close to was a 327 cabriolet, vintage mid-Thirties, I guess. It had been purchased by a guy with whom I'd gone to high school, Bill Muncey (later to find considerable fame as an unlimited hydroplane racer), who raced that totally unsuitable little sports-tourer in a series of outlaw sports-car races held on a dirt oval in Mount Clemens, Michigan. That was in 1953.

In 1954, I was proving to the world that I lacked the skills for the retail end of the imported-car business at a place called Sports Cars Ypsilanti in (you guessed it) Ypsilanti, Michigan, and our service manager, Ed Hancock, was a BMW 328 partisan. As I recall he owned two, both moribund, but it wasn't at all difficult to sit in those scabby crocks and imagine them rasping around the Nürburgring or wailing through the night on the first leg of the 1938 or '39 Mille Miglia. The 328 engine was a wondrous six-cylinder device that looked and sounded like it had double-overhead camshafts, but didn't. The top half of that engine was a confusing maze of pushrods and rockers and inclined valves, and the noise it made was simply terrific. It won hundreds of races. Both Fraser-Nash and Bristol used it under license from BMW, and the famous Zora Arkus-Duntov ran one in a race car called the Veritas, which he campaigned in Europe after the war.

I never saw the Veritas race, but I watched several Fraser-Nashes run in the Fifties and actually got to drive a couple of fairly decent Arnolt-Bristol roadsters. But the car that most fired my imagination was Ted Boynton's Fraser-Nash, a LeMans Replica Mk. II, a nasty bumble-

bee of a car with cycle fenders and louvers and leather straps and gor-
geously scorched chrome exhaust pipes. Boynton was one of the golden
boys of major-league amateur racing in those days. He was handsomely
white-haired, he wore a white turtleneck and white flannel trousers, his
car was immaculately white and shiny and the women in his pits were
flawless examples of the best idea God ever had.

The BMW 328 is history now, as are all the interesting cars it
inspired, but it was certainly a worthy jumping-off place for the company that BMW became, with Max Hoffman's help, in the mid-Sixties. I
bought a 2000 Tilux in Germany in 1967 and thrashed it the length and
breadth of the Continent. One day I drove from the offices of
Pininfarina in Turin to the Bouwes Hotel in Zandvoort, about 825
miles, in thirteen hours. A week later Pete Biro and I raced Dan Gurney
and Bill Dunne in their 110-mph Mini-Cooper from Amsterdam to
LeMans. On the midnight leg from Paris to the track, Dan drove my
BMW and reached deep inside himself to explain what the 24 Hours
meant to him and why he wanted to win it so badly (which he did, that
year, in a Ford).

Now we have tested another BMW. I first drove a new 633CSi
in Germany last fall. We left the Hotel Vierjahreseiten at dusk and sped
more than 60 miles to a little country inn on the road to Lindau. I drove
at 190-200 kph and never felt safer. At midnight, with an unforgettable
dinner tucked away, thoroughly content, we tore back through the
Bavarian countryside, alone with our thoughts as the scenery rushed past
at 190-plus and the headlights picked out the twists and quirks of the
empty road. I'd like to invite the new Secretary of Transportation to
repeat that experience with me some night. Dinner and the BMW might
color his thinking about a few things.

Renaissance.

I spent last week in Detroit, and it's funny how much I love the place. We stayed in the new Plaza Hotel at Henry Ford's Renaissance Center and the view from our sixty-first-floor room—west, or "down-river" as we Detroiters say—was breathtaking. The Detroit setting is ideal—surrounded by lakes, an easy drive from places like Toronto and Chicago, literally minutes away from all kinds of hunting, boating and fishing, but there's some kind of rottenness at the core, and nobody can tell if this latest megabuck attempt at a heart transplant will take or not. I hope it works. Having grown up there, having worked on those assembly lines and in those office buildings, I feel that my own health and wellbeing are inextricably meshed with Detroit's. And on a purely practical basis, given my crazed affection for all things automotive, I suppose they are. In a larger sense, I suppose all of us who care enough to either work for or read a magazine like this one have a stake in Detroit. It may not produce many double-overhead-cam V-12 engines or Alfetta GTs, but every automotive engineer and designer in the world must acknowledge—however grudgingly—his debt to Detroit. It is still the automotive capital of the world, still the place to which we Americans must look for our automotive hopes and dreams.

Car magazines, and the people who read them, are finally getting their innings in Detroit. We've begged, pleaded, cajoled and occasionally threatened Detroit, always in the hope that they'd see it our way, that they'd finally come to appreciate what it is that we love about the special-interest cars from overseas. Not just the Ferraris and Lamborghinis and other thin-blooded exotics—the Volkswagen Beetles, the Saabs, the Minis and all the other sprightly little sedans that so fired our imaginations over the past quarter-century of our car enthusiasm.

I first called on Detroit for *Road & Track* magazine in 1957. They were getting ready for the Corvairs and Falcons and Valiants that came out in the fall of '59, but they still didn't understand why. One school said it was foreign-car status; another held out for the idea that these were poor, benighted souls who simply couldn't afford to buy a "real" car and were thus buying new VWs. Only a tiny handful of Detroit visionaries understood that little cars were fun to drive, that low mass might be its own reward.

As the imported-car boom rumbled onward and upward, their confusion grew apace. By the mid-Sixties, they were building cars that borrowed four-speed transmissions and "heavy-duty" handling packages and all manner of cosmetic non-essentials from the imported competition, still without coming to grips with what was really important about the little cars from other places.

Now all that's changed. Detroit is singing our song with a vengeance. The Chevette may be ordinary in specification, but it's a terrific little car to own and operate. The new Fiesta is even better, a little car that takes the Honda Accord and the VW Rabbit head on, and needs make no apology for the fact that it was designed in Dearborn. Not to mention the smaller full-size cars that GM introduced for 1977, or the still smaller intermediates they'll introduce this fall, coincident with Ford's neat new "Fox" family of compacts. The automotive renaissance is at hand, gentle readers, and you should take pride in the fact that you and your fellow car enthusiasts are every bit as responsible for the change in Detroit's product philosophy as OPEC or Washington. If you hadn't voted with your billfolds all those years, doggedly holding out for better, smaller cars, the Detroit response to the energy crisis might have been just as complacent and conventional as its response to Ralph Nader in 1965. Now I have another reason to go back to Detroit—not only did I grow up there, *they've* grown up there!

Foyt, Fangio and the sponsor's ego.

T hrough the good offices of our former European Editor, Mr. Bill Gavin, I recently got to see the finest motor-racing film I've ever attended. Gavin is now in the film-distribution business in the U.K., and he arranged for me to get a preview of a film called *Fangio,* produced by Giovanni Volpe and written and directed by Hugh Hudson. The presentation is essentially autobiographical, and we watch as Juan Manuel Fangio retraces the steps that led him to five world championships. There's wonderful newsreel footage of his first great victory in Argentina's 6000-mile Gran Premio del Norte, which he won driving a highly modified 1940 Chevrolet coupe. There's equally great footage of virtually every important milestone in his career, and this is interwoven with fantastic sequences in which the retired Fangio puts on his old Herbert Johnson helmet and blue T-shirt again and goes out to drive a 250F Maserati, a 1956 Ferrari Lancia D50, an Alfa Romeo Type 159 from the Alfa museum, the great W196 Mercedes that won him the championship in 1954, '55 and '56, and a really trick Chevrolet-powered single seater that he drove in the postwar years in Argentina.

As the film progresses, it becomes more and more preoccupied with all the men who've died in racing cars. The deaths of Marimon, Ascari, Rodriguez, Rindt, Bandini and Siffert are all documented in painful details, as is Levegh's fiery slaughter at Le Mans in 1955. There's also a sequence of unidentified accidents happening everywhere from postwar Indy to unnamed European circuits in Edwardian times. Much of this seems gratuitous, especially since many of the deaths shown happened either before or after Fangio's racing career, but the point is well taken nonetheless. As one who stopped attending races when Bruce McLaren was killed, who felt that four-dozen dead friends in fifteen years was too many, I have to say that I was receptive to the point being made. Yet everything else about the picture reminded me of the breath-taking majesty of racing and the superb quality of the men who drive the cars.

Amid all this, Fangio reflects on the overwhelming commercialism that's become part and parcel of international racing since he retired in 1958. He makes the observation that in his day the cars were painted in their national colors and men raced with a sense of patriotic pride and purpose. "Now," he says, "a driver may die for a brand of chewing gum...but at least he dies rich."

With that thought in mind, I came across the news that Mr. Fred Stecher, the man who runs Citicorp's megabuck racing hobby, so disapproved of Mr. A.J. Foyt's public behavior that he threatened to turn off the tap and withhold Citicorp's $400,000 investment in USAC Champ Car racing next year. Mr. Stecher is the latest in a long line of hype-moguls who presume that their company's investment in racing makes them more important than racing itself. They presume too much. How A.J. Foyt behaves in public or anywhere else is none of Fred Stecher's business. If he wants to promote Citicorp through racing, that's fine. But he has to take racing as it comes, warts and all. He may be spending a ton of money for his ticket to the races, but a ticket is all racing owes him. And, incidentally, A.J. Foyt probably sells more tickets than anybody.

I've always been able to control my enthusiasm for A.J. Foyt without too much effort. But if his antisocial behavior gets him out of line, that's USAC's problem, not Citicorp's. Foyt *is* racing. Foyt, for better or worse, is what automobile racing is all about—just as Juan Manuel Fangio was in his day. No sponsor should ever lose sight of that fact. They pay their money, and they take their chances. It could be argued that racing wouldn't exist without sponsors, but it's even more difficult to imagine racing without drivers.

What it all means.

～❦～

I t is exactly six o'clock on a Sunday evening and I'm sitting in my office reflecting upon the splendid day that's just winding down around me. Yates called me at ten, and we went around the corner to a delicatessen for breakfast, accompanied by my sixteen-year-old son Matthew and hedonist Porsche-racer Steve Behr. Bagels with cream cheese for Yates, ham omelet for Behr, toasted bialy with cream cheese for yours truly and corned-beef-and-swiss-on-an-onion-roll-with-Russian and a Coke for my kid.

The breakfast-table conversation was about what you'd expect: the identity of Enzo Ferrari's mistress; how Achille Varzi's girlfriend turned him on to hard drugs and ruined his life; whatever happened to Achille Varzi's girlfriend and how old would she be; who had the first Cad-Allard in the United States; the time Captain George Eyston was honorary chief marshal at Watkins Glen in 1954 and black-flagged my pal Del Lee for dangerous driving, and what Del said; which Brooklands cars and which Land Speed Record cars were designed by Reid Railton and for whom; the current whereabouts of Cord-designer Gordon Buehrig; the inadvisability of sleeping with women who threaten to commit suicide in your apartment; how much Jim Haynes paid for his Miller and where he got the money; the Columbo-engined twelve-cylinder twelve-liter luxo tourer that Luigi Chinetti would like to build; how dull things are without Max Hoffman; and whether or not Behr could get better rides if he had a rich wife. I may have left one or two items out, but that's what I remember.

Matthew and I then walked down to the Red Ball Garage, arguing his views that 1. Pontiac Firebirds are Macho cars and I shouldn't like them so much, and 2. whether or not one should put wire wheels on Cadillac Sevilles. In a minute or two the Volvo 242 GT came rolling off the Red Ball elevator, and we stopped by home to pick up his stuff. He was returning to school in Connecticut and his "stuff" consisted of two duffel bags (one mine, one his), one Brooks Brothers garment bag (mine), one pair of soccer cleats, one orange quilt, one L.L. Bean FiberFill II rectangular sleeping bag, one pair L.L. Bean insulated hunting shoes, one pair Red Wing "Red Setter" boots, one large mirror (plastered with Terlingua Racing Team and Gurney Eagle decals), one small blue bag filled with clothes he'd outgrown last year (and couldn't remember the reason for packing), one compact Sony stereo with speakers, one large stack of records, one desk lamp and one mounted Jackalope head (souvenir of Sheridan, Wyoming). Missing were the E.M.S. down jacket (orange) and the framed picture of Babe the Wonder Dog (the Golden Retriever we lost in last year's divorce settlement).

Loaded thus, and looking like Gypsies fleeing the Cossacks, we headed north into the wilds of western Connecticut. My blood was up, and I was more than ready to attack my favorite bit of test road, between Route 22 and New Milford. It's uniquely rough and winding, and it takes the Mickey right out of some pretty good cars. The Volvo stuck like glue, handled pretty well and rode—to be charitable—unevenly. We flew.

We arrived at Canterbury, where a dozen or more station wagons and Wagoneers were disgorging similar boys with similar loads of junk, and the GT's chin spoiler and killer paint scheme caught every adolescent eye. Not like last term, when I showed up in a red Porsche 924 and they lost their cool completely, but not bad. The Volvo got a lot of cool, appraising stares, like one might direct toward a nubile redhead if one were sixteen and on fire with fantasies. With Matt safely in his new room, I hurried back over my favorite road again, alone with my own Mille Miglia fantasies playing like movies on the insides of my eyelids.

On location.

Y ou are on your way to the Frankfurt Automobile Show. You have agreed to meet your wife, J.L.K. Davis, in Paris and drive over. You emerge from the customs funnel at Charles de Gaulle Airport and there she is, at the wheel of a metallic blue Citroën CX2400GTi. This Citroën will carry you almost 700 miles before you're through with it, and it will take almost that long to get used to the car's remarkable and idiosyncratic personality.

The looks take some getting used to for a start. The car's shape is simply unlike anything any American driver is accustomed to looking at. Not as strange as the older DS-19 and DS-21 were to U.S. eyes, but still a sort of audacious French poke in the eye—a take-it-or-leave-it approach to how cars are supposed to look in this day and age. It is a four-door streamliner and its appearance reeks of aircraft technology.

Inside, it seems still farther out. The seats are squishy-soft and all the spatial relationships seem to be about ten percent out of register. Nothing is quite where you'd expect it to be. The upholstery fabric is a cross between Navajo and Art Deco and the instruments seem to be the latest thing from Atwater-Kent—old fashioned console-radio dials and controls upgraded for the Seventies. The speedometer and tachometer are the drum-type, rolling the numbers into view from right to left, constantly bathed in yellow light to make them visible in their deep rectangular recesses. The instrument panel is as much *Flash Gordon* as *Star Wars,* but once you find everything, it's a joy, because it all works at the touch of a finger, and the only time you need to move a hand from the steering wheel is when you want to move the five-speed shift lever or grope the lady who's harnessed herself into the right-hand seat.

The CX2400GTi is no less remarkable in motion. The ride is billowy-soft, softer than any American car, but here the softness is your friend. The Citroën howls down the *Autoroute* at its top speed of 180 kilometers per hour as true as a die. For all this lap-of-luxury softness, it handles. Granted, it doesn't behave like anything else on the road, but it will give any other sedan in its price and displacement class all it can handle on a nasty mountain road. The four-cylinder fuel-injected engine is a little noisy at its peak, but the system works so well as an integrated whole that you don't mind. The Citroën is an automotive experience nobody should miss. It stretches your mind and makes you aware of automotive alternatives you hadn't considered before. American practice has dictated that a 2.3-liter engine with four cylinders and an overhead camshaft was strictly power for the proletariat—something to propel dull Vegas and Pintos slowly over unchallenging roads. In this car, a 2.3-liter engine with four cylinders hurls the family along at an easy 180 kph and the "family" is apt to be the Rothschilds, or the President of France.

After Frankfurt, we drove to Munich. On Sunday morning we were awakened by the Oktoberfest parade going right past our windows, so we threw on our clothes and rushed out into the rain where we must have shot ten rolls of film as the local shooting champions, their fellow villagers and their marching bands paraded past. The Munich police, acting as roving parade marshalls, were mounted on immaculate white BMW cafe-racers and wore bright green skin-tight leathers. Even the California Highway Patrol riders in their immaculate boots, britches and jackets are eclipsed by Munich's cops-as-GP-riders.

On Monday we visited BMW and picked up a new 733 sedan. The Citroën rested for the next five days while we ran the BMW as hard as it would go, all the way out to Graz in the southeastern corner of Austria, west into the Algau for a disappointing visit to Alpina and through a dozen or more dramatic Alpine passes. The seven-series BMW sedan is everything the 630CSi coupe isn't. It looks very much like a four door version of the coupe, but with a redesigned front suspension and more wheelbase the sedan is a lively, aggressive car with exactly the same character as a 2002 or a Bavaria. Let's pray that American emissions controls don't emasculate this new BMW luxo-sedan because, in its European form, it may be the best BMW sedan yet—genuinely first class, a true sports-tourer in the classic sense.

The drive from Munich to Graz took six grueling hours, but it was worth it. One is almost forced to use the main truck route from Western Europe to the Middle East to get there, and it's two lanes and wall-to-wall trucks all the way. Thank God for the BMW because every time you pull out to pass it's an adventure. The Citroën, lacking mid-range power, would have been hard-pressed to get us there the way the 3.3-liter BMW did. A great car for bad roads.

In Graz we visited Steyr-Daimler-Puch and saw them building the *Car and Driver* Project Pinzgauer. A Pinzgauer is a hardy horse that works in the Austrian Alps, and Steyr-Daimler-Puch builds a wonderful off-road vehicle by the same name. The American arm of the Austrian firm has asked us to drive one for a while, to bash it around North America for a few months, and we have gleefully agreed. The Pinzgauer comes either as a 6x6 or a 4x4 and it is distinctly military in appearance and function. What makes it unusual is the fact that it drives like a car! For all its forbidding martial aspect, it is more civilized on the road than a Land Rover. We drove it up a series of goat-roads and creek beds to the top of a mountain near Graz in Styria where we could see Italy, Yugoslavia and Hungary, all at once. The Pinzgauer is like a trails bike. It doesn't go fast but it goes anywhere. Sherman and I can hardly wait to get that little sweetheart over here and go adventuring.

We regretfully left Graz and drove back to Munich where we returned the BMW, climbed into our Citroën, and had to get to know it all over again. We hit the Munich-Stuttgart-Karlsruhe Autobahn at exactly the same moment as the entire U.S. Army in Europe started home from maneuvers and it was a 100-mile traffic jam—the worst! A night spent in Baden-Baden restored our good humor and we made it to Paris without difficulty the following day. Goodbye continental Europe, goodbye Citroën, you intriguing spaceship, you.

A day later, in England, we visited the Aston Martin works at Newport-Pagnell. Here we got a plant tour, a look at the incredible new Lagonda, lunch at a public house called "The Swan Revived," a ride in the managing director's airplane, and the loan of a shiny black DBS coupe. The Aston Martin DBS feels as determinedly old-fashioned as the Citroën CX is modern. Dinner that night was at the Wild Boar Inn in Cheshire with some pals from Rolls-Royce and the States, and the drive through those hedgerowed lanes in that big black beast was a thrill. Next day we hammered it all over Wales, then met Charles Fox and his son James for dinner in Abergavenny. As the miles rolled up, we never got over the feeling that it was too big and too heavy, but we did develop a great deal of respect for its brakes and road-holding. It goes, stops and sticks like hell, but its 5.3-liter twin-cam V-8 engine drinks gas at a scandalous rate and its seats are guaranteed to aggravate your sciatica. Definitely a car for the wealthy toff who thinks it all went to hell in the Sixties.

Do yourself a favor. Cash in the Christmas Club, sell your IBM stock, raid the savings account and take a vacation in Europe this year. Enjoy two weeks of real honest-to-God freedom in an automobile. It'll clear the cobwebs from your workaday head and get your automotive adrenalin flowing. You'll never take 55 for an answer again.

Aged in the wood.

❧

So old Sid Jeffee, the Vice President-Engineering at Chrysler Corporation, loads me into this very snazzy Diplomat with absolutely *everything* on it, man, and we drive through the Engineering Garage, headed for I-75 and Little Harry's restaurant. As we idle down between the rows of parked cars I suddenly spot—Wait a minute!—*wood!* I swear to you, there was this new LeBaron station wagon and it had this *wood* all over it. The new LeBaron Town and Country, by God. For an instant, I thought it might be real wood, but I was kidding myself. Polyurethane wood from the polyurethane forests of Davidson, a division of McCord, located in New Hampshire. But for an instant I suspended my willingness to disbelieve and they had me. Boy, a half-timbered Town and Country, just like the good old days. When the first Chrysler Town and Country came out in 1946, I was a sophomore in high school, generally regarded as weird, and hopelessly in love with a *zaftig* girl with red-gold hair and soft woolly curves, whose name was Natalie. She was majoring in Chastity and she shared the common view of me and my distorted approach to life. I read *The New Yorker*, for one thing, and talked about it, for another. I went to the midget races at Motor City Speedway once a week, and girls like Natalie with mothers like Natalie's mother did *not* go to midget races. I read *Esquire* and wanted desperately to dress like the guys who graced its pages—former officers and war heroes, all of them—guys who'd inherited millions of bucks, bachelor's degrees and '39 Mercury convertibles when they'd turned sixteen.

There were pictures of Chrysler Town and Country convertibles in those magazines. They were big, soft round cars, not unlike Natalie in concept, every bit as seductive and equally beyond my grasp. The idea was to combine the sportiness of the convertible with the elegance of the station wagon. That's right, the *elegance* of the station wagon. Station wagons were still elegant in those days, half-timbered charabancs dispatched to the station to fetch the former officers and war heroes and their well-born women to festive weekends at country places. The name, *Town and Country,* reeked of prewar status, of fast-fading adherence to the rules of F. Scott Fitzgerald. Town was a place called "Fifth Avenue" or "The Loop" or, in Detroit, "Washington Boulevard." It was a wonderful place where men wore worsteds and flannels, never tweeds, where they talked business over lunch and met sleek, highly sexed women for cocktails. *Country,* on the other hand, was the place where one wore tweeds and shetlands and cheviots with a passion, where shirts were soft and patterned and ascots were permissible, as were knitted ties. *Country* was the place where they shot the ads for *The New Yorker* and *Esquire,* the place that always seemed to combine a tennis court, a putting green, a pool, a manor house with a curving drive and a new car being admired by about two dozen former war heroes and their well-born women, all of whom seemed to be having a good time. I had a feeling that if I owned a Chrysler Town and Country, it would take me there, like a horse returning to the barn, but I despaired of ever finding it on my own.

About the time the agony of high school ended for me, I saw my first Jaguar XK120. It was small and black and looked like it could do laps inside your average 1949 Chrysler. I abandoned my search for *Town and Country* country, and never looked back. That Jaguar fueled the fantasies that have danced before me ever since. Town and country ran together, ticky-tacky along the Interstates, and doubleknit polyester seemed to make all questions of worsted versus tweed irrelevant. That Jaguar helped me to reach escape velocity, but the LeBaron Town and Country in the Engineering Garage took me back for just a moment, and it wasn't too bad.

Agony of choice.

❦

Car *and Driver* magazine and I will be moving to Ann Arbor, Michigan this spring. This is a wonderful thing for the magazine, complicated and in some ways traumatic to be sure, but a wonderful thing nonetheless. I just bought a nutball house with a three dog kennel and a four car garage, and now I face the car enthusiast's eternal dilemma: What kind of wheels am I going to buy?

The deal fell through on my '77 Bronco. I really thought I had it all put together—I'd even sent the dealer a check—but then I came face to face with the little brute. Instead of my dream Bronco with four seats and four on the floor, there was this two-seater with three on the tree and all the charm of a post office van. The salesman turned his back for a moment and I slunk away like a thief. It was his screw-up, but for some unexplainable reason *I* felt guilty. Now I have the check back, but once again the agony of choice is upon me.

All my adult life I've been sitting around examining this burning question with one pal or another, usually in a place where alcoholic beverages are sold. No matter how the conversation starts out, sooner or later somebody says, "If you could have any car you wanted, what would you…" and that leads to a couple of hours of arcane discussion not unlike questions of how many angels can dance on the head of a pin. It's not easy, even when I don't actually have to make the decision and buy a car, but now I really need to buy a car and I'm hopelessly at sea.

This one will not be a sports car. J.L.K. Davis has already decreed that one of the four slots in the Davis garage will be reserved for a Lotus Elite, dark brown with a beige pseudo-suede interior. This is fine with me for a variety of reasons. First, I'll enjoy driving the Lotus a lot, at least on those occasions when she lets me. Second, it will make her happy, and I enjoy nothing so much as basking in the warm glow of a happy woman. Third, and perhaps most important of all, it's one automotive decision I won't have to make. Mrs. Davis, in that nice no-nonsense totalitarian way that women have, has simply decreed that the Lotus Elite is it and no others need apply. I have no such resolve. I am tortured by alternatives.

Now that the Bronco has gone west, I find myself considering everything from a Rolls-Royce to a Dodge Colt station wagon. I *know* that a Corniche convertible would be a terrific investment. I could drive it for the rest of my life and leave it to my kids, and it would undoubtedly be more valuable than any stock portfolio I could amass in my sunset years. Unfortunately, the down-stroke on the Corniche got squandered on the nutball house with the four car garage. What then? A Mercedes? A BMW? My new car must be small yet roomy, practical yet fun to drive. It must get reasonable gas mileage but it can't be slow. It has to take me and my dog to the grouse coverts and duck marshes, but it must be respectable enough to transport VIPs to and from the airport. It must be able to tow boat and motorcycle trailers, and it has to be good in snow.

Denise McCluggage blew in from Vermont to report that her aged Land Rover is breaking in half and that she, like half of New England, has decided that the Subaru 4WD wagon is the greatest thing since short skis. I've considered the VW Thing and the Z28 Camaro, but they're not quite right. Last year I loved the Jeep Cherokee and Buick LeSabre wagons, but this year the Chevy Malibu is the wagon that grabs me. A four-wheel-drive Suburban would be terrific, but you need an uncle in OPEC to run one. Yates loves his Honda Accord and Dodge pickup, but I don't trust him. Never have. Besides, I can't get enough people in a pickup, and I really like the Fiesta. I'd buy our 25,000 mile test car but Sherman says they won't sell it to me. I know, I'll buy Bedard a beer and ask him. "Listen Pat, if you were going to buy a car, and…"

Allards, Ariels and Attila the Hun.

I got a nice letter from Bill Wood the other day. Bill's a guy who helped launch the Sports Car Club of America in Detroit years ago and whose last name graces one of Michigan's largest imported-car emporia. The car deal was pretty slick: First, it plugged Bill into an endless supply of shiny new machinery and, second, it got his brother Don off the street. I worked there in 1953, and it was too good to be true. The showroom was about the size of your dining room and usually contained something really commercial like an Alvis drop-head coupe. The shop consisted of three gas-station bays and we did in fact pump Mobil gas out front.

A few miles away the notorious Delevan S. Lee held forth at Louis Deeb Cadillac. Del raced a J2X Cadillac-Allard, mainly in hill-climbs, and his was one of the best in the country. It was metallic blue with chrome Borrani wire wheels and he gave gas-station attendants twenty-dollar bills to run it up on their hoists for safekeeping whenever he wanted to chat up the girls in one salon or another. The Allard matched his Cadillac convertible and race-car trailer and, all in all, it was an impressive entourage.

Christmas 1954 found me and Del working together at Lawrence Falvey's Jaguar/Mercedes-Benz/Austin Healey/Bristol/Rolls-Royce store. Del was the sales manager and I was a salesman who seemed doomed never to sell anything. Del tried to be smooth, but he generally came on like Attila the Hun in flannel slacks and a cheviot jacket. His speech was both garrulous and foul and he was no respecter of persons.

A wealthy doctor dropped by for the first checkup on one of two Jaguars he'd bought the week before. As he pulled into the shop he spotted a Type 37 Bugatti Del had left under a nylon cover in the corner. Those shiny cast wheels pulled him like a magnet and he cautiously lifted one corner of the cover. "Hey you," Del boomed from the doorway, "getcher goddam hands off that car!" That was our sales manager.

Another time, a man of considerable taste and charm, José Cavillo, came to take delivery of his new silver Mercedes 300SL gull-wing. José usually bought one of every new car to come along and we usually treated him with a lot of deference. On this Saturday José showed up, only to find that his silver Mercedes was green, olive green. Del had sold the silver one to Holley Carburetor. Childlike anticipation abruptly changed to rage and fury, and Mr. Falvey barely managed to calm him with the promise of the best free paint job money could buy. Our customer was standing there shaking his head sadly, when Del roared in at the wheel of his jet-black XK120M. "Jeezus, Joe," he hollered breezily, "you shoulda got silver. That green paint makes that sonuvabitch look like a goddam light-reconnaissance vehicle!"

Del had an Ariel Square Four motorcycle that was as immaculate as his cars, and he rode it down to Ohio one weekend for one of the last Put-in-Bay road races. On the way back, a guy in a Lincoln Cosmopolitan convertible cut him off at about seventy. Del went after the guy, scared the bejeezus out of him in a bout of fender tag, then tore away at about a hundred, flat against the tank. When he thought he was safe, he let go with his left hand, raised his arm and gave his chastened adversary the finger. The Ariel peeled off into the woods, through a fence, only stopping when it had hit most of the saplings in Ottawa County. They say people had to come out from the ASPCA in Toledo and bring Del down with a tranquilizer dart.

Bill Wood's letter told me that Del had died of cancer. I can just see him crashing the pearly gates in his Allard, taking the Lord's name in vain and flipping Saint Peter the bird. Cancer may have beat Del Lee, but I'll bet the disease was severely mauled in the process.

Henry Ford: The Windmills of His Mind.

Henry Ford was a remarkable man who revolutionized America without ever really understanding the place. Fortunately for all of us, most particularly his grandchildren, he had about a dozen really good ideas that more than offset—both financially and historically—his hundreds of bad ones. The Henry Ford Museum and Greenfield Village were probably good ones. Old Mr. Ford was always vaguely suspicious of factory workers, his own included, and he even went so far as to have them spied upon and their home lives subjected to the scrutiny of his "Sociological Department" lest they squander the good money he was paying them. On the other hand, farmers, like his father, were the salt of the earth, and he always felt badly about his own responsibility for dragging them away from the soil and into the teeming cities he so detested. Greenfield Village helped him to assuage whatever guilt he may have felt by enshrining the American rural past and instructing future generations of Americans in the fundamental nineteenth-century verities.

The flip side of Henry Ford the Would-Be Farmer was Henry Ford the Populist Technocrat. Even if his factories risked destruction of the simple America he loved, the products he built there would ease the lot of the simple man. Thus he saw no conflict between his idealized view of the nineteenth century and the burgeoning technology of the twentieth. That's how Greenfield Village managed to encompass, in the folds of its ample agrarian bosom, such a technological thrill show as the Henry Ford Museum. By filling a vast hall with all the technological toys of the transportation age—his toys—he built a monument to himself and his own magpie, packrat, mechanic mentality.

On October 21, 1929, the museum was opened with a splendid gala. The guest of honor was Thomas Alva Edison, who said that the Menlo Park workshop had never been as neat and tidy as it appeared in the Ford restoration. Gathered to honor Edison was a crowd of luminaries that included President Hoover, Madame Curie, John D.

Rockefeller, Jr., George Eastman, Walter P. Chrysler, Ransom E. Olds, Orville Wright, Charles and William Mayo, Cyrus Eaton, Lee De Forest, Harvey Firestone, Sr., Jane Addams, Charles Dana Gibson and Will Rogers. It has been said that no greater assemblage of inventors and breakthrough researchers has taken place in this century.

The facade and main entry area meticulously replicate Philadelphia's Independence Hall. It was rumored that Ford actually tried to buy the original but the city fathers of Philadelphia stopped him. The display area is a vast single room, floored with eight acres of hand-laid teak. The architect, Robert Derrick of Grosse Pointe, Michigan, wanted to do a three-tiered affair—basement, main floor and balcony—but Ford wasn't having any. He dictated the all-on-one-floor layout because he wanted to be able to stride through one end of the building and see all the way down the aisles to the other, just in case any of his workmen were loafing. Cost was no object and Ford spent five million 1929 dollars on the building alone. The Ford dealer organization was instructed to buy and ship virtually anything that pertained to early America and its technology, and they did: everything from silver candlesticks and ladies' hats to farm tools and railway locomotives.

Today the place holds 170 cars, mostly American, with another 35 in storage (including Jimmy Clark's '65 Lotus Indy winner and Gurney and Foyt's '67 Le Mans-winning Mark IV). There are sixteen aircraft, including eight of the twelve voted most significant of all time by General Doolittle's commission in 1961. There are 21 motorcycles, including Charles Lindbergh's 1919 Excelsior and the world's first production bike, the 1894 Hildebrand & Wolfmuller. All this is garnished with an eye-popping fleet of locomotives. Damnedest thing…

The museum has been criticized for years as a sort of unplanned, Raggedy Andy agglomeration of unrelated stuff. That's what it is, and, what's more, that's what makes the place so much fun. I'm probably unique among motoring journalists in that I've never been very comfortable with either Harrah's automotive collection or the idea of Bill Harrah. The cars are too perfect. The place is so technoid and sanitary that it always makes me think of a Nazi trade fair. Nowhere does humanity seem to intrude upon the seamless technological perfection of it all. Henry Ford probably wouldn't have liked it much either, because whatever else he was or wasn't, he was human, warts and all. He didn't like people who made their living making money. He loved making money, but he saw that the money had to come as proof that you were doing something worthwhile and doing it better than the other guy. The Harrah moneymaking machinery, impersonally and automatically converting human foolishness to liquid assets, would have given that quirky old man the creeps. It gives me the creeps. I much prefer the musty clutter of Greenfield Village.

As you roam aimlessly through the place, you're reminded again and again of the purely human aspect of technology. It's no better and no worse than we are—an occasionally funny, always fascinating mechanical manifestation of our own foibles and frailties. It's like hiking through the nostalgic tinkerer's creases in Henry Ford's brain. Like all of us, he bought more toys and curios than he needed and, once he owned them, couldn't for the life of him figure out what to do with them. There's the '31 Pitcairn Autogiro, bright red, with *WWJ—The Detroit News* gaily painted on the side. Over here's a tall black Tucker, poised to burn up the road between Detroit and Chicago in 1948. The 1929 Cleveland four-cylinder motorcycle with petrified tires. Walter P. Chrysler's red '32 Imperial limousine, painted to match a vase in his collection of Chinese porcelain. Charles Lindbergh's house trailer. Fire apparatus, buggies, Edsel Ford's little Grand Prix Bugatti, rigged with fenders and splash guards to protect him from the famous Detroit slush. My God! That's the Lincoln limo Franklin Delano Roosevelt was riding in the time my grandmother Simpson made my father chase him down Woodward Avenue between Pontiac and Birmingham so that she might get a closer look at him, to hate him with even greater ferocity.

The place is perfect. Like a lifetime of conversations with Bruce McCall and Warren Weith, it ambushes me again and again with forgotten nuggets of technological trivia. Henry Ford may have had a narrow mind and a nasty disposition, but he created the greatest attic in the world for people like you and me.

Notes on the passing of a
152-pound halfback.

❧

I probably shouldn't be writing this in *Car and Driver,* but since *Car and Driver* is the only magazine for which I write on a regular basis and since I feel obliged to get it down for somebody to read, here goes.

I never cried for a dead race driver, even though 30 or 40 dead race drivers used to be friends of mine. God knows it's not because I can't cry. I've wept as I left the Nürburgring, because the race was over and I was leaving my summer friends and going back to New York, and because the Eifel Mountains and the Ahr River and the morning were all so beautiful. As a nineteen-year-old boot at Great Lakes I got all choked up in my first big review when those thousands of guys came to attention and the band struck up "Anchors Aweigh." Women have made me cry, and I cried in 1955 when I first saw what the Sacramento race track and my own imprudence had done to my face. As I've gotten older, though, tears have come harder, and at greater intervals.

Yesterday it happened to me again. I was flogging our Volvo Boss Wagon across the back roads of Ashland County, Ohio, crying like a baby, while my wife and a Brittany spaniel pup tried in vain to comfort me. Driving hard and fast seemed like the only cure, so I kept on the wood until my eyes dried and I could breathe normally. It had finally come to me, in a rush, that my father, who'd died a few days before, was really dead.

I knew he was going to die because they'd all said there was nothing to be done for the cancer they'd discovered only two weeks earlier, but I'd allowed myself to believe that he'd last long enough for one more deer season, even if I had to help him into the woods and sit with him. Maybe I needed that more than he did, but I wanted very badly for him to see the sun rise in deep snowy woods again, and maybe scare up a grouse, or sit silent while a cedar squirrel crept up to sniff his boot sole. But with 73 years and probably four dozen hunting seasons on him he dozed off one Sunday morning and his heart just stopped.

He wasn't a car enthusiast, not in the sense that you and I are car enthusiasts anyway, but he did love cars and he was an automotive person. He drove fast and well, most of the time, although he occasionally suffered the same kind of lapses we all do. When he was young he hit a mule with an open Buick touring car, said mule landing inside the car with him and nearly kicking him senseless. Another time in the same car he and a couple of drunken friends were on their way to a dance, having stopped for a jug of what he called "Who Shot John," and got stuck in some trackless waste near Hazard, Kentucky. He blearily announced that he'd get out to see what was wrong, opened the door, stepped off the running board, and fell twenty feet into a rocky creek bed.

I remember a '34 Ford, a '37 Plymouth, a '40 Oldsmobile (that saw us through the war), then a '46 Olds that got rolled, and a '47 Olds that he stuffed into the center of a railway abutment, maiming himself for life and very nearly ending it all right there. Most of my earliest memories involve night rides, often in the rain, sleeping on the back seat with the harsh mohair upholstery abrading every exposed surface on my body. I was enveloped in car smell and car noise and I'd wake fitfully from time to time, hear the sound of my parents' voices or the rowr-rowr snick-snick of inefficient old windshield wipers, and feel uniquely safe and secure. We drove everywhere, sometimes hundreds of miles at a crack, and he never surrendered the wheel. My mother claims that I got my automotive start earlier, as a baby, when I used to sleep on the parcel shelf of a Model A Ford coupe with our Boston bulldog, Bozo. My favorite toy, she tells me, and my best-loved teething device, was the hard rubber shift knob from that Model A. When my dad sold the car, he had to come home and retrieve the gnawed shift knob from my playpen and my mother got the sniffles.

When he died last week he had an aged but sound Dodge van, which he called "The Bluebird," and a pristine Nova coupe. He and my mother covered most of the eastern United States and Canada in that van, buying antiques for their shop, and it was treated like a member of the family. On the way to the funeral she said that he'd have given a lot to be riding in our trick Volvo instead of the hearse to which they'd consigned him, and she was certain that he'd have been impatient with our crawling pace going to the cemetery.

I know that I got involved with racing because of him. He'd been a fine athlete in his youth, played college football with Bo McMillin at 152 pounds, played semi-pro baseball in a coal miners' league in Welch, West Virginia, and done a fair bit of boxing and pool hustling. All his life he was that same athlete, arm wrassler, wise guy, storyteller, needler, and headstrong adventurer. I needed to prove myself his son and heir, yet I was intimidated by his prowess in all the standard games. After a lack-luster and halfhearted athletic career, I stumbled onto motorsport and never looked back. He never saw me race, but I think he got a kick out of the idea, and I know that he was pleased when I drifted into writing by way of *Road & Track* magazine. One of his own dreams was a career in journalism.

He taught me about jazz, and the big bands of the Twenties. He taught me about good furniture, and Bennington pottery, and mercury glass. He taught me about laughter. He taught me to drive his way, fast and aggressively, and imprinted me with his Kentuckian's distrust of governments and do-gooders. I got his love of hunting and fishing with my genes and, like him, I'd rather be outdoors than in, going somewhere rather than sitting still. He knew the woods as most suburbanites know their lawns. He was a natural shot, a hunter who never missed—as near as an awe-struck adolescent could tell—and he did not suffer fools gladly.

For the first twenty years of my life I was under the impression that he was trying to kill me. At his direction I once backed a Ford Okiebox camper off a six-foot clay embankment, and when my mother and I went through his things we found the very Pflueger Supreme casting rod with which he buried all the treble hooks of a six-inch Bass-Oreno in my fourteen-year-old shoulder one night on Pontiac Lake.

For the past 28 years he was in pain, yet he stumped through life on his bad leg and had more fun than any three healthy people I know. He brought beauty into a lot of households—building beautiful furniture, and restoring battered and broken antiques that lesser craftsmen might have discarded—and his own household was one of the happiest and most entertaining places I've ever been. As I drove away with his lovingly maintained hunting and fishing gear in the back, I suddenly choked on the realization that he really wouldn't be using it anymore, and I just couldn't handle that. He was David E. Davis, Jr., until his father died, and then he dropped the Junior. I can't do it though. For me, he'll always be the original.

The night Willie Nelson and Junior Johnson played the White House.

~·~·~

Bedard walked in with it. An invitation. "Thought you might be interested in this," he said. I took it from him, turned it over in my hand, and discovered that it was an invitation to a buffet dinner at the White House. "The President and Mrs. Carter invite you…" Oh my God. We called the White House just to be sure it wasn't a gag. No, it wasn't a gag, Mr. and Mrs. Davis *were* invited to a party on the South Lawn honoring NASCAR, with Willie Nelson as special guest.

Now I'd never been to the White House before, not even as a tourist, and the invitation simply blew me away. Never mind about who's in office, the invitation came from *the president of the United States!* What's more, outlaw Willie Nelson is one of the very few people I would trust if they ran for the presidency, and this promised to be an excellent opportunity to see and hear him—right up close—so I accepted the invitation faster than Lucas wipers can quit in a rainstorm.

It was an affair harking back to the days of Andrew Jackson's administration; the red-necked *nouveaux riches* of NASCAR mixing it up with the good old boys from the red-clay county of Georgia. H.L. Mencken's booboisie on parade. Top boob honors probably go to HEW Secretary Joe Califano, who'd apparently taken time off from impersonating the Statue of Liberty to make an appearance, but the NASCAR biggies and their parasitic corporate camp followers were never far out of contention.

Bill France, Sr., allowed that he'd come only because he'd gotten an invitation, saying, "Frankly, I've always been a Wallace man. If he hadn't been shot, I think we'd have been here four years earlier." When asked how he felt about Willie Nelson, he said, "Marty Robbins has always been my favorite country singer." Richard Petty displayed similar style and grace when he told a reporter that the country had been in much better shape under Nixon. Meanwhile, the hustlers and deal makers never stopped moving and mumbling. Bringing the biggies together.

"You wanna meet Miz Carter? Why you just come right along with me here, son. Hey, you boy, get a pitcher of this! Go ahead now, give her a hug." NASCAR on parade looks like a convention of small-town real-estate men. Three-piece polyester and complicated hair are very much the NASCAR style these days, as are hyper-aggressive wives huckstering their husbands for fame and fortune. Willie Nelson's roadies were the most colorful and interesting people present, in cowboy hats, Levi's, and thrift-shop chic.

Rosalynn Carter was the class of the evening, closely followed by Willie in a red Adidas T-shirt, a bandanna on his brow. Her husband, the president, was off at Camp David with the Israelis and Egyptians, and she was by all accounts a gracious and charming hostess. I'd always thought of her as a stiff, but she turns out to be a very together lady; she did a great deal to bridge the chasm between the suspicious NASCAR hippie-haters and Nelson's fun-loving band of free spirits. Willie did his bit by singing "Up Against the Wall, Redneck Mother" with enthusiasm and verve. It was perfect.

It was ironic as hell. The NASCAR people covet respectability more than wealth. The Willie Nelson people have taken a long, hard look at it and thrown it away. The ex-outlaws and the would-be outlaws sat down together for roast beef, Georgia ham, three-bean salad, and carrot cake, and Mrs. Carter poured. Junior Johnson nailed it. He looked around and said: "They've cleaned us up a whole lot, I guess. There's just a few of us old-timers left now, like the cowboys and Indians. It's getting sort of sophisticated-like. I guess the West has been won."

Mea culpa.

s I write this, a Porsche factory mechanic wearing electric-blue bib overalls is probably wandering around under a chocolate-brown Porsche 928, shaking his head. As he expertly pokes and prods, like a doctor feeling for broken bones or mysterious lumps, he pulls tufts of grass and weeds out of various cracks, crevices, and joints, runs his fingertips over the contours of a grapefruit-sized dent in the muffler, and wonders about the origins of a non-standard hydraulic line on the automatic transmission.

The first thing he'd have seen is a long, whitish scrape on either door, indicating that the car had gone rather quickly between two white-painted objects—two objects too close together to allow easy passage of a Porsche 928. If he looks closely, he'll probably be a little puzzled to find that the scrapes apparently run from back to front, indicating that the car had abraded its flanks on those white-painted objects while backing up. It will also be apparent to his practiced eye that someone has attempted to remove as much of the alien white paint as possible, evidently with a rag and some kind of liquid car-cleaning compound. His final discovery, when the doors are repainted and the new muffler is in place and the automatic transmission has been checked for damage, will come when he takes the car for a test drive. Then he'll discover that the Pirelli P7 tires, at about 400 DM per tire, have been flat-spotted. Not horribly flat-spotted, mind you, but just enough to feel vaguely out of balance.

I told them I'd pay for the damage. I tried to describe the depth and breadth of my magazine's insurance coverage. But the hospitable members of the Porsche press department just smiled and allowed that those things happen, not to worry, that the damage would be repaired. Little did they know. I will mull this over and fret about it to my dying day. I'll wake up in the middle of the night, years hence, and blush with embarrassment, remembering the night I went off the road backwards in

45

a borrowed Porsche.

We'd picked it up the week before, in Stuttgart. We drove to Austria, by way of Munich. On the Stuttgart-Munich autobahn, we found that Saturday traffic was sailing along at about a hundred, with little groups of serious guys getting it on at 120 or so. We fed the Porsche into the flow at 120, then picked up a Mercedes-Benz 6.9 and a Porsche 911SC Targa who wanted to run at about 130. In the absence of any vestige of self-control, and savoring the joyous liberation of the autobahn after months of tense lawbreaking on American Interstates, I joined the fun. It is roughly 210 kilometers from Stuttgart to Munich (130 miles), and we made it in an hour and twenty minutes. Even so, the guy in the Targa got tired of my dawdling along at 200 kph toward the end and flashed his lights to pass. I let him go, and he clearly wondered what kind of pansy I must be.

One night in Munich, then on to Graz, where we would be the guests of Dr. Egon Rudolf, technical director of Steyr-Daimler-Puch, and his wife. We went south of the main road, the trunk route that carries trucks from England to the Middle East, and kept to country roads. J.L.K. Davis got to drive the best leg, from the vicinity of the Österreichring to Graz, which took us over the highest pass in that part of Austria and saw her nipping in and out among the tour buses and yowling through the hairpins like Eddie Barth in the Mountain Championship. At dinner that evening, we learned that Marcus Rudolf, the eldest son of our host and hostess, disapproved of the 928, thinking it a rather "American" car, suggesting that a Porsche could not be a Porsche if its engine was located anywhere other than the traditional Porsche location, astern. I vowed to give him a demonstration of the 928's virtues when we'd finished our hunting trip with his parents.

Four days later, I had to make good on my promise. Now Marcus Rudolf is a serious young man of seventeen, a good scholar, a knowledgeable car enthusiast, already showing signs of considerable engineering talent; why it was so important for me to show off for him that night, I cannot say. I didn't know the road, but my blood was up and I was determined to impress him with the spectacular capabilities of the 928. One turn after another. Hard on the brakes, throttle flat on the floor. A couple of times I thought that I was probably going faster than I'd ever gone before in that sort of car. Then, over a blind crest, swinging hard right, we hit a frost heave. Nothing to it, really, only the rear end was momentarily airborne, then we were spinning, headed for the next corner, an uphill left. I saw a tree and a row of white fence posts and knew that the car was about to become a total. Then we were stopped, backed up the bank, having slithered right through between the fenceposts, backwards, at about 65. I put it into gear, gingerly drove it back onto the shoulder of the road, got out and looked for damage. There was no body damage, only scrapes. Apologizing profusely, feeling like the most irresponsible clown in all Christendom, I started off again, testing the controls timidly, listening for some clue to the awful damage that I must have overlooked in the dark. Five minutes later, just when everything had checked out okay, the automatic transmission seemed to become confused. It began to hunt for a gear, and it was taking increasing amounts of throttle to keep us moving. Thoroughly overcome with self-hatred, I coasted through a village and made it to the Texaco sign I'd seen glowing in the dark. Automatic-transmission fluid was coming out of somewhere like blood from a shot liver, and I was in trouble. We called Marcus' father, reluctantly, and he came to get us.

Not only that, he made arrangements for the local Porsche distributor to pick up my wounded steed and, further, had a new part made in the Steyr experimental department when the Porsche people didn't have what we needed. I sincerely hope that all his helpfulness wasn't just because he wanted to get rid of me. I was considerably luckier than I deserved. What if I'd written off a $25,000 Porsche? What if I'd injured Marcus Rudolf, or worse? What if there'd been a 200-meter drop-off, instead of a steep bank? What if the fenceposts had been closer together? And yet none of those things would have made any difference whatsoever if I hadn't been driving over my head on an unknown road. *Driving sensibly means never having to say you're sorry.*

If I were King...

ᴠᴏᴇᴠ

ast winter, our editor-publisher was invited to speak to the Detroit Society of Automotive Engineers. Violating every known rule of hospitality, he proceeded to accuse them of leaving the door wide open for the federal government and the imported-car industry to steal the thunder from the domestic industry. He said rude things about everything from the Chevrolet Vega to the consumer movement, and he didn't eat his dessert. Toward the end of his remarks, he revealed himself in his true colors—as pretender to some non-existent American throne—and wound up his assault on the audience with the following bill of particulars. Make of it what you will.—The Editors

Let's say that I realized a lifelong ambition and managed to become king of the United States of America. Mine would not be some bogus limited constitutional monarchy, folks, mine would be benevolent despotism of the very best kind. Benevolent despotism being what it is, I'd be able to do pretty much what I wanted to do, and here's what I'd do for a start. I've thought a lot about killing all the lawyers, but I've decided that it would be best to simply slaughter half of them, just to get the other half's attention. Then I'd kill any automotive engineer who hadn't contributed a useful idea in the past twelve months. It goes without saying that automotive engineers working for the government would be wiped out. Boring SAE papers and doubleknit polyester suits would be punishable by imprisonment or selective amputation.

Then I'd direct the president of the United States to assemble a blue-ribbon commission, responsible to him personally, to hammer out a national transportation policy, with the clear understanding that the country could have no coherent energy policy until it had a properly developed transportation policy. The secretary of transportation could be a member of the commission, but not its chairman, since he is so abysmally ignorant of America's transportation needs and desires. The secretary of energy couldn't be on the commission, because he'd be in a home for the terminally dim.

Among the many pieces of enlightened rulemaking I'd demand from this commission would be the following:

1. Both houses of Congress would have veto power over federal regulatory agencies.

2. The United States must join hands with Europe and Japan in the rationalization of existing safety and emissions standards, and the development of any future standards. Further, the federal government must do everything in its power to encourage the internationalization and export potential of our auto industry.

3. Americans would be expected to pay the free-market price for gasoline. Dr. Paul Chenea, of GM's research laboratory, said something to this effect: "America's energy politics are such that, should we be fortunate enough to have the last gallon of gasoline left on earth, we'd probably sell it for 76 cents."

Two-dollar-a-gallon gasoline will do more to accelerate the swing to smaller, more efficient cars than any other move we could make, and revenues thus raised could be used to better maintain our existing highway network.

4. Drunk drivers must be removed from the roads. They are easily identified and segregated, and their driving privileges should be unconditionally revoked.

5. Incompetent or impaired drivers must be either removed from the road or drastically limited in their use of motor vehicles.

6. Automobile-insurance underwriting policies can no longer be skewed toward the lowest common denominator on our highways. Underwriters must, in the future, discriminate in favor of skillful, safe drivers in well-maintained cars. There will be no prosecution for product liability in any case where negligence, drunkenness, incompetence, or any form of overt silliness is present.

7. Driver's-license requirements must be stiffened. Better training and higher skill levels will become mandatory.

(These last five items would do much to create the viable constituency for mass transit that it has lacked until now.)

8. The 55-mile-per-hour speed limit, having proved itself nothing more than a meaningless placebo for the safety-at-any-price freaks, and a pernicious form of police harassment against all others, will be modified as follows:

•The national speed limit on all rural Interstates will be 80 mph.

•The speed limit on urban Interstates and freeways will be 55 mph.

•The speed limit on first-class rural highways will be 55 mph.

•All other traffic laws, including local speed limits in cities, suburbs, and villages, will be standardized.

•These speed limits conform, in general, with those of most Western nations, and represent a reasonable balance between considerations of safety, energy conservation, and improved traffic flow.

9. The current policy of staffing regulatory agencies with personnel who are certifiably hostile to the industries and businesses they regulate is hereby declared bankrupt and abolished. Henceforth, department heads and administrators will be forced to prove their openmindedness and complete freedom from any taint of advocacy—except for the wholehearted belief that whatever they regulate must work as efficiently and profitably as the law and the competitive give-and-take of the open market allow.

10. All laws pertaining to product design and liability, and all federal regulations pertaining thereto, will henceforth be framed in the belief that citizens of voting age are capable of making decisions in their own best interest, and do so at their own risk, unless they have been certified as impaired or incompetent by the courts.

I will set my royal seal to all the above because I want this country and its automobile industry to hit a bases-loaded home run in the next few years. I want us once again to set the technological pace for the rest of the world. I wonder if the sleeping giant of American technology may not have been doped by the bad guys in Washington. He should be back on his feet and working in no time at all, once I take the throne. I see nothing in any of this that might cause cancer in Canadian mice or set fire to your Pinto, but I'll ask the Swine Flu people to keep an eye on things, just in case. They haven't had enough to do anyway.

Drunk, just across the quay from the ducks.

~~~✦~~~

S *aturday afternoon, Geneva:* I am seated at a small table in the Restaurant de la Cascade on the Quai des Bergues. I have just completed five hours at the Geneva Automobile Show, which I attended more or less by accident, and now I am just a tad drunk, surrounded by Italian waiters busily serving Alsatian food to the local Swiss. On the table before me is the yellow legal pad upon which I write, a large greasy platter that held *choucroute garnie,* and a small plate littered with minute traces of strawberry tart, the latter two guarded by an empty half-bottle that only minutes ago gave up its last drop of kick-ass Gewürztraminer. In my right hand is my customary green Flair pen. In my left hand is a glass of stumpwater-colored *marc de Bourgogne,* which I love dearly, and which promises to further fuel the fire that got me started writing this in the first place. Outside, across the quay, this end of the lake is crowded with some of my favorite brands of ducks eating duck junk-food. I've often thought I'd like to be a wild duck, but today the difference between our luncheon menus makes me wonder if I'd enjoy it all that much. Today I'm glad I'm a hedonistic automotive journalist adrift in Geneva.

This has been a real Artur Keser lunch. Almost twenty years ago Keser introduced me to the *marc* family of fine alcohols. That was the same day he told me that any large wooden pepper mill was called a "Rubirosa" by the European racing community of the Fifties, a reference to the much publicized sexual capabilities of the Dominican playboy Porfirio Rubirosa. Artur Keser taught me a lot, much of it having to do with the good life, but the most important part having to do with the responsibilities, obligations, and mysterious delights of running a major-league car magazine. He was press director at Daimler-Benz and very much a man of the world. I don't know how many languages he spoke, or in how many dialects, but he was an ace communicator wherever he went. One late night I asked him, "How can you live in Stuttgart? You, who enjoy London and Paris and Munich and Baden-Baden so much?" "Stuttgart is perfect," he answered. "Every night I can go to bed at nine o'clock, certain that I am missing nothing!"

When Artur Keser died the other day, his sister, Lilli, decided to have a memorial service for him in a suburb of Basel, hard by the place where they'd lived together following his retirement, and not far from the south-German town where they'd grown up. I decided that I owed it to Artur and his sister and myself to attend, so I hopped on a plane and flew to Stuttgart, met Leo Levine (who introduced me to Artur Keser, years ago), and drove to Basel in a red turbo-diesel Mercedes. That was day before yesterday. Lots of old friends were there: Karl Ludvigsen, once editor of this magazine, now a Fiat executive; Dirk Strassl, once Keser's assistant at Daimler-Benz, now, at BMW, the hottest automotive PR man in Europe; my ride, Leo Levine, for years the *Stars and Stripes* auto-racing maven in Europe, later the automotive guy for the *New York Herald Tribune,* now press chief for Mercedes-Benz North America; and, as they say, a host of others. The feeling was strangely solemn. At the reception after the service there was wonderful food and drink in harvest-table quantities, but we all felt, somewhat guiltily, that we should have been drinking champagne by the magnum and raising all kinds of hell in Keser's honor. Had Keser been in charge, I'm confident that he would have run it that way.

I wondered, briefly, whether it might be inappropriate to combine my trip to his memorial service with a visit to the Geneva show, then knew that few things could have been more appropriate. The best thing that could happen to an automotive writer at any European show in the last three decades was to look up and see Artur Keser striding across the floor with an impish grin and arms spread wide. So I hopped the evening train for Geneva, checked into the Hotel Bristol, and dived into William Faulkner's first novel, *Soldier's Pay.*

Read till three in the morning last night. Breakfasted all by myself in the very elegant Hotel de la Paix, just around the corner on the lakefront, then cabbed to the show in a lovely, clean '78 Chevrolet Caprice. There's a surprising assortment of American GM products on the streets of Geneva. Camaros and Firebirds, big Chevys, the odd Corvette, but most impressive are the new Malibu sedans and station wagons. The Chevrolet Malibu looks as though it was designed for Europe. The car is perfectly at home in these surroundings, looking elegant and purposeful all at once. I'll bet that the F41 suspension would get Mr. Well-To-Do Swiss Burgher and his Malibu through the Alps pretty smartly too. Not as well as a BMW or a Rover 3500, perhaps, but a lot better than any American car that preceded it.

Today was opening day for the public, and the show was jammed, with multi-national crowds piled up at the ticket windows. I paid my six francs, got my ticket, and passed through the main entrance right into the specialty coachbuilders' area. The famous Italian firms have apparently lost their respective ways, being mired somewhere between *Star Wars* and the old Fisher Body Craftsman's Guild, producing wet dreams that range from silly GT coupes to silly off-road vehicles. Pininfarina's Jaguar XJ Spider was just awful, and Ghia's Fiesta-based GTK was bad origami. Only Giugiaro at Ital Design seems to know where he and the automobile are headed. The rest of them just go on rehearsing their own confusion. Off-road vehicles were literally everywhere, and four-wheel-drive madness is almost as far advanced in Europe as at home, only with a different constituency. In Europe, it's the province of the rich and almost-rich, and the blue-collar crowd need not apply.

Interestingly enough, the real-world off-road stuff was generally more stimulating than the stylists' fantasies. Geländefahrzeug GmbH, child of the marriage between Daimler-Benz of Germany and Steyr-Daimler-Puch of Austria, exhibited the full range of Mercedes-Benz G-series off-road vehicles, attracting hordes of would-be-off-roaders. These vehicles look terrific, and we can only spin our prayer wheels and hope fervently that they'll come to the United States. VW showed a civilian version of its 4wd Iltis (Polecat) military vehicle, which seems to fall somewhere between the Citroën Mehari/Mini Moke and more conventional vehicles like the Range Rover and the G-wagen. British Leyland, or whoever they are these days, responded to the latest German challenge with an eye-popping display of Land Rovers, plus a strange and wonderful six-wheeled Range Rover that only drove four wheels.

The long-awaited Rabbit (Golf) convertible was also on view, and it's so ugly that you'd have to chain it to your porch at night just to keep it from uglying away on you.

Geneva is an interesting show. Not as vast and varied as Frankfurt, but a terrific place to run an EKG on the automobile business. Based on my examination, I'd say that the car biz is hale and hearty for a patient in his early eighties, and good for another eighty, provided that the Naders and Haddons and Claybrooks of this world are prevented from assassinating the old codger.

That has to be it for now. The waiters are hovering over me, sucking their teeth and watching for my fingers to loose their grip on the stem of my brandy glass. Tomorrow I'll buy four ounces of fresh caviar at the duty-free store and when I get home Jeannie and I'll go to bed with that, some fresh toast, and a bottle of champagne. And if that isn't a fitting tribute to Artur Keser, I can't imagine what is.

How did George Washington manage without a secretary of transportation?

nice lady named Frances Lewine called from Washington a while back to say that the secretary of transportation, Mr. Brock Adams, wanted to see me. "Oh nice," I brooded, "he finally got fed up with all the rude things this magazine has said about him, and he's going to have me spirited away in the back of an Interagency Motor Pool panel truck and I'll never be seen or heard from again." There could be no other explanation. The Kafkaesque forces of darkness at DOT were being mobilized against me. They don't like rabble-rousers down there—unless they're named Nader—and now I was going to pay with my life.

I showed up at New York's crummy old Biltmore Hotel on the appointed day, ten minutes early, and was ushered into the most depressing hotel room I've seen since World War II. Small, roughly the size of an Eldorado's trunk, it contained two chairs, a bed, a chest of drawers, a lamp, and a beardless youth in a three-piece suit of sincere cut and material. "Brock'll be in in just a minute," he said with warm familiarity,"and Terry Bracy will be sitting in." "Who's Terry Bracy?" I asked. "Oh, Terry's a really bright guy, a public-affairs specialist. He's doing a kind of Jerry Rafshoon thing for Brock." To these jaded ears, "doing a kind of Jerry Rafshoon thing for Brock" translated directly into hyping the secretary's public image, building him up in the public eye for his long-predicted run at a Washington Senate seat. Terry the Flack has his work cut out for him, I'd say.

"Just a minute" becomes a half-hour, then Terry the Flack strides in, all business, followed by a cheery secretary of transportation wearing a bell-sleeved alpaca golf sweater and an open-collared white shirt. Just one of the guys. "Good morning, Mr. Secretary, may I tape our conversation?" Of course. No sweat. My fears were groundless. Adams isn't going to have me killed. A couple of minutes of small talk clearly establishes that he has only the foggiest idea who I am, and that he's never read this magazine in his whole entire life. His breezy charm is at first disarming, and I fret inwardly, wondering if perhaps I've wronged him in all the editorial shots I've taken at him over the past two years. But no, as the conversation begins to develop, I'm more and more reassured. This warm, likable man is the same one who's been getting it wrong about automobiles ever since James Earl Carter foisted him off on an over-regulated body politic.

As a heavy hitter, our secretary of transportation falls somewhere between Dagwood Bumstead and my golden retriever, Red. He is a genuinely nice man, and he seems to mean no harm, but Warren G. Harding would have creamed him playing Twenty Questions. He believes things that aren't true. He looks for solutions to national transportation problems in technoid fantasies—his own and other people's. He is more beguiled by Buck Rogers than by Boss Kettering. God help the Republic if George Barris or Mickey Thompson ever gets his ear.

We sat in that ghastly little room for an hour while he earnestly poured out his confusions and frustrations concerning cars and the people who manufacture them. As he talked, I became less and less able to keep my mouth shut, and ever vigilant Terry the Flack was similarly afflicted, shouldering his way into our conversation every few minutes to amend or amplify some point the secretary made, or to scourge me for my periodic outbursts of pro-car crime-think.

The secretary's main concern seemed to be the domestic automobile industry's unwillingness to accept his public challenge to "reinvent the automobile." He quoted no less an authority than former General Motors vice-president John Zachary De Lorean—Detroit's answer to Margaret Trudeau—saying, "When I was talking to John De Lorean the other day, he said that with all of our efforts, in the last few years, of fuel economy and downsizing and all of this, we've arrived about at the 1956 Chevrolet." For the benefit of those who've somehow missed Mr. De Lorean's media blitz, he is the man who hopes to build the new American sports car...in Ulster, using a French engine, an Italian-designed body, and English engineers. He is best remembered in this country as the man who brought us the Pontiac GTO Judge and the 1973 Chevrolet Monte Carlo, both high-water marks in automotive taste and farsightedness.

The secretary went on to bemoan the fact that no one in Detroit wanted to build a car for the late Eighties as fresh and innovative as De Lorean's. It was at this point that Davis the partisan blew the interview for Davis the journalist. "But De Lorean's car is an old car!" I interrupted. "But it's stamped out of new materials," he came back. "I don't mean that we're going to be able to use that for the general public, because he's got a high price and he's really competing with Porsche and, in other words, he's got a lot in that, like, you know, zero to sixty in eight seconds and things like that...." My turn again: "De Lorean's car is older than a number of cars that are on the road right now, including several that GM has already introduced. De Lorean has hacked together a prototype using existing pieces from all over the United States and Europe." "Except he's got a new body," was the secretary's defense. I wanted to say that I'd heard De Lorean had a face lift, but I didn't know anything about a new body; but I restrained myself and simply suggested that John Z. was "stuck with stainless-steel body panels."

As I sat there listening to this friendly man with the Hubert Humphrey voice worry about our automotive destiny, it occurred to me that as secretary of transportation he was also responsible for trains and that there was probably a train derailment going on somewhere at that very moment. (There's usually one happening somewhere.) Maybe we should all send telegrams and urge him to worry about trains instead. Even Terry the Flack acknowledged that Adams knows more about trains than automobiles. Derailments have become epidemic in our country. We lead the world in miles of improperly maintained roadbed. Something must be done! Mussolini made great political hay out of the doubtful claim that he made the trains run on time. If Brock Adams will stop listening to all those people trying to lead him down the garden path and listen to us, he may be a senator yet. Forget our automobiles, Mr. Secretary. We'll just try to struggle along without your help while you fix the railroads.

Well, we still beat 'em at baseball
(for the time being, anyway)...

~

In flight, JAL Number 6, Tokyo—Anchorage—New York: Historians and World War II buffs will record that I finally agreed to a separate peace with Japan on May 22, 1979. The battleship Missouri not being available at the time, I chose a Nissan experimental electric bus as the platform for the official end of hostilities between me and the Land of the Rising Yen. The warming trend in the Davis-Japan Cold War begin in 1960, when I bought a Miranda 35mm camera, the best I ever owned. By the mid-Seventies I had been seduced by Japanese products ranging from the Datsun 240Z and the Winchester Model 101 shotgun (made by Miroku) to a Marantz sound system. My Sony Trinitron had grown closer to me than at least two of my children, but I was still unwilling to go all the way and accept the possibility that Japanese technology had co-opted me.

Oh sure, they made a lot of terrific stuff, and they seem to be getting better every year, but they were short, their language was unintelligible, and camera-toting busloads of them were constantly engulfing me at the world's major airports and historical monuments. I was inclined to the belief that some latter-day Commodore Perry ought to go over there and open their gates to the full cornucopia of American throwaway merchandising. It was immoral somehow that they sold us all their exportable cameras and cars and television sets, yet politely refused to buy any of ours. I turned down a couple of invitations to visit Japan because Japan made me uncomfortable. Germany and Italy enjoyed the sunshine of my smile years before the third partner in the Axis big three ever got anything but a curt nod. Each time some Datsun or Toyota pleased me, I felt like a traitor to John Wayne.

Then, two months ago, I got a phone call from California: Would I visit Nissan in Japan? Would Mrs. Davis care to join me? I accepted offhandedly. Then, ten days later, had misgivings. My kid would be graduating from school in Connecticut the day after we got back. I had too much work to do. I wouldn't like it in Japan, and I resented the Japanese. As late as two days before our departure I was warning the staff that my head cold might keep me from going. Three days later I was in Tokyo, embarked on my tour of Nissan's automotive works. I guess my resentment had grown out of the feeling that the Japanese had outsmarted us somehow. That became clear as we tramped through the Tochigi plant, watching Datsun 310s roll off the line. The Japanese are doing a better job at realizing their version of the American dream than we are with ours. Japan turns out to be merely sensational. I feel like Lieutenant Pinkerton in *Madame Butterfly*. I'm in love, and the grudge I've nursed since adolescence is healing like a lanced boil.

A Japanese car factory is cleaner and quieter than its American and European counterparts. The people who work there—blue-collar and white-collar alike—may be "workaholics living in a rabbit warren" as someone so gracefully put it, but they aren't automatons or lobotomized tools of the great trading companies. Assembly-line workers make about a thousand bucks a month, plus a good-sized bonus, and they enjoy a pretty fair package of benefits. They like their work, and they're proud to work for one of the industrial giants. The academic maunderings of the American intelligentsia about "blue-collar blues" have not yet filtered down to the Japanese factory worker, with the result that he doesn't know he's supposed to be miserable. A Nissan worker has to have a high-school education, and he receives comprehensive training and indoctrination before he starts screwing Datsuns together. We saw horseplay on the assembly line, bows exchanged between workers and bosses, and snappy salutes tossed by gate guards, but not once did we see mass calisthenics by obedient proles, or kamikaze workers' choirs belting out the company song.

The thing that's most remarkable about Japanese industry is not the fact that they build some fairly ordinary cars—in addition to triumphs like the Datsun Z-car, the Honda Accord, and the Mazda RX-7—but that they've made such extraordinary progress in just two decades.

Japan suffers badly from congestion, and her cars have suffered in execution from their humble, English-cars-built-under-license origin and an 80-kph speed limit. Japan's drivers are generally thought of as crazy, but this is slander. They're opportunistic, and they lean on one another at merges and intersections, but we never saw one do anything genuinely silly. Cars built for a moped speed limit in a country where you're never far from the madding crowd probably won't be hilarious fun to drive, not in the sense of the BMW 2002 or the Alfa GTV anyway, and Japanese cars have lagged behind their European competition in this respect. But the Japanese, unlike the Americans or the British, can look at a market and learn something from it, and the Japanese have. Each new model to come from Japan lately is dramatically better than the car it replaces, and soon most Japanese cars will meet American and European standards of fun, performance, and appearance. Datsun's new Silvia and Gazelle, Toyota's Corolla DOHC, and Subaru's 1800cc Leone are knockouts, and there are more where those came from. After visiting Nissan, I am moved to speculate about what's going to happen here when Japanese cars are not only reliable and inexpensive to operate, but beautiful and fun to drive in the bargain.

The General Motors X-cars have gotten everybody's attention—here and abroad—for the moment, but they can't do it all by themselves. Japan's auto industry is moving much faster than ours to meet the dual challenges of the energy crunch and America's growing passion for little cars. We asked Nissan's president, Mr. Ishihara, about plans to build Datsuns in the United States, and he said that their main concern was for quality and that they had some doubts about American plants being able to deliver Japanese quality. Fellow traveler David Smith, editor of the highly regarded *Ward's Auto World,* then put forward the proposition that "quality is a management decision"; that the reason for Japanese quality is Japanese manufacturers' insistence upon it, not the mythic superiority of Japanese workers or the Japanese manufacturing process. Mr. Ishihara is a tough guy, a former rugby player who looks as if he could bend samurai swords with his teeth. He talks the same pious double-talk as most Japanese leaders when questioned about Japan's barriers to import, but he made one point loud and clear. "We send English-speaking managers to America, and we do plenty of market research. We send cars well-adapted to that country. We succeed because we do our homework."

Tell the jury, please, Mr. Sherman, just what you and Mr. Duntov had in mind when you entered this courtroom in a full powerslide.

ora Arkus-Duntov should be given a place in the Smithsonian. I used to think that he'd make a nice national park, but I'm not sure that the government would fund a white-haired national park with a Russian accent. If they ever did, though, it would be a terrific place to drive cars and chase women. But the vastness of a national park would blur the Duntov effect. At the Smithsonian, in the intimate room I have in mind, you could sit in the shade of the pits at the Nürburgring, sip an aperitif, and listen to Zoraika tell stories. In the background you'd hear a blend of hysterical exhaust noises and the cheery French café music that was always used for the great British motor-racing films of the Fifties—Muzak, but Muzak with cojones. Zora Arkus-Duntov would sit beneath a Martini umbrella wearing linen trousers and an Hermes shirt, very soft Italian loafers, and a silk scarf, origin unknown (but subject to a lot of ribald speculation by his friends). Nearby would be a display featuring the Ardun cylinder head, which made OHV screamers out of flathead Fords, and the Duntov cam, which was like a dose of goat glands for early small-block Chevys. In the background, we'd see an 1100cc Porsche racing car, like the ones that Zora drove to class victories in the '54 and '55 Le Mans 24-Hour races. In the foreground, of course, there'd be a great thumping ZL-1 Corvette, capable of running eleven-second quarter-miles all day long, and probably the apogee of American performance-car development. That small area, all by itself, inhabited by a white-haired engineer and his remarkable wife, Elfie—possessor of the finest giggle in all civilization—would attract car enthusiasts the way the National Air and Space Museum attracts everybody else.

Now, I get word that Duntov—inventor, engineer, raconteur, award-winning roué, and most European of Europeans—is thinking of suing us. I guess he's sore because Sherman referred to the current Corvette's independent rear suspension as "ill-conceived." As it happens,

Zora holds a patent on that particular design, and he doesn't think it's ill-conceived at all. I guess a lawsuit is all I needed to make my relationship with Duntov complete.

Zora and I have been friends, more or less, for about 25 years. In 1960, when I wrote Corvette and Corvair advertising, Zora used to complain to my bosses and his bosses that my Corvette advertising wasn't as filled with *sturm und drang* as he'd have liked it to be. In 1961, when I was responsible for a team of Corvair rally cars in Canada, Zora sent John Fitch to spy on me because he was confident that I'd screw it up (happily I didn't). Somewhere in the middle Sixties, Zora wanted me to sample the delights of a prototype 396-cubic-inch Stingray with a Powerglide transmission. This involved him screaming around the little track behind Chevrolet Engineering at speeds well above the transmission's upshift point, which proved absolutely nothing about the possible usefulness of an automatic transmission in a Corvette, but did cause us to go off the road, backwards, in the north turn at about 95 miles per hour. (Zora had been getting farther off-line for the four previous laps, and I could have predicted within a few feet the point at which we'd exit the banking, backwards, but he was drunk and the heady wine of sunshine and an empty track and the hard contralto yowl of that 396.) After we'd stopped slithering through the grass, backwards, and picked our way back onto the track, Zora drove very sedately to the Engineering garage and proposed that I not mention my thrill-packed ride to anybody in authority at Chevrolet Division of General Motors. This is the first time I've mentioned it. I do so, now, because Zora has been retired from Chevrolet for lo these five years, and because his superiors at Chevrolet found out about our high-speed surveying trip anyway, and subsequently blistered him for tearing up the grass, or something. Now his lawyer says he's suing us. It figures; he wasn't able to get me fired, and he couldn't kill me, so now he's taking me to court.

Thus, this isn't the first time that Zoraika has been annoyed with me, and it probably won't be the last. I just hope it isn't permanent. We live in perilous times, when more entrepreneur-engineers like Duntov could be helpful to the cause of the automobile. Too many of the young technocrats who walk the halls of American automobile-engineering buildings today are virtually interchangeable with the young technocrats who walk the halls of government agencies. In a time when they should be arch-rivals, they are sisters under the skin. For every one who might share Duntov's passion, there are a hundred who are perfectly willing to design cars for a 55-mph speed limit—cars with brakes like those on the new GM X-cars, designed to meet the government standard, no more, no less, and who cares if the car gets sideways every time you really hammer the middle pedal? Where Duntov is a man of the world, a colorful personality forged in two wars and a half-dozen countries and on a hundred racetracks, these guys want to keep their heads down, take no risks, and keep making the payments on the boring houses in the boring suburbs. Where Duntov nearly killed me, the new generation of engineers is moved to complain when I make the tires squeal. I don't know how many times he got it right, or how many times he got it wrong, but God knows he was never afraid, and he was never boring.

Should *Duntov vs. Sherman, Davis, and Car and Driver* actually make it onto the docket in some Detroit courtroom, it'll be some terrific scene, certainly a cut above Perry Mason, or the recent Indianapolis 500 silliness. Sherman and Duntov are more than a match for each other, both best known for great clouds of rubber dust, and terrified passengers. I'll be along for the ride, so to speak, but what a ride! *Thrills and spills, hearty laughter.* Maybe we should include a videotape of the proceedings in the Zora Arkus-Duntov Room at the Smithsonian. Think of its value for future generations of American engineers, if they can take time out from designing low-priced copies of Japanese cars.

Rabbits vs. foxes, and crash tests for migratory waterfowl.

❧

I had a chance to have dinner with the smartest man in Detroit the other day, always a treat, and he not only provided me with a pretty nice lobster, he gave me a lot of food for thought as well. He's not as depressed as he was five years ago, but I don't know if that's because he's mellowing or because he sees some hope for the future. Judge for yourself.

Halfway through the second pre-dinner Perrier, he said: "You know, this'll be the first generation since the dawn of time that was actually slower than the one that preceded it. I am prevented by government decree from driving as fast as my father did, even though he was driving really crude vehicles on roads that were essentially unimproved. Speed saves time, and time is not only an unrenewable resource, there's no substitute for it. Horses go faster, year after year. Airplanes go faster. Men *run* faster than ever before. But our government has decided that progress in ground-transportation technology has to stop here. This is as fast as man should go. Historians in the next millennium will look back on this period and call it the Dark Ages. What we now call the Dark Ages will look like the Enlightenment by comparison. Medieval scholars can be forgiven for all their foolishness and superstition; they didn't know what we know, nor did they have the tools that we have for mining information. Equipped as we are, knowing what we know, I think we can absolutely count on God to exact some awful punishment for our profligate misuse of these gifts.

"I only hope that my great-grandchildren, looking back on this period with all its stupidity and institutionalized superstition, will appreciate the fact that I was against everything. Take crashworthiness. Nothing else made by man or God is designed to crash. Ships aren't designed to sink. Jet aircraft aren't designed to crash. Only cars. Try to imagine a rainbow trout or a tiger that was designed to withstand a 30-mile-per-hour barrier impact. A wild duck designed to survive the federal barrier test would be the funniest-looking organism you ever saw. It wouldn't be able to lift off the water, much less fly. Have you ever noticed that virtually everything in nature is beautiful? That's because it's been allowed to evolve along lines that make it most efficient for the tasks it has to perform. Nature protects her creatures from crashing by providing them with mobility, and the instincts to take advantage of that mobility. Creatures that persist in crashing into barriers don't become better adapted to barrier crashes, they become extinct, as they should.

"The same thing holds true for corporations. Doug Fraser says that the government ought to bail Chrysler out. I don't know about that. Will Chrysler make it? I guess I don't care. GM and Ford were *supposed* to beat Chrysler, just as Chrysler was supposed to beat GM and Ford. If memory serves, about 1996 car companies have bitten the dust since the beginning of the automotive era. I don't know how badly those guys, the losers, got skinned up, but maybe it's just as well that those original 2000 got pared down to four. There are about 10,000 automotive product variations available right now, and that may not be enough, but it's a better choice than you get with panty hose or underarm deodorants.

"Right now it costs about a billion dollars to tool up for a car that you sell to the public for roughly the same price-per-pound as hamburger. The industry seeks a natural balance, much like the foxes and rabbits. Slow rabbits get eaten by fast foxes. Slow foxes don't eat. Both species fool around with colors, long ears, sharp noses, keen eyes, and a lot of other high-tech evolutionary stuff. If the rabbits get the edge, their numbers begin to increase, which then provides extra food for the foxes, whose population goes up in turn. At some point there may not be enough rabbits to go around, but the foxes never eat them all, and the best rabbits survive. When the rabbit population dwindles, the bottom line for the foxes falls off, and invariably the incompatible foxes are the first to go. So everybody makes out. It's a perfect plan as long as nobody screws around with it. I guess I feel sorry for those slow little rabbits, but I sure don't think they ought to be protected from those foxes. Chrysler Corporation may never get to be one of the foxes, but it could evolve into a faster rabbit, provided the government doesn't step in with a lot of money to guarantee that it'll be a half-dead rabbit forever.

"The adversary relationship between our government and our industry must be altered, however. If something doesn't happen to ease the burden on the automobile companies, we'll wind up with General Motors fighting single-handedly against the Japanese for automotive supremacy. And GM won't be fighting a Japanese automobile industry that's all alone—it'll be fighting the combined resources of the Japanese government, the Japanese scientific community, Japanese labor, and finally the Japanese auto industry. Without the support of its own government, General Motors will ultimately lose that fight. There are adversary relationships that work and there are others that don't. They only work, it seems to me, in completely independent or parallel relationships like Dodgers vs. Yankees, or Ford vs. General Motors, or foxes vs. rabbits. They don't work at all in interdependent relationships like catcher vs. pitcher, engineering vs. manufacturing, labor vs. management, or government vs. industry. As adversaries, these interdependents are bound to self-destruct. The fundamental forces for improving the breed are pulling in opposite directions. They become problem-makers, not problem-solvers. Their selfish survival instincts point away from the common objective. Just to keep the whole thing from becoming self-energized requires almost as many umpires as players. Very few consumers are adequately equipped to make decisions in their own self-interest. It's a terrible burden to put on the best informed, let alone the poor slobs who only know that the bad guys are the ones with the most money. It creates an environment in which con men and opportunists like the ones who perpetrated the 84-mpg-Capri hoax can flourish, to society's detriment. The fact that so many members of our government were taken in by those clowns is eloquent commentary to their fitness to make regulations affecting the cars we drive. What it tells us about the daily press is unrepeatable."

For sale: tacky plum-and-white '73 Javelin. Basic transportation for cultural throwback.

~·~

Dear Mr. Davis,

This letter is to inform you that under Michigan law, a repair facility has the right to place a mechanics lien & sell the vehicle for the cost of repairs.

We have made numerous contacts with you, all to no avail. Therefore, if the bill for $110.30 is not paid & the vehicle not picked up by 9/1/79, we will commence a $5.00 per day storage fee & file for the mechanics lien to dispose of the vehicle.

> *Sincerely,*
> *Margaret A. Kormash*
> *Secretary/Treasurer*
> *Campus/American, Inc.*

Dear Ms. Kormash:

Do you have any idea how difficult it is to be a parent these days? Perhaps you are a parent yourself (a mother, most likely). If so, you will appreciate my position, provided there is even the tiniest drop of the milk of human kindness flowing in your body (nothing personal, Ms. Kormash). The 1973 Javelin in question belongs to my son, the budding Punk or New Wave song-stylist and rhythm guitarist, who left high school some years back, having decided to give himself completely to churlishness and self-pity. Inasmuch as this particular son and heir has reneged on every commitment to which he's been a party since he was fourteen years of age, I can't really say why I was dumb enough to co-sign on his car loan, but if television has taught us nothing else, it has consistently (and correctly) shown that fathers are stupid.

You may wonder why I'm telling you all this, Ms. Kormash, but I was touched by the understanding tone of your letter, and I need to talk to someone.

I am not what Dr. Spock would hold up as a shining example of fatherhood, but I'm proud that none of my three children has committed either murder or suicide, and that—so far—they've all resisted the temptation to go Korean and join up with the Unification Church, or worse. Although the son in question frequently appears in public with hair done in decorator shades of green and orange, and in spite of the fact that his wardrobe is not up to the *Esquire* magazine/Savile Row goal I set for myself when I was a post-adolescent, he is the one who is most like me. I tremble to tell that truth, but there it is; this forlorn malcontent, this congenital deadbeat, is the spiritual image of his father at that age. I just wish he had better taste in cars.

He started out with my Honda 250 dirt bike, which he got via his mother's divorce settlement and promptly sold. His first car was a six-cylinder automatic Firebird, vintage 1968, or thereabouts, which he attempted to turn into a street racer by dropping in a Chevrolet V-8 and a four-speed manual transmission. Why he didn't *start* with a V-8 engine and a manual transmission, I cannot say. All I know is that they assembled the racer-motor in such a way that certain important oil passages were blocked—something to do with bearings installed backwards, I believe—causing the engine to seize absolutely rock-solid after it had been running for about five minutes. A stock Chevrolet 350 V-8 was then obtained and the car was made to run, but it always looked like a sheep pen inside, and the only things of value in there, as nearly as I could tell, were the great, tumescent Hurst shifter and the sound system. Don't ask what the outside looked like. My kid was a cultural throwback, until the Punk movement came along. He got into street racing ten years after all the other guys had left Woodward Avenue and gone off to Naval Reserve drills, or whatever former street racers do. I figured he was studying to be one of the bad guys on "Happy Days."

The poor old Firebird never really came to grips with the identity crisis that was a natural result of all this mismatched cobbling, and went on the block. The proceeds went for better and flashier guitars and amps. Father, the fool, offered to help with the purchase of another car. That involved furnishing the downstroke and co-signing the note. The car selected was a '73 Javelin finished in rich plum with a white vinyl roof—in almost every respect a car to make an aging automotive aficionado like me unload my lunch right there in the used-car lot. I tried, Ms. Kormash, God knows I tried. I showed him ads for clean '69 Beetles. I took him to the local Toyota dealer and tried to talk him into driving a nice cherry Corolla. You may not know this, but your typical New Wave Fifties Throwback wants nothing to do with small cars reeking of practicality and good taste. What my kid *really* wanted was a '73 Monte Carlo. What he settled for was this terminally ill (as it turned out) impractical joke from American Motors.

It was more than a match for him in churlishness, and it was tacky enough to become the official Punk car. I should have known I was in trouble when people started harassing me about missed payments on flashy guitars and amps. Then, with about as much good sense and foresight as I'd shown in co-signing on the deal, I threw him out. Naturally, he ripped the sound system out of the poor old plum-colored misunderstanding and disappeared. Now it's mine. His name is still on the note, but I'm pretty sure he won't pick up the payments if I decide to follow his example and default. I brought it to your place to get it fixed. It wouldn't start. Your people charged $110.30 to tell me that it would cost roughly six big ones to fix the busted timing gears, replace the battery, and repair the brakes. I told them to wait until I'd regained control of myself. If it seems as if you've had that plum-colored corpse out back for a long time, I can only say that it's taken me that long to regain my composure. No matter how you slice it, Ms. Kormash, I'm going to be out about two grand on this deal and my kid gets to chortle over the way he's stuck it to his old man. What I'd *like* to do is pay the $2000 to some guys Ken Purdy used to know in Chicago to steal the car and run over my kid with it. I hope I haven't bored you, but I can tell from your letter that you're a thoughtful, sensitive person who'll understand. In the meantime, you might keep *your* eye open for a plum-colored Javelin driven by some guys Ken Purdy used to know in Chicago.

"Nobody else has found himself in the same conditions as we Italians have found ourselves in our own country."

❧

I have loved Fiats, more or less indiscriminately, ever since I saw a Balilla roadster race at Cumberland, Maryland, in 1953. At one time or another, I've yearned to own a Fiat-Abarth double-bubble coupe, a 600 Multipla (the rolling toaster), and —Oh, God, hold my hand—one of those gorgeous Ghia coupes built in the early-middle Fifties with the 60-degree V-8 engine. Right now I am negotiating the purchase of an old Topolino. It has bothered me, a little, that Fiats always seemed to be better cars on their home turf than they were here in the Big PX, but I simply ascribed that to Italian temperament, and didn't worry about it too much. Last fall I spent the best part of a week visiting Fiat in Turin, and the high spot of that visit was a conversation with the head of Fiat's automotive operations, Mr. Umberto Agnelli.

How much do you love your work? How much do you love automobiles? Would you get up each morning, walk to your car, and drive to work, knowing full well that at any moment some wild-eyed post adolescent Red Brigade crazy might blow the back of your head off? Umberto Agnelli does. Umberto Agnelli is a lovely man—in the very best, Celtic sense of the word. As vice-chairman of Fiat, or brother to Giovanni Agnelli, he is usually presented as a sort of cipher, with different meanings for different vested interests.

But as I sat talking with Umberto Agnelli in a Fiat conference room last fall, I tried to match the man to all the labels that have been hung on him over the years and none of the stereotypes seemed to fit. What I saw was a warm, enthusiastic executive who spoke excellent English, was immaculately dressed in a light brown tweed of what appeared to be a cashmere and silk blend, and wore his wristwatch over the cuff of his shirt. I was surprised at his easy candor and moved by his obvious vulnerability. A Fiat executive had been murdered by the Red Brigade as he left his home the day before we arrived in Turin, and I kept marveling to myself that Mr. Agnelli would see us at all, under the circumstances.

Fiat, like Ford, is a very human car company. Cut either one of them and it bleeds. This is partly because both concerns qualify as family businesses, and partly because of the very human strengths and weakness of the families involved. Right now, they're both bleeding. Ford's wounds are self-inflicted, but Fiat is suffering from the interrelated Italian diseases of low productivity, declining market share, and comic-opera national politics. The Italian labor situation is on a level with Great Britain's—i.e., the "Let's destroy everything so we can have a better life" school of labor economics. Clearly it is Umberto Agnelli's responsibility to prevent this from deteriorating to the disaster level of, say, BL or Chrysler, but the odds against him are enormous.

We had visited the most automated of the Fiat factories, Rivalta, and had seen the fantastic Robogate machines building car bodies almost without human supervision, but we'd encountered some hostility on the final assembly line, and had watched the start of a wildcat strike. We asked him about that:

"This is a very difficult time, if you think about last week's murder. It's a time when trade unions are a bit under accusation because they have been covering up some of these terrorists. This is a very tense moment. It's along the assembly line that they have this problem of terrorism. They've got people inside the factory, some of them at the very low levels in the unions…and who are the people they're counting on most? Those coming into those very poor jobs on the assembly line, those who started very young with fairly high school degrees, quite unhappy at the beginning, so they mount these people up for violent strikes, for violence inside the factory."

We asked how the Fiat management people we'd met kept their composure in such dangerous times:

"In Germany it was sudden. Here it's been a slow escalation, and unfortunately, you get used to it…. We've had nineteen people shot in Fiat. This is the third one who's been killed. Unluckily, once you get used to it, there's very little confidence in how the state is able to react to it…. So people just take it as you might take a car accident. That's the dangerous part. Not now, but it could become very dangerous. Today the management people are still trying to do their jobs at their best, but if it goes on they won't be able to act anymore…. But I think I see progress."

We asked about the immediate future of the automobile:

"Let's take it on the energy side first, which is going to be the most important thing for the next ten years. You can't think of really changing the society; you have to change the automobile a little bit—which is happening in your country with enormous investments and things. You'll have different production, more intelligent production, there's going to be more brains in the automobile than there's been in the last twenty years, but I don't think the general picture is going to change very much in the next ten years."

On Fiat's problems:

"I don't know if they gave you figures of compared productivity with other countries, but take Robogate…It was built with the same investment as VW made for the Golf [Rabbit]. We have an assembly line of 80 cars an hour, while the same amount of money gets an assembly line for 100 Golfs. VW builds about 90 of these potential 100 cars. Out of our potential of 80, we build 50. This makes a little difference. And we started with a built-in advantage because we were much more flexible—we could change bodies using the same investment, which they couldn't. If we could have reached 80 percent of our potential we would have had a reliable, moneymaking investment, but use it with that difference and you're out."

Asked how long Fiat could absorb that kind of deficit, he said:

"Not long. If the country doesn't realize that, then Fiat is going to become a subsidized company and it can last forever. Then it's another thing. I really hope that won't happen."

We asked him how he kept going:

"It's a thing of not only fighting fear, you're fighting for your own country. You think that in doing your own job you're also doing something to keep your country in a direction you think is the right one. It's difficult to compare, but I would say that in equal conditions in other countries you would find many people who would continue to do their jobs in the same way."

I wonder.

Officially enshrined as the gas guzzler's gas guzzler, the Rolls-Royce sails majestically into 1980 sans opera windows, sans Twilight Sentinels.

~~~

These must be interesting times for the makers and sellers of billfolds, wallets, money belts, money clips, decorator home strongboxes, and large canvas bags marked with dollar signs. Money blankets America like the dead leaves of November, and Gucci, Hermès, Louis Vuitton, Smythson's of Bond Street, and a gaggle of others outdo themselves in coming up with ever more imaginative and expensive containers for the stuff. And it follows that if you've spent the price of a late-model used car on a billfold, you're not going to carry it—or yourself—around in some ratty, low-roller $15,000 econobox.

This has spawned a whole school of kitsch-kar builders—Clénet, Sceptre, Stutz, DiNapoli, and God Don't Know Who-All—companies conceived exclusively for the purpose of separating the simple-minded *nouveaux riches* from their bucks. For most of the wealthy boobs who willingly place themselves in the hands of these cutpurses and footpads, questions of automotive taste or technical sophistication are as remote as rumors of schismatic tension among Nepalese Buddhists. They buy them because they cost a great deal of money and, furthermore, because they telegraph that single central fact with every overwrought line and stolen flourish.

Happily for that dwindling segment of the population with both money *and* taste, there is an alternative. Standing disdainful and alone at the other end of the Super-Omigod-Big-Bucks Automotive Spectrum is the Rolls-Royce. Unlike the kitsch-kar builders, Rolls-Royce is a real car company building real cars. The descendants of Rolls and Royce do not attempt to synthesize classics from such unlikely components as MG Midget bodies and Mercury chassis, nor do they comb wrecking yards and Buick parts bins for pieces from which to assemble their luxury flagships. You may think that a Roller is as big a rip-off as a DiNapoli. That's okay with me. It's okay with Rolls-Royce, for that matter, because they'll barely crank out 3500 of those big old beauties this year, and fewer than

1500 will find their way to these shores. It goes without saying that there are lots more dope dealers, rock stars, corporate heavies, and orthodontists who want Rolls-Royces than there are Rolls-Royces—even though about half of all the Rolls ever built are still in existence.

I just spent ten days and 3000 miles with a Silver Shadow II, which, at about $77,000, qualifies as the Rolls-Royce price leader. (One imagines some alert consumer group getting R-R hailed into court for running a bait-and-switch operation—luring people into their 68 American showrooms with the El Cheapo 77,000-grickle number, then trying to coerce the poor ninnies into buying $140,000 Corniche convertibles.) It was as good as ten days in Jolly Old England itself, for a Rolls-Royce is as much a state of mind, or a place, as it is an automobile. Our borrowed Silver Shadow II was finished in Caribbean Blue, with a blue leather (Connolly hide, please) interior, and Michelin radial tires. It was, as they say, a credit to its race.

Three times I've visited the Rolls works at Crewe, hard by the Welsh border, and I doubt if I'll ever tire of watching them match the hides and make the upholstery, or forget the little gent who selects and matches all the walnut veneers for the instrument panel and windowsills. When the Shadow II was first introduced, Mr. David Roscoe—the firm's PR chief—pointed proudly to the new Burman rack-and-pinion steering. "You see," he said, "they went to that little bit of extra trouble to center it on the chassis." To which I responded, "But couldn't they simply have left it at the end of the steering column, as it is on the Rover 3500?" "Of course they could have," was his comeback, "but don't you find this quite a bit more elegant?" And of course he was right.

On the subject of that steering, I borrowed a Silver Shadow I, with the old recirculating-ball steering, for the Thanksgiving holiday three years ago, and spent the first hundred miles or so wondering if I'd forgotten how to keep a car between the hedges. The steering was atrocious. I called Zora Arkus-Duntov on my return home to tell him of my difficulty, and he said: "When I am last in England, I am loaned Rolls-Royce by brother-in-law. Driving this car is like attempting to ride bicycle ver-r-ry slowly…weaving, constantly weaving." Now, I'm happy to report, the Silver Shadow II goes down the road—even a snowy one—as straight and true as a set of Johansson gauge blocks.

I drove the Shadow II on as many kinds of road as possible, but my favorite came on a cold Saturday morning when my dog and I were off to harass the grouse at our farm. We headed east on our old test road, M-14, straight into the December sunrise. It was all lavender and creamy-gold and it reflected in the sharp, creased planes of the wonderful hood like a Salvador Dali flag. My affection for the Rolls is like my affection for pubs in Hampshire, and thornproof suits, and Churchill XXV shotguns in fitted oak cases. It is not like my passion for a Porsche 928 or a Mercedes 450SEL. The Rolls is long on comfort and style, but it lacks the sinewy grace of the German cars. It is smooth and solid and it irons out all the unpleasantnesses—major and minor—that its tires encounter in an 85-mile-per-hour charge from Ann Arbor to Manhattan, but it detests the wiggly bits. It is a big Irish hunter, not a quick little cutting horse.

Like horses, like many things British, it is more interesting than foolproof. If it lacks the athletic skills of the Porsche and Mercedes V-8s, it also lacks the bland perfection of an Olds Ninety Eight Regency sedan. All four doors were hard to close on our blue Roller, and the windshield washers froze at the first sign of seriously inclement weather. If there was a rear-window defogger on the car I couldn't find it, and it was an absolute horror to drive for the first twenty minutes of a cold morning, stalling every time I lifted my foot. Wind noise was a problem around the right front door, but the chauffeur who brought us the car explained that the noise wasn't air, just improper adjustment. Is it silly to want one? Emphatically, no. Is it worth the money? Certainly, provided you have the money. If you can't afford a Rolls-Royce, you shouldn't waste your time speculating about whether it's any good or not. Concentrate on what's possible. It's always worked for me. Sure it has.

"Hey, uh, if you're not busy this weekend, howdja like to exercise my Ferrari?"

~ఴ~

Bill Pearce owned some pretty terrific cars back in the late Fifties, early Sixties. That was before all of his attention and disposable income were captured by a 32-foot double-ender called "Temptress." When I met him he had a Porsche 1500 Super cabriolet, probably a '54, and I have fond memories of a vast sand-colored Mercedes-Benz 300S convertible coupe that was loaded with Old World charm and hardly ever ran at all. Pearce and I were soul-mates in many ways. We enjoyed the same cars, we never tired of bench racing together, we loved to eat and drink to excess, and we were similarly enthusiastic about the jazz that blared as background whenever we indulged in any or all of the above pastimes. Once in 1953 or '54 we even went out with the same girl, briefly, but he had the good fortune to marry her. If we differed in any important way, it was that Bill seemed to be accident-prone. I recall that most of his cars either ran into things or got run into, and I also recall that he had a tendency to fall down stairs and off porches whenever his alcohol level became safe to about 60 below.

That may be why he let me drive his Ferrari as often as he did. I sometimes puzzled over his willingness to place one of the most wonderful cars ever built at my disposal, but I wasn't going to look a gift horse in the mouth and I drove the hell out of it. It was a 250GT coupe, a racer that was reputed to have been driven to victory in the '56 Tour de France by the colorful Alfonso Cabeza de Vaca, Marquis de Portago ("Fon" to his friends), but probably wasn't. I can't remember whether the body was built by Farina or Scaglietti—they looked alike—but it was definitely one of those '54-'55-'56 competition coupes that preceded the better-known short-wheelbase Berlinetta. The body was aluminum, the sliding side windows and rear window were plexiglass, and the interior was bare-bones serious business. Whenever I think of that car, the thing that comes first to mind is the shift knob, which was sort of triangular, was made of some kind of fake ivory-looking stuff, and featured a small red jewel looking up from its center—like one used to find in the centers of taillight lenses years ago. Strangely enough, I don't remember the sounds of the car very well, perhaps because there were so many of them and in such overwhelming volume. I suppose, however, that it sounded exactly as any other Ferrari racing car of that period would have sounded, allowing for the fact that this one was equipped with rudimentary mufflers for street use.

It was a car that would flat knock your hat in the creek, just sitting there. Blood red, it was, with great skinny sixteen-inch Borrani wire wheels and louvers and slots and humps, and scruffy-looking aluminum hardware to open and close the doors and keep the hood from flying off. It wasn't terribly comfortable, but I'll bet that the throne of the Holy Roman Empire wasn't exactly a La-Z-Boy recliner either. The steering wheel was large in diameter, small in section, an aluminum frame with some kind of pale wood steamed and bent to form the rim. The instruments were large and legible but strangely out of date, both in terms of contemporary graphic design and measured against the tech-level of the surroundings. It was like a roomy World War II fighter plane with gauges by Seth Thomas.

The designation 250GT meant that it was a three-liter Grand Touring machine. You knew it meant three liters because Ferrari at that time identified his engines by their single-cylinder displacements: ergo, 250 cubic centimeters multiplied by twelve cylinders gave three liters. This nomenclature encompassed a whole slew of cars built from 1954 to 1965, and included some of the nicest Ferraris ever made—a variety of coupes and open cars, powered by three distinct generations of engines having the same bore and stroke dimensions (73 by 58.8mm), but differing a great deal in many other respects. The engine in Pearce's car was a direct descendant of the original Ferrari racing engine of 1948, the supercharged Type 125, designed by Engineer Colombo, with subsequent development by Engineer Lampredi—who would be responsible for the next generation of Ferrari V-12s as well. It was a wonderful engine. In this form it probably produced no more than 230 horsepower at 7000 rpm, but it was a work of art, aesthetically, metallurgically, and technically. Many of the Ferrari's most devoted followers regarded it as the firm's all-time great powerplant. Single overhead camshafts, two valves per cylinder, six-port heads, three four-barrel downdraft Weber carburetors, forged crank and rods, and a beautifully compact overall design made this engine a lovely thing to behold, as well as drive.

Driving it, at the risk of sounding sexist, was man's work. Ferrari had not yet discovered the wonderfulness of Porsche-type synchronizers, and shifting required timing and determination. The clutch was heavy and the flywheel was light. Revs were always kept up, over 3000 usually, partly because we believed it was necessary to prevent plug fouling and partly because we liked the noise. It had primitive shocks and a solid rear axle to go with its narrow Englebert tires, but it worked. Once, when it was in my custody, I drove out to Pine Lake to pick up a friend who at age 40 or thereabouts had never sat in a Ferrari. It was a bright Sunday morning, early, and I gave him all the ride my skill, the black arts of Enzo Ferrari, and limited prudence would allow. As we approached a nasty little ess-bend that ran through a gully and across a humpback bridge, I changed down at about 90, hard on the brakes, hanging the tail out, and shouted over the unholy din, "One of the problems with this damned thing is that you have to double-clutch every downshift." Frozen in his seat, eyes wide, he hollered back, *"I don't know, it looks like an awful lot of fun to me!"* He had that right.

How Pearce could let me have all that fun in his Ferrari I'll never know, but I enjoyed it indecently. Blasting around the back roads of Michigan, tearing off to Toronto for a long weekend of fun and frolic, I kept the plugs clean and the tires warm. "Joy" is too puny a word to describe the feeling that welled up in me each time I pushed that strange-looking key home and that engine whomped to life. If the fates had been kinder to Bill Pearce and his Ferrari I might still get to drive it every now and again. But it was not to be.

Maybe Bill needed money for the boat or something, I don't know, but he sold the Ferrari to a kid who'd been saving all his coins for the express purpose of buying it. He bought it, loved it, and went to work cleaning it up, and it caught fire and burned to the ground. I doubt if the new owner ever got to drive it a quarter as far as I did, and God knows I never drove it as far as I wanted to. Now Pearce is gone, the 250GT is gone, and I don't know what happened to the boat that enticed him away from cars. If the pattern held, it probably sank like a stone.

We'll just hop into the Mercedes and go have dinner with a living legend.

~~~~

Juan Manuel Fangio won the World Championship five times: once for Alfa Romeo in 1951, once for Maserati and Mercedes-Benz in 1954, once for Mercedes-Benz in 1955, once for Ferrari in 1956, once for Maserati again in 1957, and first, last, and always for Argentina. He was the best racing driver ever, a giant. Best known of all the former world champions, his personal impact on motor racing all over the world was simply greater than anybody else's. In Argentina, he's a national hero. The Argentine man in the street speaks of him as he might speak of a saint, or a great noble. Fangio, for his part, returns the compliment. He'll turn 69 on June 24, yet he can still go faster than a lot of younger men, and he loves his country and its people at least as much as they love him.

I have a picture of Fangio in my mind, like a black-and-white slide that I can project on the insides of my eyelids any time I want to. He is standing on the pit wall at Monza during the Italian Grand Prix of 1956. His Ferrari V-8 has gone out with steering failure, and he hopes to take over one of the other Ferrari team cars. Luigi Musso makes a pit stop, but refuses to hand over. Portago's car is already out, having blown a tire. So is Castellotti's, having narrowly missed a serious crash. Fangio isn't particularly tense, even though all hope for another World Championship depends on this race. Peter Collins, lying second, makes his pit stop on schedule, and is asked to hand over to the Argentine. In spite of the fact that Collins could himself gain the World Championship by winning here at Monza and setting fastest lap, he steps out of the car, vaults onto the pit wall, and hands over to Fangio. Fangio finishes second to Stirling Moss, gets three more points, and nails down his fourth World Championship. While all that was going on, I was recuperating from my own racing accident, and one of the things that helped to see me through the months of plastic surgery was Gregor Grant's weekly *Autosport* magazine. One week that fall, *Autosport* arrived, and the cover photo was of Fangio standing on the pit wall at Monza, shouting last-minute instructions to the mechanics as Collins decides to give up his race car. The picture is black and white, but I know that Fangio's helmet is a brown shellacked Herbert Johnson and his T-shirt is pale blue. The photograph is silent, but I know what the pits at Monza sounded like that afternoon and I know that Fangio's voice was strangely soft and high-pitched, yet the mechanics heard every word through the clangor and din of the race. I can see it now, as though I'd just ripped the wrapper off drunken old Gregor Grant's magazine.

Today, Juan Manuel Fangio is president of Mercedes-Benz Argentina and a successful dealer as well. He looks much as he did when he was racing, although he seems to be a little thinner. Like more and more people we know, he came through a heart problem a few years ago and now seems fit as a fiddle. My wife and I had dinner with him on our first evening in Buenos Aires, last January, and we whooped and laughed until one in the morning—until jet lag overtook yr. obt. svt., to be exact—and as we left the restaurant he was still arguing that we were making a big mistake by not visiting one of the clubs and trying our luck at the tango. If the tango is one of the national sports in Argentina, Fangio is a national monument. It was a wonderful feeling to walk into the Hueso Perdido's garden dining area and see every head in the place snap around as he came down the stairs. I expected to hear ruffles and flourishes and "Hail to the Chief."

Mercedes' fortunes in Argentina are as good as they are everywhere else in the world. They have a lock on the lion's share of the city and suburban bus market, and we saw their trucks everywhere. They don't build any cars in Argentina, but a tiny handful are imported, at prices that would drop you to your knees. We traveled from place to place in a five-speed-manual European-spec 280SE, which was terrific, but sold for more than $100,000 in Buenos Aires.

Argentina is terrific, itself. We tramped through factories, met with the Argentine automobile manufacturers' association, and played every night. The country is ravaged by post-Perón inflation, but everyone we met gave the new military government high marks for simultaneously stopping terrorism and getting a leash on inflation, which has fallen from 300 percent to 50 percent in just three years.

We went to Buenos Aires expecting it to be like other Latin American cities we've visited, but it isn't. Argentina is a European country that just happens to lie at the tip of South America. The main population groups are Spanish, Italian, and German, with strong minority populations of French and English. We were greeted at the airport by

Mercedes-Benz Argentina executive Ricardo Ross, an Argentine native who speaks English with a very strong *Irish* accent, inherited from his grandfather. The country has no noticeable black population, and their Indians were virtually wiped out in the nineteenth century, in Indian wars much like our own. Argentina is like this country in many ways. It's vast and beautiful, it too can claim to be a melting pot, and its people are an enormously attractive blending of Europe's best. There's a feeling of old-fashioned let's-get-on-with-it optimism in the air, and an American senses—somewhat ruefully—that this is what it must have been like here 75 years ago, before we confused ourselves.

Fangio, like the other Argentines to whom we talked, is a totally dedicated, un-self-conscious patriot. At dinner, sitting next to one of his most rabid fans, J.L.K. Davis, he talked rapturously about how much we'd love his country, how important it was for us to get out into the countryside and meet the real people. He also volunteered to introduce me to some of the real trout that live in the mountains, but Mercedes-Benz Argentina had us on a tight schedule. I'd like to go back and fish with Juan Manuel Fangio, and I'd like to wander through his home town of Balcarce, and eat *carne asado* with him again. He restores my belief in heroes.

Bulldog, Bulldog, Bow-Wow-Wow!

~~❧~~

The way I get it, this very high-powered sheik ordered what is now known as the Aston Martin Bulldog as his personal 200-mph whizaround, only his kid locked him up in one of the family palaces before he could take delivery. Aston Martin, not wanting to get stuck with an incredibly expensive design prototype, and not wanting to offend the sheik—who, presumably, will regain his freedom someday, make his way to Monaco or Geneva or someplace, and order some more Astons Martin—decided to make the best of a bad deal and turn the Bulldog into a show car. It has now done the tour, winding up at Los Angeles's Auto Expo, and I would say that it has been an unqualified success. Car magazines have chronicled its progress from Newport Pagnell to Los Angeles, and it has created something of a stir.

Aston Martin's man in America is Morris Longstreth Hallowell IV. I encountered him on the second day of the show, hovering around the Aston Martin stand, looking for all the world like a man who expected some kid to toss a melting Eskimo Pie through the window of his $500,000 prototype, except that the windows don't open. He invited me to climb in. To facilitate this, he opened a little panel next to the driver's gull-wing door and pushed one of a cluster of small square buttons, and the door began to rise. "Erng, erng, erng, erng." It whined like something from science fiction. A wonderful servo-motor noise that might have been taped somewhere inside the Space Shuttle about five minutes before takeoff. With the door in its full-upright position, the whole left side of the cockpit was laid bare, from the floor to the roof, such a gaping hole that one wondered if the car had any structural integrity at all. I went in gingerly, head first, expecting the Bulldog to sag in the middle. It didn't. Morris Longstreth Hallowell IV slid his somewhat more lissome self into the passenger seat and pushed some more buttons. Stereo "erng, erng, erng, erng." Both doors closed and we were alone. Morris Longstreth Hallowell IV moved the short lever on the right side of the steering column upward, one notch. Inside, all manner of digital thingies lit up on the dash. ("Hello, Earth, we have data display.") Outside, the parking lights, marking the extreme front corners of the vehicle, as well as most of the rear end, came on. Then he moved the lever upward, one more notch. The slotted panel covering the headlights silently fell away. One last upward push and the battery of five—count 'em, five— seven-inch rectangular Cibié quartz headlamps came on. The crowd fell back, arms thrown over faces to defend against the white light. Touching the turn-signal lever on the opposite side of the steering column, Morris Longstreth Hallowell IV switched on the high-beams. A little over 200 yards away, across the show floor, a CPA from Downey—who'd sneaked away from his wife and kids at the Clénet display to call his girlfriend on the pay telephone—was incinerated by the Cibiés' harsh glare, patches of his lime-green doubleknit leisure suit sticking to his flesh like napalm, his shadow permanently etched on the back wall of the phone booth. The Aston Martin Bulldog gets our highest check-rating for lights.

The CPA from Downey had hardly stopped sizzling when my genial host suggested that if I return to Auto Expo the following weekend, then the show would be dismantled, he would give me a ride in this mighty wedge with the canine name. I accepted, and eight days later was delivered to the rear door of the Convention Center by our own burnout, Steve Smith. The Bulldog was waiting, crouched in the freight entrance. Morris Longstreth Hallowell IV was circling it warily, fending off the attentions of interested inner-city residents. All was in readiness. I clamber into the driver's seat, and am told that Morris and only Morris can drive it. I can be passenger/observer/shotgun-messenger. Rats. I fall out of the driver's seat, bang my head on the gull-wing door, trudge around the rear to the other side, and again perform my patented headlong plunge into the soft, brown Connolly-hide interior. Morris Longstreth Hallowell IV slips into the seat I just left and hits the buttons for the doors. "Erng, erng, erng, erng." ("Earth? Bulldog. We have closure.") The only man in all North America allowed to drive the Aston Martin Bulldog pores over the controls, feels around behind the steering wheel, smiles at me uncertainly, and says, "I've never driven it before."

We are not daunted. A twist of the key brings about 700 great big English horses to life, snorting and pawing the earth. The Bulldog's engine is the standard Aston Martin double-overhead-cam V-8, pumped up with a pair of Garrett AiResearch turbochargers, one for each bank, fed by Bosch fuel injection instead of the standard engine's four dual-throat 42DCN Weber carburetors. All this is snarling and snapping just behind my left shoulder. We move off. Morris Longstreth Hallowell IV complains that the shift lever is too close to the rear bulkhead for his forearm. I figure he should get his arm shortened. We are supposed to follow one Cecil Harper, who is driving a Volante convertible. Cecil Harper roars off toward Olympic Boulevard and Morris Longstreth Hallowell IV cries "*Jeezus,* Cecil!" and strives to keep up. "How is it?" I ask. "Mutter, mutter." "Does it feel like 700 horsepower?" I ask. "Mutter, mutter." "Are the controls heavy?" I ask. "Look," he says, "it would probably make more sense if you just drove it yourself." And with that, he swings it into the curb. As we disembark, I hit my head on the upraised door, and Steve Smith's black Saab Turbo pulls up alongside. "The license plate fell off back there about six blocks!" he yells. Cecil Harper hauls the big Volante around in a squealing U-turn and goes back to search—in vain, as it turns out—for the lost plate. We stand at the side of the busy street and try not to get killed by the curious, who think we're shooting the sequel to *The Empire Strikes Back.* ("Earth? Bulldog. We have encountered indigenous alien personnel.")

Cecil returns. We take off. I mean we really take off, you guys. I am determined to stay with Cecil as he tears through Sunday-night traffic. Glorious. The seat is a tight fit. The controls are crisp and easy to use. I can't read any of the digital thingies glowing red on the dash because of my farsightedness, but Morris Longstreth Hallowell IV is watching them like a hawk anyway. It doesn't feel like 700 horsepower. With the 200-mph gearing and the huge P7 tires, it's fast, but not dragster fast. Furthermore, the engine isn't quite right. It tends to stumble and bang a little at low rpm. Ask me if I care. This is hog heaven. All too soon we arrive at our Bel Air destination and the great British beast disappears into a garage. (Sigh.) They didn't want me to drive it, they said, because it was still in very rough prototype condition—creakings, rattlings, the aforementioned engine bothers, stuff like that. But it doesn't make any difference, because I've promised Morris Longstreth Hallowell IV that I won't tell anybody. It's a secret, right?

1980...
It was the best of times,
it was the worst of times...

⁓⁂⁓

Another year ends. Paradoxically, what was surely one of the worst years in American automotive history was, I should hesitate to mention, the all-time best in *Car and Driver*'s. The magazine winds up 1980 in better shape than even its most optimistic supporter (me) could have anticipated, but although we're delighted with our own long-sought success, we'll feel a lot better about things when our friends in the car business have switched back to black ink in their ledger-keeping. Barring a full-scale Moslem Holy War, I'd speculate that by this time next year they'll be back on the track as well. It won't be easy for any of the manufacturers, and Ford and Chrysler face truly Herculean labors as they struggle to recover from the blows rained upon them by the free-enterprise system, but business is getting better.

I guess the greatest thrill of the year past was, for me, going to Argentina and visiting with Juan Manuel Fangio. Bleeding hearts have criticized me for enjoying myself down there, but I couldn't help it. It's a beautiful country, populated by good-humored, industrious people, and I loved it. Fangio has a chair waiting right at the top in my personal pantheon, and I need not defend either his greatness as a racing driver or his patriotism as an Argentine citizen. If I have any regrets at all regarding my visit there, they would have to do with the fact that I have no firm plans to go back right away. Until I do get to return, I'll hang out in Argentine restaurants in New York, drink the country's blood-red wine, and think about mountain streams full of trout with my name on them.

A great car found its way into my garage in 1980. When I visited the Fiat Museum (Centrostorico) in Turin last year I was given the chance to drive their Fiat 500 Topolino—a 1936 model that had belonged to the car's designer, Dante Giacosa. At that time I told the museum's director, Commandante A. Costantino, that I'd always cherished the hope that I might someday own a Topolino. After all, it was the first modern economy car; a car that I'd always admired in purely aesthetic terms; and one that had contributed suspension parts to an awful lot of racing cars that captured my fancy when I first took the veil of fully committed car enthusiasm. Six months later, a message was forwarded from Mr. Costantino, to wit: "We've found you a 1946 Topolino, burgundy with black fenders, almost as good as the one in the museum. What should we do with it?" Pat Bedard was on his way to visit Ferrari, so I borrowed $3000 and sent it off to Italy pinned to the inside of his blazer. The Topolino was mine! Late last summer it arrived at the office on a beat-up eighteen wheeler, traveling in company with a Ferrari 308 and a Rolls-Royce Silver Shadow. It was everything I'd been told it was…excellent original paint and upholstery, sunroof in perfect working order, engine and running gear in mint condition…a little jewel box. I intend to write the full Topolino story in the next few months, but right now I just like to back it out of the garage into the sun and celebrate the fact that it's actually mine.

I recently wrote about attending the Experimental Aircraft Association Fly-In at Oshkosh, Wisconsin. The basic mode of transportation on that trip was an Airstream motorhome, but I failed to mention the official *Car and Driver* transport auxiliary—an enormous Harley-Davidson 80-cubic-inch FLH Classic with sidecar. The Classic is the motorcycle that most people have in mind when they think of Harley-Davidsons. It had everything but electric windows and power seats. For 30 years I've been told by my biker friends that Harleys vibrate, and that I should never, ever attempt to ride in any kind of motorcycle equipped with a sidecar. Well, brothers and sisters, the word "vibration" does not, cannot, adequately describe the tremblings and throbbings of a Harley Classic. The Harley's big V-twin wouldn't move the needle into the big numbers on the Richter scale, but it could be felt in neighboring states. On my first long ride from Milwaukee to Oshkosh I had the distinct impression that my hands and feet had gone permanently to sleep.

As to riding with a sidecar, I would advise prospective sidecar cyclists to always wear gloves, lest their white knuckles glowing in the night confuse oncoming motorists. A motorcycle equipped with a typical sidecar cannot camber, does not lean into the corners, and you have no idea how important the cambering dynamic of a two-wheeler is until you get on one that doesn't do it. My first corner, in downtown Milwaukee with the assistant chief engineer of Harley-Davidson in the sidecar, saw me run wide and crowd some poor clown in a van right into the parking lane. God knows what the effect upon the assistant chief engineer must have been. You soon learn that left-hand turns are quite safe, but right-hand turns are challenges requiring *cojones* the size of the award-winning cabbages at the state fair. Otherwise, it's a piece of cake. In fact, when we left Oshkosh on the return trip, the intrepid Missus Davis was at the controls of the big Harley and thundered all the way down to Milwaukee at an honest 75 miles per hour. A never-to-be-forgotten memory of the summer of 1980.

The autumnal equinox was celebrated in proper Celtic style with a trip to West Virginia, where I was chief judge at state senate candidate Bill Neely's Hillbilly Chili Cookoff. West Virginia being one of the most beautiful motoring environments in North America, and the cast of characters at this affair being heavily studded with colorful automotive personalities, I elected to drive down in a brand-new English car of impeccable enthusiast credentials, which will remain, as they say, nameless. The day was warm, and when we tried to turn on the air conditioning we found that it was inoperative. When we put the electric windows down to compensate for the lack of air conditioning, we found that the one in the right front door wouldn't go back up. When we stopped for lunch, we discovered that the central door-locking mechanism refused to lock the driver's door. What's more, when we opened the locking gas-filler door, there was no gas cap inside. Oh yes, and the radio wouldn't work in the AM mode. Other than that, it too was a piece of cake. They say there'll always be an England, but sometimes one has to wonder.

Final note: The Topolino wasn't my only transportation purchase in the past twelve months. We picked up a '65 VW Squareback with 28,000 miles and no brakes on it, and I also bought my late father's '65 Dodge van from my mother. She couldn't bring herself to drive it, and she couldn't bear the idea of selling it to some feckless youth and someday meeting it on the road with its rear end jacked up and shag carpet everywhere, so I bought it. Sherman and I went out to start it the other day and I discovered that the ashtray was still full of my dad's old cigarette butts...strange feeling. I don't quite know what I'm going to do with these two vehicles, other than spend money on them. Maybe that's why I'm buying the Suzuki GS1100E—I need something a little more practical, a bit more utilitarian for day-in, day-out transportation in 1981.

Eighty on 80.

꿍

Regular readers of car magazines have absorbed a lot of romantic nonsense about the limitless delight of the German autobahns. Wrong. The U.S. Interstate highway system is better in almost every respect. The big difference is that Germany has no speed limit at all on the greatest part of its superhighway network; and enthusiast-drivers—who make up a much larger percentage of any European driving population—can really honk it on over there, between traffic jams. As a matter of fact, I'd say that autobahn traffic, especially the more aggressive traffic that's such an important part of Germany's mix, really goes *too* fast for comfort or safety. I've spent as long as an hour traveling in excess of 130 miles per hour on the Stuttgart-Munich autobahn, not by myself, but in a tightly knit little convoy of a half-dozen cars, each driven by a complete stranger, running almost nose to tail. Add to that situation gathering dusk, and maybe a little rain squall somewhere between Ulm and Augsburg, and you have a sure-fire recipe for a tension headache.

France is a perfect compromise between the slothful driving habits of America and the *blitzkrieg* style of West Germany. The French autoroutes are wider and less crowded than the autobahns—less crowded because they're hideously expensive toll roads—and traffic generally moves a bit faster than the 80-mile-per-hour (130 kph) speed limit. The pace is more conducive to pleasurable touring on the not-so-freeways of France or Italy than the balls-out autobahns of Germany.

America's Interstates, which President Eisenhower modeled after the German autobahns, should be perfect and very nearly are, flawed only by the willy 55-mile-per-hour speed limit and their steady deterioration—a direct result of the neglect implicit in the last decade of anti-automotive public policy. Given better maintenance and an 80-mile-per-hour limit, our Interstates would be pure joy for tourists and serious drivers alike. As you probably know, the *Car and Driver* staff tends to ignore the 55. Thus we already know what the Interstates are like at 80. They're terrific at 80, that's how they are. They're terrific even at the old (pre-Energy Crisis I) speed limit of 70 miles per hour. One covers the ground at a decent pace, and the danger of nodding off that's so much a part of driving long distances at 55 is greatly reduced.

In the last month I've spent a lot of time and about 4500 miles on the Interstates—I-80, mainly—and day after tomorrow I'll hit it again for the 650-mile run to New York City. It all started about 30 days back, when my friend Ed Labunski went to sleep at the wheel of his BMW and kept going straight where the road turned. He was dead when they got him out, and I hopped into our Volvo GLT Turbo for a 24-hour round-trip dash to Milford, Pennsylvania, for the funeral, 1200 miles. For once, going to sleep at the wheel was not a potential hazard because I had Ed's example constantly out there on the other side of the windshield to keep me awake. At eight in the morning I was eating a scrapple breakfast in Stroudsburg. Four hours later I was stopped at the roadside, the funeral over, watching two dozen wild turkeys pick their way across the floor of a brushy valley like grazing sheep.

Then came my fiftieth birthday. I carefully set aside about six weeks for commemorative carousing and celebration at venues ranging from Michigan to Wyoming to the north of England. It has been my great good fortune to have a new Turbo Diesel S-class Mercedes to drive from place to place through this unfolding orgy of self-indulgence. I'll drop it off in New York, grudgingly, this weekend when we embark for God's Own England. It has transported us from point to point in the grand manner, with the cruise control somewhere between 75 and 80 during my driving stints, smack on 85 when Missuz J.L.K. Davis was at the wheel. My own rough-and-ready long division tells me that we never got worse than 24 miles per gallon at those speeds, and once, with a strong westerly tailwind in Wyoming, we did 350 miles at a tad more than 28.9 mpg.

For all the brave talk about how fast Westerners drive, we were only passed a couple of times, once in Wyoming by a determined-looking young guy in a Toyota Celica with Washington plates, cruising along at about 90, his car jam-packed with luggage and a Fuzzbuster standing guard on the dash; and once by a couple of cowboys in a Ford pickup that looked as if it was probably full of empty Coors cans and Charley Pride cassettes. The longest stretch without a peep from our radar detector was Sheridan, Wyoming, to Rochester, Minnesota, and we can report that more and more cops are equipping themselves with pulsing radar of the KR-11 type. Our Escort would generally spot these roving bushwhackers when they fired their signal at some car ahead of us, but a couple of times it was stand on the brakes and pray that the man in blue wasn't paying attention.

We went west on I-80 and returned east on I-90. I-90 gets the nod, being smoother and having less traffic, fewer cops, and better scenery than I-80 to the south. At Cody we hunted deer and elk on horseback for a week, and there is nothing like a succession of eight-to-ten-hour days on a horse to make one appreciate the modern automobile. Cody is like a Merle Haggard album come to life. Aside from the magnificent Buffalo Bill museum, it consists of a dozen or so honky-tonk bars with the necessary logistic and residential support, peopled by used-up-looking cowboys and a breathtaking assortment of agri-groupies drawn by the smell of horse sweat and unlaundered denim. Sideburns are the rage in western Wyoming. The place looks like the General Motors Building circa 1972, haircut-wise.

Coming back on I-90, we detoured through the Black Hills and visited Mount Rushmore. If you've never done that, do it. I had no idea what to expect, even though I felt I knew those four stone faces by heart, and when we came around the last bend in the road to find ourselves face to face with Washington, Jefferson, Lincoln, and Teddy Roosevelt, the sight fairly took my breath away. Our roads may not be in such great shape, but our national monuments will compare favorably with any in the world. The whole experience was made perfect by the fact that we were parked next to an old Chevy wagon full of Iranian college students, and when we returned from our close-up appreciation of Mount Rushmore we found the male members of the Iranian contingent busily trying to get one of the Mercedes' doors open. How absolutely, poetically appropriate. I was unable to properly express my feelings at that moment. They appeared to be moderately embarrassed when Missuz Davis commenced yelling at them, gesturing in good-humored helplessness their inability to cope with the English language. The Mercedes trunk being well equipped with fancy hunting rifles, I was tempted to shoot one of them, but nobody there was trophy quality. Having just ridden a horse all over our purple mountains' majesty and driven back and forth across the fruited plain, I can't blame the shah for dying. It must have been really humiliating to have been in charge of such a cut-rate country.

With Subaru, Suzuki, and Cessna through not-so-darkest Africa

ritish Airways 054 Nairobi-London—The song says, "They call me a cockeyed optimist," and I suppose that applies to me as well as to whomever they were singing about. I've gone through life having enough fun for an entire family of hedonists, and I've always expected it to be even better tomorrow. Thus, I wasn't surprised when I opened my passport a couple of weeks ago, saw that it now contained a visa from the government of Kenya, and felt all those anticipatory shivers once again. British Airways, the Kenya Ministry of Tourism, and American Sports, Incorporated, had joined forces to transport me to Nairobi to cover the Marlboro Safari Rally.

I look back on almost 30 years of adventures—automotive and otherwise—and I see that my fascination with the people involved has always been more than equal to whatever I felt for the machinery. High-performance cars come and go, but high-performance people have a special, lasting effect. I met a lot of high-performance people in Kenya, and I was pleasantly surprised at how many of them were women. Indian girls in saris, wearing jewels in their noses. Indian girls in cutoffs and T-shirts. Black girls in sling-back heels and tapered trousers. Tanned, athletic girls who looked English, only better, even. What little I knew of East Africa and the Safari Rally had not prepared me for this aspect of life at the equator.

Another woman who used to get my attention was Mehitabel, the free-spirited alley cat who couldn't say no in Don Marquis's Archy and Mehitabel. The only thing that kept Mehitabel going through a life that was, in her words, "just one damned kitten after another," was her unshakable belief in the Pythagorean Theorem of Transmigration of the Soul, which supported her claim of having been Cleopatra in an earlier incarnation.. Sharing Mehitabel's enthusiasm for Pythagoras, I'd always thought that it would be nice to come back as a wild duck—a bluebill, to be specific—because I like the way they fly and the places where they hang out. Now I'm not so sure about that. After my two weeks in Kenya I'm beginning to think I might like to come back as Willy Roberts—for pretty much the same reasons; i.e., I'm nuts about the way he flies, and I'm blown away by the places where he hangs out.

Willy Roberts is a good-looking blond guy of 34 or so who owns a two-tone green Cessna 180 with which he gave me a unique view of Kenya and the Safari Rally. He looks athletic and Anglo-Saxon, and he has the brownish flush of a fair-complexioned European who's spent a great deal of time in the tropical sun. He flies for the love of it, and, in spite of the fact that his airplane serves as both car and pickup truck, he is always first and foremost an enthusiast—part bush pilot, part sport flier. He has a Maserati Sebring garaged in London that he hasn't seen in a while, and he wonders what it might be worth in the States. It's all original, with less than 30,000 miles on the clock, and I encouraged him to bring it over here and sell it to finance the crop-dusting training he'd like to get somewhere in the American West.

He showed me the country from his Cessna, his aged Toyota Land Cruiser, his helicopter-pilot friend's Fiat 131, his brother's Suzuki pickup truck (800cc, four-wheel drive), and his brother-in-law's 4wd Subaru station wagon. The place is breathtaking, like the American West at its springtime zenith, but with sudden mountains that leap into the sky almost without warning. I doubt that guys like Hemingway and Ruark ever did it justice. Maybe Hemingway, but certainly not Ruark. It is so big, and so exotic. One encounters faces in every tone from lily-white through brown to enamel-black. Swahili is spoken everywhere, but as in the Scandinavian countries, there's always someone in earshot who speaks English. It's a friendly, hospitable place, and the only remotely hostile people I encountered were minor bureaucrats of the sort who are hostile in every country. I walked miles through the noisy, crowded streets of Nairobi. I visited Mr. Dinoo in Biashara Street, who tailored me a safari suit (made to measure, basted try-on, ready in five days, 85 bucks). I argued politics with earnest university students, ate samosas (deep-fried Indian burritos) from greasy paper bags, drank Tusker Premium beer, and tried to imagine the day in 1909 when Teddy and Kermit Roosevelt's safari marched away from my hotel with 500 porters.

When the rally was about over, Willy Roberts said, "You ought to see some more country. Maybe we could fly down to my bro's farm in the Mara." So the morning after an epic prize-giving dinner dance, the highlight of which was a men's-room fistfight between one of the Brits and a platoon of Asians, we flew off to the Masai Mara country and brother Andy's farm. Again, as in the rally, we climbed across the escarpment and over the Rift Valley, but this time we went due west. Traversing a vast plain like the top of a big mesa, we saw zebra, giraffe, warthog, hippo, eland, oryx, wildebeest, impala, and topi, and for twenty minutes we were never out of sight of great herds of wild game. Willy played tour guide, identifying various species as we passed, and suggested that "tonight we should see some elephants and buffalo…they're a real problem around my bro's farm." This noncommittal reference to elephants as common pests reminded me forcibly that I wasn't in Michigan.

We landed beside a thousand-acre cornfield and walked a half-mile to the camp where brother Andy lives until he can get his house built. The land was leased from the Masai last year and cleared, and now it'll grow two good crops per year. There was nobody home except two Africans working in the shed that serves as a kitchen, and four wonderful hounds who were delighted to have some company. Willy and I went back to the plane, took off, and searched the winding little Jeep trail for Andy and his brother-in-law, who'd be toiling in through the bush in a Subaru wagon. We spotted them, buzzed them, and went looking for elephants. The land was crisscrossed with game trails, sometimes a quarter-mile wide. We found a herd of elephants, circled them just about eyeball to eyeball, then went back to meet the others. As we returned to camp, two tiny dik-dik leaped across the road ahead of us.

That night we lay around the campfire in the rough grass-and-tin camp that brother Andy calls home, drank whisky, and ate strips of roast meat seasoned with Tabasco—canapés cut from a shoulder that lay sizzling on a piece of industrial screen over the fire. Dinner was a rich red stew, washed down with a local Riesling. Andy Roberts, like many white Kenyans I met, is a colorful character, straightforward to the point of bluntness, a survivor, and an uproarious storyteller. After I went to bed I lay awake listening to some large animal crashing around in the bush outside camp. An elephant? I asked about it next morning, but nobody else had paid any attention.

Breakfast in those rustic surroundings was, believe it or not, classical British fare—two fried eggs, bacon, sausage, and broiled tomato, served with tea—all prepared over the kitchen campfire. After breakfast we took the Subaru to get the native workers started on their day's chores, then went to check a place where a waterbuck had broken the fence during the night. The Masai spearmen who'd patrolled the edges of the cornfield all night reported no elephants.

We loaded the Subaru with Willy's sister and her little boy, Willy's son Richard, and me and my gear, and set out for the heart of the Masai Mara. This is a vast corner of Kenya that abuts Tanzania, a national game refuge dotted with Masai villages and herds of Masai cattle, and thickly populated with the greatest number and variety of wild animals that anyone could imagine. Before the morning was over we'd seen buffalo and elephants, hundreds of antelope, a hyena, baboons, waterbuck, many of the species we'd seen the day before, even lions. The remarkable little Subaru took us through everything from axle-deep mud to vast sheets of shoe-topping water concealed by waist-high grass, but the lions were playing hard-to-get. So we went to the place where we'd scheduled lunch, Governor's Camp—a former hunting camp that's become a haven for German tourists—and picked up a native guide. Within a half-hour he'd led us cross-lots to a point where we spotted a big male lion silhouetted under a tree. As we got closer, I could see that he was accompanied by another male, a couple of lionesses, and a half-dozen cubs. We drove almost close enough to touch them. They were napping fitfully in a great heap, utterly oblivious to us. I shot an entire roll of film as I watched one cub awaken, try to stir something up with his brothers and sisters, then climb the tree in disgust.

Brother Andy and brother-in-law Jamie McLeod flew the airplane to Governor's to meet us for lunch. My return home was imminent, and thoughts of weight control had begun to creep back into my idyll, so I grudgingly skipped the beer and had a salade Nicoise instead of the moussaka and lamb that everybody else was hoovering. We ate outdoors, and watched the camp's pet mongoose romp on the lawn for the benefit of the Germans. Two hours later we were back in Nairobi, and 48 hours after that I was on this airplane. Willy wants me to bring my wife back next year, to camp in the Mara and hang out on his island in Lake Baringo. If it's humanly possible, Willy, we'll be there.

Indianapolis and the Anti-Destination League

⚜

Iwent to the Indianapolis 500 this year. I hadn't sat through a race since Bruce McLaren was killed in 1970. It wasn't that I felt any closer to Bruce than to a bunch of other good guys that got killed in racing cars, but his death did get to me in a special way. I was in the advertising business, and one of our clients—John De Lorean, then with Chevrolet—called to say that Bruce had crashed while testing at Goodwood. As racing people do, I immediately started the mental and emotional process of rationalizing his death, making it all right, and by the time I got home from work that night I had insulated myself from the reality of what had happened 4000 miles away.

I walked into the kitchen, where my then wife and all three kids were getting set for dinner, and casually gave them the news. They were wrecked. My daughter, just into her teens, was especially hurt because Bruce had given her a lot of his time and attention at Elkhart Lake the previous autumn, where he'd won the Cam-Am race. He was the 47th friend of mine to die in a racing car since I'd started racing in 1953, but he was her first. I suddenly realized that there was something unhealthy about a process that allowed one to accept the death of an old friend without grieving; that shaking one's head and muttering trite homilies about that being the way he would have wanted it, or some such claptrap, was not an appropriate response. So I stopped going to races. I went back to Watkins Glen one year, but didn't go to the track. I had to go to the Daytona 500 on business once, but managed to catch a plane home before race day. People badgered me to attend various races, particularly the Long Beach Grand Prix, and a couple of times I made reservations, contacted the press officers involved, then decided to stay away at the last minute.

Twelve months ago, I talked to illustrator-friend Bill Neale at his office in Dallas and told him that I wanted to do the Indianapolis 500 story with him this year. I hadn't attended a 500 since 1966, and I figured that if I was ever going to get back into it, Indy was the place to start. He agreed to come along, to dress up my words with his illustrations. It was all set.

I talked bravely about spending most of the month of May at the track, as I once did, but the track opened on May 1 and I wasn't there. The first weekend of qualifying came and went, and I missed it. Ditto the second weekend.

Finally, it was time for the race, and I was out of excuses. We loaded our cameras and luggage into the Mercedes and set off for Indianapolis. We used back roads part of the way, and somehow each dairy farm we passed, every courthouse and volunteer fire department we drove by, made me feel better about what I was doing. By the time we rolled up in front of the Columbia Club on Monument Circle in downtown Indianapolis, all my qualms were gone. We tore off to Al Bloemker's office, got our passes, toured the museum, watched the film, and bought T-shirts for our kids at the souvenir shop. At a party that night, attended by a large share of the Indianapolis establishment, I realized how few people I knew anymore, and how old many of the people I did know had become since 1966. But no matter, I was back.

Neale called the next morning to report that his life had become complicated and he wouldn't be able to join us. That was okay too. We'd miss Bill, but he could do the illustrations from photographs, and his absence would give me an excuse to stop off and see him in Texas to—ahem—discuss the project. We went to the track for carburetion tests. It had been some time since anybody ran a carburetor at Indy, but never mind. Finally, I saw some people I knew: Jim Hall, Mario Andretti, Linda Vaughn, Dan Gurney. I was beginning to feel as though I'd never left. The next day we attended the drivers' meeting. Danny Ongais gave his brand-new Valvoline jacket to my wife, telling her, "I think they wanted you to have this." Sure they did. After that, we had reserved seats for the parade. We sat near the public library on North Meridian Street and had the time of our lives. Cops whizzing by, standing up on the seats of their Harleys. Linda Vaughn looking like a movie star, upstaging all the other celebrities. The Third Infantry Fife and Drum Corps in full colonial-army regalia. High-school bands, the Purdue Golden Girl, a Marine band, an Air Force band, Shriners in old Formula V cars, sheriffs' posses on horseback, and floats from all over North America. The U.S. Navy band played "Anchors Aweigh" as they swung past our seats, and I took it as a personal compliment.

I've reported on the race elsewhere in this issue, but I wanted to use this space to celebrate a little, to say how nice it was to be immersed in a great automobile race again. I've already made my reservations for next year, for both weekends of qualifying as well as the race itself, and I don't think I'll have the slightest bit of trouble keeping those dates. Racing is a hell of a mess here and abroad. Television has, paradoxically enough, trivialized it while turning it into a megamillion-dollar activity. The voice of the Indianapolis Motor Speedway used to be the late Sid Collins, but now it seems to be a Greek chorus of multimillionaires debating the best ways to restructure it all to their own benefit. But nonetheless it's nice to be back again. Racing has outlasted most of its problems, and it may even be stronger than the profit motive.

I did get to see Bill Neale. We sat on his dock and fed earthworms to the bluegills, and talked about life, told stories, shot at turtles with a BB gun, and even chatted about the illustrations he'd do for my Indy story. We drove up to his place at Cedar Creek from San Antonio, where I'd given a speech to a small local cell of the Armadillo Breeders Association, and I discovered that Texas too has become afflicted with an automotive syndrome that seems to be sweeping the country. The left (fast) lanes of America's Interstate highways have become clotted with self-righteous jerks cruising along at or near the speed limit, refusing to move over for faster traffic (which outnumbers them ten or twelve to one), and generally making a dangerous nuisance of themselves. Are they members of Steve Smith's Anti-Destination League, or are they just common pests? *Quick, Henry, the Flit!*

Cars à la mode.

❦

I t is 1967. You left the Nürburgring 1000-kilometer race early because you were bored and because you had to drive all the way to Torino that night to meet Rick McBride. You are driving a white BMW 2000 Tilux, purchased in New York and picked up at the factory. Somewhere south of Frankfurt a Citroën DS19 appears in your rear-view mirrors. You didn't overtake him anywhere along the line, and he doesn't seem to be overtaking you, but there he is. Your BMW will run a little better than 110, and that's how fast you've been going ever since you hit the autobahn at Koblenz. You know that your car is faster than the Citroën. You can see that he has three passengers to slow him down, while you're all alone. But there he is. You will push your BMW as hard as it will go, but you won't lose that Citroën until he turns off at Baden-Baden. It will drive you nuts, so much so that you'll still remember it fourteen years later sitting in an office in Ann Arbor, Michigan. French cars are like that.

The Germans invented the automobile, and the Americans turned it into a disposable appliance, but it was the Italians and the French who taught it to sing and dance. It didn't take Italian cars long to acquire all the machismo hang-ups of the Italians who built and drove them. Everything about a good Italian automobile struts and postures a kind of "mine's bigger than yours" arrogance. French cars turned out differently, as one might expect. The smallest and least expensive ones go at it like something out of *Mr. Hulot's Holiday.* Their personalities are vivid, challenging; their appearances—often as not—startling.

I don't know of more than a half-dozen Americans who appreciate the charm of a Citroën 2CV, the corrugated car with the window-blind roof and the yo-yo-mode suspension. Everything about the 2CV makes perfect sense, yet it looks silly to American eyes. My wife was once driving her two sons from Paris to their great-grandmother's house at Le Mans in a 2CV. She was passing a truck on a narrow three-lane road when a bus roared by from the opposite direction. There was an explosion of sorts as the folding canvas roof was blown loose from its moorings on the windshield header, then a blast of bright French sunshine as the aforementioned roof trailed out behind the car at 100 kph like Isadora Duncan's scarf.

America hasn't exactly opened its heart and its pocketbook to Renault's Le Car either. I get sidelong glances from my fellow *Car and Driver* contributors whenever I express my long-held enthusiasm for this jaunty little box, but I continue to admire it for its resolute unwillingness to become a homogenized clone of everything else at that end of the market. The Le Car's biggest brother, the 18i, is a much more conventional car—at least insofar as any French car could be called conventional—yet it still unnerves unimaginative Americans. Our first 18i test car, a year ago, even put *me* off. It didn't seem that the melding of Franco-American product philosophies had borne the hoped-for fruit. It was not, as they say, a together car. Now we have another one, a red one, with an automatic transmission. This one has charmed the hell out of me. It seems much more representative of a single automotive concept than the first one, as though AMC and Renault are finally really working together, not just collaborating. The 18i is now perhaps a little less French than the Le Car or the 12 from which it sprang, but it sure isn't American yet.

Peugeots are something else again. Peugeots have always struck me as being French, but with just a trace of a German accent. Their Frenchness brooks no nonsense. A Peugeot appears not to care whether you like it or not. It is there to do a job, and, like any Frenchman worthy of the name, it probably considers itself superior to the person who owns it. I have owned two Peugeots—a 1959 403, which I had equipped with all manner of exotic French speed equipment, and a 1961 404, which I foolishly thought would be an even better car than the 403. The 404 was Peugeot's only mistake up to the moment a few years ago when they decided to buy a bunch of properties that were losing money for Chrysler overseas—and which have continued to lose money for these nice people from Sochaux. The Peugeot 504 seemed to be very much the inside automotive proposition for the "No Nukes" and "Warning! This Vehicle Brakes For Animals!" crowd; a sort of Super-Volvo for those people who believe that Ford and General Motors have been responsible for every disaster since the Dust Bowl. The Peugeot 505 seeks to redress this imbalance in owner-type. The 505, either gas or diesel, is targeted at a broader sweep of America's affluent managers and professionals—the same sort of people who buy the car in France. I wish them well, because

Americans of this stripe need to be exposed to the Peugeot's solid-citizen bourgeois virtue.

A couple of years ago, following the Frankfurt Auto Show, I drove down to the great Max Hoffman's home at Tegernsee, near Munich. I was driving a Citroën CX2400 GTi, which I parked in a graveled area just beyond his garage doors. When we had our drinks he strolled over to one of the huge windows overlooking the lake and asked, "What do you drive today?" Then, looking down from the window, answered his own question: "Ah yes, the car of the future…two and a half liters, front-wheel drive, wheels pushed all the way out to the corners for more room inside, good aerodynamics…everyone in the business must soon build this kind of car." I can hardly wait. I caused the Citroën people all kinds of headaches a while back when I tried to work some fiddle that would have allowed me to import a single Citroën CX for my own use. It just wasn't in the cards. They saw nothing but service problems and people calling from the hinterlands wanting to know where such cars could be bought in their own home towns, and I guess they were right. I gave in and backed down on my dream. But, boy, would I like to own one of those. Svelte, feline, disturbingly comfortable, even with an obsolete four-cylinder engine it is simply light-years ahead of sedans costing thousands more dollars to buy. It differs from other manufacturers' conceptions of the modern car to about the same degree that *Star Wars* is different from the old Flash Gordon Saturday-afternoon serials. It is exactly what Maximilian E. Hoffman said it was that day in Tegernsee: the car of the future that Europeans are fortune enough to buy right now.

Yesterday, while I beavered away at the lead for this column, I got a call from Bob Cumberford, the automotive designer and expert who occasionally contributes to our magazine. I asked him for a capsule opinion of French cars. He said, "Hmmm, French cars. Idiosyncratic, out of step with the rest of the world, and probably right."

Max Hoffman

❦

Max Hoffman died a while ago. He was 78 year old, and I would not be surprised to learn that he was giving some individual or institution a hard time at the moment of his passing. If there is a hereafter, he has already spotted its flaws and spoken sharply about them to the present management.

Max Hoffman didn't invent the sports car, but he introduced it to an awful lot of us. He loved his wife, state-of-the-art cars and architecture, and the sweet science of making money—in what order we will never be sure. He opened all of our eyes to the possibilities of Porsches as racing cars in the very early 1950s, when he imported a pair of then hyperexotic Glöckler Porsche spyders and drove them himself with considerable verve and moderate success—verve and success sufficient, however, to launch Porsche on the trail of North American racing laurels that led directly to today's IMSA 935s. It was natural that he'd go for it in that way. First, because of his prewar racing successes with motorcycles and cars in Europe, and second, because Max Hoffman always believed that he could do most things better than anyone else anyway.

He was tough. It may have been more difficult being his friend than his enemy, since he made no demands on his enemies. Enemies were beneath his contempt, but friends weren't. If you were his friend, he called daily to badger you about whatever was on his mind, and that could have been almost anything. If you were his employee, he checked every single move you made, and his manner toward you was that of a Marine DI speaking to a particularly stupid and recalcitrant boot. If you were his wife, it was apt to be all of the above. Lots of people couldn't handle it. I suppose there are not too many among the automotive press who loved him as I did. Similarly, there are many among the managers and ex-managers of the car companies with whom he did business who find it difficult to be complimentary about Max Hoffman. Jaguar Cars' Sir William Lyons referred to him as "our former friend, Mr. Hoffman."

That "former friend, Mr. Hoffman," for his part, referred to Jaguar as "Junk! English Junk! But ah, David, such a business."

Through his very small company, Hoffman Motors, he brought us Alfa Romeo, Allard, Cisitalia, Delahaye, Facel Vega, Fiat, HRG, Healy, Jaguar, Jowett, Lagonda, Lancia, Lea-Francis, Mercedes-Benz, Porsche, and—at the peak of his career—BMW automobiles, and there were others as well. He served all of these, at one time or another between 1946 and 1975, as importer, distributor, and dealer. But he was more. He got involved in every phase of the business, driving engineers and stylists crazy with his detailed suggestions, criticisms, complaints, and direct orders. Had it not been for Max, there would have been no BMW 2002, no BMW Bavaria, no BMW 507, no Porsche Speedster, and the list goes on.

It has often been suggested that he would have been more happy as an automotive engineer or manufacturer, but that simply isn't true. Engineering or manufacturing would have bored him to death. He was a high-handed, high-flying entrepreneur, an automotive merchant-prince. Had he been on the inside of some automobile factory looking out, he would have been forced to put up with people he didn't like, to *schmooz*, to be a team player. Unthinkable. As a team player, he would have made a great archduke. His eyes were gimlet-pale, shaped by a thousand-year-old Eastern European gene pool, and they conveyed the unmistakable implication that, if you continued to make stupid suggestions, he would turn you into a Poland-China brood sow faster than you could say "Sorry, Mr. Hoffman." He loved fighting it out in the trenches of the automobile business, the retail showrooms. He enjoyed visiting the centers of power, the headquarters of the great car companies in Europe, but he never made the currently fashionable mistake of forgetting that the heart and soul of the automobile business lies in the age-old ritual of negotiations between buyers and seller.

We used to lunch together once a week. His office was in the Seagram Building, and the opulent Four Seasons served as his personal company cafeteria. Although the food there has always been superb, I'd hazard the guess that Max liked the place more for its spectacular architecture and decor, since food never seemed to be that important to him. We'd argue about cars. What should he buy for Europe this year? Something nice. "Well," I'd begin, "why not get a Ferrari?" "I've had Ferraris, they no longer interest me." Venturing into deeper water, I'd offer, "What about a Maserati?" "Junk," he'd say, "Italian junk. Like an Italian car made by Englishmen. A fake Ferrari." Not having the sense or the strength to change the subject, I'd go on: "Why not get a Mercedes

600?" He'd look sad, then muse, "I tell you something. Listen here, the Daimler-Benz people are the best in the world, absolutely the finest. They build the best cars. I have never done business with such high-class people, except for BMW. But this time, with this 600, they have made a mistake. I drove it last year on the autobahn by Munich, and I spun it at a hundred miles per hour. It is not a safe car." That year he wound up buying a Rolls-Royce, he told me, because it was the only new car that interested him and the only one he hadn't owned in a long time. "I know. I know what you think. You think I am a fool to buy English junk. Well, I don't care. The Rolls-Royce people are also very fine people. You know, I dealt with them before the war."

When I saw him in Germany, that fall, I asked him how the Rolls had worked out. "English junk," he spat back. "I drove it home from the distributor's place in Munich—the owner, he is a very good friend of mine—and I hated it. I called him the same day to come and take it back. I have learned my lesson. There is nothing like a BMW."

BMW was his last hurrah. One by one, as the years went by, the various car companies he'd represented here set up their own importing and distributing arrangements and bought Max Hoffman's contracts. In some cases he made more money giving up their cars than he'd ever made selling them, but it always hurt when another one would go west on him. His willingness to invest his own talent and treasure so heavily in enthusiast cars, and his single-minded, autocratic approach to the business, made him very, very wealthy, but it also made him unique in the automotive world. He was willing to bet everything on cars like Porsche, Lancia, and Alfa Romeo—even when Alfa Romeo took his money after the war and shipped the cars to somebody else—and that made him a pioneer. His detractors will say he was a bad guy, but I look at all he did and all the automotive joy he brought to people like you and me, and I paraphrase the Marine recruiting slogan…"The car business needs a few bad guys, guys like Max Hoffman."

Smug young wimps for a safer America.

I saw Mr. Jack Gillis, late of the Department of Transportation, hawking his updated version of *The Car Book* on television the other night. He told us with trembling jowls of the carnage on the highways, and he compared our awful death toll to hypothetical weekly 747 crashes. Every time he said "Automobile," he said it with a capital "A," with the same sort of barely controlled horror that Elizabeth I's Lord Walsingham must have displayed in references to Mary, Queen of Scots. Now, for just $4.95, we can all buy an updated and enhanced version of Miss Joan Claybrook's Big-Lie valedictory. The Almighty has shown Mr. Gillis a way to save countless thousands of lives and make a few bucks at the same time. There can be no greater calling than the profitable pursuit of righteousness.

Mr. Gillis's publisher also appeared briefly, but he obviously felt no outrage, so puffed up was he at the prospect of America's loons and dimbulbs leaping up from in front of the six-o'clock news and rushing out to spend their Christmas Club funds on the "new" *Car Book.* If Miss Claybrook's original lies and half-truths were such a hit, then surely Mr. Gillis's Xeroxed lies and half-truths will make him the hottest property since Savonarola, fear-and-loathing-wise.

Watching these two smug young wimps on my Trinitron, it occurred to me that I'd been watching smug young wimps try to save me from myself and the depredations of the Industrial Revolution ever since Ralph Nader got it wrong about the Corvair and became uncrowned king of the common good. I decided that I should try to learn more about Smug Young Wimpism, so I went to their national headquarters and met with the Head Wimp.

An attractive young guy with something of the graduate student in his bearing, he wore a nondescript knockoff of the standard-issue Brooks Brothers natural-shoulder suit, nicely accessorized with run-over Earth shoes and a rayon tie that appeared to have been rinsed in a mixture of minestrone and granola. He wasted no time in small talk, making it clear that he was a busy person. "I wish there was a way to make you car enthusiasts appreciate the immeasurable harm you do this society," he snapped. "You can practically hear the cries of the victims of this nation's preoccupation with automobiles, yet you people make fun of us, vilify us, whenever we try to do something about it...like shutting down the automobile industry."

I held my ground against his opening gambit and let fly with a sly question designed to throw him off stride.

Car and Driver: Exactly who are you people anyway?

Head Wimp: We are attorneys, academics, and EST graduates determined to save society. We represent the great majority of people in the United States who worry about things like the effects of Jeep CJ-5s on laboratory mice. Roll a Jeep CJ-5 over on a laboratory mouse sometime and see what happens. It'll turn your stomach. We're also heavily into the whole issue of mothers' milk.

Car and Driver: You mean it might be carcinogenic?

Head Wimp: That was our original concern, but then we found out how they actually feed that stuff to those poor little kids. It's terrible. They stick their...It's too awful. I can't talk about it. Try to imagine putting a part of some woman's body in your mouth! Without antiseptic! Aack! Those *poor* little kids.

Car and Driver: I had no idea.

Head Wimp: Of course not. People like you simply don't care. People like you don't care if *everybody* dies.

Car and Driver: But everybody *is* going to die. Not even old Henry Agard Wallace had a fix for that.

Head Wimp: That's Fascist talk. That's exactly the kind of crap that's coming out of the Department of Transportation these days. What would be the point of getting a doctorate from Columbia if you were going to die? What would be the point of getting published in the *New York Review of Books?* None of that would be important if we were just going to die some day. Your problem is that you buy the AMA party line. If it wasn't for cars and saccharin and handguns and the Department of Defense and nuclear power plants, nobody would have to die. Well, maybe a few really *old* people, you know, but certainly nobody who'd ever been to graduate school, not a *good* graduate school anyway.

Car and Driver: What was it that got you into this line of work?

Head Wimp: I can tell you exactly. All my life the other kids laughed at me because I couldn't catch a ball. They made fun of the fact that I ran like a girl. Me, an all-A student. Well, practically all-A, until I failed driver training in the eleventh grade. Is it any wonder that I hate the automobile? If it hadn't been for my superior SAT scores, that stupid E in driver training might have kept me out of Harvard.

Car and Driver: But that doesn't seem like much of a springboard for social change. Criminy, a lot of people couldn't play split end for the Dallas Cowboys.

Head Wimp: See, there you go. I try to talk about my innermost motivations, and you immediately get into the risk-taking and competitiveness that's bred into our society through antisocial activities like pro football. Those people hurt one another deliberately! What kind of society encourages great big animals like that to hurt each other? It's worse than the draft. My God, it's worse even than the General Motors executive bonus program, and you're too blind to see it!

Car and Driver: Then I suppose you must really get tensed up when you think about automobile racing.

Head Wimp: No, we love automobile racing. I mean, who could sit in front of a television set and watch those cars traveling at speeds well in excess of the speed limit, see them crashing, listen to the incredibly banal remarks by the television commentators, and not comprehend that automobile racing is the whole catastrophic interface of man and the automobile in microcosm? And besides, we don't worry too much about automobile racing.

Car and Driver: Why not?

Head Wimp: Boy, are you dumb. It's simple. Eliminate automobiles and you eliminate automobile racing.

Car and Driver: Sorry, I guess I couldn't see the forest for the trees.

Head Wimp: *Trees!* God, do you have the slightest idea how dangerous trees and their byproducts are? Are you aware that they make bows and arrows out of trees? That that slippery floor you walked across coming to my office was made from trees? Why, when I was at Yale there were young men—liberal-arts people, probably—who actually *climbed* trees! Been doing it since they were little children! Oh, the stories I could tell you...

Car and Driver: Yeah, I guess you got a million of 'em. Did all you wimps attend Ivy League schools?

Head Wimp: Oh, no. I mean, I won't try to deny that it's a definite leg up in our movement, but it's enough if you're able to prove that you're pathologically frightened by all the risks that other people take for granted every day.

Car and Driver: Have you ever considered running for office as a means of accomplishing your goals for our society?

Head Wimp: Never. Not even once.

Car and Driver: Why not?

Head Wimp: Are you kidding? Who'd vote for a wimp like me?

Car and Driver: I guess I can see where you're coming from.

Our philosophy and eating Eggs McMuffin.

hat are we here for? Hugh Hefner spent a lot of his time a few years ago trying to explain, month after boring month, exactly what he meant by the *Playboy Philosophy*. It occurred to me the other day, while hurtling through a blizzard in a Saab 900 Turbo, that I could do the same thing without taking up too much of your valuable time. Here it is, folks, the *Car and Driver* Philosophy:

We prefer small cars to big cars, light cars to heavy cars, fast cars to slow cars, interesting cars to boring cars. We believe fervently that low mass is its own reward. We also believe that gasoline should be subject to an excise tax that would provide enough money to *properly* maintain the U.S. road system, and we are dedicated to the proposition that the speed limit on all rural Interstate Highways and similar limited-access roads should be 80 miles per hour. Beyond that, we only want you to be nice to each other and have a good time. Eat your heart out, Hefner.

The Egg McMuffin and I. One of the benefits of our work as automotive journalists is that we get to bat around all over the automotive world eating and drinking in a style to which only millionaire hedonists and writers for the slick epicurean magazines ordinarily become accustomed. There may be some with blighted palates among us who don't see that as such a golden opportunity, but I, for one, keep a hall of fame in my head at all times, where great meals wear the same laurels as great cars, great experiences in cars, great shots on geese, great fish, and great moments with women.

That is not to say that I've become so jaded that I only enjoy meals in four-star restaurants. Heaven forfend! I will take a back seat to no one as a scuzz-food fanatic. Truth to tell, I probably rate no better than gourmand, as a description of my ranking among trenchermen, but that's okay because it allows me to Hoover my way through all manner of national and regional cuisines, small-town road food, ballpark hot dogs, and innumerable meals cooked over open fires out in the hills. All the above has been said as a preamble for this next bit of soul-baring, to wit: I regard the Egg McMuffin as one of the ten or twelve greatest accomplishments of Western Man.

Eggs Benedict are quite lovely, but not the sort of thing one eats with one's fingers while driving hell-bent-for-election between San Antonio and Eagle lake at 7:45 in the morning. It was Mr. Herb Peterson, owner-operator of a McDonald's franchise in Santa Barbara, California, who in 1972 came up with the combination of ingredients that turned messy Eggs Benedict into a manageable sandwich. Saint Herb, he should be called. Between the fork-split halves of an English muffin, old Herb placed one large grade-A egg (fried in a ring, the yolk broken), one slice of real, honest-to-God Canadian bacon, one slice of mild American cheese to replace the runny hollandaise, a little butter (real butter, mind you), and the Egg McMuffin was born. How many unpromising mornings has Herb Peterson saved for me and my passengers? I have driven fifteen miles out of my way in search of the Golden Arches, secure in the knowledge that, no matter how barren the culinary wasteland through which I was driving, the McDonald's down the road would provide me with an Egg McMuffin, coffee, and orange juice, and the day would brighten perceptibly.

We could convene symposia to argue the goodness of McDonald's hamburgers against the claims of Burger King, Burger Chef, Wendy's, and White Castle. Powerful men can dispute the relative merit of the Detroit/Cincinnati "Coney Island" hot dog, the Nathan's New York hot dog with its sauerkraut, or the steamy franks dealt by loud-mouth vendors in ballparks all over the country. Every city in North America believes that it has the one true source of decent pizza. But surely there can be no argument about the early-morning superiority of the Egg McMuffin as a means of nourishing one's self while motoring from where one is to somewhere else. For me, the Egg McMuffin hangs right there with the works of Kettering, Edison, and the Wright brothers.

"How about one for the road?"

~~~

About seventeen years ago I trooped up to Manhattan's West Side and into the cramped little studios of National Public Radio for an on-the-air conversation with Ralph Nader. Nader was a hot ticket in those days. His book, *Unsafe at Any Speed,* was the new bible of the new consumer movement, he'd caught GM's inept flatfoots messing around in his private life—a private life so apparently barren of excitement as to make Henry David Thoreau look like a rampaging profligate by comparison—and he was the darling of a Congress determined to scourge America's Big Business community.

In the course of our discussion, I called him a demagogue and suggested that if he really wanted to save all those lives over which he was wringing his sensitive hands, he'd mount a campaign to (first) get all the drunk drivers off the roads, (second) make everybody wear seatbelts, and (third)—if after all that the death rate was still too high for his taste—he could force the driving public to wear crash helmets. My thought was that fully half of the people killed on our roads are either drunk themselves or the victims of drunk drivers, and that about 10 percent of all highway fatals are head injuries, so matched sets of Bell Magnums for Mom and Dad and the kids make a lot of sense. The seatbelt thing just seemed to me to be too obvious to require any supporting argument.

Boy, was I wrong. Old Ralph could barely conceal his contempt for my limited gifts of logic and persuasion. What was obvious to Ralph was that the major corporations of America were deliberately killing their own customers and this slaughter could only be stopped by the strong arm of the federal government. As I recall, he suggested that it was simply too complicated and too difficult to get the public to do anything in their own best interests, that the way to turn this thing around was to put the greatest pressure on the easiest target, the manufacturers. And so, in the next decade, he did.

In the years since his dishonest little tract appeared and frightened GM into killing the Corvair—a rather pleasant compact car that was written off because nobody loved it but the customers—we've seen Ralph the Pure and his Roundhead acolytes get their way in virtually every area that could catch and hold their interest. Nowhere was his power more manifest than in the area of automotive safety, the high-water mark being the selection of his ward, Miss Joan Claybrook, to head the National Highway Traffic Safety Administration in the Carter administration.

Times change, the pendulum swings, and now America's intelligentsia are more concerned with saving what's left of the nation's former industrial might than they are with Ralph's ravings about corporate excess. And, as he gets older, Nader sounds less like a valiant crusader and more like a whining nuisance. What nobody seems to have noticed is that he was wrong. We were killing roughly 50,000 people a year in the late Sixties, and we're still killing about 50,000 people a year. Federally mandated, Nader-inspired safety equipment is supposed to have saved tens of thousands of lives. The 55-mile-per-hour speed limit is supposed to have saved tens of thousands of lives. If that's true, why are we still killing roughly 50,000 people a year? The rate is down, but the Safety Nazis never trusted death-rate data when used in the automobile's defense. I'd now like to remind America's Own Savonarola of my hipshot thesis in that grungy little radio studio seventeen years ago, to wit: *the way to cut the traffic-death total is to remove the drunk drivers from our roads and to somehow get the American driving public to use seatbelts.*

If you'd like to murder somebody, try this: get yourself blind, staggering, out-of-control drunk some night and just run over the poor bastard as he walks across his lawn to the mailbox. Chances are the law won't lay a glove on you. Especially if you're white, middle-aged, and middle-class or above. Our courts apparently believe that the only bad drunks on highways are young, poor, and/or nonwhite, and that any liquor-related incident involving "the better class of people" is simply a lamentable accident, one of God's little practical jokes.

The real tragedy is that problem drinker-drivers are an easily identified and isolated minority of our population. Every time some drunk kills a kid in a crosswalk, a dozen of his friends and associates will ruefully admit that they knew it was just a matter of time until he killed *some*body. They'd seen him drunk too many times, heard of his many close calls, maybe even seen him haled into court once or twice, but knew he'd never change until something *really* terrible happened.

It appears that very few Americans want to point the finger at friends, neighbors, business associates, or relatives who are potential killers. They figure it's none of their business, and anyway, isn't that what the cops are for? Unfortunately, the police generally only come face to face with the deadly problem drinker after he's done something awful enough to capture their attention. However, something constructive has happened, at last. Several states have begun a get-tough policy with drunken drivers, and a group called MADD (Mothers Against Drunk Drivers) has sprung up at the grass-roots level to spur government concern about the problem. The results of the campaign at this writing are encouraging, but the "nothing can be done" crowd pooh-poohs all the good that's been done so far with the warning that every state or county that's tried the stern approach to the problem has seen it lose momentum and run down after a while. The publicity scares social drinkers at first, it's said, then gradually they learn that the police can't catch *everybody*, and they drift back to their drinking-and-driving ways. Well, if it was strictly up to the government, I guess I'd be cynical about the outcome myself. But I've seen the good women of MADD on television, heard them on the radio, and read about them in several newspapers and weekly news magazines. Many of them have lost children or other kin to drunken drivers, and I don't think that they're about to let America's dangerous boozers off as easily as might the courts or the local police.

Early in 1968, I wrote in this space: "Social drinkers will be discouraged by the prospect of revoked drivers' licenses and punitive jail sentences. Problem drinkers and repeat offenders can be effectively isolated and treated as addicts or criminals, depending on the circumstances….Repeat offenders should be given long, long jail terms, and *permanently* denied the right to own or operate any kind of motor vehicle….Such people are no more socially acceptable than homicidal child molesters or ax murderers, and should be similarly removed from contact with a vulnerable public when they have been proved potentially lethal."

Now, if some group like Mothers Against Drunk Drivers will only come along and stir up similar interest in 100 percent use of seatbelts, we'll be well on our way to saving a bunch of those lives that Ralph Nader and his Safety Nazis have been caterwauling about for the past decade and a half.

Detroit and the Grand Prix:
Right place, right time.

S omewhere in the pack-rat welter of my personal belongings there's a memento of a great road race. It's a piece of bright red-and-yellow harness tack, the sort of thing you'd use to decorate your plow horse for a big religious festival, particularly if you live in Sicily. I bought it by accident. I was watching the Targa Floria with Henry Manney in 1967. We were in the Sicilian village of Collesano, where the cars came down-shifting into town from high on the mountain, negotiated a hairpin, then screamed back up through the gears out of town and into the valley beyond. (Nino Vaccarella, a law professor from Palermo and a local hero, managed not to negotiate this hairpin, while leading the race, and put his factory Ferrari P4 into the old stone wall just like a dart.) I too was making my way downhill, along the main drag, trying to find another vantage point. Each time one of the Porsche 910s or the Ferraris or the Phil Hill/Hap Sharp Chaparral would pass me, I'd be forced to step quickly into the nearest doorway. The cars were about a foot away, and traveling at about 130. At one point I backed up and blundered into a dark little shop where a dark little man made and sold harness, both workaday and festive. On an impulse, I bought a piece to commemorate the occasion. Now I can't find it. I hope my first wife didn't throw it out with the rest of the marriage.

I never got to see the Mille Miglia. Alfonso Cabeza de Vaca, Marquis de Portago, blew a tire and went into the crowd on the way north from Rome just about a week before I started work at *Road & Track* magazine in 1957. The Italian government put a stop to the Mille Miglia as a result, so I never saw the race, something I will regret to my dying day. I have watched the Grand Prix at Monaco, however, and I did get involved in racing 'round the houses at Watkins Glen and Put-in-Bay a couple of years before *Car and Driver*'s new art director, Linda Golightly Moser, was born. Now I can say I've watched Grand Prix cars racing through the streets of Detroit, Michigan. It's hard to believe.

Detroit is only the second world-class automobile race I've ever attended where one could walk from the pits to a world-class hotel or restaurant without leaving the racetrack—Monaco being the first. *Car and Driver* had a gorgeous 40-foot Custom Coach Land Cruiser parked in the paddock, heavily stocked with food, drink, friends, and Betamax cassettes. Renault, having interestingly enough assumed the role of home team, had a splendid hospitality tent on one of the terraces of the Oz-like Renaissance Center overlooking the pits and Turn Three. Ford and Moët et Chandon had another hospitality area on another terrace. My room was on the 66th floor of the Westin Hotel, where we could see five turns—the entire east end of the circuit. Bernard Cahier and his wife were one floor above, and they could see the entire west end of the circuit. If there was ever a better place or a manner in which to observe major-league motorsport, I didn't know of it.

The Detroit race track was not perfect, but neither was it terrible. Frank Williams, of the Saudia-Williams team, offered the thought that "there are six or seven circuits worse than Detroit, and Monaco heads the list." The track, laid out by Chris Pook early last year, featured too many 90-degree corners, one 23-mile-per-hour hairpin that was one too many, and some rough pavement. Even so, the drivers found that there were only a couple of bad bumps that couldn't be avoided in a normal race lap. The streets' manhole covers that had so spooked the drivers (one journalist actually suggested that the great suction of the racing cars with their downforce aerodynamics would suck the manhole covers out of their manholes and send them clanging into the crowds) turned out to be no sweat. They simply drove around them. The drivers' oft-quoted fear that there'd be no place to pass also turned out to be baloney. In driving to victory, John Watson passed McLaren teammate Niki Lauda, Eddie Cheever's Talbot-Ligier, and Didier Pironi's Ferrari, all in the same lap. Jackie Stewart got it exactly right on the ABC television coverage of the race when he suggested that the problems were not with the course, but with the cars.

There was one major screw-up. When Patrese and Guerrero crashed on the sixth lap and Patrese's Brabham started to burn, the chief steward's decision to throw the red flag was stupid and unprofessional. The official involved, Bob Swenson, has played the same official role at Long Beach and Las Vegas and should have known better. He panicked, and events were out of his control for the next hour. Patrese's fire was barely sufficient to roast marshmallows, and both cars were well off the line and against the wall. The hour's delay was disastrous for the television coverage, and it probably didn't help the surviving cars and drivers either. Part of the delay was occasioned, however, when the SCCA officials discovered that Patrese, Guerrero, and someone named Winkelhock (who'd crashed his ATS in the opening laps) were on the grid for the restart in their backup cars and had to be removed. If at first you don't succeed...

Going back to that summer of 1967—on our way from Monaco to the Targa Florio, in fact—Henry Manney and I stopped off in Modena. After dinner, we dropped in to the bar in the Palace Hotel just in time to hear Alf Francis (a large, colorful man who'd been Stirling Moss's mechanic in those golden seasons) declaim to a collection of layabouts and out-of-work race mechanics: "There are no more hairy-armed heroes!" One wonders what Alf would say about the present lot of Grand Prix prima donnas. Not only is there a lack of hairy arms, one would not be surprised to learn that half of them shave their legs. Analysis of them, as a group, would reveal about a hundred times too much John McEnroe and Ilie Nastase and a hundred times too little Richard Petty and Dan Gurney. The faction led by Pironi and Lauda is among the great kvetchers of all time, behaving as though each race coincided with the apogee of some monstrous cycle of menstrual discomfort. If they hate racing so much, they should stop taking the money. There must be plenty of better-humored heroes who'd like their seats.

Drive-in democracy.

have an unusual assignment. Somebody in the State Department
has asked me to write a piece about Americans and their automobiles for *America Illustrated,* which is an English-language
magazine our government distributes in the U.S.S.R. I am now about a
month late on the assignment. I've never been to Russia, and I must confess I'm a little intimidated by the place. I'm sure I'd like the Russian
countryside, and I know I'd like the people because I've liked every
Russian I've ever met. But I think I may enjoy silliness and wild talk too
much to qualify me for a place in the bosom of the Russian bear.

What on earth do I tell the Russian people—or those librarians,
technicians, and schoolteachers who might read *America Illustrated*—
about Americans and their automobiles? If I was sitting around a bottle
of vodka with a little group of like-minded Russians, I could tell them
about my old man hitting the mule with the Buick touring car, or I
could tell 'em about the time some friends and I tried our hand at boot-
legging in their Model A cabriolet and had to flee the Ontario Provincial
Police along the beach and how, the next day, we got broadsided with me
asleep in the rumble seat and the cops had to lever me out with a crow-
bar after they set the old Ford back up on its wheels. I could describe
Lindamood's recent adventures driving in a demolition derby, but they
might think that demolition derbies were clear evidence of capitalist
decadence, and they'd probably be right.

An interesting conundrum, that. America's working class is supposed to be suffering under the heel of the Republican oppressors, yet all
over the country hearty blue-collar types are gaily whanging into each
other every night with automobiles for which the average Russian bureau-
crat would gladly swap his position in the party pecking order. That may
be why I'm blocked on this story. I'm really put off by the idea of all that
useful transportation getting destroyed in demolition derbies, yet I really
cherish the idea of a country where demolition derbies can happen.

I've been dying to tell someone about the couple I saw at the car-wash the other day. As I was pulling in, they came out through the big blowers in what appeared to be a brand-new Datsun, made a U-turn in front of me, and went right back to the start. I followed them through their second run, and when I came out into the sunlight, there they were, preparing to take pictures of each other beside the car. Who says the love affair is over?

But then it'd probably not come as news to the average Russian upward-striver that Americans love their cars. Any Russian who could get his hands on a car would love it too. Perfectly natural. What might give them more enlightenment about us and our cars would be the other Datsun I saw the other day. It was an orange pickup with a slick little Okie-box on the back and the bumper sticker that read, "Real Americans buy what they want." My Russian readers might find that a little hard to swallow, but if I could somehow convey the incredible fact that American consumers really can buy just about anything they want, that nothing is rationed, that there are no limits of any kind on what American wage earners can do with their money, then I'd be telling them something important.

It might be equally important to try to explain the fact that Americans can climb into whatever automobiles they own and go any-where they choose. Not only can they whiz from state to state, from one end of North America to the other, they can cross into Canada or Mexico with only minor delay for a routine and perfunctory customs check. Ceppos says they won't believe me. He tells a story about a Russian couple who visited friends in the United States and spent the first two weeks convinced that their hosts' house and car had been fur-nished by the government as window dressing to give them a false, favor-able impression of this country.

Sociologists in the U.S.S.R. might be interested to learn of the lowriders, to comprehend the ingenuity and expense required to develop slow cars with no ground clearance, cars that hop up and down at the press of a button, cars that seem to be designed to simultaneously cele-brate and perpetuate the Chicano's underdog role in the United States. Perhaps engineers would be intrigued by the defiance of basic physical principles embodied in drag racing. Explain *that* to a solemn group of technoids in Leningrad. "Well, comrades, here's what they do: they work for months, spend thousands and thousands of dollars on a passenger vehicle with skinny little motorcycle wheels and tires in the front and enormous underinflated baloneys in the rear and about a trillion horse-power in the middle. They never drive these cars farther than a quarter-mile, and that hardly ever takes them more than ten seconds, usually quite a bit less."

What would they think about our motels? How many of them have ever stayed in anything as nice as the average Holiday Inn? I wonder if there are a dozen hotels in all the Russian provinces as comfortable as the Holiday Inn in Texarkana? Fast food. If it wasn't for America's relationship with the automobile there wouldn't be an Egg McMuffin or a Wendy's double-cheese with mustard, onion, and ketchup. Not only is Soviet culture lacking these things, it doesn't even have a car window to pass them through.

Nowhere in Europe can one get a decent ice-cream cone. Imagine the childlike delight of a second- or third-level commissar from the Russian boonies on being ushered into his first Baskin-Robbins 31 Flavors. He might try to give the impression that he was fully accustomed to having a choice between Pralines 'n' Cream and Bubble Gum flavors back home, and he might even try to suggest that such a range of choice was not in the consumers' best interest, but deep in his heart he'd be wondering about the odds against a successful defection. Would he be able to see the connection among an ice-cream cone, the privately owned passenger car, and personal freedom? I wonder. I wonder how many Americans make the connection. It's perfectly obvious to me.

What we have here is a drive-in democracy. Thomas Jefferson would probably have been troubled at the prospect of all those ordinary men and women in restless motion, enthusiastically exploring the unique combination of social and automotive mobility that is life in these United States. He'd prefer us to have stayed on the farm, I think. Benjamin Franklin, on the other hand, might have hugely enjoyed the run from Philadelphia to Los Angeles in a Ford van. Difficult as it may be to imagine Lenin or Stalin driving a Cadillac across Texas with two six-packs of Pearl and some old Ry Cooder tapes, I think that might be the best way for Russians to come to grips with America's automotive ethic. Maybe I'll suggest that when I finally sit down to finish my piece for *America Illustrated.*

Personal best.

W|hen I originally thought of doing this month's first annual "Ten Best" issue of *Car and Driver,* I warmed to the notion of me sitting here autocratically doling out the old hyperbole, ignoring any counsel or dissent from my staff, having the time of my life. Alas, democracy still flourishes here at *Car and Driver,* and egalitarian rot immediately began to erode my perfect vision of ten times ten best. Other people were allowed to express themselves. People like Ceppos, Griffin, Csere, Lindamood were given the ballot. I didn't even enjoy *primus inter pares* status anymore, I was just one vote. Damn. Well, making the best of my dashed fantasy, I will now come at it from another direction.

Best Status Car: This magazine has long maintained, and correctly so, that Japanese cars have succeeded by becoming the best little American cars money could buy. However, there is one little Japanese car that is too often overlooked when deliberations of this kind are taking place. That car would be any Subaru with four-wheel drive. Henry Ford I, Boss Kettering, and William Crapo Durant would have seen the wisdom of my words in a flash.

The Subaru is as American as baseball, hot dogs, apple pie, and Chevrolet. It is good old Yankee know-how, expressed in terms that are pure make-a-better-mousetrap free enterprise. It is just, in this case, that these terms are being expressed by the people at Fuji Heavy Industries. It is my good fortune to have in my garage one Mercedes-Benz station wagon and one four-wheel-drive Steyr-Daimler-Puch Haflinger. If I were forced to replace those two with a single vehicle capable of doing both jobs, it would have to be a four-wheel-drive Subaru station wagon. Happily, if I actually did that, it would leave me with enough money to build myself a house in the Rockies or take my wife around the world on the *QE2,* because Subarus don't cost very much money. What the hell, the estimable P.J. O'Rourke feels right at home in his 4wd Subaru wagon; my friend George Alexander, a judge no less, opts for a Subaru when commuting to and from the trout streams and grouse coverts; and I forget the names of countless thousands of straight people who drive them every day. It is the car of choice for all kinds of folks who have to drive up mountains or through snow, and there's an overlapping constituency that sings its praises just because it's inexpensive to operate and it hardly ever breaks. ("Warning, this vehicle breaks for nothing.") It is the ultimate expression of automotive status.

Best Comeback by a Fallen Idol: When it transpired that John Z. DeLorean was unable to manage the affairs of one of the world's smallest automobile companies, and nobody wanted the cars that company was building anyway, the people who concern themselves with such things thought he might be off the front pages for good. But no, in a public-relations coup of unpredecented proportions, Mr. De Lorean propelled himself back into the limelight with yet another of those innovative impulses that had so marked his career with General Motors. Hardly pausing for breath, the silver-haired philosopher-prince turned his back on the ethical-sports-car business and—according to certain departments of the United States government—set out to buy his way into the infinitely more exciting importing field. How like the newspaper and television people to fall into his trap and turn a simple change in career path into the news story of the year. Mr. De Lorean has proved to his detractors that his main goal in life is not just the betterment of the human condition, nor the construction of colossal false-front empires in the style of Mr. Cecil B. De Mille. No, Mr. De Lorean, a simple man from simple beginnings, only wanted to get his name before the public. In this he has succeeded, probably beyond his own wildest dreams. If his ethical-sports-car business and his importing business have gone down the sewer, we can blame the British and American governments for once again meddling with the honest, straightforward workings of the free-enterprise system.

Best Dinner: The best meals I have eaten in the United States have come from my own kitchen. Mrs. Davis spent her time wisely during her eighteen years in France, Switzerland, and Italy, and came home to the States with a sure hand in the culinary arts. However, *haute cuisine* is plenty *haute* on the continent of Europe, and the best meal—actually the two best meals—I've eaten in the past twelve months have been served at the Alte Post in Stuttgart, home of both Porsche and Daimler-Benz. Mr. and Mrs. Siegfried Riegger are young, charming, and handsome, and their restaurant is a treasure. They could serve me anything from their venturesome menu and I'd be delighted, but I would challenge fire, flood, and the forward wall of the Dallas Cowboys for one order of their goose-liver pâté, the finest I have ever tasted. It is as smooth and creamy as custard, and when it warms on your tongue there's an aromatic explosion that must surely rival the effect of various controlled substances. The Alte Post's cuisine is probably classical German, not the sausages and potatoes of the German stereotype, but subtle, refined continental dishes like those worked up for the palates of pre-Bismarck Germany's noble families. Game, veal, chicken, lovely fresh fruits and vegetables, and for dessert—second only to the incomparable goose liver—nonrepresentational paintings done in homemade fresh-fruit sherbets, every plate different, every one a pale of swirl of favorite flavors. If you intend to take European delivery of a Porsche or a Mercedes, or if you're just planning a business or vacation trip, Alte Post is in downtown Stuttgart with the Rieggers' Porsche parked right out front, closed on Sunday, and there's no goose liver on Monday, because it won't keep over the Sabbath. Trust me on this one.

Of Larry Griffin, Porsche headlights, Vanagon campers, and the Jean Lindamood of pickup trucks.

~·~

I t is 7:35 in the morning, and the sunrise outside is coming up a brilliant purple. I got to the office about a half-hour ago and found our long-term Blazer sitting in the parking lot, obviously having been there all night. The building was locked but our burglar alarm was shut off, so I figured one of our folks was inside. Sure enough, I opened the front door, walked in, and heard Larry Griffin's typewriter tapping away behind his door. That meant he'd been here since nine or nine-thirty yesterday morning, working against the same deadline that oppresses me today.

The days are pretty nice here in Michigan. There's something wonderful about getting up early, showering, dressing, addressing one's goodbyes to a tumbled bed full of wife, cat, and two hunting dogs, then driving a Porsche 928S over the winding road past the lake to the office. The 928's headlight pods are silhouetted against their own white light, and you just sort of keep the road between them as you let the engine warm up till you can hammer it in third and clear your head. Nana Mouskouri is singing softly about unrequited love on the tape deck, and all's right with the world.

If I stand up at my desk and look out the window, Detroit is squarely in front of me, 45 miles to the east, and to my left, for the next 500 miles or so, stretches a parade of lakes, forests, farmland, and pretty little towns. I have to confess that last fall saw at least as much of me in and around the lakes and forests as in the city of Detroit. A living obviously has to be earned, and this is undoubtedly the best way for a car enthusiast to do that, but nonetheless I happily forsook this desk and the centers of automotive power in Detroit as often as possible.

Two friends helped to make it possible for me to do that. One was Jean Lindamood and the other was Herb Williamson. Herb Williamson was the associate editor of this magazine back in 1961 and '62, when it was changing its name from *Sports Cars Illustrated.* He wrote one of the definitive Beetle books, *Today's VW Guide,* and became one of the stalwarts in the Volkswagen PR department, where he's been ever since. Herb lent me his Vanagon camper—his own company car—for the months of October and November, my two favorites here in Michigan. We made a dozen trips in that Vanagon, and ran up hundreds of miles on its odometer. During the deer season, my stepson and his wife slept in it a couple of nights when the temperature was down around zero in the woods and J.L.K. Davis and I had prudently retreated to a nearby motel. Sometime soon, I'll do a piece on the vehicle, and describe its many delights, but I just wanted to make sure Herb knew how much I appreciated the use of his wheels.

Several times during the same period, I found myself in need of a four-wheel-drive truck, and my pal and associate Jean Lindamood came through in grand style. The Lindamood family truck is a 1978 Dodge stepside Power Wagon—burgundy, with white Jackman wheels and nearly bald tires—that they use mostly to haul firewood, and she lent it to me without a whimper. I cannot tell you how much I love that dumb truck. The engine is a 318 with a Direct Connection high-performance distributor (which, Lindamood proudly points out, she recurved her very own self with a broken nail file), a four-barrel Carter Thermoquad carburetor, and a set of Cyclone headers.

Jean and Tom ordered it with the heaviest-duty suspension Dodge offered, then added Delco air shocks and extra leaves in the springs at the front, and extra-heavy Delco shocks at the rear. The driveline is all Chrysler, featuring a Torqueflite automatic transmission (plus oil cooler) and full-time four-wheel drive; certainly a painless approach to trips through the muck and mire. The truth is that they ordered it with every option you could get, except for a radio and a rear bumper. It still lacks a rear bumper, and for reasons unknown to me they installed a little FM/cassette system that's just about useless when you're way out in the boonies trying to get a weather report at five in the morning. (We will now doff our caps and share a moment of silence in honor of AM radio with its hourly news and weather and its incredible range.) I'm not sure how the cassette player worked, because the headers usually made so much noise that you couldn't hear it anyway.

The interior of Mood's truck is special. The seats are covered in thick, shiny black vinyl, and the left one has been liberally patched with a combination of electrician's and duct tape. The power amp for the FM/cassette is low on the dash, millimeters away from the driver's left kneecap, and there's a bracket for a missing CB radio waiting to cripple the passenger in the event of a collision. The aftermarket sunroof leaks when it's raining, or whenever the heater starts melting the snow on top of the cab, and the water runs unerringly down the passenger's collar. There's another leak at the top of the windshield directly above the steering column, but this simply drops water onto the floor.

The road ahead is really where the driver's attention should stay fastened with Mood's truck. The combination of bald tires, super-stiff suspension, and bags of power tends to give the old maroon beauty a mind of its own. It darts, hunts, nibbles, and weaves on a high-crowned country road. That may be because, in its present setup, it's really an off-road vehicle. On-road is not exactly its forte. Off-road, at low speeds, it will aggressively go anywhere you're brave enough to drive it. The only drawback here is that one tends to get thrown about the cab because of the non-absorbent shock absorbers and the barely flexing springs. However, at high speeds off-road, it is another matter altogether. It is exactly like an unlimited hydroplane, and every bit as physical. You point it where you want to go, open all four holes in the Carter Thermoquad, and it actually planes, squirting over the rough stuff, only touching down every now and again to let the four balding Goodyears get another bite. In this mode, the driver will not be inclined to change tapes or tie his tie. In this mode, the driver is hanging on for dear life, grinning like a fool, knowing in his heart of hearts that the Safety Nazis would in no way approve of his behavior.

We used it to haul huge loads of carrots, to haul lumber, to haul assorted beer drinkers up hill and down dale, and to get us back into the inner wilds of Michigan, to wild places where Herb Williamson's Vanagon wouldn't go. It is a good-humored "Rubens nude with a big motor," the Jean Lindamood of half-ton pickup trucks.

Between Texas and Michigan, the mind wanders...

~~~

T he new BMW 318i was introduced to the American motoring press at Boerne, Texas, in the heart of the Texas hill country. We drove one of the cars back to our Ann Arbor headquarters after the preview was over. Having a terrific cold at the time, we didn't talk much but watched the scenery roll by in glum, congested silence, thinking about everything under the sun. What follows is a random sampling of those thoughts.

Why do American cars have such heavy doors? Swing an American door open, letting it go to the limit of its travel, and it invariably bounces back at you, trying to trap your left ankle and cut your foot off. I hate that. A BMW door—or virtually any other contemporary imported-car door, for that matter—is lighter and shorter than a typical American door, and it stays open, even when the car's parked on an upgrade.

Who do you suppose decides how the family front yard is supposed to look? This thought struck me as I was driving through a ghastly wasteland along Route 67 south of Pocahontas, Arkansas. Do Mom and Dad sit down after the kids have gone to bed and thrash it out? "Listen, honey," Dad opens, "I've been thinking a lot about your pile of rusty prewar lawn chairs. What if we moved them closer to the busted washing machine? That way people going by on the highway could get a better look at the old ton-and-a-half stake body with the missing engine and still see our whitewashed tractor tire with the dead geraniums in the center." It doesn't seem possible that these elaborate arrangements could just happen by accident.

Where is the factory that produces the entrees for America's blizzard of Cork 'n Cleavers, Beef 'n Bourbons, Eat 'n Parks, Branigans, Flannigans, and Snarl 'n Slobbers? Since all of these places have more or less identical help ("Hi, I'm Debbi, I'll be your waitperson tonight, and if there's anything you want, just ask me"), it follows that they must all get their main courses from the same source as well. There's the veal Cordon Bleu, the fresh Rocky Mountain rainbow trout, the chicken Kiev, the flounder stuffed with crabmeat, all squeezed out of similar sets of extrusion dies, all undoubtedly coming out of the same foodlike-substance factory in some place like Secaucus, New Jersey. It is a scandal. Avoid these places like the plague, but if you're taken there by kidnappers or for any other reason you're unable to avoid dining in one some night, keep it simple: order a steak. Any conversational riposte from you that's more than four one-syllable words in length will cause Debbi (or Kerri, or Kevin, or Bruce, or whomever) to fix you with a blank stare and say, "I'll have to go back and ask about that."

The Fiat X1/9 seems to have replaced the Vega as the car in which Americans most like to be marooned at the roadside. For several years now I've watched Vegas, usually rusted-out Vegas, coasting to stops in the middle of nowhere, their drivers' faces masks of resignation, the tiny bit of horsepower they could still generate finally curling up from the edges of the hood in the form of smoke, steam, and other effluvia signifying an early and undignified death. Now, apparently, most of the Vegas have gone on to that Great Car Auction in the Sky (hopefully, God has forced the late president of General Motors, Mr. Ed Cole, whose brainchild the Vega was, to drive one till Judgment Day) because we don't see too many of them anymore, dead or alive. Their place in the dead-car park has been taken by the Fiat X1/9. These poor, benighted little cars, evidently conceived as transport for midget clowns in Italian circuses, have now rusted to the point that one can usually see through them, lengthwise, and are coughing their insides out, miles from home, all over the republic.

Bottles and cans, along with blown mufflers and shards of truck tires, used to be the kind of junk that one most often encountered at the side of the road. Now one finds dreadful snarls of tape, sometimes rolling along on the breeze, sometimes blown into the bushes or wrapped around the Armco barrier. My own experience tells me that these must be the innards of dead eight-track cartridges, since eight-track is a notoriously unreliable sound system and the cartridges, with all their winding around and going back down their own throats, as it were, seem to jam much more frequently than cassettes. Thank heaven for cassettes.

It is impossible to get a decent cup of coffee west of the Mississippi River, maybe west of Chicago. Good coffee is rare enough on the eastern seaboard, but the farther west one goes, the weaker the coffee gets. I know the legends about cowboy coffee that rots the spoon and all that, but I'm here to tell you that the average cowboy would faint dead away at his first sip of the stuff routinely drunk by convent girls in Philadelphia. The Davis Long-Distance-Driving Team has a fix for this. Buy a small jar of any instant coffee and keep it close at hand as you travel the American West. When the coffee comes, you discreetly slip about a half-teaspoon of instant into the local brew, and it becomes darker, more aromatic, in every way more like real coffee, as it was meant to be drunk.

Vans are making a comeback—only, it seems, with a different constituency. Mom and Dad are buying them these days, and they're not buying stripped commercial models, either. One gets the impression that outfits like Starcraft must be working three shifts to satisfy the demand for plush luxovans with captains' chairs and Venetian blinds and teak trim, flanks perforated everywhere for enormous GM motorhome-type panoramic type windows, and flashing *Star Wars* decals. One more sign that the economy is struggling to its feet.

Finally, there are still a few leftover hippies out there. Every once in a while I pass some benign throwback to the Sixties hunkered down at a remote Interstate interchange, smiling as though he was the bearer of his own secret tidbit of good news, wrapped in an old GI overcoat and about four feet of hair. These types are harmless, but there's another breed of longhaired throwback out there with whom one would be wise not to mess. Curiously enough, the very rednecks who used to harass the hippies, focusing more often than not on their hair, now have long, greasy hair of their own. Their role models are more apt to be aggressive senior citizens of the Hell's Angels persuasion than the Beatles or Timothy Leary, but there they are, tossing their locks and affixing "Buy American" bumper stickers to their listing Mercury Turnpike Cruisers. Hopefully, this too shall pass.

Our man Bedard goes to Indy, while ABC drifts beyond the boredom barrier.

O ur Mr. Patrick Bedard is no longer a rookie at the Indianapolis 500. At age 41, in his third attempt in as many years, he qualified seventeenth, right in the middle of the field—sixteen guys ahead and sixteen guys behind. On lap 26, while lying 22nd, his car ran wide of the line exiting Turn Four and struck the wall. By all accounts he did a masterly job of saving what could have been a disastrous situation by keeping the broken car straight and out of the path of Bobby Rahal, who was overtaking him at exactly the moment that he bounced off the wall and back into the 200-mph traffic. We're sorry that he didn't finish, but glad that he's okay.

Obviously, we're very proud of him, and we're all doubly proud to be associated with him on a daily basis. No other automotive journalist has ever made the field at Indianapolis. Paul Frère, the Belgian writer, has done all kinds of races and won his share, and quirky little Denis Jenkinson, of *Motor Sport,* raced side-hack motorcycles in his younger days and wrote one of racing's great pieces when he rode with Stirling Moss in the winning 300SLR in the 1955 Mille Miglia, but making it into the 500 has challenged and beaten some of the greatest names in motor racing's history. Pat's feat is unique in the annals of this business and sets him apart as a very special member of our subcategory within the journalistic community.

Somebody suggested that what Bedard did should become mandatory in all sports, beginning with heavy-weight boxing. Imagine the joy of the fans when Howard Cosell steps into the ring to go fifteen rounds with Leon Spinks at the Garden.

While Mr. Bedard was suiting up and steeling himself to the prospect of 500 miles at an average speed of 160 or more in the world's most prestigious automobile race, I was preparing to go out and catch a mess of bluegills with a wonderful little midge-weight fly rod. While he fought an understeering car around the most famous racetrack in the universe, I stood in a small boat on a spring lake and threw a tiny black spider at short-tempered little fish. I heard most of the race on a portable radio, and I must say that it was infinitely better than being there—especially when someone I liked so much was driving one of the cars.

The radio coverage of the race was superb. The several commentators were uniformly professional, informative, and enthusiastic, and they provided me with more information about the race than I could possibly have assimilated had I been there. Their technique of flashing from commentator to commentator as the cars went around the track wasn't new, but it was gripping and conveyed a feeling of immediacy that really kept the listener's attention. Also, we were able to hear real racing sounds, sounds directly related to the events being described. Furthermore, they kept me advised of various backmarkers' performances, along with a wealth of pertinent statistical information. The whole thing served as a vivid reminder of the power of radio, when properly used.

The television coverage, on the other hand, was a very bad and tedious joke. It is clear that our friends from the American Broadcasting Company have become jaded, bored with "The Greatest Spectacle in Racing," and are simply unable to get themselves up to do a workman-like job of race coverage anymore. Of the entire mob of commentators, only Chris Economaki was able to convey useful and timely information. Watching the televised proceedings that night, I got the feeling that Messrs. Flemming, McKay, et al., were determined to structure their presentation as a conceptual cross between coverage of the Iran hostage crisis and "That's Incredible!" Never has such a stirring and remarkable sporting event received such trivializing and utterly listless electronic attention.

In the three hours that ABC devoted to this year's 500, there was perhaps an hour of actual racing coverage, and that was so badly done that anyone who hadn't been to the speedway before, or heard the radio broadcast, could have been forgiven for believing that there might be only four or five cars in the race. The rest of the time was devoted to endless revelations of the record-breaking shallowness of the TV people themselves.

Jackie Stewart—ordinarily a bright and engaging interpreter of the sport—sat in disconnected isolation at some mythical place called "Race Central." This might as well have been London, for all the sense of immediacy it conveyed. He shuffled papers and looked lugubrious, only showing signs of life when the network cut to an utterly inappropriate sidebar of The Wee Scot himself standing at the entrance to the pits and harping away for what seemed like 30 minutes on how it could all be made safer.

Jim McKay crept on verbal hands and knees through a mine field of disinformation, while Sam Posey gave androgyny a bad name with his endless yips and squeals about the parallels between today's race and his own largely forgettable career as a racing driver. Poor old Sam. For two weeks before the event he's maundered on about how dangerous it was going to be, and then it turned out to be one of the safest races in memory and the wind seemed to go out of his sails. The absence of blood and gore really seemed to be a downer for all concerned. One imagines that those *National Enquirer* readers attracted to the show by Sam's pre-race hand wringing must have been annoyed indeed. Not even the rollicking fun of a spoof pit stop by the ABC announcing team or a film clip of Paul Newman in *The Verdict* (Paul Newman is co-owner of Mario Andretti's car, get it?) could raise anybody's pulse rate above that of a garden slug.

We learned how John Mecom's guests felt about it all, and we heard one of ABC's cheery but empty blazers proudly announce that he'd never been there before. (Oh, *excellent!*) Then their token woman sportscaster recited a round of doggerel with predictable rhyming punch lines mouthed by lovable moppets from among the mob—a ghastly bit designed to let us know why children come to the 500—and we watched the animals at play in the infield to the soulful strains of a Carole King ballad. Decorously missing were any "Show Us Your Tits!" signs, apparently out of consideration for the lamebrain bird conducting the tour, or perhaps to enhance the mood conveyed by Ms. King.

All in all, it was a near-perfect demonstration of network television's special gift for making the exciting and uplifting seem banal and ordinary, while celebrating all that is truly second-rate in this society. Our Patrick Bedard and 32 other very special individuals deserved better.

Routine business correspondence.

~·~

omorrow I leave for the mountains of Wales, where Messrs. Yates, O'Rourke, and I will participate in a four-wheel-drive shoot-out with the rowdy Australians who produce Great Britain's *Car* magazine. We will be armed with a Chevy S-10 Blazer, a GMC S-15 Jimmy, a Ford Bronco II, and a brand-new Jeep XJ Cherokee. They're supposed to show up with a new independent-front-suspension Land Rover, a five-speed Range Rover, a short-wheelbase Mercedes-Benz Geländewagen, and a European-spec Mitsubishi Montero. Our Oswestryan correspondent, Mr. Philip Llewellin, has reconnoitered the route and is hoping for the worst. We will do our best to see that he isn't disappointed. We will prove that the doctrine of Manifest Destiny is not dead, just facing east, back across the Atlantic.

With the prospect of a long absence from the office ahead of me, it has occurred that I should handle some of my correspondence. Therefore, I've selected this space as the best venue for some overdue letters. Here we go…

To *The Wall Street Journal*
Gentlemen:

You no doubt appreciate what a thrill it is for a bunch of simple kids from the Midwest to make the front page of your prestigious gazette. We were proud, pleased, and perfectly amazed to learn that you intended to do a feature story on *Car and Driver,* and when the day of publication arrived, we were all waiting around the mailbox in breathless anticipation.

The piece was wonderful, everything we could have hoped for. We found ourselves portrayed as tough-talking macho types who'd rather flout the law and crash and burn than waste our time with the tiresome details of getting Ann Arbor's leading car magazine out each month. Fair enough. Not exactly what our mothers had in mind for us, nor is it the sort of thing our superiors in New York like to read about us, but it's our legend and we're stuck with it.

However, there are one or two teensy-weensy details that your winsome, high-school-graduate correspondent got wrong and we feel that these should be called to your attention.

In speaking of our "arrogant" editorial taste in cars, she said: "Special targets are big sedans from Detroit and efficient little cars from anywhere." We felt a little abraded by that one, since we've been prophets without honor in our own country, trying to hasten the nation's acceptance of smaller, more efficient cars, and for the past quarter-century. And given your writer's thesis, how do you explain our recent selection of the Chevrolet Caprice as one of the ten best cars?

Seated in my office, questioning me about the nonenthusiast constituency for cars like Volvo, Saab, and Subaru, your inquiring debutante-journalist apparently neither listened nor took notes very carefully. She quoted me as calling the owners of *practical* cars "granolas." I will not recite the entire statement. "*Protest* [emphasis ours—Ed.) cars have always been with us. Years ago, there were Nashes, Lafayettes, Hudsons, Essexes, Kaisers, and Frazers, lots of cars for the guy who wouldn't allow himself to be hoodwinked into buying a car from one of the Big Three. As the American independents fell away, one by one, the imports took their place as protest cars. Protest cars, like Volvo, Saab, and Subaru, have been bought in large numbers by the granolas, anti-car people who want to save the whales, ban the bomb, and wear dirndl skirts." I believe you'll agree that there's a vast semantic gap between "practical cars" and "protest cars."

Our own Jean Lindamood is described as one "who crashed cars into a wall for a living." To the best of our knowledge, Mrs. Lindamood has never crashed a car either for a living or as a form of relaxation—unless we count her daring exploits at the Chelsea, Michigan, Demolition Derby. Mrs. Lindamood *was* a test driver at the Chrysler Proving Ground, and she *did* work in the crash lab as a welder, but she most assuredly did not "crash cars into a wall for a living."

There are seven or eight other journalistic miscues, but there's little to be gained in whipping a dead horse. We remain delighted that you deigned to give over the center of your most valuable front page to a feature about us and our magazine. The next time you choose to extol our manifold virtues, send a professional, or send somebody cute, but don't send Mary J. Pitzer.

To the Spartacus of the Seventies
Dear Mr. Nader:

Sorry I wasn't here when you called the other day. Always a pleasure to hear a voice from the past. I understand you were really exercised about the pro-K mart letter we ran from some guy who signed your name. Surely you're not against K mart, Mr. Nader. I mean, you might not like the corn dogs, but the men's suits are…the suits are…well, the suits are just you, Mr. Nader, and there's no gainsaying the fact.

We all felt terrible when you attacked us in *The Detroit Free Press* on this issue. "It epitomizes the yellow journalism of this chrome-plated conflict of interest and fraud called Car and Driver," you said. As nearly as we can divine, you don't like us because we disagree with you about cars. You'd apparently like us better if we were *Mother Earth News* or something more in your ideological ballpark. Alas, we can't help you on that one. I'm afraid we're forever doomed to dwell in the shade of your distaste. We can understand why you might get testy, though. It can't be too easy wasting your life, waiting for the nation's loons and dimbulbs to name you benevolent despot by acclamation. They may be a constituency, but they're still a minority. Maybe if you had a trade…

To *The Wall Street Journal*
Gentlemen:

I don't want to be a pest, but you guys did it again. Two days after you published your revelations about *Car and Driver*, you seemed to go berserk over the new Mercedes-Benz 190. Very strange. Your author, Amal Nag, the one who was named after an acronym, first broke a deadline to which all the journalists at the 190 preview had specifically agreed, then suggested that the new mini-Mercedes was a flop, and cited the opinions of several members of the motoring press in support of his view. He blew it. I have canvassed a representative number of the writers who attended that preview, and they all loved the car.

Is it possible that your man overlooked the presence of a gasoline-engined model in the line? All of his remarks seemed to relate to the diesel version, as though every 190 that comes to America will be diesel-powered. An erroneous assumption. Furthermore, diesel or no, I would be happy to demonstrate the sporting character of the 190D on the road to Lindamood's farm any time Mr. Nag wants to try his luck.

You worry us. If you can be so utterly wrong about something as easily quantified as the performance of a Mercedes-Benz 190, should we trust you when you publish what purports to be the inside skinny about Bill Agee and Mary Cunningham? Facts, gentlemen, give us the facts.

Freedom & Whisky!

Go 2500 miles, at a hundred or better, without a moment's care for the cops.

⤜⤛⤜

The Federal Republic of Germany continues to allow people to drive as fast as their cars will go on the autobahns. Not long ago, however, they did begin to suggest that 130 kilometers per hour (81 mph) would be a more prudent speed, but they weren't *pushy* about it, by any means. Germans being big believers in law and order, a surprising number of them have in fact slowed down. J.L.K. Davis and I spent two weeks and some 2500 miles driving from London to Austria to Frankfurt and back to London again, and we were struck by the fact that traffic, generally speaking, seems to have slowed a little on the glorious wide-open roads of West Germany.

Ford's garage in London's West End was only a block from our hotel, so I strolled over on Tuesday morning and picked up a snappy Sierra XR4i—bright red, but otherwise similar to our November test car—which turned out to carry German registration plates and left-hand drive. I had prepared myself for the rigors of driving a right-hand-drive car on Europe's left-hand-drive roads and I felt just a trace of disappointment. This feeling quickly disappeared, though, when I pulled out of the alley and into Berkeley Square's rush-hour traffic and found myself seated on the wrong side of the vehicle. I handled it with the use of a mantra taught me by Mr. Brock Yates, several years ago. Yates's way is to constantly remind yourself, sotto voce, "Keep left, look right." If you do this religiously, the only time your life will be in actual peril is during the execution of right-hand turns.

We loaded all our stuff into the XR4i, shook hands with Messrs. Yates and O'Rourke on the sidewalk in front of the hotel, and set out for Dover and the Hovercraft that would carry us to Calais. Round-trip Dover-Calais by Hovercraft costs $208.80 for a car with two passengers, and it's a kick, crossing the channel in 39 minutes, compared with 90 minutes by ferry. The Dover Hoverport is pleasant, and the Hovercraft personnel are courteous and friendly. Even Her Majesty's Customs seemed to be a bit more laid-back at the Hoverport than they normally are at places like Heathrow Airport. We rolled into the pre-boarding area after a 90-minute run south from London, then drove aboard.

The Hovercraft carries cars, trucks, and tour buses, and the drill is to park where you're told, lock your vehicle, then go to the passenger area and find a seat. This aspect of Hovercraft travel is rather like riding the bus. We got window seats up forward and sat back to watch. When the engines start, they're felt as much as heard; then the Hovercraft begins to rise on its cushion of air until it appears to be at the full extension of its rubber skirt, maybe six feet off the ground. That accomplished, the four big topside props are used to both drive and steer the craft down the paved docking ramp, across the sand, and onto the water. The channel had been wracked by four days of gales before our crossing, and it was moderately choppy, but our Hovercraft was in no way discomfited by the roughness. She would occasionally slew into a trough, then stagger up again, but 95 percent of the time one could only marvel at her composure—especially when the captain came on the squawker and said we were proceeding at 63 miles per hour!

Once clear of the Calais docks, and unable to restrain ourselves, we tore straight up the road to Ardres and the Grand Hotel Clement, where we celebrated our arrival on the Continent with a long and memorable French lunch. Then it was due east toward Belgium. You know instantly that you're not in Connecticut. Traffic *moves*. Guys in 1.1-liter sedans pass as though they were driving small-block Chevys and unkillable. You quickly get into the spirit of the thing. The XR4i is a fast car by most standards, and the amount of power available in the midrange, combined with the beautifully staged ratios of its five-speed gearbox, makes it hard to beat in back-road cut-and-thrust.

We stayed near Bastogne in Belgium. It's eerie to drive through a countryside where every crossroads is marked with the names of places we all remember from the Battles of the Bulge and the Ardennes. Saint-Vith. Malmédy. Aachen. When I was a kid every neighborhood held at least one father who'd been gassed in 1918. I regularly saw Spanish-American War veterans marching on Decoration Day, and I knew one or two veterans of the Civil War. Time passes. Now the senior survivors of World War II have begun to fall from old age. We drove by fields full of guys who've been waiting for them since 1944.

In England, the speed limit is 70 mph, and everyone drives about 80 to 85. In Belgium, the speed limit is 120 kilometers per hour, and everybody drives about 150. In France, on the underutilized not-so-free-ways with their staggering tolls, the speed limit is 130 kph and everybody drives at 160. In Germany, I'd promised myself that I wouldn't become speed-crazed and drive flat-out from border to border; 160 kph, just under a hundred miles per hour, that seemed like a reasonable speed to me. Well, it can't be done. If you're in the fast lane, you have to go 180 or better to avoid being run down by the Opel Asconas. At 200, you are still overtaken by big Mercedes and an occasional Porsche going quite a bit faster than you are. Meanwhile, the slow lane, with all its trucks, is moving at about 110. This tends to make the autobahn two one-lane roads. Once in one lane, or the other, you kind of have to stay there, for better or for worse. The Ford's acceleration was a big help in this regard. A big 500SEL would come roaring up astern at 225; we'd whip into the right lane at the first opportunity, drop down to third, and, when he'd passed, nail it and swiftly resume station in the left lane.

There are damned few left-lane bandits in Germany. Drivers watch their mirrors and move over at the approach of a faster car. What does happen sometimes, however, is that a Mercedes or Audi Turbo driver cannot believe that the silly red Ford behind him is actually trying to get by. This leads to light-flashing and forehead-tapping, but sooner or later even the most stolid diesel driver will move over for the hot Fords and Volkswagen GTIs.

Austria gave us the chance to whip around on narrow Alpine roads, again taking full advantage of our midrange power and good gear ratios. By now we were fast friends with our red XR4i. We were a little sad to come down out of the mountains, not far from Salzburg, and find ourselves headed up the on-ramp to another autobahn stretching 500 kilometers or more to the Frankfurt Show. Except for one day at Frankfurt, when we took P.J. O'Rourke down the famous Romantic Road to lunch at the Hotel Eisenhut in Rothenburg, we were on autobahns, autoroutes, and motorways all the way back to the outskirts of London. But there was one last great dice. From Canterbury to London's Vauxhall Bridge we were stuck into a very enthusiastically driven Mitsubishi Cordia coupe. Traffic was heavy and we enjoyed one of those nutball spur-of-the-moment contests that deplete your adrenalin supply for two days afterward. If the driver of the white Mitsubishi reads this, I'd love to hear from him.

There is no goose down in an Eddie Bauer Bronco II.

～ひら~

The most practical clothing I own—for long-distance drives, at least—is a Filson cruiser jacket and pants. As I understand it, this is actually a U.S. Forest Service uniform that the Filson people manufacture in Seattle. The jacket has four outside pockets in the front, one inside breast pocket, and a large poacher pocket across the small of the back. The material is a military twill that never seems to lose its press. I've worn mine so much that we had to bind the ragged trouser bottoms with leather, and now the cuffs on the jacket are starting to go. But what the hell. I bought it in 1974; it ought to be a little worn. It's such a terrific outfit for driving that five years ago I bought five yards of the same material from Filson and took it to Anderson & Sheppard in London to have a three-piece business suit made—heavy, but it stays pressed when I wear it to drive from Ann Arbor to New York or Chicago, it keeps me warm when I'm filling a 40-gallon tank at the self-serve pump, and that's no bad thing for someone who drives and wears suits as much as yr. obt. svt.

I bought the original outfit from the Eddie Bauer store in Chicago. I think it was the first item I'd ever purchased from them that didn't come out of their catalog. I have a red Eddie Bauer down shirt that I dearly love, in spite of the fact that my retriever, then a puppy, tore off one pocket and ripped the sleeve. My whole family's baby-blue Duofold long-handles came from Eddie Bauer. My duck-hunting hat came from Eddie Bauer. My Patagonia polypropylenes came from Eddie Bauer. My sleeping bag came from Eddie Bauer. My mountain boots came from Eddie Bauer. Heck, my entire household wears sheepskin bedroom slippers from Eddie Bauer—bedroom slippers, again, in varying stages of dog-related destruction.

All of this has a payoff. A few weeks back, I received a mailer from Eddie Bauer, a folded Manila card, eleven by fourteen inches, which introduced me to the new Eddie Bauer Special Edition Bronco II and invited me down to the local store to celebrate the Eddie

Bauer/FoMoCo collaboration. It described a top-of-the-line Bronco II, loaded with options, with its own special two-tone Eddie Bauer paint treatment, special cloth upholstery in an Eddie Bauer motif, Eddie Bauer signature emblems on the front fenders, with an Eddie Bauer Cordura nylon gear bag thrown in. It also suggested that because I was such a good customer, this very piece of Manila-colored cardboard would entitle me to anything I wanted to buy from the Michigan Eddie Bauer store at a generous discount. Oh, my God.

Well, I mean, how are you going to pass up a deal like that? Harriet Stemberger and I rushed in and presented the certificate. "Oh," the man said, "you're a Ford employee." "No," I replied, "I'm not. The thing there says that I'm entitled to all this largess because I'm a regular customer." He shrugged, smiled, and waved his arm to indicate that the whole place was mine, subject to that generous discount. I was a wreck. Would I buy a new Filson cruiser suit? No, they don't sell them anymore. Would I buy J.L.K. Davis the mate to my sleeping bag so that we could zip them together and play Sleeping Bag Monster in the middle of the woods in the middle of the night? Again, no, they've changed their style of their bags and the new large-and-long heavy-duty rectangular down-filled sleeping bag won't mate with my old large-and-long heavy-duty rectangular down-filled sleeping bag. Well, at least I could buy a new Thinsulate-insulated Gore-Tex camouflage parka for duck hunting. Mrs. Stemberger, meanwhile, took advantage of my good fortune to buy her husband a terrific Christmas present.

Reflecting on all this, I decided that I had to put some miles on an Eddie Bauer Bronco II. The one I got was maroon and tan, and it got a lot of attention wherever it went. Downsized Broncos have been with us for a while now, long enough to have become commonplace, I should think, but this one, with its Eddie Bauer livery, really seemed to grab the onlookers. It was a V-6, of course, with an automatic gearbox, and it was a neat piece. No manually locking front hubs to mess with; just jerk the transfer-case lever from 2HI to 4HI, or 4LO, and a little greenish light pops on in the center of the dash to tell you what you just did, and away you go.

I've put about 2000 miles on it now, and I've come to know it pretty well. The rear hatch opens easily enough, except that you always need the key to operate the two-way handle (twist to the left to open the rear window, twist to the right to open the whole door, which swings up and pretty much out of the way). Ford's swing-away spare-tire mount works well, too. No need to use the feet, just a stout lever that you lift about an inch and the whole thing unlatches and swings way out to the right, well out of your way when loading or unloading. The rear seats fold quickly and easily without any need to clamber in and fight with the latches: seat bottoms fold forward against the back of the front seats; seat backs then fold flat, making a perfectly flat floor and more than doubling the available cargo space.

The Eddie Bauer Cordura nylon gear bag, with its roomy nineteen-by-thirteen-by-seven-inch main compartment, zip-out portfolio, twin side compartments, webbing handles, and detachable shoulder strap with leather cushion, had apparently been ripped off, because we couldn't find it. Neither could we find the no-extra-cost Eddie Bauer map holder, "a four-compartment folder that comes with a handy penlight and can hold maps, your Bronco II owner's manual, Ford care booklet, and more....All included when you buy your Eddie Bauer Bronco II," it says here, but missing from our little off-roadlet. Not having the gear bag or the map holder to throw into the back, we hauled furniture, groceries, luggage, dead deer, large Coleman coolers, hunting dogs, people, and cases of beer where the Eddie Bauer gear bag and the Eddie Bauer map holder might have gone.

Broncos II have very stiff springs and shocks. Too stiff, for our taste. The ride motions at normal off-road speeds, off-road, are sudden and occasionally sick-making. It could be that the spring rates and shock valving are appropriate for high-speed stuff off-road, but what owner is going to be stupid enough to run his own trucklet at Baja speeds while out admiring the wildflowers? At normal around-town speeds, around town, bumps will tend to pitch the Bronco II sideways in a particularly nasty fashion. Happily, this doesn't seem to happen at Interstate speeds, where the Bronco II is really in its element, but it's an attention getter, even at 40. Aside from this, the Bronco II is mighty nice. In its Eddie Bauer Special Edition form it's no mightier, but even nicer. I hope lots of outdoor types buy them.

In the meantime, I'm waiting to see if there's going to be a Brooks Brothers Blazer.

Three four-by-fours to go, with a side of beans and plenty of salsa.

aybe it wasn't the high point of the entire week's vacation in Baja California, or of the epic New Year's Eve celebration at the Hotel Misión de Loreto. But when Tom Yelvington got up and solemnly proposed a toast to Slim Pickens midst all the balloons and paper streamers and empty Corona bottles, by God, it was a golden moment. The party could have been improved only by the presence of old Slim himself, dead less than a month when we set out for Loreto, some 700 miles down Baja.

Nine of us decided to spend the week after Christmas in Loreto, B.C. Well, actually, P.J. O'Rourke and I decided that it would be a good thing to do last year, and then it was just a matter of dragooning a handful of like-minded drinking pals into our fantasy. We gathered in San Diego, collected our ground transport, and headed south. I selected the vehicles purely on the basis of my own enthusiasms and prejudices. One diesel-powered, four-wheel-drive GMC Suburban, one Subaru BRAT Turbo, and one Mitsubishi Montero.

We drove down in a day and a half. First day, San Diego to San Ignacio, 528 miles, was a bit too long, what with holiday traffic, a stop in Ensenada, and the inevitable milling and stem-winding that accompany each pause for gas or food when you're traveling with several vehicles and a bunch of folks. The second leg was only 200 miles, San Ignacio to Loreto, but we managed to turn that into almost a whole day's drive by the time we'd visited the eighteenth-century mission church in San Ignacio, stopped to clamber around on the old mining trains and traction engines and watch the pelicans and cormorants feeding in Santa Rosalía, and spent more than two hours over lunch in the garden at the Restaurante Candil in Mulegé.

We engaged the services of a good travel agent and worked out all of our hotel reservations, deposits, et cetera, in advance. In our case the agent was a company that specializes in hunting and fishing trips, called Frontiers (P.O. Box 161, Wexford, Pennsylvania 15090). They scoped out the whole trip for us, handled airline reservations, hotel reservations, got all the skinny on hunting and fishing, and generally handled a lot of the preliminary details. At their suggestion we got our papers through the Mexican Hunting Association in Long Beach, California, and arranged car insurance well in advance through MacAfee & Edwards, Mexican insurance specialists, in Los Angeles.

Our time in Mexico, as a result, was delightfully trouble-free. We lived like royalty, saw the countryside, feasted on *langosta*—Mexico's lobsterlike crayfish—and every kind of Mexican specialty imaginable, drank Corona, Tecate, Carta Blanca, Pacífico, and both Dos and Tres Equis, along with the occasional glass of Tequila *Conmemorativo,* and generally enjoyed ourselves. Our days were thrice blest, first because the hotel manager's brother-in-law, José Luis, volunteered to be our guide; second because he introduced us in turn to one of Loreto's leading citizens, a Señor Green, who very generously offered us the run of his vast agricultural properties north of town; and finally because the weather each day and night was a little more perfect than it had been the day or night before. Carroll Shelby called from Los Angeles to see how we were doing, and, on hearing how well we were doing, dropped everything to fly down in his Aerostar and help us celebrate.

Baja California is a car enthusiast's paradise for one reason: Highway 1. Highway 1 is only ten years old, in its paved form, and it is a road to conjure upon, winding more than 1100 miles from Tijuana to Cabo San Lucas, and placing a premium on shock absorbers, steering, and superior automotive reflexes. It would be a glorious venue for the return of the old Mexican Road Race, and I pray each night that I'll someday be able to drive it in an Audi Quattro with *carte blanche* from the Mexican police. Shelby ran the old Carrera Panamericana in an Austin-Healy 30 years ago, and it was easy to sit beside him wheeling our Suburban through the mountains and imagine what that must have been like.

Baja California is *not* a car enthusiast's paradise for another reason: Pemex gasoline. Pemex quality varies widely from tankful to tankful, but none of it is of sufficiently high octane to please a modern engine. Our turbo-charged BRAT and our Montero detonated like mad, and, in the BRAT particularly, one had visions of large holes melting in the crowns of pistons on long uphill stretches. Another Pemex problem is the typical Pemex station's toilets. The women in our group were agreed that a short walk into the cactus was vastly superior to the filthy, malodorous facilities offered by the government's petroleum monopoly.

Our vehicles proved to be everything I'd expected them to be. GM's Suburban is not suburban in any way. It is, instead, America's premier back-country Mother Ship, and that's exactly how we used it. By removing the third seat, we created a cavernous cargo hold that swallowed six hard shotgun cases, seven or eight large duffel bags, at least that many other pieces of luggage in various shapes and sizes, two cases of shotgun shells, and six gallon jugs of safe water. Thus burdened, the Suburban could still carry five passengers, cruise smoothly at 70 miles per hour, and get 450 miles on a tank of Pemex fuel oil. The clatter of the 6.2-liter diesel at low speeds with the windows open was about unbearable, but at one point—with ten people inside and O'Rourke and Yelvington riding the hood like Secret Service men—we followed Señor Green's Ford pickup several miles cross-country to an estuary he wanted us to see, and it was just fine.

The Turbo BRAT was the liveliest vehicle in our little motor pool, and its engine was loved by one and all. There's little question that a similarly equipped Subaru wagon would have been a more practical choice, but when you set out for the beach with the roof panels removed and two hard-core tanning freaks riding in the outdoor seats, practicality is not your primary concern. One would think the U.S. government would outlaw the BRAT, if only because it's such outrageous fun. If it had a drawback, it was the fact that its thirteen-inch wheels made it a nightmare in the potholes.

The Mitsubishi Montero was, as is now becoming commonplace in our experience, a little dreamboat. It is quiet and comfortable—in both front and rear seats—and it'll happily cruise at 75 or 80 if that's what you want it to do. It's a superior highway machine, as four-wheel-drive vehicles go, and we've now proved to our complete satisfaction that it'll go anywhere you point it. If my boss called and ordered me back to Baja this afternoon, I'd probably take the Montero.

Hold it, was that the phone?

Regarding René and Maurice.

~~~

met René Dreyfus—and dined in Le Chanteclair—for the first time in 1957. I was taken there and introduced to him by my then employers, John and Elaine Bond, of *Road & Track* magazine. We had come into New York on the overnight DC-7C from Los Angeles to honor Phil Hill as America's top international racing driver.

I was stunned by the restaurant. It seemed to contain, in a rather small area, everything that was important to me as a car enthusiast. The walls in the bar were covered with motorsports photos and memorabilia. The bar was short, no more than a dozen stools, yet at least one of those stools always seemed to support the weight of someone whose opinion about cars and racing really mattered. You could stand by the cash register, where René's sister, Suzanne, was enthroned, and scan the room for familiar faces—either friends or the famous—while René's brother, Maurice, organized your table. (René himself would usually be chatting with someone at another table, and would slide by to say hello and exchange the day's gossip after you were settled.)

To have René Dreyfus stop by your table, to be recognized by him, was to be safely in the bosom of a worldwide community of car people. I still rely on contacts, friendships, made in the bar in Le Chanteclair, like-minded individuals to whom I was introduced by René or Maurice. When I moved to New York City in the autumn of 1958, I went to Le Chanteclair for lunch the following day and was made to feel like a regular, even though I walked through the door filled with a hayseed's trepidations. When my first son was born early one April morning in 1959, I visited with my wife for a while, went to the office to check the mail, then walked over to Le Chanteclair, where René bought my lunch. I ate alone in the southeast corner of the restaurant; then René and I drank the new kid's health with a strong, smoky marc de Bourgogne—the first I'd ever tasted.

René Dreyfus is a gentleman, if not by the obsolete definition of the term, certainly by his bearing, his generosity, his accomplishments, and his flawless taste. He drove racing cars, starting with club races in the south of France in 1924 and finishing with the Indianapolis 500 in 1940. His first big victory was the Grand Prix of Monte Carlo in 1930 (my wife's French mother-in-law was there with her new husband), and he became champion of France in 1938. Along the way, he drove for Bugatti, Maserati, Alfa Romeo, Talbot, and Delahaye. During World War II he served as a master sergeant in the U.S. Army, having been stranded in this country by the fall of France. He spoke only about a dozen words of English at the time of his enlistment, but he served through North Africa and Italy, finally linking up with his brother and sister again just before Nazi Germany's collapse in 1945. Maurice had managed to stay one jump ahead of both the Gestapo and the Vichy authorities throughout the war, working as an underground publisher and a courier for the maquis.

René brought brother and sister to America after the war and launched himself in the restaurant business, succeeding on two levels: first, by providing a hangout for the international automotive crowd, and second, by providing damned good French cuisine in a comfortable environment where many of the customers where unaware of the proprietor's heroic past.

Le Chanteclair is gone now. The daily regimen of up-and-out before five in the morning to do the buying, and problems with Maurice's health, convinced René that it was time to get out. The building isn't even there anymore. Which is probably just as well.

Notes on a yellow pad…Elaine Bond is dead.

~~~~~

It's hard to imagine the powerhouse who ran *Road & Track* for so many years gone, but gone she is. It'd be stupid to say she died before her time, because her time had obviously come, but she might have bought herself a few more years if she'd been willing to undergo a second round of brain surgery for the recurrent tumor that finally got her. She just didn't want them hacking at her anymore.

Elaine Bond was a tough babe. She couldn't control her weight, her hair was apt to be oily because she always ran her fingers through it when she was feeling the pressure, which was most of the time, her malapropisms made her the butt of office jokes, and I loved her dearly. I came within an eyelash of making a pass at her one night when we'd been drinking and arguing about magazines into the wee hours. For once, we were in total agreement that something was a dumb idea.

She couldn't write a lick, she was neither an editor nor an automotive engineer, and she was too often an awful judge of character and talent, but she nonetheless made *Road & Track* the hot property it is today. Her husband, John R. Bond, played a key role too, but it was Elaine who put it all together and made it work, and it's time she got the credit that is her due. Like most people who deserve credit, hers comes posthumously, but she'd appreciate the irony of that, I'm sure.

Her vision of *Road & Track* was simple, and gorgeous in its simplicity. Almost 30 years ago, she said, "America has no magazines like *Autocar* or *Motor*. What we need is a magazine like them, that will cover the same subject matter, even the same cars, with the same air of authority. But *Autocar* and *Motor* are really boring magazines by American standards. Therefore, we have to marry the content and authoritative air of the English car magazines with the wit and wry point of view of a distinctly American magazine."

She chose *The New Yorker* magazine as her model. It had style, it was timeless, it was slyly good-humored, and it had an air of authority all its own. The marriage was a success and the resulting magazine made the Bonds rich, but it wasn't easy. She worked all the time. She drove people hard, and was in turn driven by her husband, who always made sure that she did the dirty work. Dirty work that included getting rid of people who'd fallen from favor or become frazzled in the struggle, that also included selling the magazine to CBS, to the stunned disappointment of the staff, who'd innocently believed that they'd be offered first refusal in the event of any decision to sell. But Elaine always shouldered the blame, always took the brunt of the anger, always made sure her husband was safely out of harm's way when the shooting started.

Like the genius who created *The New Yorker,* Harold Ross, she was imperfect. But like him, she stirred the stew that became a very successful magazine, she controlled the heat, and she made damned sure the mixture was seasoned to her taste. She taught me how to run a magazine, and the last time I talked to her—a few months before she died—she told me she thought I was doing a pretty good job. I cannot tell you how much that meant to me.

Think about an October vacation.

❧

I happen to think that October is the finest month in the year, at least in the northern temperate zones where I spend most of my time. What October offers has been pretty thoroughly chronicled, but I thought I'd make a suggestion, just in case you might be stimulated by the notion of an October vacation in Paris and along the Normandy coast.

This is a special year for Americans in Normandy. No matter how blasé you think you are, you'll be deeply moved by Omaha Beach, Utah Beach, Pointe-du-Hoc, Ste. Mère-Eglise, and the American cemetery above Omaha. So here's what you do. You make arrangements to attend the Paris Automobile Show, which opens on October 4 and lasts for ten days, then you drive to Normandy. The dollar's strength makes European delivery of a new car a very good deal this year. The savings can pay for one round-trip ticket. Order your car for delivery on or about October 1, use the intervening days to motor gently to Paris— unless you order a Peugeot 505 Turbo or a Renault, which you could pick up right on the spot—and get comfortably ensconced in your hotel in time for the show's opening. I have every intention of being there myself come autumn.

Unless you have a favorite hotel in Paris, I'd recommend mine, the Regina, in the Place des Pyramides across the street from the Louvre. It's not a zoo like the various Hiltons, Sheratons, and Inter-Continentals. It's a very comfortable, very charming place to stay that's in easy reach of everything, and only two or three short blocks from a Métro.

Everybody has a favorite restaurant in Paris, including your friends who've never been there. I wouldn't presume to say that one Paris restaurant is best, or even better—there being so few bad ones—but I will give you the name of one to which I will always return. It is the Auberge Pyrénées Cévennes, and what I will always eat there is cassoulet, a crusty stew of white beans, pork, mutton, little sausages, and duck that has never been known to exceed, maybe, three million calories. The Pyrénées Cévennes has no stars, but that doesn't prevent my mouth from watering whenever I recall the bright coppery sheen of that restaurant and the pleasant din of French voices raised in gustatory celebration.

Mrs. Davis's favorite for many years was the Grand Vefour, but she seems to have tempered her love for the place since it was bombed by terrorists and slipped from three stars to two. Whether it lost the star because it was bombed, or was bombed because it lost the star, I cannot tell you.

You'll need to spend a couple of days at the show. It's better to browse at an easy pace, leave when your feet start to get tired, and go somewhere for a drink and a nice meal than try to cram everything into one day and go back to the hotel exhausted. One of the things to do in the afternoon when you've subwayed back from the show is to visit the W.H. Smith bookshop in the Rue de Rivoli—sort of halfway between the Place de la Concorde and the Place des Pyramides. Smith's has a large stock of English and American titles, everybody speaks English, and after you've bought your book, you can go upstairs for a very civilized English tea and watch elderly French ladies eat poundcake with knife and fork as you read.

When you've done the show and seen the Paris sights, you get your new car out of the parking garage and head for Normandy. If you leave after breakfast, you can be there for lunch, unless you decide to sightsee along the way. I intend to drive straight down on the *autoroute* in order to get every minute that I can in Normandy, but you can take the parallel *Route Nationale,* which is free, and which traverses some beautiful and historic country at a more touristic pace. Europe offers the best maps and guidebooks in the world, and you need have no fear of setting off on your own into Terra Incognita. What's more, once out of Paris it's much easier to survive on high-school French. The people are easier-going, and more apt to enjoy you and your thick American tongue. In Paris, unless your French is quite good, speak English and save yourself some abrasive encounters.

Normandy will remind you a little of New England. It is beautiful, and much of the countryside seems to be done up in miniature. Villages are small, seaports are intimate, and restaurants, except for the very grand ones, never seem to be much more than a dozen tables. When you arrive in October, you'll find that most of the tourists have fled and you have the best of it to yourself. Mealtimes are absolutely incredible. Imagine the best French food you ever ate in your life, all of it prepared with a nifty regional twist that dictates plenty of rich Norman cream, and lots of dishes prepared with apples or cider or Calvados (the famous local apple brandy). The seafood is world renowned. Oysters, gorgeous little shrimp, lobsters, and sole that might have been caught within sight of your hotel.

We stayed in Deauville the last time. The Hotel Normandy is excellent, and most of the delights of Norman food and drink are available there, or right across the river in Trouville-sur-Mer. The only problem with the Deauville/Trouville area is that it's a long way from the D-Day beaches. We didn't mind, because the network of country roads that parallels the coast is tailor-made for car enthusiasts. They're fairly narrow two-lanes that run through hedge-rowed farmland, punctuated with picturesque villages that show very little evidence of the steamrollering they took in 1944. Caen is the region's capital city, and it's a real city. I'd suggest staying in any one of the dozen or so hotels there, or going to Bayeux, which is not only endowed with a couple of spectacular places to stay, but offers a thousand years of history antedating all thoughts of World War II. Food is not going to be a problem. Caen has three one-star restaurants, and in this area even the little joint on the corner will serve you better food than any motel dining room in North America.

I may stay in Chef-du-Pont, just a hoot and a holler down the road from Ste. Mère-Eglise. The Hotel Normandie there has a few rooms and the only restaurant in town, and that's where I want to be, where the 82nd and 101st Airborne landed on the night of June 5, 1944. I'd stay right in Ste. Mère-Eglise, if there were an inn or a hotel, because, of all the D-Day stories, the ordeal of the American paratroops is the one that chokes me up the most. On our last visit we met one of the survivors, a cop from Derry, New Hampshire, named Howard Manouian, who at age nineteen—that night, 40 years before—dropped into a Frenchman's garden 100 yards behind the church where paratrooper John Steele was hung up on the steeple watching the Germans pick off his pals, like mallards coming in. The Frenchman pulled Howard into his kitchen and kept him there for two hours, until the noise died down, then sent him back to war.

So order your car now, buy the *Michelin Guide,* and start planning your trip. If you don't want to buy a car, rent one. Either way, I'll probably see you in Paris or somewhere along the *Route du Dèbarquement.*

Saved (twice) by a Volkswagen.

~~~~~

Sports Cars Ypsilanti was the name of the place. It was a struggling imported-car store on the main drag in Ypsilanti, Michigan. I worked there in 1954, after I'd worked in one similar place in Grosse Pointe, and just before I worked in another in Ferndale. We sold Volkswagens, Porsches, Jaguars, Arnolt-Bristols, MGs, you name it. If it came from Max Hoffman in New York, Edsko Hekmann in Grand Rapids, or Wacky Arnolt in Chicago, we could get you one.

Business was terrible. Business was so terrible that our leader, Doug Mahoney, was moonlighting as a model and actor in Detroit, trying to keep corporate body and soul together. We were about 200 years ahead of our time, as far as the Upper Midwest was concerned. There were the faithful, of course, but not very many of them, and the few there were only bought cars one at a time. We were dedicated enthusiasts, and we fervently believed that ought to be enough.

One night, when I'd delivered an MG to a guy in Coldwater, I called in to let Doug know I'd be late. We were supposed to answer the phone in an alert, optimistic voice. *"Sports Cars Ypsilanti!"* we'd bark into the mouthpiece. But on this night I could tell the general public's indifference and cynicism toward our small-car crusade was getting to Mahoney. The phone rang about four times, then he answered, "(Sigh), funny little cars," voice dripping with resignation.

My pal Bill Rowley bought an MG TF 1250 from us, yellow, with red leather and wire wheels, and I offered to drive him to Chicago to collect it from S.H. Arnolt, the distributor. We drove over in a piece from the used-car lot (which was actually the space between our building and the sidewalk), a 1953 Volkswagen Beetle, light blue, one of the last ones with cloth upholstery. It was a gorgeous summer morning, and we enjoyed it to the limit. We were in Chicago before lunch, and even got to shake hands with Wacky Arnolt himself, ankling around the place in a pair of low-cut cowboy boots. While there, we saw a brand-new cycle-fendered Nardi sports racer and got our first in-the-flesh exposure to the exquisite little Arnolt-MG convertible.

Bill started back while I collected the paperwork, and by midafternoon I was on my way. I decided to stop in Marshall, Michigan, where I knew several women, and where, sure enough, a warm, loving bar hostess was glad to see me. She worked till eleven, and what with one thing and another it was about two ayem when I got back on the road.

Before I crossed the town line I knew that I was going to sleep. I tried all the usual cures—beating on the steering-wheel rim, blowing the horn, yelling at the top of my lungs, and that old standby, pinching the skin under my chin. Nothing worked. As I approached Albion (O perfidious Albion), I knew I'd have to bed down somewhere pretty quick.

The next morning I awoke with considerable pain and a lugubrious young state trooper sitting on a straight chair at the foot of my hospital bed. He informed me that I had struck a parked 1953 Buick Roadmaster four-door in downtown Albion at a rate of knots sufficient to destroy it. The Volkswagen, he said, was in bad shape, but could conceivably be repaired. I remembered nothing. He allowed that as soon as I felt up to it, he'd convey me to the local justice of the peace. Swell. I put off feeling better for another half-hour or so—I had suffered a broken nose and some cracked ribs—then resigned myself to the wrath of Albion's judiciary.

I was a mess, but the justice of the peace was not exactly an oil painting himself. He appeared to be about a thousand years old, and he had cataracts so advanced that his rheumy old silver-blue eyeballs were badly wrinkled. He heard the state trooper's description of my crime, then charged me with reckless driving.

I was horrified. I had already amassed points sufficient to cost me my license, and a reckless-driving conviction was certain to make a pedestrian of me. I begged the old gent to reduce the charge to careless driving, insisting that I'd had every intention of removing myself from the road as soon as a suitable spot presented itself, but sleep had overtaken me. Surely this was not recklessness, I pleaded, but, at the very worst, the forgivable carelessness of a lad who would awooing go.

He fixed me with those awful eyes and said, in a voice that seemed to come from the upstairs closet in an abandoned house, "Young man, anyone who attempts to operate a motor vehicle upon the highways of the state of Michigan, while sleeping, is driving recklessly." Case closed, license lost, hope gone.

I was not yet through with that VW, however. Some months later, when a Washtenaw County deputy sheriff arrested me, again for reckless driving...

Uh, I must interject that I was not driving recklessly at all on this occasion. I was driving a '51 Beetle that was equipped not with flashing turn signals but with trafficators, the little semaphores that lit up and flipped out to indicate the direction of your turn, when I met a friend coming toward me in a similarly equipped MG Y-tourer. It was the fashion then to flip the trafficators up and down, side to side—like Pluto's ears, sort of—in greeting, and we did so. The deputy sheriff saw this from behind the sign of a darkened drive-in theater and gave chase. I spent the night in the slammer, when it was determined that my license had been revoked for cause, and the following morning the deputy, probably annoyed that he'd been taken away from his milk route or something, testified that "he wasn't speedin' or nuthin', Your Honor, but when I seen them little lights goin' on and off, I knew he was up to somethin'."
…but anyway, that morning the '53 VW came back from the dead to save me. It was in the river, behind the shop, where we'd pushed it after stripping off everything useful, but its title was in a desk drawer in the office. That worthless title was enough to let me make bail and walk the streets a free man again—that is, until my case came up and I had to finish serving the mandatory 72-hour jail term that went with a driving-with-a-revoked-operator's-permit conviction in those days.

My time inside was not wasted, however. While locked up I wrote a letter proposing marriage to my future first wife and became friends with a very nice Florida citizen who was awaiting extradition to the Sunshine State on a robbery-armed charge. For some reason, neither of us was invited to join the other guys, who'd gone out to the county farm first thing after breakfast. I have no idea what finally became of Mr. Robbery-Armed, but I have a pretty clear fix on what became of me. I hope he made out as well as I did.

Jeepers Jamboree: Gummi Bears and Jack Daniel's under the stars.

~~~

You could drive a Camaro Z28 or a Porsche 944 from Georgetown, California, to Lake Tahoe in less than an hour, if you pushed it. You could drive it in less than an hour and a half in a Jeep, even if the Jeep had a soft top and no doors. People do. We took another route, however, skipping both Interstate 80 and U.S. 50. We went by the old stagecoach road, and it only took us about fifteen hours—three days, if you count some serious rest and rehabilitation up in the mountains.

We were part of the 32nd annual Jeepers Jamboree. Our friends at AMC had suggested we might like to try it, and as former Jeep owners and occasional off-road drivers, we accepted in a flash. Our vehicle was a perfectly stock four-cylinder, four-speed CJ-7, running on Goodyear Wrangler radials. It didn't have a radio or air conditioning, but it did have a large cooler lashed into the back.

Instead of a back seat, we carried one bag each, plus J.L.K. Davis's cosmetic case, two sleeping bags, two air mattresses, a pop tent, and miscellaneous camera, binoculars, rolls of toilet paper, ground cloths, and Swiss Army knives.

A hundred years ago you could go from Georgetown, California, to Lake Tahoe on a pretty good road—good enough for the stagecoach, anyway. About halfway there, Rubicon Springs offered the hospitality of the Hunsucker brothers' hotel, where one could wash off the trail dust, catch trout in the Rubicon River, and take a quick cure in the nearby mineral spring. Today the road is all but gone, and the hotel is a scattering of old foundation stones, watched over by the river, the trout, and the mineral spring. No stagecoach ever built could make it into Rubicon Springs today.

As the name implies, the Jamboree is preeminently a celebration of the Jeep's virtues, of which there are many. You could make the run in some other kind of vehicle—it's done regularly—but when you roll into

Georgetown on the day before the Jamboree, you'll feel like a pariah if you're not driving a Jeep. We saw World War II Jeeps with small-block Chevys trying to claw their way out of the engine compartments. We saw rusted hulks that seemed barely able to wheeze into town for the start. There were five dozen variations on the big-tired, jacked-up theme.

In recent years the Jamboree has become too popular, and the organizers have gone to a lottery system to keep the total number of entries down to a manageable level. Even so, they now run a second, smaller Jamboree a week after the main event to handle some of the overflow. This year 401 vehicles turned out for the first weekend, a four-day extravaganza, and 150 were on hand for the three-day affair a week later. We ran the second weekend. The four-day event costs $180 per person. The three-day version costs $120. An incredible bargain, less than the cost of one night in a second-rate New York hotel.

The fee includes all meals—which are of the hearty lumberjack or hunting-camp variety—and the services of the world's most agreeable and reassuring backup team. A helicopter, paramedics, mechanics, and a crew of experienced four-wheel-drivers, called Rock Rollers, who act as course marshals, are all out there to protect you from fate or from your own stupidity. There's nothing nicer than approaching the worst pile of jagged rocks you ever saw, hanging twelve hundred feet above the United States of America, and seeing a pleasant young guy in green coveralls who says, "Okay, put your left-front wheel right here, hard left, now goose it. Nice! Nice!" Watching some crews struggling to make it over various obstacles, one also hears pleasant young guys in green coveralls shouting things like "No, no, goddammit, keep your foot off the clutch!"

The level of driving skill varies widely, and often the toughest-looking outfit is driven by the most feckless, sometimes downright terrified, chauffeur. We watched housewives motor serenely through stretches where it seemed no four-wheeled vehicle could ever go, then waited for an hour or more for some Indiana Jones macho type to white-knuckle his way over the top in a Jeep that looked as though it had been constructed by NASA for assault on Mount Everest.

Like Brenda Lee, the route itself is short, but overwhelming. The bad part, from Wentworth to Chambers—that is, from the end of the good dirt to the sudden appearance of pavement near Lake Tahoe—is only seventeen miles, but these are the most grueling seventeen miles you've ever driven. Long stretches of grapefruit- to basketball-sized stones that shift and roll as you climb through them, interspersed with real, honest-to-God boulders and granite ledges that simply appear to close the trail before you. Worst of all is the steep downhill gully called the Sluice Box, which leads into Rubicon Springs, a half-hour that seems like a lifetime of scraping, banging, literally crashing down from rock to rock without pause or relief. The Sluice Box is demoralizing to one, like me, who is more a car enthusiast than a four-wheeler. I felt pangs of guilt and agony each time some part of the undercarriage screeched over a pointed rock, and when we slipped slaunchways off the boulder and smashed the rocker panel, I wanted to cry. Other vehicles broke shock absorbers, springs, and steering boxes. Parts were helicoptered out to marooned vehicles.

Going slowly enough is everything. First gear, low range, and stay off the goddam clutch, as the young man said. In this mode the Jeep seems to walk through and over obstacles. It is quite miraculous. When you must stop, you simply turn off the key without declutching. Then, when the way is clear ahead, you simply key the engine to life, again without the clutch, which prevents those heart-stopping moments when the vehicle rolls backward toward oblivion as you try for something akin to smooth engagement.

At Rubicon Springs we were serenaded by a burly pianist who wore cowboy boots with his tailcoat and formal trousers. An excellent piano player, he was also a finish carpenter, playing a grand piano that had been brought in dangling from a helicopter flown by a pilot who hopes to become a chiropractor.

On Saturday night we were surprised by a pipes band in full Scots regalia, marching into our clearing from the big trees along the river. Later, two Honda generators provided the wattage for a fusion band (country/rock/you name it), which played until after the witching hour. Earlier that day we'd stood in a glacier-cold pool in the river with off-road racer and Jeep-genius Brian Chuchua, who told us about the arrowheads he'd found in these mountains. Now in the pitch blackness, we stood around a Jeep's tailgate and ate Gummi Bears and corn curls with our Jack Daniel's and envied nobody in the whole wide world.

Dirt.

~ʊɛ~

In 1959, America had 3,503,354 miles of roads. Of these, some 1,007,566 miles were unsurfaced. The most recent survey we could find tells us that in 1982 the Republic's road net had lengthened to 3,866,296 miles, and only 467,486 of those miles remained unpaved. We now have 3,398,810 miles of paved road in this country, almost as much as our *total* in 1959. I hate that. Not that we have more roads—although there are a few I could do without—but that our dirt roads are steadily becoming extinct.

U.S. 27, the main drag from the Straits of Mackinac to Miami, ran right through Burnside, Kentucky, where I was born, and my mother remembers town meetings in which the citizens petitioned the state of Kentucky to please pave U.S. 27. This may partially explain my affection for unpaved country roads. They are as much a part of me as the sidewalks of New York were part of the Honorable Fiorello La Guardia.

I grew up on a dirt street in Royal Oak, Michigan. When my father and some of the more progressive neighbors decided our street should be paved, they had to get a cash commitment from everybody on our block to supplement whatever funds the town's politicos would allocate. This was at the tail end of the Depression, and when my old man called the family across the street, poor as mice, they told him they couldn't get involved because they were tithing the full ten percent of their income to the Reverend Ed Weinzerl's Radio Temple. Some years later, when the Reverend Ed Weinzerl headed for his hereafter, he had his choice of his limo or his own airplane to make the trip, and I'll bet the streets were paved. If America's latter-day broadcast evangelists should ever express concern at the fact that I regard every last one of them as a charlatan, I'm going to refer them to that dirt street and the Reverend Ed Weinzerl's motor pool.

A popular form of motorsport, in those days, was sledding over those dirt streets seated on a metal sign (Orange Crush signs come to memory) towed by Junior DeLeeuw's Model A Ford. We bent the old Orange Crush sign to resemble a toboggan, punched two holes in the front for the rope, then tried to see how fast we could go around corners before the kid on the sign got mailed off into somebody's front yard. (On reading these lines over my shoulder, my assistant, Harriet Stemberger, said, "We used to do that. We used to hit mailboxes and everything. It was *great!*")

On one occasion, I was riding on the right-hand running board when Junior hurled us into a corner that had been freshly graveled. The Model A got up on two wheels, scared the whee out of me, and I jumped off, suffering rather severe gravel rash on both knees and both hands. A hundred feet farther down the road, old Junior just laid 'er over on her side in the grass—the side where I'd been standing. Knowing that I wasn't sandwiched between somebody's front lawn and Junior's Model A more than made up for the pain in my knees and hands.

A good dirt road is a thing of beauty and wondrous joy. I prefer true dirt to gravel, but gravel roads also have their charms. Unfortunately, most states, and most highway authorities, now regard gravel as merely a transitional state between real honest-to-God dirt and pavement. Very few new gravel roads are being built. Generally speaking, existing gravel roads are getting paved. When the last unpaved road in America gets smothered with asphalt, I'm going to be an unhappy car enthusiast. (Happily, by then I'll probably be a dead car enthusiast.)

According to Donald Tuggle, of the Federal Highway Administration, a major county road is defined as one that's traveled by fewer than 50 cars a day and is supposed to be twenty feet wide, with a two-foot shoulder on each side. It should be well graded and drained (with culverts), and its maximum gradient should be no more than seven to ten percent. The designed maximum speed on such a road is 40 to 50 miles per hour. This will surprise a number of experienced rally drivers.

To build such a road, you first remove all the trees and big rocks and strip the topsoil. The second step involves "the removal of unsuitable material," which in Michigan is apt to be muck, but could be anything that won't support a roadbed. In this process the high spots are scraped off and the low spots are filled in, and dirt is spread on the surface in nine- to twelve-inch layers. Each layer is rolled and tamped to a specific density that can be checked in a number of ways, but the really heads-up highway engineer of the Eighties will use a nuclear density device that will give him density readings in pounds per cubic foot. The Michigan standard for such a road decrees that the dirt base will then be covered with a twelve-inch granular subbase made up of stones ranging from a maximum of three inches in diameter down to pebbles no larger than grains of sand. This facilitates the process of compaction, and prevents the larger stones from rolling under vehicles' wheels. This done, the road is finished with a six-inch layer of gravel, well graded, running from edge to edge.

There are road standards covering everything from two-track Jeep trails to what the engineers call a "local seasonal access road," which they describe as "unimproved earth, eighteen feet wide." That sounds like my favorite, the road for which four-by-four V-8 pickup trucks and Audi Quattros were conceived. The U.S. Forest Service builds even better ones. They call them Public Access Roads, and they are a mere ten to twelve feet wide, without shoulders. They are drained by dips and fords, for the most part, and their maximum gradient is supposed to be twelve percent. Design speed is ten to twenty-five miles per hour. This, too, will come as a shock to a guy like John Buffum. These are built to accommodate ten to thirty vehicles a day, but just in case you do meet a fellow dirt-road enthusiast coming from the other direction, passing turnouts are provided every thousand feet or so. Basically, these are little more than old trails that have been touched up with a grader, then covered with a couple of inches of gravel.

Last month, guided by my wife, the ace map reader, I drove a Jeep Grand Wagoneer over 130 miles of such roads in the tops of Wyoming's Bighorn Mountains. We were in our element. The big Wagoneer, which is a good enough horse on the highway, really came into its own on the Forest Service roads. Once, when the road got bad and warning signs were posted, we contemplated going to four-wheel drive, just to be on the safe side. Then we saw a plume of dust approaching up ahead, and a moment later a young couple in a Chevrolet Cavalier whipped past, proving again that some warning signs really have to be ignored. These were too small to sit on, or I might have asked J.L.K. Davis to tow me behind the Wagoneer for a couple of miles, just for old dirt's sake.

Carbohydrate preloading for car enthusiasts.

～じじ～

I f anybody asks me, which sometimes happens, I say that Giorgetto Giugiaro is the best automotive stylist I know or know *of.* I loved his Lamborghini Miura. I owned a Volkswagen GTI, which was his work, and I'm crazy about the Isuzu Impulse. What's more, I really want to add one of his Alfa Romeo GTVs to the small but growing Davis family car collection. If I find one of them after the Citroën *Traction Avant* is fully restored, and before I locate the 1938 Buick Century that rolls through my dreams, it'll be the next car to take up residence in our moldy four-car garage.

I'll probably pass on the De Lorean, which was also a Giugiaro design—not because of Giorgetto's work, but because I overdosed on Corvairs in the early and mid-Sixties and I can't have any more of those. (It is noteworthy, however, that the price went up on De Loreans when the jury announced their not-guilty verdict in Los Angeles. One envisions Mom and Pop sitting by the old Muntz television set, getting the news. Pop turns to Mom and says, "You know, Hildegarde, I was half afraid to buy one of them goddam things, as long as it looked like old John Z. was headed for the slammer, but now, by golly, I think we ought to run down to our neighborhood Pontiac-GMC-Toyota-De Lorean dealer and pick one up before they're all gone." Mom nods sagaciously over her crewelwork and replies, "We'd better hustle, Harlow, because now that he's beat this rap, everybody and his aunt will want one of those suckers." One wonders if the price of Canadian Ace beer went up each time Scarface Al Capone slipped through the grasp of the law.)

But to get back to Giugiaro, if you don't have enough money in your kick to buy a Lamborghini Miura, or one of the last hundred De Loreans in Columbus, Ohio, you'll soon be able to buy one of Giorgetto Giugiaro's very latest designs for very little money, and you'll be able to buy a whole bunch of them just about any time you want some. We refer here to the much heralded Giugiaro-designed pasta, called *Marille.* We tried to get some for our annual brunch at the Chicago Auto Show—in fact we tried to get Giugiaro himself—but neither it nor he was available. Months passed, and still no *Marille* found its way to my expectant palate. Friends and associates went to Italy, but came back empty-handed. Giugiaro himself ignored the earlier request and sent no 50-kilo crates of designer pasta via Alitalia.

Now, at last, one true friend has come forward. Craig Morningstar, who does something for Alfa Romeo—I've never understood exactly what—sent me a small (500g) bag only this morning, accompanied by the following letter:

> *David,*
>
> *I seem to remember a conversation at the Chicago Auto Show morning-after-the-night-before brunch, during which you said you were unable to get Giugiaro pasta in the U.S.A. In our last shipment of Spiders, I found this strange bag of macaroni product. The thought of actually eating something called durum-wheat semolina disgusts me, so I am sending it out to you...*
>
> *I would like to suggest Salsa Matriciana...*
>
> *In a medium-sized saucepan...*
>> *1) Brown ¼ lb chopped bacon, retain fat.*
>> *2) Just before bacon is finished, add 1 medium thinly sliced onion. Cook 2-3 minutes.*
>> *3) Add 1 lb drained (but not thoroughly) peeled Italian tomatoes.*
>> *4) Spice to taste with garlic—plenty, salt, hot pepper, oregano, basil, chocolate chips if you prefer.*
>
> *Simmer this till the sauce is a nice viscosity 10-15 minutes, add 2-3 tablespoons of olive oil about 3 minutes before cooking is complete.*
>
> *Buon appetito,*
> *R. Craig Morningstar*

It is well known that I would eat a pile of rocks if I thought there was pasta made of "something called durum-wheat semolina" hiding in there, so I immediately called Miz Davis and begged her to come to the office to prepare said Giugiaro *Marille* for lunch. Being a woman of infinite patience and good humor, she came. Instead of Morningstar's Salsa Matriciana, she served it in a sauce of bacon, onion, garlic, and a little olive oil, the drained pasta being tossed with ground Parmesan in the same skillet. What followed was sort of a road test. Jean Lindamood,

Harriet Stemberger, Csaba Csere, and Linda Golightly Moser joined me and J.L.K. Davis in the evaluation. Our pasta was accompanied by Mr. Robert Mondavi's 1980 Cabernet Sauvignon, a glass of which now sits beside my steam typewriter.

The *Marille* noodle is quite large and quite thick. (According to our technical department, overall length uncooked is 38.5mm, cooked 50.0; overall width, uncooked 36.5mm, cooked 41.5. Wall thickness between ribs is 1.42mm uncooked, expanding to 2.60 after boiling. All cooked measurements obtained *al dente*.) According to J.L.K. Davis, who lived in Naples for a couple of years, that bulkiness is typical of the pasta most Italians eat at home, in contrast to the lighter-gauge stuff we get over here. *Marille* looks to be about as wide as a matchbook, and rolls back on itself in a double loop. According to Maestro Giugiaro, the shape is that of an ocean wave, hence the name. The benefit of those loops and whorls and that extra width is that there's more area to hold sauce, inside and out.

I loved the weight of the *Marille* noodle, the thickest pasta I've eaten, and thus the one with the strongest "pure pasta" character. Miz Davis thought that the noodles were really designed for men, that they were a bit of a mouthful for most women. Harriet Stemberger agreed, but went on, "We all talked about how heavy it was, but we just kept shoveling it in. If this is authentic Italian, I want to be Italian." Linda Moser went back to her office and was not heard from again. Lindamood said "Giugiaro's *Marille* is hearty, hefty peasant pasta with the appeal of tortellini or manicotti, but without the filling." The Hungarian technoid volunteered this: "The astonishing variety of flavors and textures in this very substantial noodle makes it clear why the pasta rather than the sauce is the heart of true Italian dishes." (Your Hungarian technoids tend to talk like that.)

Well, there you are. Giugiaro's *Marille* should be a smash hit. I would like to try it once with butter, basil, and garlic, or in a tomato sauce with fennel sausage, before I go all the way and say that it's as good as his Lamborghini Miura or his Alfa GTV. But this limited test has convinced me that the world's greatest car designer has done a great service for enthusiasts all over the globe. For us committed car people, there is only one course. *Marille* must become our official food. Watch this space. As soon as it shows up on American shelves, we'll holler.

What do you do for an encore when your name is Porsche?

❧

Iwas thumbing through one of those fattening pre-Christmas issues of *The New Yorker*, and there on page 27 was an ad for the most beautiful pipe I ever saw. It featured radial fins, like a Porsche cylinder barrel, and it was exquisite. It was by Porsche Design, and, thus, it was not too surprising that the bowl was finned like a Porsche cylinder barrel.

I'm not a pipe smoker. A cigar is more to my taste. Like Fred Zeder, when he was engineering vice-president at the Old Chrysler Corporation, I have some trouble with pipe smokers. I always wonder if they aren't using the pipe and all its paraphernalia to prolong pointless conversations, or to avoid coming to points. "Well, yes, um, um (knock the pipe against something, peer into it, blow through it), yes, that's um, that's um (hold the pipe between the teeth while searching the pockets for a tool, find the tool, open the tool, scrape at the inside of the pipe, blow through it again), that's, um, an interesting area for speculation. I, um, I, um, recently read (fill pipe, tamp charge, suck reflectively, search for matches, light pipe, lean back in chair), I recently read something that…" At this point his pipe goes out. If you were old man Zeder, you arranged on the spot to have the pipe smoker discharged from Chrysler's employ. If you're like me, your mind drifts and you imagine the look of amazement on his face as you slip the engraved Colt Detective Special from its concealed Hermès shoulder holster and plug him right between the ums.

But never mind pipe smokers, it's pipes that launched us on this course. This perfect Porsche Design pipe suddenly reminded me of a visit I made to Porsche Design in Austria several years ago. We'd been to Steyr-Daimler-Puch, in Graz. We'd watched them building Pinzgauers and bicycles and tiny motorcycles, and we'd seen a prototype of the forthcoming Mercedes-Benz Geländewagen. After the factories and the test drives and the long strolls through the medieval streets of Graz, we went into the mountains, to the S-D-P hunting preserve at Donnersbachwald. As arranged in advance, through yet another division of Steyr-Daimler-Puch, J.L.K. Davis took delivery of her birthday present, a Mannlicher-Schoenauer carbine, and we hunted stags. Hiking up pitch-black mountains at three in the morning. Stags and their harems, nostrils steaming, slipping through the brush above the timberline. Sausage and cheese and coarse bread from a rucksack at ten. Washing it down with a long, reflective pull from a small bottle of apricot schnapps. Looking down on a black eagle patrolling the valley. Great country dinners in rooms older than the United States. Then, after three days, driving off to the northwest toward Zell am See, headquarters for Porsche Design and family seat of the Porsche clan.

We arrived in Zell am See on Saturday night. It's a small, thriving resort town, but this was autumn and it was raining, and the place was not a hive of activity. We checked into the St. George Hotel (which belongs to the Porsche family), ate dinner, went to sleep. Sunday morning we slept late, had breakfast in bed, and lay there watching a procession of pink-cheeked couples, all ages, hiking up and over the top of the mountain across the road. We did not join them.

First thing Monday morning, the phone rang. It was a young English-speaker from Porsche Design. Were we ready? He would be out front, in a Range Rover. We hurried downstairs, hopped into our car, and peered out through frosted windows at the Range Rover. There were two people and a dog inside. They led us through town, along the lake front, and into the manicured parking lot of Porsche Design, Butzi Porsche's studio. As we clambered out of the car, we saw, to our horror, that the driver of the other vehicle was Ferdinand "Butzi" Porsche himself. What with fog and frosted windows and foreign languages, we'd thought that he was a company driver, sent to fetch us. He was very gracious, but his dog, a businesslike Schweisshund, was impatient. Enough small talk, guys, she wanted to hustle inside and get the week started.

The Porsche Design studio is a small, two-story building, contemporary German high tech contrasting with the Tyrolean stucco of the town and the surrounding countryside. The man himself was older than we expected him to be, fiftyish. Although I'm a junior myself, I always expect other juniors to be younger. He is the oldest of five brothers, and, until the blowup that removed all the Porsche and Piëch siblings from the direct day-to-day management of the Porsche automobile business, Butzi was chief of design. (Tony Lapine, chief designer at Porsche today, has said of that time: "Dr. Porsche hired me from Opel to build a stage for his son Butzi. One day I looked around, and I was standing on that stage all alone.")

In a conference room dominated by a beautiful scale model of the Porsche 904, the dog hopped into the chair at the head of the table, and we all sat down to rich Austrian coffee and biscuits. Our host spoke no English, but the three of us shared limitless enthusiasm for cars and the out-of-doors and things that work properly, and language barriers quickly began to disappear. It was clear from his manner and from small indications in word and gesture that Butzi Porsche would have preferred to continue as the chief designer of Porsche cars. That being no longer possible, he had transferred his considerable talent and his inherited passion for innovative industrial design to other fields. I got the feeling that he could not have emulated his cousin—Ferdinand Piëch, who went from Porsche to Audi—and moved to another automobile company, if only because his name *is* Porsche.

We saw Porsche Design watches, crash helmets, sunglasses, ski-bobs, and shoes. We saw a speculative design for a monocoque bicycle. We talked about cars. He told us how his 911 came to be. We ran our hands over the sensuous curves and planes of his scale-model 904, surely one of the prettiest and friendliest racing cars ever to turn a wheel. I asked him about a possible revival of the Austrian car industry. Would he, like his grandfather, one day design another Austro-Daimler? Or maybe a Puch? He sighed with resignation. No, it wasn't in the cards. He sometimes found cars taking shape on his drawing board, but they were just fantasies, daydreams.

Three hours passed this way; then we went to the prosperous farm that has been home to the Porsche family for hundreds of years. Their Schütt-Gut hotel is there, but before we went in to lunch, we walked across the grass to a small chapel, a shrine dedicated to the memory of old Professor Ferdinand Porsche. I know several grandsons of founding fathers in the automobile industry, here and abroad, and the Americans generally refer to their grand-fathers with a kind of self-conscious jocularity. There was no trace of this in the shadowy little chapel outside of Zell am See. There was unabashed reverence, even awe, as we looked at the old man's likeness. This morning, as I think back on that, I can imagine the old engineer turning a new pipe over in his hands, and speculating about heat dissipation from a pipe bowl finned like a Porsche cylinder barrel.

Money may not buy happiness, but it could sure add spice to my motor pool.

At the end of *The Prisoner of Zenda*—one of the great adventure stories of all time—Fritz von Tarlenheim says to the heroic Rudolf Rassendyll, "Heaven doesn't always make the right men kings." I might say that I agree with young Tarlenheim, and I'll go him one better. Heaven doesn't always make the right men rich, either. I'm not sure why heaven chose to deliver me to an attractive young woman in a house without running water or electricity in Kentucky's Pennyroyal, a house farther from the pavement than several places where I've pitched tents in the years since. I could have been born just as easily in a mansion in Asheville, North Carolina, or overlooking the Atlantic in Newport, Rhode Island. I had very little to say at birth anyway, and a silver spoon in my mouth would have been an inconsequential impediment, at worst.

I would have been really good at being rich. I have hung out with rich guys, and it's been noted that I fit into those surroundings very well indeed, just like a Chippendale chest-on-chest, or a set of gold-plated bathroom fixtures. I suppose that I could still become rich, but I have no wealthy relatives to leave me fortunes. I don't feel that I can really depend on the Michigan lottery, and my chosen profession tends to provide more fun than profit.

My problem, see, is there's a whole bunch of stuff I want to buy. Like a C-type Jaguar. I really *need* a C-type Jag, a late-model customer's car, with disc brakes and a British-racing-green paint job and a pair of chromed exhaust pipes with inner diameters about the same as the barrel of a mountain howitzer. The Jag would sit in the garage right next to the Frazer Nash Le Mans Replica Mark II, which I also want. I would hope that I could buy Ted Boynton's old car, which was painted purest refrigerator white to match his white flannel trousers and white turtleneck, not to mention the white perfection of the blond women who seemed to gravitate to the Boynton pit at places like Watkins Glen and Elkhart Lake.

The C-type and the Le Mans Replica Frazer Nash wouldn't be too good as street machines, so I'd have a 1500cc HRG, also British racing green, and a metallic-blue J2X Cadillac-Allard to drive to Vic Tanny's every morning. On mornings when it rained, I'd drive my Porsche 928S or my Lincoln LSC with the full AMG-lookalike treatment. The Porsche would be metallic hunting green, and the LSC would be gun-metal gray. A rich guy would want something with four doors, too, so I'd have a 1972 300SEL 4.5. Some of you will chide me for not buying a 6.3 or the later 450SEL 6.9, but I owned a 4.5 once, in my other life, and found it to be an exquisitely satisfactory high-performance car.

Have I told you about my desire for a private railway car? No, I guess not. I want to find a decent example of a private railway car somewhere, and ship it to Rail Passenger Services, Inc., in Tucson, for restoration. I don't want anything flashy. I really like the way the Orient Express people have done their trains, and I'd be happy with a private car done pretty much in the manner of Venice-Simplon. Tasteful art deco. A pool table wouldn't make much sense in a moving conveyance, but I'd want a fully stocked bar with stools for six, a partner's desk for me and Mrs. Davis, several hundred books (including *The Prisoner of Zenda* and a complete set of *Automobile Quarterly*), a small but complete restaurant kitchen, and a large master bedroom that opened onto the observation platform.

We'd use the private railway car to commute back and forth to the country place at Buffalo, Wyoming. I visited Argentina in 1980 and fell in love with a traditional Argentine ranch house where we stayed for a couple of days, not far from Juan Manuel Fangio's home town of Balcarce. This ranch house was built in a square: four separate one-story buildings surrounding a garden, with a veranda all the way around the inner court to shade the occupants and protect them from inclement weather. Obviously, one of my four buildings would be a garage and shop, since it would be a little ostentatious to travel across country packing all the necessary hunting vehicles and runabouts on the train with us.

Inasmuch as we already own a Steyr-Daimler-Puch Haflinger, we'd have that shipped out to Wyoming, and we'd get a half-dozen four-footed (hoofed?) Haflingers to go with it. That's for my wife. I'd get myself an air-conditioned Volkswagen Vanagon Synchro, the new VW bus with more power and S-D-P "thinking" four-wheel drive. I am presently part owner of a 1959 Allis-Chalmers gasoline powered tractor named Alice. I would use my overwhelming financial clout to buy out my partner in the tractor, which would then be sent to California, where I'd have Phil Hill do a complete restoration. If I couldn't buy new implements and accessories appropriate for a '59 Allis-Chalmers, I'd buy used ones and have Phil restore them too. I wonder if anybody's ever asked him to restore farm machinery before? (Rolls-Royces don't count.)

There would be a small fleet of dirt bikes for friends and family, probably Husqvarnas, but I'd ride a BMW R80 G/S myself, being older, richer, and much more dignified. In the winter, Kawasaki snowmobiles would replace the motorcycles. In this same vein, I'd have Brian Chuchua build me a Jeep CJ-7 for my private hunting and fishing use. It would be powered by a Chevrolet 350-horse, 327-cubic-inch hydraulic-lifter V-8, my all-time favorite American engine. I would supply the engine to Brian from my private stock of twelve, which I would keep on a walnut rack in my bar/library/snooker room. The Jeep would be done up like one I saw him driving last year, with a Scrambler cab installed, turning it into a neat little bobtail pickup, complete with canvas tonneau cover. The chassis and the suspension would get the full Chuchua treatment, and there'd be enough skid plates under there to allow you to drive it all the way down Mount McKinley with the wheels off, if that was something you felt you ought to do.

Most guys in my position would probably have some kind of high-performance Bell helicopter in the yard for trips to town, but I guess I'd prefer two cars instead—an Audi Quattro for bad weather and a Mercedes-Benz 500SEL for the good days. The nice thing about that arrangement would be the fact that the Mercedes would also function very satisfactorily as an executive jet, should I ever have to rush home to the real world faster than the private railway car would take me.

I think that about does it. Obviously a ménage like mine would require a good-sized fleet of support vehicles, and these would run to Ford vans, Dodge Power Wagons, and Chevy Suburbans. My step-daughter has announced that she should have a yellow Porsche (pre-fender flares) 911 when she graduates from high school. She doesn't understand reality. Speaking of commemorations, it should be noted that all of my pals would receive Mitsubishi Monteros—replicas of the ones that blew everybody off in this year's Paris-Dakar—for my birthday. Happy birthday.

Driver education in the view of a man whose stepdaughter is taking same.

O ur home state, Michigan, was hit harder than most in the recent recession. This led to cutbacks of all kinds. There were nice ones, like fewer state police out on the roads, and some fairly grim ones, like the one I learned about this morning when I gave a speech to a conference of Michigan driver-education professionals. What I learned was that Michigan no longer requires a driving test for a kid to get his or her driving license. Go through the motions in driver ed, fill out the forms, take your chances with the written test, and you're free to drive until you've killed so many people that they can't ignore you anymore. Herewith, an excerpt from my remarks...

I learned to drive sometime during World War II, using a 1940 Oldsmobile that belonged to my father.

During my second or third hands-on driving experience, I turned a 90-degree corner from one gravel road onto another, failed to center the steering successfully, and put the car into the ditch, quite a steep, deep ditch. My mother, who was recovering from a serious illness and using a lot of phenobarbital, and my five-year-old sister, who is now the principal of a middle school here in Michigan (and could probably use a little sedation herself), were a bit more disturbed by the experience than perhaps they needed to be, but I can still hear their shrieks as the horizon tilted and that Oldsmobile slid inexorably into the cattails.

Less than ten years after that I was applying for a racing driver's license, so that I might become an amateur road-racing driver in events sanctioned by the Sports Car Club of America. I had absolutely no experience as a racing driver, save a few outings at gymkhanas, or time trials on frozen lakes, or the odd hill climb. Nonetheless, I was duly given a license to go risk my life and those of others at road-racing circuits all over the country, which I did.

It wasn't until 1963 that I actually attended a driver-training school. By then I was the editor of *Car and Driver*, and the school was the Carroll Shelby School of High Performance Driving at the Riverside racetrack at Riverside, California. I was there for three days, driving a 289 Shelby Cobra while a guy named Pete Brock showed me the fine points of hundred-mile-per-hour cornering, late braking, lift-throttle over-steer, and a host of other things that I find of enormous value in my daily drives back and forth to the office.

Since then, I've also spent time at the Bob Bondurant school at Sears Point in California, and the John Powell driving school at Mosport Park, near Toronto. Sometime this summer, I hope to go to a school for rally drivers in Wales. Right now, I'm sending a daring and good-humored woman who works for me—Jean Lindamood—to check it out before I commit myself.

Furthermore, I'd like to do a refresher course at the Bondurant school, during the next year or so.

I'm not doing any of these things because I still harbor any delusions about being a racing driver. I have attended those schools, and will continue to do so, because I believe that driving a car is considerably more demanding and dangerous than flying an airplane, and I want to be reasonably certain that my skills are everything they should be each time I slide behind the wheel of a car. Which is often, because I presently drive about a hundred thousand miles a year.

My stepdaughter, a gorgeous fifteen-going-on-twenty-eight-year-old, is presently enrolled in driver education. As part of that program, she's had one very brief stint in the driver-training car, and she's now in possession of her parent driving permit, which enables her to practice in various cars with a white-knuckled mother.

As it happens, her mother is an extraordinarily good driver, having driven in Europe for twenty years or so, and having been through the John Powell driving school at the same time that I went through. She learned to park in Paris, and any driver who can park in Paris is a tough mother indeed.

I, too, will serve as a driving instructor from time to time, but I'll emphasize a more advanced, more aggressive aspect of the driving experience. I'll emphasize smoothness, quickness, and alertness.

I'll teach her that she has more options in a life-threatening situation than simply stomping on the brake and sliding into the accident with the wheels locked up and her eyes closed.

I'll try to make her understand that there are no dangerous cars or dangerous roads, only dangerous people.

I'll show her that a car can still be controlled when it is leaning clear over onto the bump stops and in such a state of yaw that smoke is pouring off of all four screaming tires. In this way, she may learn that automobiles are seldom out of control, but people often are.

When I'm through, I hope she'll understand that the modern automobile—any modern automobile—offers reserves of dynamic safety that are far more valuable than its passive ability to simply withstand a crash.

I wish she'd learn all these things in drivers ed, even if it meant a second semester, but I fear she won't.

I'm afraid she'll be exposed to a lot of prepared material saying that speed kills, when she should be made to understand that drunkenness, failure to wear seatbelts, poor skills, and inattention kill the vast majority of our driving dead.

To offset this, and to improve both her understanding and her driving reflexes, I'll send her to Bob Bondurant's driving school in California as my gift for her graduation from high school. I do this in spite of the fact that it's virtually certain that Bondurant will make a pass at her.

I don't expect her to become a race driver. Actually, she'd like to be a ballet dancer. I just want her to be as well armed as is humanly possible when she takes to the roads with all those millions of inattentive, undertrained, unskilled, often impaired, and occasionally psychopathic Americans who got their drivers' licenses because they knew how to parallel-park.

Finally, when she's been through all this, and understands that there are risks...that there are consequences...I hope for a synergistic effect quite unrelated to the standard driver-ed curriculum.

As a driver, I want her to understand—in dynamic, real-world terms—that for every action there is a reaction. I want her to gain a sense of her responsibility for her own actions. I want her to begin to perceive that she will be responsible for the state of her own life and for the impact which her actions will have upon the lives of the people around her. I want her to understand that this is a good thing.

I want her to enter the stream of life, like the stream of traffic, alert, in control, fully aware of the risks involved, but filled with a sense of fun and adventure.

Roadside trash.

❧

T*he sun shines bright on my old Kentucky home...'tis summer, the Interstates are covered with the shards of blown-up truck tires.*

Warm weather seems to be the season for debris along the roadside. In the northern tier of states the arrival of spring is particularly hard on lovers of roadside neatness and beauty. First off, the melting snows reveal an entire winter's accumulation of trash. Worse, the migratory water-fowl and various representatives of the nation's smaller fur-bearing population are seized with the need to wander far afield in search of the opposite sex. Rabbits, skunks, raccoons, and possums give up their lives nightly—squirrels by day—and the shoulders of the roads begin to look like the pastures behind the Normandy beaches when Allied shelling killed all the dairy cattle.

A little later, the mallards make their nests and settle into a kind of sedentary stupidity that's absolutely heartbreaking. I saw three dead mallard drakes in the gutter on my way to work one morning. They just don't understand. It's even worse when the proud mallard mothers start marching their kids back and forth across the roads. I have stopped traffic in both directions on suburban streets and country roads to let them pass, but I know that there are people who deliberately steer for them, as though a mallard left dead in the road were a sign of human superiority.

My headlights illuminated a young rabbit kicking his last by the Veterans Hospital the other night. I wanted to stop for him, but I knew how futile that would be. Once, in downtown Detroit, we passed a black Labrador pup trapped on the median, barking his fear and defiance at the traffic whipping past at 60 or 70. I finally managed to get stopped, in an attempt to call him, only to see him bolt into the rush of cars and trucks and...God*dam* if he didn't make it to the other side!

In Nevada one morning, on I-80, we came face to face with a big downed coyote lying athwart the center line, his toothy grin and lolling

tongue belying the fact that he was disemboweled and doomed to be
struck again at any moment. I think about that coyote a lot, and I always
hope that shock had relieved him of the burden of terror. But at the same
time, as an enthusiastic coyote watcher, I think of the breed's incredible
wisdom and toughness, and wonder if maybe he wasn't lying there daring the eighteen-wheelers to try to take him out—like John Wayne or
John Garfield propped up along the trail, too badly hurt to move, waiting for the bad guys with one full clip and a couple of grenades.

In 1974 the Federal Highway Administration reported to
Congress that the crud on the highways broke down as follows: 59 percent paper; sixteen percent cans; six percent plastics; six percent glass
bottles; thirteen percent miscellaneous. Litter volume was found to cor-
relate directly to traffic volume, and I suppose that coyotes and mallard
mothers got lumped into "Miscellaneous." Someone at the Highway
Administration suggests that those trashy numbers would be pretty
much the same today, but I wonder.

For instance, what about the miles of dead audio tape that fes-
toons the bushes from here to the nation's perimeter? I see loops and furls
of cassette tape glistening in the sun wherever I go. Cassettes fail from
three main causes: first, heat, which causes the tape to curve and prevents
proper threading, and finally destroys sound quality; second, uneven
winding caused by the constant starting and stopping of car-stereo
equipment; and third, vibration, because tapes left rattling around in a
car unpack themselves, then jam when they're plugged into the player.
Nobody seems to know why people then throw them out their car windows in the first place.

I'm certain that various states' bottle laws have made a big difference in the amount of glass and cans on the roadside. Connecticut,
Delaware, Iowa, Maine, Massachusetts, Michigan, New Hampshire,
New York, Oregon, and Vermont now have such laws, and they've made
a very positive difference. New York reports a 70-percent reduction in
roadside glass as a result of the law's enactment, and Michigan says that
bottles decreased from sixteen percent of total highway litter in 1978 to
less than three percent in 1981. Michigan also reports that half of the
bottles still found along that state's roadsides are nonreturnables from
out of state. A former chief engineer at Chevrolet once told me that glass
was the largest single cause of tire and road damage, so reductions of
these magnitudes are welcome news indeed. Now we need biodegradable
fast-food containers, or maybe edible ones.

Which brings us to shredded truck tires, which, like Big Mac
containers, are neither biodegradable, edible, nor particularly attractive.

David E. Davis, Jr.

Marshall, Michigan, where Davis lived as a "semi-vagrant" and "Don Juan in training" in the very early Fifties. His first car, a 1935 Mercedes-Benz custom-bodied roadster, purchased for $1000 from an Air Force colonel who liberated it in postwar Germany.

Bob Knoll

Cumberland, Maryland, SCCA National, 1954. A cool and debonair Davis leans on his MG TD as he awaits his debut as an also-ran in sports car racing.

The helmet Davis wore in his famous crash at Sacramento, California, in 1955. The racing car, an MG, got upside down and the author's head was caught between the back of the seat and the pavement. In a thirty-yard slide, he suffered the loss of his nose, the eyelid on the left eye, the roof of his mouth, and all but a few of his teeth, as well as 130 compound fractures of his upper and lower jaws. A lot of damage was done by the helmet's broken visor. The dark stains are the author's precious bodily fluids.

Nürburgring 1000 Kilometers, 1967: Evi Butz, of the Porsche Press department, interrupted by the author while conferring with engineer Hans Mezger, father of the Porsche 910. In 1969 Fräulein Evi Butz became Mrs. Dan Gurney and lived happily, if hectically, ever after.

The author and Dan Gurney examine Gurney's Indy car at the Indianapolis Motor Speedway in 1964.

New York International Automobile Show, 1964: Davis, Jim Wangers, Bob Anderson, and John Delorean. Wangers was the man who inspired the Pontiac GTO. Anderson was DeLorean's buddy, a Chrysler vice president and later president of Rockwell International. DeLorean was Detroit's hottest young automotive executive and that city's answer to Margaret Trudeau.

Stuttgart, West Germany, 1965. Davis drives the Mercedes-Benz W196 Grand Prix car in the pouring rain at the factory test track. The mechanic in the cap is Herr Bunz, last member of the great Mercedes racing teams of the Fifties to be employed at the factory, and a man profoundly concerned about Davis driving this car in the rain. In the event, his fears were well-grounded.

Mexico City Autodromo, 1965. Davis with Jackie Stewart before practice for the Mexican Grand Prix. This was Stewart's first trip to North America, and he had just savored his first hamburger and first chocolate malted at Sanborn's Drug Store with Davis as his guide.

Bill Gavin

Bridgehampton, New York, muscle car comparison test: Davis with Brock Yates, "the best conversationalist, and finest companion one could have on any long automotive journey"—which describes their respective lives pretty accurately.

P.J. O'Rourke leads a motley crew of Harley riders to Bloomington, Indiana. Behind him are DED, Jr., Land Rover's Bill Baker, and at the rear the infamous engineer, racing driver, racing car designer, and unlikely satyr Trant Jarman.

Davis with Trant Jarman, toward the end of a long Harley-Davidson ride to dine with the editors of *The American Spectator* in Bloomington, Indiana.

John and Elaine Bond, the husband/wife team who reinvented
Road & Track magazine, charted a course for every upscale car
magazine that followed, taught the author everything he needed to
know to run a magazine of his own, then fired him for disloyalty
and incompetence.

The great Max Hoffman standing beside the long-awaited BMW 507—a car for which he should share design
credit with the designer of record, Count Albrecht
"Zeppo" Goertz.

Ford Motor Company

Oulton Park, England: Davis with Jackie Stewart, Ford Cosworth Sierra, after the successful completion of a one-day course at the Stewart Driving School and three days at a Jackie Stewart Sporting Clays Tournament at Gleneagles Hotel, Scotland.

Road & Track

Henry N. Manney III, the best writer who ever graced the pages of *Road & Track* magazine, with Phil Hill—America's first world champion, driving for Ferrari in 1961, and a funny, quirky, knight errant of U.S. motorsport.

Rene Dreyfus, restaurateur, racing driver, and perfect gentleman, poses at the wheel of a Bugatti GP car.

The author with five-time world champion Juan Manuel Fangio in his Mercedes-Benz office in Buenos Aires. Kidney and heart disease had taken their toll, but Fangio was still gallant, still graciously hospitable.

J.L.K. Davis

Davis, flanked by Ruben "Toto" Fangio and Luis "Negro" Barragan at the Autodromo Juan Manuel Fangio in Balcarce, Argentina. Toto Fangio was Juan Manuel's younger brother, and his chief mechanic in the early days of his racing career.

J.L.K. Davis

Alan Rosenberg

Last view of Juan Manuel Fangio, shortly before his death. After a long hour with a group of American admirers, he grew tired and was taken away by his nurse. Note the bowed legs which earned him his nickname, "El Chueco," as a young soccer player, and how elegant he was, even when terminally ill.

Davis standing where he has absolutely no business—beside a Rolls-Royce. He loves the Rolls not as a great car, but as an immensely charming English eccentric.

Humphrey Sutton

Moroso Park, Florida: Styling and profiling in George Shelley's 4.4-liter Ferrari 121. This is the car driven by Eugenio Castellotti at Le Mans in '55. It didn't work any better for the author than it did for Castellotti.

Greg Jarem

One of the great automotive experiences—driving a factory-owned D-Type Jaguar from Coventry to LeMans, exactly as the factory team used to do in the Fifties.

Greg Jarem

1988 Mille Miglia Storica: Davis guns the Mercedes-Benz 300SL through the crowds as co-driver A.B. Shuman records the moment on videotape.

Davis with Mike Dale, president of Jaguar in North America, in the painfully beautiful 1953 C-Type Jaguar they shared in the 1998 Mille Miglia Storica—1000 very fast miles on the roads between Brescia and Rome.

Davis at the wheel of a Ferrari Short Wheelbase Berlinetta, Ferrari Club national convention, Summit Point, Virginia.

Jerome Magic

To David: The fun came first, the fire came later! Bob.

The author with Robert Lutz, then president of Chrysler, about to experience his first ride in a prototype Dodge Viper at the Chrysler Proving Grounds, Chelsea, Michigan. The car caught fire and was extinguished by Viper chief engineer Roy Sjoberg, using pitchers of ice water from the nearby dining tent.

Carroll Shelby embraces our hero: "Shit, David, I'm sorry you lost $50,000 on them cows, but I lost my money too! I already told you that I can make it up any time you want a plane-load of rare-breed chickens."

J.L.K. Davis

Davis with designer, author, former racing driver and OSS operative John Weitz at a charity autocross in New York City.

Edsel Ford II—an enthusiastic husband and father, qualities that were somewhat lacking in his own father, Henry Ford II. He is also an occasional quail hunting and drinking/dining companion of the author, which practically guarantees him a seat in the pantheon.

Davis with Jack Telnack— at Telnack's retirement. Telnack was Ford's design chief until 1998.

Davis learns the truth from Lee Iacocca, while a PR man averts his eyes and hopes for the best.

J.L.K. Davis

Davis and Carroll Shelby with the Kougar Jaguar purchased from Tony Hogg's widow. Davis was for many years the last person to actually want a Kougar Jaguar in the entire civilized world.

J.L.K. Davis

The Davis Ferrari 328S is winched onto the trailer to be hauled away after a raccoon destoyed its interior. AAA paid over $17,000 to repair the coon's ravages.

Aaron Kiley

The author with Duke, aka Duc Thieu, the orange cat built like a meatloaf. Behind Davis is Red (Mioaks Red Menace) the wonder dog, official dog at the launch of *Automobile Magazine* and best dog Davis ever owned. One Fiat Topolino 500A, one Steyr-Daimler-Puch Haflinger, one Dodge van (formerly property of author's antique-dealer father), and one Volkswagen GTi—the Davis fleet in front of the Davis house.

Standing in front of the Inn at Perry Cabin, on Chesapeake Bay, with Bob Tullius and Stirling Moss—each one an unusual racing talent, each one a fascinating man, yet as different from each other as a can of diet Coke and a bottle of porter.

Brumos Porsche chairman Dan Davis (no relation), the author, Ron Baraba, Bob Snodgrass, Jacksonville Jaguars kicker Bryan Barker, and crew chief Jim Bailey—the Brumos Motors vintage racing team at Daytona Speedway in 1997. On this occasion the author drove Hurley Haywood's Daytona-winning Porsche 911 RSR, Dan Davis drove a 962, Ron Baraba drove his own RSR, general manager Snodgrass drove a 935, and Bryan Barker and Jim Bailey drove 914-6 GTs.

The author prepares for a shot at Big Sur during the filming of the TV commercial that would launch *Automobile Magazine* for viewers of late-night full-contact karate cable programming.

Davis consults with Officer Bob during the filming of *Automobile Magazine*'s launch commercial. "Bob, they want me to go faster across the bridge. I'm already doing a hundred. Is that okay with you?" "Oh sure, when Honda and Kawasaki do motorcycle commercials up here, they generally run about one-fifty."

Visiting with the lovely Cristina Ferrare (formerly Mrs. John DeLorean) on "Good Morning L.A." as part of a nationwide media tour to launch *Automobile Magazine*. Cristina: "Did you hear that John is planning to introduce another car?" Davis: "No, I did not. What sort of car?" Cristina: "Oh, same old bullshit."

Davis poses with his girlfriend and lead bird dog—Bella, Italian Spinone—at Red's Bog, his farm in northern Michigan. The two-hundred-acre farm doubles as an off-road testing ground, and the Land Rover Discovery had been seriously stuck the previous evening.

The author as chief judge of the West Virginia Championship Chili Cookoff, near the birthplace of Stonewall Jackson.

David E. Davis, Jr. with J.L.K. Davis at the White House, to celebrate the beauty and wonder of NASCAR. Willie Neslon opened the evening's entertainment with "Up Against the Wall, Redneck Mother," which seemed perfectly appropriate for everyone present.

JT

*Please present this card
and personal identification
at
THE EAST ENTRANCE
September 13, 1978
at seven o'clock*

NOT TRANSFERABLE

*The President and Mrs. Carter
request the pleasure of your company
at a buffet dinner to be held at*
The White House
*on Wednesday evening, September 13, 1978
at seven o'clock*

South Lawn

One tire-industry spokesman told us that blowouts are seldom the cause of these scattered chunks of strips of tread, since most truck tires are tubeless. If I may play devil's advocate for a moment, I'd like to report that I was passing an eighteen-wheeler on the Ohio Turnpike one summer night at about 2:30 when the inside tire on the trailer's front set of duals blew, and I mean blew. There was a noise that drowned out my Joe Cocker tape, a huge black cloud of smoke or dust and debris, followed by a veritable barrage of rubber projectiles. My windshield didn't break, but the silver paint sure caught hell.

Most of the truck tires that blow, or otherwise fail, are retreads, but our industry spokespersons were quick to point out that this is no indictment of retreads. To a man, they stoutly maintained that the retread industry has become so sophisticated today that their product is as good as or better than the original-equipment tires supplied with the truck. One source said that poor maintenance causes most of the truck-tire failures, while another suggested that road hazards are the number-one problem. We do know that underinflation and overloading are both causes of overheating, and overheating causes tread separation. Everybody agreed that universal acceptance of radial-ply tires by truckers will go a long way toward alleviating the problem, and proper maintenance of their equipment by both fleets and independent owner/operators would only improve on the improvement.

Finally, I wish we cared as much for the condition and appearance of our roadsides as the peoples of northern and western Europe do. Italy and Greece may look like the United States at its most unkempt, but France, Germany, and Scandinavia really do a job. I've seen dead people lying along the road in Africa, but never a beer can in Germany. Only a third-rate creature fouls the place where it lives.

Bored by "Stingray," thrilled by '86 Corvette, and heading on down the road.

❧

Cars on television. By now, you may have seen NBC's attempt to clone "Miami Vice," which was called "Stingray," and was only marginally dumber than "CHiPs" or "the Dukes of Hazzard" in its treatment of cars.

I happen to think that the '65 Sting Ray was one of Western Civilization's high points, and it offended me to see some lounge lizard creeping around Beverly Hills trying to look menacing in a black one with tinted windows and an automatic transmission. Lord have mercy!

It has always been my belief that a driver with skill and good sense does not spend a lot of time driving with the tail hung out. Drivers on television, however, cannot seem to drive any other way. The swarthy person in "Stingray" was no exception. He couldn't keep it straight at all, and I wondered that the car's flanks were so jewel-like in their perfect blackness, since he must bounce the old dear off the odd solid object pretty regularly as it slues back and forth in his hands. What bothered me, and ought to bother everyone of taxpaying age in the Republic, was that the story line told us the Sting Ray of the title actually belongs to the White House motor pool. This hamfisted klutz was actually out there slaloming through L.A. traffic in our Sting Ray! A letter to the president is called for.

P.J. O'Rourke stoutly maintains that the mere presence of all those good cars on the streets of California is no reason to believe that there is any matching number of car enthusiasts to go with them. Certainly television does little to reassure us on this count. Television is where a guy in a Ferrari 308 has difficulty escaping from six or seven other guys packed into a 1937 Buick limousine. Television is where you always know which car in a chase is going to tumble down the cliff onto the beach. Of course! It's the '65 Plymouth station wagon. (Modern production budgets do not allow us to trash Ferraris and Porsches.) Television is also where the car that somersaults into the surf invariably catches fire and explodes. I regularly confound small children and elderly ladies by counting off the seconds between final impact and explosion and having the gas tank go up right on cue every time.

It seems to me that TV commercials do a far better job of presenting the automobile than TV dramas. Unfortunately, automobile commercials are as apt to present cars badly as a typical "CHiPs" episode, but the beer and soft-drink people generally have a nice eye for automobiles and how they move. Sometimes cars magically become featured players in films, as in *A Man and a Woman*, with its Mustang, or the assassins' Citroen 11 in *The Conformist*. At the risk of being assaulted by my sophisticated friends, I must confess that I never miss a chance to see *Chitty Chitty Bang Bang*, nor do I ever fail to get all choked up the first time Chitty takes wing to save Caractacus Potts, et al., from the threatening tide. I will admit it even if you will not: Many's the time I've pulled back on a steering wheel and imagined the car rising into the air. Unfortunately, the only time one actually did that with me aboard, the results were ghastly.

Dreams come true. I started writing Corvette ads in the spring of 1960. The last ones I wrote were for the 1963 Sting Ray announcement, just before moving to New York and becoming editor of this magazine. Corvettes have provided me with a lot of thrills over the years, in addition to paying the rent and food bills from April '60 to November '62. A particular favorite from those years was the 1962 model, which looked almost exactly like the 1961—blending the Sting Ray's tail with a fatter, four headlamp version of the traditional Corvette front end—but featured the new 327-cubic-inch engine, which could be had in power outputs all the way up to 360 horsepower.

More recently I fell in love with the idea of the all-new 1984 Corvette. Don Sherman came back from an impromptu session at the GM proving grounds and reported some interesting scuttlebutt about the car and its capabilities, and I went home for lunch that day and said, "We may have to buy one of these new Corvettes when they finally come out." Well, Chevrolet had a little trouble getting that first year's production right. They rode like light reconnaissance vehicles and shook like aspens in the breeze. I felt personally betrayed. It wasn't until the 1985 model came along that the Corvette and I stopped carrying the torch for each other and reaffirmed our love.

Not long ago I was asked if I'd like to drive an '86 Corvette prototype in Germany. I could pick the roads and recommend a place to stay. Naturally, I accepted faster than you could say "Zora Arkus-Duntov." I said that I'd like to drive the car on and around the two-lanes that link up to make the famous Romantic Road, or Romantische Strasse, from Wurzburg in Franconia to Fussen in Bavaria. Furthermore, I suggested that the Hotel Eisenhut in Rothenburg ob der Tauber would do just fine as a place in which to spend those hours when I wasn't driving.

The roads were predictably beautiful. I'd driven almost all of the Romantic Road in trips over the years, and it was every bit as good as I remembered. The hotel at Rothenburg was comfortable and charming and we ate like kings. I visited the German Motor Museum at nearby Langenburg, and, among its treasures, came across Porsche design chief Tony Lapine's candy-apple-and-white Chevy-powered sprint car, which had been a pile of parts when Tony showed it to me in the basement of his home a few years ago.

Best of all, it rained for two days solid, and I had every chance to try the Corvette's Bosch ABS II anti-lock braking system. It is clear that the Bosch people let no grass grow under their wheels between ABS I and II. If possible, the system is even more effective than the earlier version. Again and again I let go of the wheel and spiked the brakes at 75 or 80 on rain-swept little country roads, and never experienced a bad moment. The car was virtually flawless on bad roads in bad weather. If it had a glove box and some luggage space, I'd pronounce it perfect. It doesn't seem fair that the Corvette should have become so much younger and more vigorous in the past 25 years, while I have simply gotten older. Ah well.

Happy Trails. This is the last time I'll write this column for this magazine. I came back to *Car and Driver* nine years ago to the day. I had planned to stay at this typewriter, writing these notes to you, my friends, until they carried me out. Unfortunately, things don't always work out as we'd like them to. I love all of you as I love this magazine, and I'll miss you—as I'll miss *Car and Driver*. See you somewhere down the road.

The Automobile Magazine *Years*

Where the good life gets rolling.

~~~

With those first tentative whacks at my old Adler 21d electric typewriter (about to be replaced by an ITT XTRA computer), I officially launch what promises to be a great automotive adventure. We call it *Automobile Magazine,* because, we figured, why not call it exactly what it's going to be?

Automobile Magazine is a celebration of quality—quality in automobiles, quality of life, and quality in magazines. We seek adventure and the good life, and we seek them in cars that are fun to drive. We'll drive exciting cars to unforgettable places. We'll go wherever the roads go, and sometimes beyond. We'll wring out and review some of the finest, fastest, and most interesting cars in the world each month, and we'll bring them to life with the most evocative photography and illustration money can buy.

We won't waste your time with tiresome tales of boring cars.

If you glanced at our masthead as you opened *Automobile Magazine* for the first time, you may have noticed a gaggle of famous automotive writers, artists, and photographers. That's because this will not be a lowest common denominator magazine. We're determined to produce a quality product for a quality audience. Second-rate writers attract second-rate readers. We want to reach the best and brightest of America's car enthusiasts, and we know only one way to do that. The magazine you hold in your hand is our opening salvo.

We're immensely proud of what we've accomplished in only a few months. A couple of weeks ago I wandered through our New York offices at lunch time and saw desks covered with correspondences and promotional brochures, partitions covered with messages from important people, ample evidence of busy professionals deeply involved in a thriving enterprise. I immediately called our business manager in Ann Arbor, Harriet Stemberger, who came with me from *Car and Driver,* and said, "My God, Harriet, you should see this place. It's hard to believe that last August all I had was a handshake with Rupert Murdoch."

I spent fifteen years as editor/publisher of *Car and Driver* and departed—much against my will—first, because CBS seemed to regard the magazine publisher's job not as I did, as a lifelong vocation, but as a sort of final exam for some ghastly punishment like "marketing vice president"; and, second, because CBS announced that they were suing my former boss, Bill Ziff, for fraud and misrepresentation in connection with their purchase of twelve Ziff-Davis consumer magazines, including mine, for which they evidently thought they'd been overcharged by about thirty-nine million big ones. When CBS management made their announcement, I made my announcement.

I have always regarded Ralph Nader as one of the truly pernicious forms of urban blight afflicting the Republic, yet I have to admit that there is bound to be a tiny handful of Americans incapable of acting in their own enlightened self-interest and requiring the attendance of Ralph or one of his acolytes at their elbows when they go through the checkout line. However, when the cash register rings up a number like 362.5 million and the poor boob is already accompanied by a small army of lawyers and accountants, I figure caveat emptor has to apply there somewhere, and if the poor boob pays forty or fifty million too much for something, that's his problem. It wasn't that I feared for Bill Ziff's honor; it was just that the lawsuit made CBS seem so feckless.

I didn't know quite how I was going to do it, but I knew that I had to continue to be involved with an automotive magazine. This is my life. Friends like Carroll Shelby and Bill Ruger—understanding that—spent long hours counseling me, and even offered to help me put a deal together that would allow me to start a magazine of my own.

I flew back and forth to London to meet with Ian Fraser, managing director of Great Britain's *Car* magazine—in my estimation the best automotive publication in the world today—to see if we could somehow form an alliance. My attorney, Johnny Norris, invested a lot of time, talent, and travel in my predicament. Time dragged on.

Just when it seemed that I might have to go back to the automobile assembly line of my youth—I'm a damned good drill press operator—the phone beside my bed in Ann Arbor rang one Friday morning at seven o'clock. It was an old friend calling from New York, who said, somewhat breathlessly, "David, I want you to listen very carefully to what I'm about to tell you. This is very important. Are you listening? Okay. Rupert Murdoch's people just learned that you've left CBS, and they want to put you back into the car magazine business. David, take this very seriously, because these people are committed." I flew to New

York, and after five minutes of conversation with the president of Murdoch Magazines, Marty Singerman (since promoted to president and chief executive officer of the parent company, News America Publisher), knew exactly what I was going to do with my career. Thus began *Automobile Magazine*.

I am a car enthusiast. I love automobiles, especially the great ones. I have chosen this line of work because it keeps me in intimate, hourly contact with automobiles, along with people who drive them and the people who design and build them. I am not an automotive expert, nor a pundit, nor an analyst. I am a car nut, better informed than some, perhaps, because I've been able to eat, sleep, and drink cars for the past thirty-five years, but a car nut, nonetheless.

I cannot think of a better way to celebrate the one-hundredth birthday of the automobile than this—creating the magazine I've been in training to do since I joined *Road & Track* in 1957.

I'm delighted that you decided to join me, and I'll look forward to being with you next month and in all the months of *Automobile Magazine* that'll follow.

Broderick Crawford, call your office.

ur correspondent from the Welsh border, the redoubtable Philip Llewellin, refers to television as "the haunted fish tank." If you watched the haunted fish tank much this spring, especially ESPN, you may have seen an *Automobile Magazine* commercial soliciting subscriptions. As it happens, I was the featured performer in that little opus, though in order to obtain network clearance, I had to sign an affidavit stating that I was not an actor playing myself. Hah! My wife and all my friends know beyond a shadow of a doubt that I *am* an actor playing myself. The joke's on the networks.

If you did see the commercial in question, you know that I got to rip up and down California's justly famous Highway 1 in a Ferrari 308GTS, a bright red Toyota MR2, and a navy blue (and occasionally purple, depending on the light) Porsche 911 Turbo—the very same car that Mrs. Lindamood drove across the country in our April (premiere) issue. What you may not know is that I got to do all that ripping and tearing with the full cognizance and cooperation of the California Highway Patrol. O ye of little faith, you see, dreams *do* come true.

Highway 1 is apparently an extremely popular venue for TV commercial production, because Sergeant Andersen of the CHP post in Salinas doesn't bat an eye when we ask him for permission to film me breaking the laws of God and man on the most famous enthusiast's road in the Republic. We get the permit. Officer Bob Scranton shows up at the crash of dawn on the appointed day at the appointed spot, parks his big, shiny Ford black-and-white, and asks what we want him to do. I sort of sidle up to him to find out what he wants *us* to do, to which he responds, "My orders are to help you do whatever you want to do."

Oh my God, I have died and gone to heaven.

We were all equipped with little Motorola walkie-talkies—the kind used by the organizers of spontaneous demonstrations and worn by policemen on their belts—so when the director asked me how fast I was going in the opening shot, I gulped, and answered truly, "I'm coming off the end of the bridge at about 110, and passing the camera position at about 95," knowing full well that Officer Bob was monitoring my comments on his own walkie-talkie. Later, I parked the Ferrari and approached our representative of law and order to find out what he thought about all that. He said, laconically, "You guys are easy. When the Honda people come up to make a motorcycle commercial, those guys ride through here about 140!"

That afternoon, as the sun set and the breeze grew cold, we finished for the day and I asked J.L.K. Davis to drive me back to the motel in Carmel in the MR2. Just north of Big Sur, Officer Bob passed us in the patrol car, and my wife decided to draft him on that winding road. What a nice display of driving skill we got. He herded that big Ford through the dark and endless turns without once violating the center line or the shoulder. He never seemed to touch the brakes, never seemed surprised by the road or anything in it. We rushed along in his wake, having the time of our lives, which led my chauffeur to ask, "Do you suppose he's going to pull me over when we get to Carmel and arrest me?" I watched the taillights of his car dancing over the coastal hills and said, "No, he's having as much fun as you are, and besides, he wants to get home to Salinas."

Next morning, back on location, the patrol car arrived. Bob got out and walked over to where we were opening a thermos of coffee. "Who was driving the little red car last night?" he asked. Uh-oh. "My wife," I said. He laughed and allowed that he'd thought he might have to use the siren and the lights to keep ahead of her. When she showed up for lunch, he asked for her driver's license and affixed to it a miniature replica of the CHP's gold star, while she grinned her relief.

The whole experience reminded me once again of what a classy bunch of men and women populate the California Highway Patrol.

Aside from renewing my appreciation of the CHP, my three days on Highway 1 were instructive as to the personalities and performance of the three cars involved. One doesn't get too many chances to charge through the same series of corners at speed twelve or fourteen times while a policeman holds back the civilian traffic. The Ferrari was a 1979 GTS, which we got from George Mahi, at Monterey Jaguar, Rolls-Royce, Ferrari. It would have been a nice one to buy. It was cleaner than most new cars and only had about 18,000 miles on the clock. I was much braver in the Ferrari and the Toyota MR2 than I was in the Porsche Turbo. I'm only guessing, but I feel I might have been faster through a given series of turns in the Porsche, but only because I could stand on the throttle between corners and use all of that magnificent engine in great, earthshaking bursts.

The Porsche is not shy about its ability to go faster than the average idiot should drive it, but it's pure joy when driven the way Porsche racing cars are driven these days—cautiously in the corners and till hell won't have it on the straights. The Toyota was diametrically opposite— opposite the Ferrari in its comfort and sophistication, and opposite the Porsche in its calm, reassuring feel at full chat. The Ferrari feels sort of low-tech, high-effort. The 911 Turbo feels wonderful at four-tenths and scary at eight. The Toyota whispers in your ear that you can't do anything stupid enough to screw it up, no matter how fast you go, and we are grateful for that trusting naïveté.

I have long complained that Lee Iacocca's success as a pitchman on television has encouraged every half-baked manufacturer of storm windows, every overstimulated carpet discounter in America to take to the tube and make a fool of himself. Nothing against America's best-known automotive executive, but he did open a veritable floodgate of nasal, halting orators hellbent on vindicating wives' and/or girlfriends' flawed belief that "if Lee Iacocca can do it, honey, so can you."

Now I find myself among their ranks. I cringe each time the miracle of the cathode-ray tube reruns that sickly little smirk of mine—the one that was supposed to come across as glowing self-confidence and good-humored conviction. But it was worth an occasional midnight squirm in the TV room if it sold subscriptions to a few thousand old friends and former readers. Hell, it was worth all that and more just to spend three days zooming up and down Highway 1 in those three lovely cars.

Stuff on the wall.

~∿⊙∿~

Automobile *Magazine* has been in its new Liberty Street offices for about a month now, and life has improved dramatically for all hands. I like the sound of "Liberty Street." It's at once old-fashioned, midwestern, and patriotic. We're on the second floor of a building that used to house a famous undergraduate saloon called the Pretzel Bell, the venue of choice for countless generations of University of Michigan students bent on celebrating their twenty-first birthdays with a first legal bender. One hates to think of all the Betty Coeds who threw up within a hundred feet of this desk.

Happily, all trace of bygone technicolor yawns and liquid laughs has been erased by the extensive modification to the premises occasioned by the arrival of the traveling circus like ours, with all its desks, typewriters, CRTs, drawing boards, books, bookcases, and other essential goods and chattels. It was particularly nice to start fresh, with all new stuff. Except for my own office—furnished with the same desk I've used for years—everybody got elegant new furniture, and a dozen teams of local artisans have been through here in the past six months, building, decorating, and transforming. We now have a truly terrific place in which to work, here, upstairs from where the old Pretzel Bell used to be.

It is especially interesting to watch various people's walls get covered with stuff. Oh, sure, there are a few among us who, monklike, sit surrounded by bare walls, but the sort of person who devotes his or her life to this sort of occupation is generally the sort of person who combines the pack rat's lust to accumulate stuff with the nouveau riche's need to show it off. I am the worst. I have devoted several hours, some of them in the middle of the night, to hanging stuff on my walls. Now I sit surrounded by odds and bits and symbols of a life probably misspent but enjoyed to a fare-thee-well.

I sit facing west as I write this, and if I swivel my chair counterclockwise, a lot of life rotates past.

Item: A bill of sale (number 122, dated June 5, 1946) from Art Quantrell Motors in Wyandotte, Michigan, for a brand-new two-tone-green Olds 76 four-door sedan that my father bought for $1665.28. This was our first new car, and the first car I ever drove without an accompanying parent. Said document indicates that my father traded a 1940 Olds 66 two-door upon which fifteen payments were outstanding—the car with which I learned to drive during the war years. He paid $7.05 for the optional solenoid starter and $9.33 for the optional Fram oil filter. Two-tone paint was an extra $11.55. The first time he let me drive the car, I scratched the right front fender on my way over to Mary Lou Brown's house.

Item: A note to me from Lowell Thomas, dated September 21, 1974, thanking me for accosting him at a business dinner one night to tell him how much his *With Lawrence of Arabia* had meant to me as a boy. Receiving that note was almost as thrilling as if old T.E. Lawrence himself had phoned from the Great Beyond.

Item: A gorgeous Bill Neale poster based on his Alain Prost painting—which appeared in our inaugural issue—bearing the legend: "Commemorating the first issue of *Automobile Magazine,* April 1986." Bill added that line out of the goodness of his heart, and as anyone who knows him will tell you, he has a heart as big as all outdoors. My poster is number one of three hundred, signed by the artist, and—as T.E. Lawrence once said of the Rolls-Royce scout car he used for battlefield transportation—it is a pearl beyond price.

Item: A tin Carling's beer sign, which I found in the basement of the Danish-American Sportsmens Club in Detroit about twenty years ago. It depicts nine obviously blitzed policemen, each holding a clearly marked tankard of Carling's, and the discreet message, "Nine 'Pints' of the Law." When the light hits it just right you can see that some kid from the clouded past used it for BB gun practice.

Item: Two photographs of me with Jackie Stewart.

One, a small black-and-white shot of us sitting on the asphalt of the Mexico City Autodromo before the Mexican Grand Prix. It was 1965, his first trip to North America. He had already driven the U.S. and Canadian GPs, and that very morning had awakened to the awful knowledge that he'd blown right through the United States without tasting a hamburger or a milkshake. Just before practice, I took him to Sanborn's in Mexico City for one of each. I stayed with him through the following weekend's Times GP at Riverside and came away from the experience knowing that I had met a truly remarkable young racing driver.

The other, a larger color shot of us standing just down Liberty

Street from what later became this office. We'd just had lunch, about a year ago, and you can tell from the look on my face that I had no idea that my life was about to change so dramatically.

Item: What I believe to be a reprint of a gorgeous old poster for the 1953 Golden Gate Road Races, held May 16-17 of that year. I dreamed of running at Golden Gate. California really seemed like the big time to a beginning road racer, even more so than Europe at that stage of my development. An unknown reader sent the poster, and the person who opened the mail that day lost his/her name and address. I hope that the donor contacts me. I'd like to express my gratitude in person.

Item (south wall): A framed set of "Dan Gurney for President" campaign bumper stickers and lapel buttons from our abortive attempt to run the too-young Gurney in 1964. Ah, what might have been.

There are forty-some-odd pieces hanging on my walls, including the items mentioned, ranging from autographed photos of Jim Clark and Graham Hill to a 1957 Mercedes-Benz 300Sc radiator grille. Paintings, caricatures, photographs, old license plates, and a reproduction of a want ad from the *Times* of London, soliciting recruits for a 1914 antarctic expedition. It stirs me every time I spot it up there. It says: "MEN WANTED for hazardous journey. Small wages, bitter cold, long months of complete darkness, constant danger, safe return doubtful. Honor and recognition in case of success—Ernest Shackleton."

The ad pulled like crazy. It is said that guys were lined up around the block the next morning. I like to think that I'd have been lined up with them.

Lists.

American Airlines, Flight 295, New York-Dallas—I am not a particularly well-organized person, nor am I ruled by any passion for neatness, yet I do occasionally feel the need to make lists.

Sometimes these are lists of important points about test cars I've driven recently, sometimes lists of appointments, stories to be written, tasks to be performed, but more often they are merely random lists of names or cars or events that simply popped into my untidy mind.

For instance, on a flight to Los Angeles a couple of weeks ago, I suddenly felt compelled to compile a list of all the women with whom I'd been mixed up since I first began serious training for that activity in the seventh grade. The behavior of a cad, to be sure, but when the list-compiling passion is upon me, not even the normal standards of gentlemanly conduct can deter me. Naturally, cars figure prominently in the nostalgic toil of recalling all those names and faces. For instance:

"Oh, right, I was driving that British racing green XK120M, and she was a Capital Airlines stewardess. I was so eager to collect her when her flight came in that I slid to a stop in front of the terminal and leaped out without shutting off the engine or opening the door."

Or, "We went to dinner at the Richton Café in her car—it was one of the original Olds Ninety Eights, pale blue—and I kissed her for the first time through her veil and she tasted deliciously of martinis and cigarettes. I can still feel that veil on my mouth, even though my lower lip has been Novocain-numb ever since I tore up my face in 1955."

And, "I drove like a maniac all night long. It was that Peugeot 403 with the Abarth exhaust system and the busted rear hanger. I was desperate to get to her house before dawn, to show up at the door of her apartment while she was still asleep, before she even knew I was back in town. God, it just occurred to me, what if some other guy had been there?"

That inspired me to make another list, as follows:

Ten Great Women with Whom I'd Really Like to Have Dinner Next Friday:

Jean Arthur (actress), for her voice.

Mary Astor (actress), for her reputation.

Alice Caracciola (adventuress, companion of hairy-armed heroes), for the race drivers in her life.

Patricia Carbine (publisher of *Ms. Magazine*), because I love her, and because she's the whole world's Irish aunt.

Alicia de Larrocha (pianist), for her talent.

Amelia Earhart (pilot), for her willingness to take risks.

Signora Laura Ferrari (wife of Enzo), for her side of the story.

Elizabeth Junek (Czech Bugatti driver between the wars), for her memories.

Jeane Kirkpatrick (former U.N. ambassador), for her intellect.

Denise McCluggage (journalist, former racing driver), because I love her, and because she wears her soul on her sleeve.

I've probably had dinner with Denise McCluggage fifty times, and with Pat Carbine at least a dozen, but the next time cannot be too soon. I can't wait to get the two of them together with all those other high-powered babes. I did get to have dinner with Alice Caracciola one night a long time ago at René Dreyfus's Le Chanteclair when she was getting on in years, all porcelain pink and silver and quite beautiful. I'm not sure how I'll get those ladies who've already gone on to that big consciousness-raising symposium in the sky, but it seems as though it would be worth the effort.

Wanting to come up with a venue that might entice ten such women—with lots of great dinners behind them and busy schedules to be met—naturally led me to compile yet another list, this one of restaurants where I know we'd be well treated and well fed.

Ten Great Restaurants Where I'd Really Like to Dine with Ten Great Women Next Friday:

Alte Post (Stuttgart, West Germany): The second-best reason I know for picking up your new Porsche or Mercedes-Benz at the factory. The goose liver pâté alone is worth the trip.

Auberge de L'ill (Illhausern, Alsace-Lorraine): Three stars in the Michelin, the best restaurant in a part of France that apparently has no bad restaurants.

Boh! (Santa Monica, California): A great Italian restaurant run by the Western states' Lamborghini distributor.

Four Seasons (New York, New York): The very definition of first-class dining in New York City—a thrill for the eye as well as the palate.

The Lark (Bloomfield Hills, Michigan): Quite possibly the best restaurant between the Hudson River and the Los Angeles County line.

Hotel Neue Post (Biessenhofen, Bavaria, West Germany): Great, great food, just minutes away from the Alpina works at Buchloe.

Primavera (New York, New York): Where the manager drives a Dino and the roast baby goat with rosemary will absolutely knock your hat in the creek.

Pyrénées Cévennes (Paris): Off the beaten track in the City of Light, a perfect example of the classic Parisian bistro. Order the cassoulet for your first meal there.

Rangoon Racquet Club (Beverly Hills, California): A Carroll Shelby favorite. When I walk through the door here, I feel as though I've walked into a party in my own house. Noisy, crowded, and full of good sights and smells, with C.V. Wood's award-winning chili on the menu every day.

Wong's Eatery (Windsor, Ontario, Canada): Dim sum brunch, Peking duck dinner, or whatever Raymond Wong thinks you might enjoy. Absolutely terrific.

Except for Wong's, all of these are a little pricey, but what the hell, if you're having dinner with Mary Astor and Amelia Earhart, you can afford to splurge, right? Actually, if we ate at all ten, Wong's would bring the average cost per meal down to something well below the price of a good used car.

Which brings us to the ultimate list, the one I've been working on since I was old enough to tell Fords from Chevys.

Ten Great Cars for Taking Ten Great Women to Dinner in Ten Great Restaurants Next Friday Night:

1940 BMW Mille Miglia (aerodynamic roadster).

1938 Buick Century (convertible sedan or coupe).

1953 Cadillac-Allard J2X.

1965 Corvette Grand Sport.

1966 Ferrari 330GT 2+2.

1952 Frazer-Nash Mk II Le Mans Replica.

1954 HRG 1500.

1953 Jaguar C-type.

1966 Lamborghini 350GT.

1964 Porsche 904.

There'll undoubtedly be some carping about my list of great cars, especially about the particular Ferrari and Lamborghini models chosen, but they're favorites of mine. I can't help myself. I love that Ferrari because I put many happy miles on a brand-new 330 2+2 that belonged to Luigi Chinetti and loved every minute behind its wheel (and it would have room for my dogs). The 350GT Lambo makes the cut because it was the first Lamborghini I ever saw, and because I then hopped in and drove it around and around Connecticut's Thompson Speedway until it was out of gas. Also, these are good bets because they're relatively inexpensive examples of their respective breeds. The others, I feel, are self-explanatory.

I have also created lists of people, now dead, whom I wish were still around (my father, Graham Hill, Jo Bonnier, Django Reinhardt); writers I wish I had known (Tom McGuane, Shelby Foote, John Keegan, Jim Brady); and nonautomotive treasures I wish I owned (a Griffin & Howe .375 H&H sporter on a square-bridge Mauser action, a good Frederic Remington bronze, a full set of Winston Churchill first editions in good bindings, a best-grade Churchill—no relation—XXV twelve-bore, a classic Matthews wooden-hulled cabin cruiser from the Forties, and an unlimited line of credit in Las Vegas).

I'd like to read your lists. Why not think about it a little and then send me any lists that might come to mind? Cars, roads, dealerships good or bad, restaurants good or bad, mechanics, race drivers, races, places to go by car, what have you. Our main interest is automotive, of course, but we'll welcome any thoughtful lists you'd care to send. If this turns out to be as interesting as I think it might, we'll figure a way to compile your compilations and publish them in the magazine. Let's hear from you.

Watching the Fords go by.

In the past few years, the woods around Detroit seemed to be full of writers. First, it was the world's least competent dope broker, Mr. John Z. De Lorean, who attracted them, then Mr. Lee Iacocca, by his own admission the most gifted executive in the history of the automobile. However, Mr. Iacocca himself wrote such a rouser of a book that several authors then decided to try their luck with books about his former employer, Mr. Henry Ford II. Now the Ford books are hitting the stands, and it'll only be a short time before we get a new round of Iacocca books in response.

It has been a rather unattractive brouhaha, all things considered, with contending writers saying rude things about each other and friends of the subjects choosing sides. It is the sort of New York/Paris literary nastiness that seldom occurs in a smoke-stack town like Detroit, but when it does it gives a lot of folks a new lease on life.

If you grew up, as I did, in the shadow of Detroit, you grew up with all kinds of myths about the Ford Motor Company and the family that owned it. When I peddled the morning *Free Press* during World War II, my route was a chunk of town shaped roughly like a slice of pie—half a mile wide along Main Street, half a mile deep down Ten Mile Road, then back diagonally along the Grand Trunk Railroad tracks to Main Street and the original starting point. My bike was an ancient Sears Roebuck hand-me-down with a Musselman coaster brake that I never understood and splines in the front fork worn so badly that the bike and I almost never went where the handlebars pointed. So I walked. I can't remember the names of all the streets I plodded along during those years, but there were eight or nine of them, and since we lived in a blue-collar town, subscribers for a morning paper were few and far between.

Sometimes customers' houses would be a block apart, giving me plenty of time to fantasize as I folded each paper and prepared to throw it onto somebody's roof or into their bushes. In one fantasy, I was parachuted into Germany to free my Uncle Jim who was in a prison camp there. In another, the woman who supervised our church youth group melted into my arms and resolved a number of mysteries that had been troubling me for the past couple of years.

My most reliable fantasy, however, involved Henry Ford I's gorgeous daughter. I had no idea whether or not the old man actually had such a daughter (he didn't), but no matter. In my fantasy she was my age, and she looked like a cross between Shirley Temple in her early prime and the woman who supervised our church youth group. This golden-haired, nubile young bud would burst out of a house on Kenilworth Avenue just east of Main Street and gaily, unwittingly, run beneath the wheels of a huge transit-mix cement truck.

In a flash, I would shuck off my carrier's bag and sprint to her aid, snatching her from the jaws of death at the last possible instant. As I comforted her, having assured myself that she was unhurt—hem, hem—I would be interrupted by her stricken father, old Henry Ford himself, who had seen the whole thing and who wanted me to have her hand in marriage, an all-expense-paid college education, and a 1941 Mercury convertible, as my richly deserved reward.

On some predawn paper-route mornings she taught me all the stuff I'd been hoping to learn from the woman who supervised our church youth group. On others, she helped me equip the Mercury with a special intake manifold with two Stromberg 97s, a set of aluminum heads, headers, and Hollywood mufflers that were real quiet at low rpm and had a nasty blat to them when you stood on it.

I had no idea that the original Henry Ford was crazy as a loon by that time of his life, nor did I know the awful story of his never-ending campaign to crush every hope and dream his son Edsel ever had. I now know that he would have been a lousy father-in-law, and that I was probably better off without him. By the time I went to work at the Ford Highland Park plant in June of 1949, old Henry and his desperately unhappy son had both gone on to their rewards, about which, in the old man's case, I'll bet you wouldn't want to know.

I had grown up listening to my father's friends and men from our neighborhood talk about life in the Ford plants. I knew a bunch of guys my age who went to the Henry Ford Trade School, guys who'd actually machined their own Johansson gauges—"joe-blocks," they were called—as part of the Trade School curriculum. I knew all about bloody fights between UAW organizers and company goons. (At our house, the union was always the bad guys.) I personally knew men who'd been slugged by Ford foremen for smoking in the can, or not moving fast enough. Our contributor David Grath ("Eighty-Six Cars," June '86) remembers that if your father saw you slouched in a chair, reading a book, he'd say, "Boy, be glad you don't work out to Ford's. Everybody stands on his feet all day out there—even the draftsmen and the engineers."

Somehow, I don't think either of these Ford books has captured the automobile industry, the Ford Motor Company, or the Ford family, from my point of view. None of them will write about the guy who ran past our house in his underwear one Sunday morning, throwing his watch at me when I stepped off the porch to see what he was up to. It turned out he was a foreman at Ford whose house—not far from ours—had been firebombed and whose wits had simply deserted him at the thought of such a thing.

We can now safely assume that John Z. De Lorean wouldn't recognize the truth if it walked up and offered to sell him a can of talcum powder, and we'll probably never know the inside skinny about Lee Iacocca and Henry Ford II. Never mind, I'm just glad that I didn't have to save that hypothetical Ford heiress from the Indescribable Awful and wind up a member of the Ford family as a result. I couldn't have taken the pressure.

A BMW coupe, a bowl of red, and thou, hanging on beside me in the wilderness.

~~~

S latyfork, West Virginia—We rose at 5:30, dressed, and packed. I threw the luggage into the trunk of the BMW—fitting it around the cartons of cocktail glasses, beer glasses, water glasses, and double old-fashioned glasses we'd bought at Fostoria, in Moundsville, on the way down. (Sign of the times: the lady at the Fostoria factory store told us that there'll be no more blown glass coming out of the Moundsville plant; that from now on, it's all imported.)

With the luggage loaded, I washed the windows, checked the various liquids and lubricants, then climbed aboard and fiddled with the seat adjustments while the engine ticked over. J.L.K. Davis gave the room a final check, then joined me inside the 635CSi, placing a bag of fresh fruit between her feet and extracting a peach, which she began to quarter for my breakfast. It was twenty to seven.

I eased out of the ski resort's parking lot and pointed the BMW's nose down the mountain, slowly gathering speed as we and the car got comfortable and settled in for the day's drive. The sun was already lighting the peaks, and we could see thick fog in the valleys off to our left, knowing that we'd be down there in it within a few short minutes. With the transmission selector lever left in third, we whomped from one corner to the next—squeezing down on the brakes, reopening the throttle about halfway through, then standing on it again for an eighth of a mile or so, and repeating the process.

Two days earlier, we'd driven down to Snowshoe, West By-God Virginia, for the Ninth Annual Hillbilly Chili Cookoff—of which I have had the honor to be chief judge seven times. This is an affair to remember, which any gathering involving the cooking of chili, the consumption of Tecate beer and Sauza Conmemorativo tequila, and the endless rotation of country fiddlers and rock 'n' roll bands ought to be, and I always look forward to it.

But there are other, maybe even better reasons for visiting West

Virginia. My feeling about time spent driving through that state is much like the generally held feeling about fishing: i.e., that God doesn't charge you for the time you spend doing it. At least as important is the opportunity to visit the bard of Jane Lew, West Virginia—and impresario of the Hillbilly Chili Cookoff—Mr. William Neely.

Bill Neely has authored biographies of luminaries in the worlds of jazz and automobile racing, was co-author of *Stand on It* with the late Bob Ottum, and co-wrote a first-rate chili cookbook with his ex-wife Martina. His work appears regularly in the shrunken pages of *AutoWeek,* but that doesn't make him a bad person. He is one of Western civilization's great roisterers and storytellers, and I have a lifetime supply of fond memories of hours spent with him in and around automobiles all over the world.

Two of my all-time favorite roads wind through West Virginia: Route 219, from the Pennsylvania Turnpike south, and Route 250, which runs southeast from Sandusky, Ohio, to Richmond, Virginia, cutting diagonally across West Virginia as it goes. We drove down on 250 (470 miles) and were about to drive back via 219 (530 miles). West Virginia is virtually all great two-lane roads, being mountainous and about half-empty. The local infrastructure tends to be wild and woolly. Maintenance is spotty; many roads are heavily traveled by overloaded trucks, and they cross massive ridges in unpredictable loops and bounds. Springs run down the sides of the mountains and across the curves at frequent and inopportune intervals, and you'll thank all of the warlike Germanic gods every time you sail into one of those glistening wet spots and feel a set of ABS brakes at work under the sole of your right Top-Sider.

Much of 250 is rough and its verges like piecrust. The road might have been laid over the trails of wandering livestock. Radii decrease without warning, and it's not unusual for the road to go in another direction from the one for which you were setting up. You need a compliant suspension, sharp steering, lots of passing power, and even more braking power—happily, all attributes of our BMW.

Over east, on Route 219, it's different. The towns tend to be in better shape, and the road is better maintained. It runs through some of the highest parts of the state, and there's quite a lot of pretty farmland. Davis, West Virginia, which is about to blow away forever, is not far off 219 and used to boast that it was the highest incorporated municipality east of the Mississippi. Trucks are less of a hazard on 219, and you can really let your mind run free as you hurry south over its friendly contours. The curves are so perfect and so predictable, that you might have laid it out for your own pleasure.

South of the small town of Beverly, 219 offers a beautiful stretch of classic winding road that probably lasts all the way to the Virginia state line, though I've only taken it as far as Marlinton, which is the home of French's Diner (at the intersection of Third Avenue and Eighth Street, right smack in the middle of town).

French's Diner is heaven on earth for people who've driven a hundred miles farther than they meant to in search of lunch. I like it best for breakfast, but there are no bad meals on these premises. Fruit cobblers, in season, and all kinds of things you thought nobody could make like your mother—especially if you were born in the South and your mother enjoyed a more than nodding acquaintance with a big, black kitchen stove.

The BMW 635CSi is one of a handful of cars that might be perfect for this run. I've done it in a Mercedes, a Jaguar XJ6, a Volvo 760, a Chrysler LeBaron convertible, and a Dodge Voyager minivan (last year). One year we tried it in a brand-new Rover 3500, upon which everything but the engine and driveline had stopped working by journey's end. The other three occasions were handled by the former magazine's company airplane, which was quick, but absolutely no match for this BMW on the fun scale.

I was really hard on BMW's coupe when it was first introduced in 1976 as the 630CSi. It was a little like all those American cars that have been introduced with great fanfare as "BMW beaters" in the last decade. It looked like a BMW, and it sounded like a BMW, and in fact it was not unlike a BMW, but it didn't have any of the fiery competence that we had come to associate with that marque. The lack was intensified by the knowledge that German customers were able to buy real BMW coupes while we were limited to the ersatz export model, unless we wanted to patronize the gray market.

With the belated introduction of the 633CSi, the coupe got considerably better. And now that we can buy the 635CSi from an authorized BMW dealer here in the big PX, there can be rejoicing, general and unrestrained. This is a first-rate automobile, and a perfect example of what it is that seasoned enthusiasts find so exciting in German performance cars. It's strong, fast, and comfortable, and it goes where you point it with a sharp crispness that we all dream of, but seldom experience.

Our test BMW was so nearly perfect on the demanding roads of West Virginia that I am convinced anew that faster cars are safer cars. I'm an aggressive driver—though not compulsively so—and I really believe that a car with some serious acceleration and top-speed capability significantly expands my portfolio of alternatives when things get dicey. Obviously, driving such a car out near its limits has exactly the opposite effect, reducing one's options in moments of great dread. But when used properly, the fast car is, to my mind, the safer car. And, to add another qualifier, the fast car to which I refer is one that stops and steers and sticks as well as it goes. I've owned a couple of Sixties muscle cars, and they were fast, but they sure weren't safe.

I happily rest my case with the BMW 635CSi.

Four-wheel-drive funeral.

T here are no good funerals, although Hitler's might have been fun to attend, had he had one, and I do think I'd like to go to Ralph Nader's. However, I *did* participate in a burial ceremony that had some diverting moments not long ago, starting with a funeral procession that included a 4x4 Suburban, a beat-up red Ford pickup with four-wheel drive, and a Honda three-wheeler.

Last spring my Aunt Harriette died. My Aunt Harriette Simpson Arnow was a famous writer. Among other things, fiction and nonfiction, Aunt Harriette wrote a great novel called *The Dollmaker,* which over the decades became a sort of cult book in the women's movement, then gained new fame a couple of years ago when Jane Fonda made it into a TV movie.

The Dollmaker was about the migration of rural southerners to the factories in the north, specifically about a Kentucky woman who tried in vain to keep her family and its values intact when they left home and moved to Detroit and the wartime automobile factories. My mother and father, my Aunt Harriette, my Aunt Lucy, and my Aunt Willie all participated in that great migration, and although none of them came to work in the car plants, my dad did spend some time on a Ford assembly line during the Depression, as did I some sixteen or seventeen years later.

Harriette enjoyed a special place in our family's regard because she was, after all, the only one of us to achieve fame. Her first book was published in the Thirties, and it made her more than an aunt or a sister or a cousin, it made her a literary figure in a family that lived surrounded by books, a family that loved the contents of its books the way other families loved silver plate or ancestral portraits. It was my books, as much as my knock-knees, that kept me from achieving very much as an athlete. (Racing sports cars was the first and only sporting success I enjoyed, until years later when I got serious about shotguns.)

So Harriette died last year. She was a strange old bird, and though I had never been particularly close to her, I did have a great deal of respect for her and I had failed to attend her husband's funeral the year before, so I was determined to be on hand for her interment. I was also motivated to attend by tales of that earlier burial, which she had decreed—for maximum inconvenience, according to my mother—would take place way back in the Kentucky hills on a farm they'd owned since her first writing success, and which had turned into a pretty colorful adventure, what with icy, rutted trailed and a borrowed National Guard six-by-six that lurched and heaved and skidded hauling the deceased and the burial party up the holler to the grave site.

My Uncle Jim Simpson said, "You can't imagine what a sight it was with all them old women hangin' on for dear life and tryin' to keep from being crushed by that coffin slidin' around in the back of that truck!"

Harriette had asked to be cremated, so there'd be no coffin to slide around, and I figured that I could get my hands on some suitable four-wheel-drive vehicle that would eliminate the need for one of the National Guard's six-by-sixes. All we had to do was wait for the spring thaw, so that my favorite uncle, Uncle Jim, wouldn't have to dynamite a grave in the frozen ground.

I managed to recruit a Chevrolet Suburban 4x4 for the occasion. It would hold a bunch of old ladies and the burial urn, and it would go about anywhere. My sister and I drove it from Michigan to Ohio, collected our mother, motored on to the Seven Gables Motel in Burnside, Kentucky—a couple of miles from my birthplace, and as close as we come to having a family seat. (I fell hopelessly in love with a mint, snow white, 1963 Cadillac Sedan de Ville in the motel parking lot.)

All trips in Suburbans—Chevrolet or GMC, two- or four-wheel drive, gas or diesel—are pretty pleasant. This one was powered by GM's wonderful 6.2-liter diesel, which is a paragon of oil-burner virtue. The vehicle will keep up with Interstate traffic anywhere in North America, and its extra height makes sightseeing even more pleasurable. Driver and passengers can see over the guardrails and bridge railings, which is a considerable advantage. I've been the very satisfied owner of two Suburbans, a 454 and a 350, so the trip to Kentucky was like old home week in more ways than one.

My bereaved cousins were there when we arrived.

My New York cousin: a stocky, energetic female of the type who wears navy watch sweaters and rolled-up overall pants and knows more about everything than her relatives. Her attention seemed divided between the logistical details of the burial and profit enhancement opportunities of the deceased's literary portfolio and correspondence.

My San Antonio cousin: a woolly bear of a computer wizard who has lived the life of the mind for so long that he is often ambushed by cultural breakthroughs, like the discovery of room service in hotels, or blue shirts with white collars and cuffs. He told me that he used to get my former magazine at the public library, but this new one seemed only to be available on newsstands, so he hadn't read it.

My mother was tartly ironic, my sister was impatient with my mother, my Aunt Lucy was sweetly conciliatory, and my cousins ran my Uncle Jim ragged. I would occasionally go sit in the Suburban.

Saturday morning dawned and we piled into the vehicles and set out for the backwoods burial site. Most of the trail was steeply up or down, and spring's thaws had knocked the bottom out. Water ran in pretty impressive volumes through every low spot.

The New York cousin wanted to ride in on the back of the three-wheeler, which rocketed off across the muck and mire as though it were pavement. My Uncle Jim and his wife took the old Ford pickup—which was almost as good as the ATV by virtue of its knobby tires and bags of ground clearance—and broke trail for the rest of us in the Chevy Suburban.

In the last deep cut, just before we reached the old graveyard, the Suburban's rear overhang nearly did us in. While the ladies chatted, I thought grimly about the possibility of being marooned out there in the middle of the Pennyroyal, then rared back and slammed it forward—full throttle, low range, low gear. Nothing. I then rocked it violently. The ladies, innocent of our peril, continued their discourse. Finally, with a little leeway rearward, I hammered it forward again and we slithered into the hallowed ground at an unseemly high rate of knots. The ladies dismounted, and my uncle's eloquence once again proved up to the challenge. The urn was set into its resting place; Uncle Jim and his friend, the ATV owner, manned the shovels; Aunt Lucy walked off into the dappled shade to be alone with her thoughts; and my mother sniffled discreetly. I mused about how I was going to get them back out to the highway. The New York cousin then announced that she felt it would be best if she and her brother and assorted aged persons in attendance walked back up the mountain. The aged persons demurred, and I did my best to avert the brewing mutiny by darting over to the beckoning Suburban and throwing open its doors, as though the matter were all settled.

We roared out through the sticky bits, and I found that regaining the high road wasn't so dicey after all. In keeping with the occasion, I played my Waylon and Willie tape very quietly, front speakers only, and the ladies continued their chat in the soft breeze of the air conditioning. When last seen in the Suburban's big side mirrors, the New York cousin was leading her perspiring brother and a more distant cousin out of the holler on foot, blissfully at one with the rocks and ruts of her infancy.

In the deathless words of Mel Brooks, "Her in her way, me in mine."

It's a cold and lonely job, ma'am, but somebody's gotta do it.

ritish Air, Flight 621, Geneva-London—The Geneva International Motor Show is great fun, not because lots of new cars get premiered there, but because it's the first big European show each year, the place where everybody in the planet's automobile industry emerges from winter hibernation to see and be seen. The atmosphere is very convivial, and everything (and everybody) looks bright and chipper. We go to Frankfurt and Tokyo and Chicago for new cars, Geneva for old friends.

This year, my wife and I arranged to arrive at Geneva on the preceding Saturday so that we might spend a couple of days unwinding in the French Jura with a very entertaining French lady who used to be her mother-in-law. Lars Eriksson, president of Saab's Swiss distribution company, had laid on a 9000 Turbo for us, and we were really looking forward to the short dash—an hour or so, depending on how fast you drive—from the Geneva airport to the former mother-in-law's village of Thoirette.

Our luggage failed to make it to Geneva on the plane that brought us, so we piled into the Saab and drove into town to eat lunch and kill time until the next flight brought our traps. The traffic was a fright. Worse than Manhattan. Worse than Paris. Switzerland has been left out of all the worthwhile wars since the country's defeat by the French, led by Francois I, at Marignan in 1515, and this has clearly had a bad effect on the Swiss population. Aggressive, killer types who might have been expected to suffer a disproportionately high mortality rate in more warlike societies have been allowed to breed in the *Confédération Helvétique,* and all of their recessive tendencies are unleashed on their fellow motorists. The Saab is a lovely weapon in this kind of mock war, and we cheerfully chopped, faced down, and otherwise blew off several of our more disagreeable, less attractive adversaries. J.L.K. Davis, who once lived in Geneva, proved to be a formidable navigator, if we disregard that moment when we crossed the bridge and she ordered me to turn right, putting us smartly into a pitch black underground parking lot.

Lunch at L'Entrecôte, right in the heart of the bucks-up shopping district, was terrific, and we finished with exactly the right amount of time to race back to the airport and collect the prodigal duffel.

The drive into France started well enough, but deteriorated abruptly between Bellegarde and Nantua. It was the end of a French school holiday and ten miles of *route nationale* were plugged solid in both directions with carloads of skis and skiers. When our lane at last began to clear up, and traffic began to move, the oncoming side was still a parking lot, and we experienced something I hadn't seen since I drove back to the ferry from the Targa Florio in 1967—impatient, suicidal drivers who pulled out to pass, coming straight at me, sometimes at pretty high speeds, often from around blind curves or over the tops of blind crests. Once I found myself grille-to-grille with an idiot in a Citroën DS21 who—unable to force his way back into his lane—simply screeched to a halt. Thrills, chills, mile-a-minute excitement!

The last few kilometers into Thoirette were a joy. We'd parted company with the vacation traffic and the mountain road was all ours. We tore through the spitting rain from one corner to the next; manually downshifting the automatic, hard on the brakes; then flooring it and shifting up with the tach needle wiping the dial toward the redline and the latest apex falling behind us. I'd never driven an automatic Saab before, and it strengthened my growing belief that really fast, really contemporary cars no longer require manual gear-boxes. Today that choice has become strictly a matter of personal taste. I only wish that the 9000 looked more like a Saab and less like all those Renaults and Lancias. It has lost its charming quirks and become a generic Eurosedan. But, thank goodness, the part between the ball of your right foot and the pavement is still 100 percent Saab Turbo.

Madam Yvonne Korda, our hostess for the weekend, is seventy-nine, and travels more or less constantly. We arrived to find her briefly at home between a trip to Thailand and one to Cairo. Her fifteenth-century house is neither a château nor a farmhouse, yet it has the character of both. With meter-thick stone walls, a tower, and walk-in fireplaces it dramatically evokes a sense of the Middle Ages. Our bedroom looked out on a garden followed by a meadow followed by a mountain and we slept in a four-poster bed, when we weren't eating Madame Korda's world-class food and washing it down with burgundies and beaujolais from her ample cellar. (The heart of the burgundy district is about an hour away, on the road to Paris.)

We talked about her next car. Another Toyota? A Subaru? What about four-wheel drive? Her three-year-old Starlet has served nobly and reliably and shows no sign of faltering in the loyal performance of its duty, but one must think ahead. She is reassured to learn that Toyota is still the wonderful builder of cars with whom she did business three years ago, but she'd like to try a Subaru, if only for its four-wheel drive. What? A Toyota with four-wheel drive? *Incroyable!* The best of both worlds!

She has taken up snorkeling. Could we meet her in Baja California sometime? The snorkeling there is said to be excellent. We talk about the war, and what an intimate thing it was in this part of France. She tells us about the neighboring village of Dortan, where the Nazis burned all the houses, then stood the men and boys on a wall and machine-gunned them. Each year there is a dinner for the surviving heroes of the Resistance in her neighborhood. They are so proud, she says, so special. It was for each of these men the high point of his life.

On Monday morning we drive back to Geneva and the show. The roads are clear and we go like hell. Monday night is a Volkswagen dinner. Audi's vice-chairman, Engineer Piëch—he of the zealot's glittering eye and the goofy grin—drops by to explain in no uncertain terms that the so-called sudden acceleration problem has no technical solution, that it is uniquely American and uniquely linked to small women who are former drivers of GM products, who are not the primary drivers of the Audi, and who have driven it less than 2000 miles. His impolitic candor must be a public relations man's nightmare, yet I'm more inclined to believe him than I am those East Coast safety Nazis, who speculate about conspiracies.

On Tuesday we breakfast with Volvo and eyeball the odd little 480ES, which will come to America from Holland in November. On the adjacent stand is Mercedes-Benz, and the star of their show—of the *whole* show, to be honest—is the new 300CE coupe. A stunner, it would be even better with the sport grille of the 560SEC and 560SL. Pininfarina's stand features a chrome yellow Testarossa and a shiny new Cadillac Allanté which looks perfectly at home among Europe's high rollers.

Wednesday at the salon is more of the same. The *Palais des Expositions* is full of people I'm delighted to see again. Wednesday evening is the justly famous Saab dinner. On the way there, Lindamood gets us lost three times. On our third trip back down the Geneva-Lausanne autoroute, certain we've got it right this time, I lay the 9000's speedometer needle on 210kph and pass everybody. I mean *everybody*. We are not arrested, and the Saab party is well worth the getting lost. We drink aquavit, we drink wine, we skoal, we sing, we fall into bed at three in the morning.

Our flight leaves Geneva at 9:05 a.m. My eyes burn, as does my heart. The lady at the bar at the terminal refuses to give me a free glass of water that I might quaff the lifesaving Alka Seltzer stashed in my wife's purse. (This *is* Switzerland, after all.) She is probably kin to the security churl who angrily refused to hand-search the Colin Curwood films I'm carrying, insisting that I send them through the X-ray machine. Sorry, Colin.

For us, the Geneva show is over for another year. If BA keeps its promises and we make our connection in London, I'll be in the office this afternoon, fifteen hours from now. Not bad.

Enzo Campana: Imagine the cars he's driven and the adventures he's had.

~~~~~

Modena, Italy—Enzo Campana has been a Ferrari test driver for twenty-four years. To me, he looks like a racing driver of the classic era, a hairy-armed hero despite his costume of plaid shirt and baggy gray flannel slacks. He's built like a former athlete, with long ropy muscles in his arms and back, and the beginnings of a belly that seems still to be more muscle than lard. He's taller than the younger test drivers and his hair is iron-gray and cut short, which gives him an air of authority. It was my extreme good fortune to have Enzo Campana drive me back down the mountain from the restaurant where we had lunch on the second day of our visit to the Ferrari factory. The afternoon was gorgeous and sunny, our car was a bright yellow American-model Testarossa, and *Signor* Campana was in high good humor.

We'd started the day with a tour of the Scaglietti works, where they build the 328 and Mondial bodies. Then we bussed over to Ferrari's headquarters at Maranello to meet the test drivers, whom we found lounging around a small fleet of brand-new Ferraris awaiting their shakedown drives. Every new Ferrari is road-tested this way, on a route that includes congested streets, mountain roads, and some autostrada. The fleet included several Testarossas and 328s, along with a couple of Mondials. I chose a red Mondial cabriolet, destined for Great Britain, as my first ride. Its driver, Emer Campana (Enzo Campana's younger brother), leaped to get the door for me. Do I look that old? I slid into the passenger seat, wound my feet around a very large fire extinguisher that lay in the footwell in a metal frame, and got reasonably comfortable.

Once under way, idling through the busy streets of the town, we passed a fat old priest wearing light brown pants under his cassock, then came face to face with Enzo Ferrari himself being driven to work in a silver Lancia Thema. Then we broke free of the town and raced up into the hills. Looking back over my shoulder, I could see a string of cars behind us, led by a black Testarossa that threatened to drive right over us each time we braked for a hairpin turn. Campana the younger shifted at 5000 rpm, and drove in exaggeratedly choppy fashion—hard on the throttle, hard on the brakes, snatching at the steering wheel, and punching the shift lever into each new gear. This might have been part of his testing discipline, but I believe it was just his personality. We crested the ridge and found several of our compatriots already there, a yellow Testarossa parked on the right with its engine compartment open to release a cloud of smelly gray vapor. Nothing serious, just more evidence that these guys don't fool around. Each test driver then went through a set drill, poking and prying and whacking various components in turn, and making notes.

I then traded cars and drivers with *Auto Week*'s Leon Mandel, moving to a bilious green Mondial coupe, ordered by a Swiss customer, being test-driven on this occasion by Valerio Vandelli. Valerio Vandelli looked like he might have been auditioning for the road company of *West Side Story*. He wore a pink dress shirt with his T-shirt showing at the neck, Levis, white socks, black oxfords, and black Ray-Bans hanging around his neck on a cord. He drove smoothly and aggressively, shifting at 6000 rpm—an altogether different driving style from Emer Campana's.

Valerio Vandelli turned out to be just like the rest of us. He occasionally went one gear too low entering a corner and had to sheepishly upshift halfway around (with the tail hung out to *there*), and he'd often give the throttle a little supplementary blip an instant before engaging the clutch on upshifts, just as I do when I can't resist showing off. Testing the sound system involved dialing up some Italian disco, which, if anything, is even sillier than Italian rock-and-roll. Once, we almost collected an elderly couple riding down the mountain on a small wagon towed by a walk-behind garden tractor of the rototiller type (these are to be seen on the roads all over Italy, doing most everything cars and light-duty trucks do). Later, when we hit the autostrada, Valerio ran the 3.2-liter V-8 up to 6200 rpm in fifth, which the speedometer said was 240 kilometers per hour (150 mph), and which provided really dramatic closing speeds with the other traffic.

At the end of our autostrada run he paid our toll and pulled off to make some notes about a rattle in either the engine cover or the luggage compartment lid. While we were stopped, I watched putteed policemen, very correct, arresting people whose elapsed time between tollbooths was less than it should have been. In sign language and pidgin English, Valerio indicated that such things did not happen to Ferrari test drivers.

Back at the factory, we switched to a dark blue 412 automatic for the run to lunch. I looked forward to some time in a car powered by the Ferrari V-12 I've so loved over the years, though my enthusiasm was tempered somewhat by the presence of the automatic selector lever. At first I thought that the automatic had killed the famous V-12 engine noise and exhaust note, but the first time Valerio Vandelli put the pedal to the floor I knew how wrong I'd been. The noise, both in volume and tone, was actually painful.

The 412—descended from the 365GT4 2+2—is Ferrari's oldest current model, and it feels old. It's big and wide, and there's a sensation of sitting on it, rather than in it. A red Testarossa, not part of our group, came down the road toward us and pulled out to pass. Our closing speed was about 200 miles per hour and an accident seemed inevitable, yet all I could think of was how much this head-on collision was going to cost. At the last instant, the TR braked and nipped back into its original slot. Chicken. Farther on, we were entering an uphill hairpin and the 412's front end simply washed out when Valerio hit the brakes. He gathered it up with a jab at the throttle and a lot of winding on the steering wheel, but for just a moment it was the most vivid demonstration of understeer I'd ever experienced. It was clear that Valerio Vandelli was not an automatic transmission enthusiast and I was not displeased when we arrived at the restaurant.

After a large lunch and a lot of wine (which I surreptitiously watered), one of our hosts waved me into Enzo Campana's yellow Testarossa for the ride back to Maranello. We were second away from the restaurant, following the morning's black TR as though we were on a tow bar. Halfway down there was a Tee intersection where we all stopped, and the high revs we could hear coming from the black car indicated that he was determined to induce some serious wheelspin (difficult to do, because of the huge Goodyear tires on the back of the Testarossa). He succeeded all too well and instead of a 90-degree turn to the left, lost it, did an abrupt 180, and shot straight back up the road we'd just come down.

This left us in first position, and Enzo Campana took full advantage of it. In an instant we were hurtling down the side of the mountain on a two-lane road at an indicated 130 miles per hour, flashing past houses and slower traffic like a homing Exocet, with a half-dozen Ferraris of various models and colors strung out behind us—the black TR now bringing up the rear. All of the test drivers seem to prefer the tails-out dirt-track mode of high-speed travel, and it was absolutely exhilarating, not even remotely frightening, even though our car's U.S.-spec passive belts were inoperative and I had a pretty good idea of how far I'd fly if we made contact with some solid obstacle.

The first potential obstacle was a police car trundling along at what appeared to be bare forward motion. As we dived down upon it, Enzo Campana removed both hands from the steering wheel and crossed his wrists to convey the idea of handcuffs. Then, banging me on the thigh to emphasize his point, he sort of explained, as had Valerio Vandelli earlier in the day, that Ferrari test drivers were immune to police harassment. The mere fact that they weren't shooting at us more than proved the point for me.

There was a deep valley off to our right, just beyond the edge of the road, and there were beautiful farms and forests aplenty for anyone who cared about scenery. But it was the blond prostitute parked on the verge in the white Renault 5 that really got Enzo Campana's attention. She was sitting with her door open so that passing motorists could savor the full effect of her long tanned legs, feet propped on the dash, leather miniskirt concealing little, if anything, and her long hair draped over the seatback.

Again, removing his large hands from the steering wheel, Enzo Campana used graphic sign language, accompanied by a rhythmic through-the-teeth whistle, to explain what she did for a living, in case I'd missed it on the flashpast. Some of our colleagues, unwilling to risk their five-course lunches with the test drivers, passed the lady's place of business on the bus a few minutes later and reported that the black Testarossa was parked just down the road. We were told that it had thrown an alternator belt, but we'll never know, will we.

Back at the factory, the test drivers were obviously high from the impromptu post-prandial race, and there was a lot of explosive laughter and rapid-fire Italian in the courtyard behind the plant lobby. Enzo Campana tried to make me believe that the reason the cars were sideways so much was the Goodyear tires. Sure, Enzo. And I get my suits made in London so I won't have to wrap my body in animal skins. But I wasn't feeling contentious. I just stood there and smelled the brakes, and listened to the chassis creak and pop, and savored the best ride I'd ever had in my entire life.

In defense of yuppies and yuppie cars.

~ಀ~

Yuppies, and so-called yuppie cars, are getting a bad rap. The word "yuppie" invariably pronounced or printed with a sneer, is a mistake in the first place. It is supposed to be an acronym for "Young, Upwardly Mobile Professional." "Yumpie," to be precise. Unfortunately, "yumpie" sounds like a Swedish description of PMS symptoms, or other stress-related tensions, so the word was cleaned up, streamlined, and became "yuppie." Right or wrong, the word describes the people who are the movers and shakers in our society to a T, and it just drives college professors and newspaper reporters of the Sixties generation up the wall. When applied to cars, it seems to mean almost any car you or I would like to own.

Yuppies are not new, regardless of what you may have heard from the grinning oracles that bring us our news on the haunted fish tank. Nor are they all latter-day Babbitts, wearing gold chains and iridescent alumicron suits, hanging out in singles bars between insider trading scams. Young, upwardly mobile professionals were first created by the GI Bill after World War II. Young people who'd have had no chance at the good life, prewar, suddenly found themselves with easy access to colleges and universities and all the good stuff that lay beyond. Thanks to the GI Bill, they had upward social and economic mobility that their parents could never have imagined.

Those were the men and women who started the imported car movement in the United States. It has often been suggested that the passion for imported cars first sprang up among the rich and famous in places like Greens Farms, Connecticut, and Hollywood, California. Café society played its part to be sure, but they'd been driving imported cars since the birth of the automobile. This was a grass-roots movement among people who'd seen another way of life when they went off to war; who came home with an utterly different set of aspirations as a result. Along with their new-found enthusiasm for Volkswagens and Renaults and DKWs and Austins and MGs, they developed a taste for imported films, imported beers and wines, imported culture. I know, because I was one of them—too young for World War II, but waiting there with my cultural antennae fully extended when they came home.

What they sought was quality, and they bought imported products because they were convinced that European design and European craftsmanship were considerably better than what was available in the home-grown counterparts. Ironically, this led them to buy some really silly cars and some terrible-looking Grundig hi-fi sets. But silly as some of them may have been, the cars were smaller, more maneuverable, more fun to drive, more economical to operate, and they made a powerful statement about their owners' unwillingness to go along with the junk worship of the late Fifties, Sixties, and early Seventies. A powerful statement that our domestic industry has been trying to refute ever since, with minimal success.

When America's fascination with junk finally came crashing down, more or less simultaneously with the collapse of the Carter presidency, those quality seekers—along with their heirs and emulators— were ready to pick up the pieces. The search for quality had assumed national importance, and the so-called yuppies were in the vanguard.

Before this magazine was well and truly launched, I spoke to the Madison Avenue Sports Car Driving and Chowder Society at one of their justly famous New York luncheons, to tell them of our plans. I did my best to describe the magazine you now hold in your hands. I stressed our battle cry, "No Boring Cars"—that is to say, no coverage of cars that I find boring—and I promised a magazine with great photography and illustration, great quality of presentation, and the best writing available in the field of automotive journalism.

After thirty minutes of that, I wound down, and asked if there were any questions. I don't remember all the questions, but I do recall a large and imposing brunette from New Jersey who asked, distastefully, "Is this going to be some kind of *yuppie* magazine?"

I had just done my best to describe a high quality magazine aimed at high quality readers interested in cars with high entertainment value, and she was getting snarky about *yuppies*. I've thought about that moment a lot, since, and as happens in so many cases of that kind, subsequent periods of three a.m. wakefulness were filled with "I shoulda saids…"

I should have said:

"Well, ma'am, I really believe that we should stop all this discrimination against winners. Throughout the late Sixties and early

Seventies virtually the entire focus of the American press was on America's losers. If I never see another reverently photographed hippie commune, it'll be okay with me. Given a choice between the young, upwardly mobile state of mind, and the not-so-young, not-so-upwardly-mobile state of mind, to whom would you have me direct my magazine?

"I enjoy driving fast, sophisticated cars—the hated yuppie cars— to dinner parties where the people are well dressed, the conversation is memorable, the food is properly prepared, and the wine is carefully selected and lovingly served. I have no interest in macrobiotic meals attended barefoot in bib overalls. I was born in a place and time where people wore bib overalls and went barefoot out of necessity. I am a child of the Great Depression, and I know that in order to give me the Red Ryder BB gun with the cardboard lion target for Christmas in 1937, my parents had to stiff the guy who held their mortgage. I have fond memories of all that, but I work like hell so that I can order a Martin Hagn rifle for my wife without having to miss a house payment.

"I firmly believe that the founding fathers would have been more comfortable with the yuppies than with the yuppies' detractors. Strivers who work hard to better themselves, who struggle to own objects that give them pleasure, who want to feel the joyous rush of a great car on a fast road, really sound like the founding fathers' kind of people to me. It's not difficult to imagine Paul Revere making his midnight ride in a Corvette convertible, or Patrick Henry's Porsche parked in the shade outside the Virginia House of Burgesses."

Yes, I suppose this is some kind of yuppie magazine, to answer the lady's question. But we must define our terms. My yuppies aren't dope dealers or crooked investment bankers. My yuppies are solid citizens who would rather shape their lives than complain about them. And I'm on their side.

Who has the keys to the Jaguar?

Automobile Magazine celebrates its second Christmas, Hanuka, and winter solstice, as well as a few pagan rites.

~∿⊱~

T he holiday spirit at *Automobile Magazine* is as ecumenical as it is convivial. We embrace all creeds, cults, and persuasions at this holiday season. Even witless zealots from places like the Center for Auto Safety are welcome to share our Christmas tree, our menorah, our *buche de Noël,* our *Advent Kranz,* our panettone, our single-malt whisky (served with fruitcake from the Collins Avenue Bakery in Corsicana, Texas), our Stilton, and our port (Dow's, '70). Actually, if we really get into the pagan rites, somebody from the Center for Auto Safety might be *very* welcome—nobody ever said that human sacrifices had to be friends or family.

I am one of a tiny handful of men in the universe who has everything he needs. My wants are a different matter, but I will live out my days in happiness if none of my remaining wants is gratified. Obviously, I wouldn't turn down a blown K3 Magnette, and if my children chip in to buy me a 377 aluminum Chevy small-block engine, my gratitude will be unforgettable, but I really do have enough shotguns, autofocus cameras, Bell helmets, luggage, Montblanc pens, T-shirts, and running shoes to do me. I could use some more jockey shorts, and I lost my record of *Beyond the Fringe* in the divorce twelve years ago and I'd like a replacement, but beyond that...

The fact is, I bought my own Christmas present this year, a gleaming red Kougar Jaguar with wire wheels and a great whomping vintage Jaguar exhaust note. The car belonged to the late Tony Hogg, of *Road & Track* fame. His wife, Betty, called last summer to say that she'd decided to sell the dear old beast and to ask if I was still interested in buying it. Of course I was. A deal was struck in that very telephone conversation, and the Kougar Jaguar was betrothed to me.

Tony and I used to drive together on press flogs, or camp out together at hotel bars here and there around the world, and talk about that car. He loved it, and it irked him royally that his feckless Trackie co-workers failed to understand or appreciate the Kougar's magic. Well, I appreciate it, and now I own it. As personal transportation, it is every bit as cranky and idiosyncratic as Tony Hogg himself. Merry Christmas to me, and Merry Christmas to Tony.

I'm delighted to have come to grips with the Christmas holiday. For a while it depressed me, rendered me almost suicidal (I guess it *is* a peak season for people scragging themselves), but that was before I married the present Mrs. Davis in 1976, and, coincidentally, rejoined *Car and Driver*. Now, with each passing year, Christmas and I improve our relationship.

I recall another Jaguar Christmas, in 1955. On the preceding October thirtieth, I had scraped off the left side of my face in a race at Sacramento, driving my own MG. I was a walking horror, and my weight had dropped from 201 to 144, largely because my smashed jaws were wired shut. My left eye's lids were gone, as was the bridge of my nose, and all but twelve of my teeth. We were broke. I couldn't work, and my wife had spent all those weeks at the hospital looking after me— while the bills kept piling up. Our weimaraner pup—named after Manfred von Brauchitsch, the great Mercedes driver who fled to East Germany after the war when his troubles got out of hand—had surprised us by eating the arm of the maple sofa in our furnished apartment. Our only car, the red MG with the yellow wire wheels, was sitting right where the truck had dropped it, in back of the body shop in Hermosa Beach, waiting for us to come up with the money for repairs. Things looked grim.

We wanted a Christmas tree and couldn't afford one, so we bor-rowed a lovely old Jag Mark IV drophead from our friend Tom Dole, rolled the top back to the intermediate "de ville" position, and drove over to La Cañada and up onto the Angeles Crest Highway. It was a gorgeous winter day—still my favorite time of year in Southern California—and we could see for miles in every direction. Tumbleweeds were plentiful and we were searching for a perfect one. The big cream-colored Jag trun-dled along happily, apparently caught up in the spirit of the thing, and when we found the tumbleweed we sought, and made a U-turn to head back to Manhattan Beach, the old girl gathered up her skirts and tottered through the turns more like a real sports car than a cad's imitation Bentley. We rushed home with our trophy, sprayed it silver with an aerosol can, and hung it from the ceiling. Combined with some inex-pensive wine from the supermarket and telephone calls from worried parents back East, it made for a rather festive Christmas Eve.

Not as festive as this one, however. I look around me, filled with the milk of human kindness and five or six ounces of Old Marriage Counselor, and my world looks pretty fine. While this mood is upon me,

I'd like to send some thank yous and express some Christmas wishes.

To *Automobile Magazine:* Continued success, and a move into the black in the coming new year.

To the readers of and the advertisers in *Automobile Magazine:* Thanks from the bottoms of our hearts for your enthusiastic loyalty and support. Without you, we couldn't have accomplished any of this.

To Rupert Murdoch, and the stalwarts at News America and Murdoch Magazines: Thank you for seeking us out and putting us in business, and thank you for your patience and assistance as we've struggled to turn the shared dream into a profitable reality.

To the people at *Car and Driver* and *Road & Track:* A happier new year. Now that CBS has sold you, and now that it looks as if at least some of you will get sold yet again, my advice would be to have a little cognac and some warm milk before going to bed at night. And when you wake up staring into the hostile darkness at three in the morning, wondering what's going to happen to you, try remembering the cubic-inch displacements of all the great engines since World War II and visualizing each of those numbers in a different typeface. That's what I used to do.

To all the good guys in the automobile industry: We want you to get everything you desire in the coming year. Thank you for the Porsche 959, all production Porsches except the 924S, the Pontiac Bonneville SSE, the Ferrari Testarossa, the Toyota MR2, the Chevrolet Corvette, all Mercedes-Benzes (except diesels), the Mazda RX-7 Turbo, the Lincoln Mark VII LSC, the Range Rover, the Acura Legend coupe, the Cadillac Allanté, all BMWs (especially the M-cars), the Toyota Supra Turbo, the revamped Pontiac Fiero, the Ford Mustang 5.0 GT, the Lamborghini Countach, the Chevrolet and GMC Suburbans, the Rolls-Royce and Bentley, the Nissan Pathfinder, all Aston Martins, the Dodge and Plymouth minivans, all Hondas, the Ferrari Mondial 3.2, the intercooled Peugeot 505 Turbo, the Merkur Scorpio and XR4Ti, the Volvo 740 Turbo, the Volkswagen GTI, the Sterling 825SL, the Saab 9000 Turbo, the Saab 900 Turbo, the Audi in all its forms, all four-wheel-drive Subarus, and, too, for the continued survival of Jeep and Renault in the American marketplace. Also, for turbochargers, superchargers, electronic fuel injection, anti-lock brakes, traction control, four-wheel drive, four-wheel steering, active suspension, Carroll Shelby, and all the other things that make this a lively and endlessly fascinating way to make a living.

To all the bad guys in the automobile business, and every other walk of life: We sincerely hope that you get everything you deserve.

Happy Holidays!

All-Stars.

~∿∿~

owson, Maryland—It's Sunday, and I'm comfortably ensconced in the computer room at the Goucher College library, writing this to the accompaniment of the occasional discreet cough and the quiet murmur of female voices around me. Not bad. My stepdaughter, who's a freshman here, arranged for me to work thus while she and her mother and her roommate shop till they drop.

This is our first annual All-Stars issue. The whole idea of All-Stars has been much on my mind as we pulled this together, and I decided that the subject was suitable grist for American Driver's mill.

I've been on the road for two weeks—first at the Frankfurt show, then promoting our magazine in New York and Washington—with three more weeks to go. Three more weeks of midnight radio talk shows and early morning TV appearances. I'll do the West Coast, Texas, Florida, Boston, Detroit, Chicago, and wind up, finally, at the gigantic Tokyo show.

A couple of days into this trip, in West Germany, I was waiting for a press conference to begin and suddenly saw Juan Manuel Fangio—in my estimation the greatest racing driver ever to take hold of a steering wheel—coming across the foyer toward me. I greeted him deferentially and shook his hand, and was amazed anew at his strength and the hardness of that hand—he is not a kid, after all. It isn't that he squeezes hard when grasping my hand, but rather that there's a feeling of immense reserves of strength flowing from his hand into mine. For me, Juan Manuel Fangio is a god, and being that close to a god makes me wonder how I got so lucky. Had you told me that it would work out like this when I saw him race at Sebring, more than thirty years ago, I would have snorted with cheerful disbelief.

Four days ago, as part of this promotional tour, I was interviewed by a singularly ungodlike business writer at the *New York Post*. He didn't know why I was there, nor did he want to do the interview. He slammed things around, grumped endlessly to himself, and wound up breaking his tape recorder. It goes without saying that he was one of those legions of New Yorkers who think of cars only as yellow conveyances with lights on their roofs, and could only shake his head in puzzlement as I enthused over my favorite subject.

When the ordeal was over, I gloomily took my leave of the old Philistine and found my wife in the news room, awaiting my return with a sunny smile. "You know what I just did?" she asked. "I just made reservations for tonight at Michael's Pub. We'll eat something and catch Mel Tormé's music." I am a sucker for Mel Tormé's music. I went through high school listening to a local disc jockey, Jack the Bellboy, play "Foggy Day in London Town" and "County Fair" almost daily.

One might say that Mel Tormé is the Juan Manuel Fangio of jazz vocalists. His voice is like Fangio's handshake, forever youthful and immensely strong. The show that night was a tour de force from the moment he hopped onto the small stage till he disappeared out the door an hour later to thunderous applause. Mel Tormé is also a committed car freak. He owned one of the first MG TCs in the United States, and now drives an immaculate Jaguar SS-100. He loves to talk cars, and he says he'd like to write a piece for *Automobile Magazine*. I've encouraged him to do that, and, again, it makes me wonder why I'm so lucky. If the guy can write like he sings, a lot of automotive journalists had best look to their laurels.

The cynics tell us that there are no heroes. I guess that's why I feel such contempt for cynicism. I shook hands with a true hero in Germany the other day, and listened, enraptured, to another at Michael's Pub last Thursday evening. And just for good measure, I flipped on the TV set this morning while trying to convince myself that I should go out and run, and there, on "CNN News," was Karol Wojtyla, Pope John Paul II, greeting the multitudes in Detroit, my old home town. I'm not Catholic, not even a practicing Protestant, but that elderly Polish gent in the white gown and matching beanie—riding in his glassed-in Geländewagen, followed by his entourage of white Pontiac Bonnevilles—is hero enough for all of us. He may be the most heroic figure of our era, and I'm proud to share the planet with him. I wonder if he loves cars.

Four-wheel drive.

~ั้ะ~

*L*akeville, Connecticut—Four-wheel drive must be ranked not far below the wheel itself when we assign values to man's great discoveries in the transportation arts. I have four-wheel-driven through the sticks and pickers of two dozen states, seven countries, and three continents, and my off-road memories are right up there with the very best of my pavement reminiscences. In fact, I might stack the Jeepers Jamboree up against any of them. Driving securely over and through terrain where lesser vehicles cannot follow is good for the spirit, and whoever first thought of a way to drive all four wheels gets a seat in my pantheon of automotive heroes. Life without four-wheel drive would be, for me, unthinkable.

Imagine Hannibal's astonishment if he'd come over the Alps with his elephants only to have the Gauls and the Celts set upon him with Lamborghini LM002 all-terrain vehicles. Not as attractive as his pachyderms, perhaps, but certainly enough to get old Hannibal thinking about the less trying technological climate back in Spain, or Carthage.

We Americans like to think that our jets discouraged Mr. Kaddafi and put him out of the running for the title of Public Enemy Number One, but I wonder if perhaps it wasn't the Chadians and their killer Toyota pickups who convinced him he'd be safer pursuing his alternate career as Tripoli's most famous drag queen. One imagines the poor man unable to leave the family tent lest he be frightened out of his garter belt by some perfectly innocent citizen cruising past in a Toyota longbed four-by-four. I cannot imagine why our friends from Toyota City aren't running a saturation TV campaign showing their pickups swooping down out of the dunes to annihilate the Libyan T-55 tanks. The appeal is universal. The Indians attack the wagon train. The Charge of the Light Brigade. Compelling stuff! It would certainly sell trucks.

I thought about all this as I drove up the Taconic State Parkway from New York City to Dutchess County, not far from Connecticut's

Lime Rock racetrack. I was driving a Range Rover and I wasn't going to Lime Rock, despite the fact that there was a vintage car race going on. I was on my way to shoot in the Glenlivet Sporting Clay Challenge as a member of the Range Rover team. The event was a big one, put together by the British-American Chamber of Commerce, and though we of the Range Rover team were short on experience, we were long on high spirits and a healthy curiosity about the sporting life among the swells.

A tweedy, consommé-with-a-dollop-of-sherry event like this one is a magnet for the bucks-up four-wheel-drive crowd, and the parking areas around the Mashomack Fish and Game Preserve's polo field were filled with Suburbans and Grand Wagoneers, along with a surprising sprinkling of shiny new Range Rovers. I spotted one gray-market Mercedes-Benz Geländewagen, and of course there was a representative selection of Blazers and Broncos and Cherokees. But with entries from Great Britain's House of Lords, from the United States Senate (no-shows, for shame), a German team called "Epaulet," and a team of American gun writers, among others, this was not an outing for the guys driving the sky-high pickups with the earthmover tires.

Chevy and GMC Suburban owners have the highest demographics of any GM owner group, and the Jeep Grand Wagoneer has the highest demographics of *any* group of domestic car owners. Small wonder that those vehicles are seen in such numbers at horse shows, field trials, and related weekend activities. The real wonder is that Mercedes-Benz never brought the G-wagen to our shores. Surely, the success of Range Rover in North America must make them regret a wasted profit opportunity.

Similarly, the gurus of the New Chrysler Corporation must wonder how they can come up with a replacement for the klutzy old "Grand" Wagoneer. Its origins may be lost in the mists of automotive antiquity, but the guys with the fifteen-thousand-dollar bird dogs and the Stetson Open Road hats love it just the way it is, and turning it into a contemporary four-wheel-drive station wagon might prove to be its undoing. Tread softly here, New Chrysler Corporation.

As I drove north on the Taconic, admiring my fellow four-wheel-drivers' vehicles, I made mental notes of my reactions to the various examples on the road that day.

Chevy's S10 Blazer and GMC's S15 Jimmy are, to my mind, hands down the best-looking. They could use more power for highway work, and I find their rear seats virtually useless, but they win the prize for four-wheel drive in the cause of art. Ford's Bronco II is jaunty, even cute—particularly in the special Eddie Bauer model—but it doesn't quite match its GM counterparts for sheer good looks. Furthermore, it's a bit *too* small for my taste, and Ford's concerns about dry-road dynamics compromise the Bronco II in really rough stuff. A dedicated off-roader can disconnect its anti-roll bars to improve off-road performance, but one really shouldn't have to suffer such indignities.

The prize for *toughest*-looking four-by-four with two doors must go to the Toyota 4Runner. It really appears to be ready to kick Alps and take names. It has not been mentioned in dispatches from the war between Chad and Libya, but it is a fully appointed, enclosed four-seater, and this makes it difficult, I suppose, to mount a rocket launcher. Members of our staff have suggested that the 4Runner errs a bit on the trucky side, and have thus opted instead for the sleek Nissan Pathfinder. Because of this preference, we have ordered a Pathfinder for our long-term test fleet and look forward eagerly to flogging it through the worst that all four Temperate Zone seasons can offer.

The truth is that all the two-door vehicles in this class suffer in comparison with the four-doors. The Jeep Cherokee, with four doors, is half again as useful as a Blazer or a Bronco. Not just for rear-seat passengers, either. Everything is easier with four doors, be it loading your gear, folding the rear seats down, or finding the sandwich you left in your pajamas at the bottom of your duffel bag. The Cherokee is a bit more station wagon than all-out utility vehicle, but it does get the job done—provided you order the four-liter, six-cylinder engine.

Similarly, the Isuzu Trooper with four doors gives every assurance of being a really useful all-purpose utility vehicle, despite marginally acceptable power. I particularly like the looks of the LS model with its vinyl-armored sills. I saw my first one in Baja California a while back, and asked the owner if he had customized it. He was a very respectable gentleman from Washington State, accompanied by his blue-haired wife, and he replied somewhat archly that it had come that way from the factory and acted as though I'd asked if he'd passed his Wassermann. Nonetheless, I remain smitten by the four-door Trooper in that trim. We spent a very happy year with a Mitsubishi Montero (Dodge Raider), 1985-1986, and even though it must be the most easily lived with of the two-door four-by-four utilities, every time we went to Europe we looked longingly at the four-door Monteros (Pajeros) sold there. I'm convinced that four-doors are the hot ticket in this category.

The big Blazers, Jimmy, and Broncos have been made obsolete by their downsized offspring. The little ones are better vehicles in every way, unless sheer volume is one of your criteria—I suppose someone *might* wish to fill one with sand—and the big ones today seem to appeal mainly to young guys with whom you would not wish your daughter to go out. (The film *Deliverance* comes to mind.) However, add a pair of rear doors, as in the Suburban, and these old arks become something else altogether—the Montana Mercedes, as the Suburban has been called, or the National Car of Texas. They're called utility vehicles, so the more utility the better.

In two weeks, I'll be celebrating my wife's birthday with a group of friends. We're going to Great Britain, where we'll be exploring the hills and dales of Wales and Hampshire in a four-door Range Rover, a four-door Land Rover One Ten County, and a Mercedes Geländewagen. And, as a gesture to four-wheel drive in its most civilized form, four of us—two couples—will spend a second week exploring off-season Brittany in a four-wheel-drive Ford Scorpio.

Somebody alert the Gauls and the Celts.

Notes on the yellow legal pad.

hitton Hall, Shrewsbury, Shropshire, England—I spent 175,000 American Airlines AAdvantage miles for two first-class round-trip tickets to London, in celebration of my wife's birthday. Whitton Hall is a wonderful English country house, owned by Christopher and Gillian Halliday, and we will be here for three nights. There is at least one ghost, Gill's food is nonpareil, and the farm that surrounds Whitton Hall is home to 140 registered Jerseys, whom we watched being milked after tea this afternoon.

We are here through the good offices of a wonderful travel agency called Frontiers, which specializes in hunting and fishing adventures all over the world, and must certainly be the finest company of its kind. I don't know if you could just call the Hallidays and book a weekend at their home, but I fully intend to return once a year for the rest of my life, in order to shoot driven birds just across the border in Wales, to drive cars in one of the world's most beautiful places, to visit with our esteemed correspondent and drinking companion Mr. Phil Llewellin (who lives nearby), and to further examine my own Welsh roots.

We drove up from London with six other American couples, all pals, in a four-door Range Rover, a two-door Mercedes-Benz 280GE Geländewagen, a Ford Scorpio 4x4, and a long-wheelbase turbo-diesel Land Rover County—the current model Land Rover that now shares engine and suspension with its more posh sibling, the Range Rover.

So far, everybody loves the Range Rover and the Scorpio—the Range Rover because it's a full-fledged off-road utility vehicle that drives like a luxury sedan, and the Scorpio because it's a full-fledged luxury sedan that drives like a sports car (and has the most comfortable rear seat in most of our group's experience). Everyone in our little band is involved with cars, either professionally or as committed enthusiasts, or both, and their reactions are interesting. One guy, who devotes his life to selling General Motors products, sat in the driver's seat of the Scorpio, ran his fingertips over the small controls, and said reflectively, "This car is what Ford's 'Better Ideas' is all about. It's so thoughtfully done, and everything works so well." I agree, but I find it a bleeding shame that Ford doesn't ship the 4x4 Scorpio to the States.

Our Land Rover suffers a bit in their estimation because of its diesel engine, and the Geländewagen is taking a bad rap because the British Mercedes-Benz organization turned it over to us with a blown exhaust gasket. The noise is absolutely ear-splitting, and the poor old G stops everything in every village we pass through. Nonetheless, it's still a joy to drive, especially off-road. I love to play with the controls for the locking differentials, like some mad monk crouched over the out-of-tune organ in a mobile cathedral.

Mont-Saint-Michel, France—Yesterday, we drove the Scorpio down to Brittany from Ardres, at the Pas de Calais. Our friends have returned to the States, after one final raucous party at the St. James Club, in London. There's a hotel in Ardres called the Clément, just twenty minutes from the Calais ferry and hoverport. We love it. We cross the channel on the Hovercraft, nip up to the Clément, enjoy our first French dinner and a good night's sleep, then drive on to our continental desti-nation. The guys at *Car* magazine informed us of this gem ten years ago, and we've used it ever since.

Our Brittany hotel, the Château de la Motte Beaumanoir, is in the middle of nowhere in the Breton countryside. *Madam la maîtresse* looks a lot like Simone Signoret at the wrong end of her career, and likes to bitch about Americans. I am tempted to point out that if it wasn't for Americans, she and her neighbors would be speaking German. The old château, complete with moat, is lovely, but when the lady of the house tells us on our after-dark arrival that she could fix us some eggs but she'd rather not, I am ready for the Holiday Inn.

Today we drove from Dinan to Dinard to Saint-Malo to Mont-Saint-Michel. We loved Dinard, which is a charming resort town with several hotels where I'd rather be staying, and we ate traditional Breton crepes for lunch in Saint-Malo. Now we're watching the sunset from the highest battlements at Mont-Saint-Michel. Just a few minutes ago, we looked up to see two hawks locked in combat high above us. Screaming like the Furies, they'd scramble for altitude, each trying to get the advan-tage of the other. Then they'd roll into steep dives, ultimately colliding at a combined speed in excess of a hundred miles per hour. Why they didn't smash bones I'll never know. After three or four such midair col-lisions, the interloper headed for the mainland, while the champion—who apparently lived among the towers and rooftops of the old castle/abbey/fortress/prison/town—came back to the home roost, obviously pleased with himself.

Pointe du Hoc, Normandy—This is one D-day landing site I've never before visited—where the Rangers landed on June 6, 1944, scaled the cliffs in the face of ferocious German resistance, and became the first Allied unit to achieve its objective. Two days later, when they were relieved after a series of determined counterattacks, ninety of the original 225 guys were still on their feet. The place has been left as it was. Busted concrete, unfilled shell holes, barbed wire, everything much as it was when the Rangers moved out. Nothing at Normandy is more moving than the Omaha Beach cemetery, but Pointe du Hoc is a stirring memorial in its own right.

The Scorpio has done yeoman service for two weeks. It has been fast, sure-footed, and comfortable over all kinds of roads in some truly frightful rainstorms. But today, on the way down from Saint-Lô to Pointe du Hoc, I lost an argument concerning the right of way with an oncoming French eighteen-wheeler and he busted our left-hand mirror. I caught considerable hell from the female passengers, and I'm mortified. If I'd been driving a left-hand-drive car it wouldn't have happened, but the Scorpio had been so good for so long that I'd begun to believe that it and I could do anything, and I turned out to be wrong by about three-quarters of an inch.

Fuel is expensive in France. We ran four vehicles—including the Scorpio—in Britain for a week, and our fuel cost a total of $259.70. A week's French fuel—four tanksful—for the Scorpio alone cost $169.42.

The Palm Restaurant, New York—Lunch with Celine Sullivan, our distinguished marketing mind, who wanted to show me the latest demographic research on you, our readers. When we'd put business aside and cleaned our plates, she said, "I had a wonderful experience the other night. It was the coldest night of the year so far, not brutally cold, but cold enough to keep the riffraff off the streets of Greenwich Village. It was like a time warp. With all of *them* in the subways, or wherever they go, the Village looked as it did years ago, and I found it quite lovely. I walked along, kind of exulting in all this, when I suddenly saw a perfectly maintained Edsel sitting under a street light.

"It simply stopped me in my tracks, and I thought, seeing that car parked in surroundings that really haven't changed much in the past thirty years, what a wonderful way to explain to younger people who we were, and where we came from. That Edsel, with those bizarre lines and all that chrome, says so much about those times. Standing alone under the street light in Greenwich Village, it was like a Rosetta stone, a key that might have been used to unlock all kinds of mysteries and clear up all kinds of misapprehensions about the years between Korea and Vietnam."

New Pittsburg, Ohio—Dr. Emilio Anchisi, Ferrari's U.S. president, called me in England to say, "I have a Testarossa for you to drive, but only on one condition. You must come shooting with me on the twenty-ninth, or no deal." So a few hours after the aforementioned lunch with Celine Sullivan, I'm driving a Ferrari Testarossa from New York to Ann Arbor. It's the eve of a holiday weekend, and I stop in New Pittsburg to collect my seventy-six-year-old mother so that she can join the Michigan branch of the family in fun and frolic. Sort of "Over the River and through the Wood," with twelve cylinders and an Italian racing red paint job.

Based on this morning's experience I can tell you that the Ferrari will hold one Gokey canvas carry-on bag (mine), one lady's (larger) bag in nylon, one loden coat (mine), one lady's quilted coat, one lady's poplin raincoat, one round metal box of grandma-*gemacht* cookies, two antique mercury-glass candy dishes, one bag of bulbs (recently dug from my mother's garden), three frozen roasting chickens, one book (a biography of Confederate general A.P. Hill), one large standing rib roast, three large sirloin steaks, twelve good-sized hamburger patties, and three bags of frozen shelled chestnuts.

In addition to me and my mother—but only for a short time—it also held one cat carrier containing her thoroughly annoyed cat, named Bennington. New Testarossas have passive belts, like those in the Toyota Cressida, which slide along a track over the door to clasp you safely against the seatback. When I twisted the key to bring the great flat-twelve to life, it also caused my mother's belt to gather up old Bennington's carrier and press it very firmly against the aged person's rib cage. Bennington was not amused. He did his best to rip the carrier apart from inside, and the Testarossa was filled with floating cat hair.

When we set off down Route 250 toward Wooster, I deliberately nailed the throttle in first and second, causing my mother to exclaim, "This little thing certainly has good pickup." Enzo Ferrari his own self could not have said it better. She remarked that she had once gotten up to eighty-five while passing a car in her old Chevrolet Nova, and I immediately floored the Ferrari again. "Well, Mom," I said, "there's 100," and a moment later, "there's 120."

She laughed like bells ringing, and said, "It doesn't seem like very much, but you'd better be sure that one of these farmers doesn't drive a tractor out in front of us." Bowing to her wisdom, I backed out of it, and, at about eighty, was sailing past the turnoff to the cat hotel when she shouted, "Left!" I jumped on the brakes, causing the tin of grandma-*gemacht* cookies to open, showering us with several dozen, er, snicker-doodles. I repacked the cookies while a betrayed Bennington was being turned over to the cat sadists, and I can promise that anyone who eats a snickerdoodle this weekend will get a bonus of nourishing cat hair with every bite.

Dare to be smooth, with Jackie Stewart.

I was recently able to renew my acquaintance with Jackie Stewart, first at his Mechanics Grand Prix Challenge shooting competition in Scotland, then at his Ford-sponsored driving school at Oulton Park. I have taken driving instruction from Dr. M.R.J. Wylie and Max Goldman and Walter Hansgen of the old Road Racing Drivers Club. I have been through the Pete Brock/Carroll Shelby Driving School and John Powell's Mosport Racing School, the Range Rover off-road school at Eastnor Castle, and I've been instructed by mad Finnish rally drivers in the Swedish outback, and I learned from all of them. But the session with Jackie Stewart was special.

The Ford Motor Company invited five of us—John Dinkel of *Road & Track*, Mike Anson of *Motor Trend*, Csaba Csere of *Car and Driver*, and free-lance writer Mike Knepper—first to the Gleneagles Hotel in Scotland to compete in Stewart's Challenge, then on to his driving school, followed by quick visits to Cosworth Engineering and Aston Martin. The Challenge is a tournament involving twenty-six teams from the racing community shooting shotguns at clay targets at the Jackie Stewart Shooting School, which is part of the hotel's spectacular recreational plant.

I was the only member of our team who'd ever shot in competition, and my fellow members of the Ford U.S. press team astonished me with their ability to absorb the art and science of shotgun shooting literally overnight. Led by our captain, Ford's John Roberts, we finished fifteenth overall and blew off all the other press teams, as well as the Formula 1 drivers' team, which was sponsored by Longines and captained by that legendary Scot shot, Innes Ireland. We would have done better still, but I fell apart on the second day—owing either to jet lag or to a serious character flaw—and missed a half-dozen birds that I should have hit.

It was a terrific affair, with famous people all over the place.

Teams of drivers, teams of mechanics, teams of sponsors, teams of wives and girlfriends, and through it all, everywhere at once, Jackie Stewart. It's not unusual for celebrities to lend their names to tennis and golf tournaments and the like, but it is unusual for them to work so hard to make the events successful. Stewart was no figurehead. He had a hand in every single aspect of the two-day affair, and when it was all over he had raised more than $250,000 for the mechanics' welfare fund. After dinner Saturday night he rose to thank his sponsors, and this turned out to be a forty-minute presentation. God help us if he ever decides to start a car magazine.

We then drove from Gleneagles to the old Oulton Park circuit, near Chester. Oulton Park is a lovely little road course—reminiscent of Lime Rock, or perhaps Laguna Seca—no longer a Grand Prix venue but a fine track to drive, nonetheless. We spent a day there, most of which was devoted to a short, concentrated version of the master's approach to high-speed driving, as described in his recent book, *Jackie Stewart's Principles of Performance Driving.*

We were instructed by the three-time world champion himself, along with Formula 1 driver Dr. Jonathan Palmer and Divina Galica, a great-looking brunette with a wonderful Lauren Bacall voice, described by Jackie Stewart as Britain's finest woman racing driver. The drill was that we would first drive with the instructors, so that they might show us the circuit and reinforce the basics, as given us by Jackie in a preliminary chalk talk. To oversimplify, the basic concept underlying everything Stewart teaches is smoothness, pure and simple, and it begins when you shift into first gear and engage the clutch for the first time. After several laps with the instructors, we would take the wheels ourselves, each paired off with another student, the idea being to start judiciously applying the things we'd been told, driving as teams. Finally, each of us would drive with an instructor beside us, commenting upon and, when necessary, correcting our errors.

I was able to ride with all three of the instructors but drove only for Divina Galica and Jackie Stewart. I regretted not being able to have Jonathan Palmer's opinion of my performance as well, partly because I liked him enormously and enjoyed riding with him, and partly because something in my personality craves that sort of symmetry. Nonetheless, it was a rare old thrill to go smoking around a racing circuit with two such demanding and utterly different passengers.

We drove stock Ford Sierra four-by-four sedans with manual gearboxes, and they were more than up to the task at hand. Stewart and Palmer were as smooth as glass, but Divina Galica drove very aggressively, and her driving seemed oddly at variance with Stewart's philosophy. Stewart constantly referred to a hypothetical granny in the back seat who was not to be upset by hard shifts or brutal braking or driveline snatch. He did not want to hear rude tire noises, and, like the granny, the car was never to be upset, whether braking, accelerating, or turning. Granny could have been forgiven for wondering if Divina was listening during Stewart's preliminary presentation of the smoothness catechism.

I must have done two dozen laps with Divina as my observer. Her complaint about my driving was that I attempted to enter corners too fast, then lost time in the inevitable adjustments that had to be made as I tidied things up. Gradually, I learned her line and managed to approximate her rhythm, but I still got it wrong on this corner or that. Finally, she pronounced me ready to drive for Stewart. We went to the pits and waited for the master, who was at that time lapping with John Dinkel.

Stewart popped out of Dinkel's car, popped into mine, and away we went. He continued his nonstop reiteration of the basics, as he had when he was driving. Now, up to speed and approaching the hairpin at full chat, just as I'd been instructed to do by Divina, I found my new coach fidgeting mightily and finally erupting: "Why are you doing it this way? Divina Galica is the only racing driver in the U.K. who would take this line in this corner!" The next ten or twelve laps were spent with my sheepishly unlearning Divina's line and Divina's rhythms, and trying to learn Jackie's.

Stewart's complaint about my driving was the same as Divina's: too fast coming in, and, as a direct result, too slow going out. My own growing realization about my driving on closed circuits is that it suffers in exactly the way my clay bird shooting suffers: from lack of concentration. I tend to think of other things, to look at the scenery, to chat. At one point he asked me to do the bravest thing I'd ever done in a car. He said: "On this next corner, leave your hands on the wheel, but let me steer. Do exactly as I say." We were traveling at something in excess of 100 as he continued, rapid-fire: "Keep your foot down, foot down, now lift gently. Now gently on the brakes. Change down smoothly. *Hard on the brakes!* Back on the throttle." With that, he pulled the steering wheel smartly to the right, and we shot perfectly across the apex, already swinging wide into the exit, throttle wide open. It was lovely, but I'm not sure I would have done it under any other circumstances, or with any other human being holding the steering wheel.

Before the day's adventures began, Jackie Stewart promised us that no matter how proficient any of us might be as drivers, each of us would go away from his program feeling that we'd learned something valuable. The promise was kept. I've pursued smoothness as the main component of my own driving ever since I learned that the old Rolls-Royce school for chauffeurs instructed drivers to shift so that their passengers wouldn't know gears were being changed, yet I certainly benefitted from my day as a Stewart student. Maybe it was my spirit that benefitted most of all. I drove around a lovely old racing circuit at the wheel of a fast, competent car with one of history's greatest drivers instructing and encouraging me. Now, every time I squeeze the brakes on and change down for an upcoming corner, I'll remember, again, how it was that day with Jackie Stewart.

Henry N. Manney III
1922-1988

I got back to the office this morning to learn that Henry N. Manney III, for a number of years *Road & Track* magazine's European correspondent, the funniest and best of all the people who ever wrote in the English language about motorsports, died while I was in New York. Henry had been living in a state of suspended animation—comatose, following a stroke—ever since 1981, so his death is one of those events that lots of people will describe as a blessing. I have to demur. When somebody as good as Henry Manney goes away, it's no blessing. The world is a poorer place for his departure.

I first read Henry's nutball prose in Gus Vignole's *MotoRacing* in the middle Fifties and became a fan for life. He and I spent several weeks together in Europe in 1966 and 1967. He wore a green loden coat and a tweed hat in Mediterranean summer, and told hilarious stories about his largely futile attempts to trace his family's genealogy. He was a terrific traveling companion who knew absolutely everybody in European motor racing. He had moved to Europe in the vain hope of becoming a ballet dancer and had become an automotive journalist instead. He gave up his home in Paris and the life he loved so much to return to the States in late '67, naively expecting *Road & Track* to welcome him with open arms and give him a regular staff position. He had been the best thing in that magazine for a decade, and he knew it, though he never affected any airs on that score. Unfortunately, they didn't see it that way and let him know that they had no plans to use him in any important capacity.

Henry had always had a cynical streak. It was one of the things that made him so much fun at an alfresco lunch table in Modena or when holding forth wickedly to a group of pals in the pits at some GP circuit. But the cynicism came to dominate his conversation in later years, and I missed my last chance to spend some time with him because of it. J.L.K. Davis and I encountered Henry and his wife, Annie, at the 1981 Monterey Historic Automobile Races, and he was in a bitter humor about all these fools who thought that, by going vintage car racing, they could counterfeit the golden era of motorsport he had lived and breathed in Europe. Nothing, it seemed, met Henry's standards anymore. They invited us to join them for lunch, and I begged off, not wanting to listen to what had become an ongoing litany of his disappointments with his fellow humans. A short time later he had the stroke, and I'll never forgive myself for turning down that luncheon invitation. Henry N. Manney III lit up my life, and those of countless others, for a long and happy time, and I should have been willing to listen to him when he was in the slough of despond.

Thank you, Leo. Thank you, Daimler-Benz. Thank you, Automotoclub Storico Italiano. Thank you, Tazio Nuvolari.

※

otel Principe di Savoia, Milan—Fortune smiled, this weekend, and I was able to drive in the 1988 Mille Miglia. It was about two years ago that my pal Leo Levine suggested we make a serious effort to get an entry. The original Mille Miglia ran a thousand miles, from Brescia to Rome and back, between 1927 and 1957. No longer a race, but a celebration, today's Mille Miglia is a sort of rally/tour over the same roads, limited to cars that would have been eligible for the original.

The early years of my car enthusiasm were fueled by fantasies of the Mille Miglia. I'd read Ken Purdy's heartbreaking story of Tazio Nuvolari's 1948 try at the thousand miles, in which the fifty-six-year-old legend, *Il Mantovano Volante*, sick to death with emphysema, kept his Ferrari in the hunt by sheer force of character, long after it had shed or broken more than enough pieces to allow an honorable retirement.

Purdy wrote: "He came into Rome thirty minutes ahead of the pack, but the car was breaking up. At Florence the bonnet was gone and a spring had broken. He wouldn't let his riding mechanic get out to check the car. He stalked arrogantly once around it, spitting blood, and climbed back aboard. Still leading near Modena, where the Ferrari is made, the car broke down, quit cold, and that was that. Nuvolari sat quietly in the rain, in tears, as the others screamed past in the dark, until finally a priest came and persuaded him to come into the parish house."

I'd read and reread Denis Jenkinson's account of his 1955 ride with Stirling Moss in the Mercedes-Benz 300SLR, the year Moss ran the thousand miles in ten hours and seventeen minutes, a record that will stand forever. And, finally, I knew all the contending versions of the 1957 accident that killed the Marquis de Portago—along with ten Italian spectators and the Mille Miglia itself—when his Ferrari went off the road and crashed into the crowd.

Leo Levine was in Brescia that day, representing *Stars and Stripes*.

233

He'd driven down from Germany in an Austin-Healey 100, learning in the process, he recalls, how bad a car can be. He remembers that he met photographer Jesse Alexander there for the first time, and he remembers the press bulletins coming in to Brescia from all the towns and cities along the route—until one came in that said something like, "The Spaniard Portago has had trouble with a tire," and after that there were no more bulletins and all the press officials seemed to disappear.

Everybody has friends. If we're lucky, we have a handful of best friends, people we're always glad to see, people who are always glad to see us, people who'd accept our collect call from Buenos Aires in the middle of the night and send us the required bail money. Leo Levine is one of those best friends for me. A long time ago he did something I wish I'd done. He was sent to Europe by the U.S. Army in 1952 and when his tour was over decided to stay on, working for *Stars and Stripes* as a sportswriter. While he was there, he owned some outstanding automobiles, drove in rallies and races and hillclimbs—including a couple of rides in factory Porsches—and got to know a lot of people in the European automobile fraternity.

We've known each other since the beginning of the Sixties, when he finally came home from Germany, suffering the pangs of divorce and dislocation, to become the motorsports guy for the old *New York Herald Tribune*. When the *Trib* folded, Leo wrote the definitive study of corporate automobile racing, which was called *Ford: The Dust and the Glory.* About the time I left automotive journalism to become an advertising agency executive, Leo became head of public relations for Mercedes-Benz of North America. Our second wives have become good friends. When I knew that I was going to abandon the life of a corporate executive and return to the car magazine business in 1976, Leo was the first person I called.

It wasn't hard to understand why he'd want to have a go at the new Mille Miglia, and I certainly needed no convincing. Max von Pein of the Daimler-Benz Museum would help us get a 300SL, Leo said, and we'd go over and spend a week in Italy soaking up the atmosphere and relearning the things we'd forgotten about swing axles and drum brakes. Unfortunately, we didn't get an entry that year, and I figured that was all she wrote, another near miss with the thrill of a lifetime.

But then, about the time winter began to close in, Leo called again. Okay, he said, send me two passport photos and we'll get this thing started for '88. Max von Pein had come to the United States to buy some cars for the museum—the dollar-deutsche mark relationship having deteriorated to the point where hideously expensive American-owned Mercedes-Benz classics are now bargains for German buyers—and one of these was a nice black gullwing coupe that we could drive in the 1988 event. We'd be part of a three-car factory team, with Stirling Moss in the car he drove to win in 1955, and Eugen Böhringer, the great rally champion, driving one of the 1952 300SL prototypes that ran at Le Mans; the Carrera Panamericana, and the Mille Miglia itself.

About the time this year's Geneva Auto Show opened, the organizers announced the 1988 entry list. We were in! Our number was 303, last car in the field. We reminded each other that in the old days they started the slowest cars first, and the high numbers went to guys like Nuvolari, Ascari, Villoresi, Moss, and now, *Davis and Levine!*

Leo prepared by running every morning, playing golf, and test-driving our car before it was shipped to the Oldtimer Service at Daimler-Benz in Stuttgart. I prepared by purchasing a new Bell helmet—a black Mag 4, to match the car—and an equally black Mini Mag Lite flashlight with an extra set of double A Duracells. I thought about resuming my running program, abandoned last November, and I thought about losing weight, and I thought about checking in at Bob Bondurant's driving school for a refresher course, but, in the end, the helmet, the flashlight, the extra batteries, and countless nights spent playing mind movies of the Mille Miglia on the insides of my eyelids was the extent of my preparation.

I was ready.

Leo was ready, too, but with only days to go, he called and announced that he would be unable to make the trip, due to the fact that Daimler-Benz's chairman, Mr. Edzard Reuter, would be making an important visit to the United States at that time. I instantly assumed the worst. "No, no, no," he said, "you're still going. A.B. Shuman can be your co-driver." Saved again. A.B. Shuman is Leo's Number Two in the MBNA press department, a former naval pilot, former editor of *Hot Rod*, former editor of *Motor Trend*, and a thoroughly good guy. We talked. A.B. was as stunned at his sudden good fortune as I had been weeks before. Did he know anything about the arrangements? No. Neither did I. Hotel rooms? Logistical support? Car condition? We were total innocents. My last word on the subject was: "Look. Let's just get on the plane next Saturday, fly to Stuttgart, and take our chances. If we sleep in the car, we sleep in the car." A.B.'s last word on the subject was, "I'm taking my video camera."

We were ready.

Now the Mille Miglia is over for 1988. Surrounded by Ferraris and Maseratis and other automotive exotica, our car was perfect. It was fast, comfortable, and it handled and held the road like the champion it once was. An ideal way to experience one's first Mille Miglia *storica.* The organization was perfect. A good-natured team of mechanics was provided by the Daimler-Benz Oldtimer Service to look after us along the route. The organizers provided hotel rooms and meal chits, so we never had to sleep in our black gullwing. Italy was perfect. It was an utterly exhilarating automotive experience. I have never driven as fast for as long on public roads, certainly never on public roads still open to the public, and with the encouragement of the police!

Crowds lined the route, cheering. I followed Mike Sheehan's Ferrari 250 Testarossa absolutely flat out from Bologna to Modena, passing everything, often on the wrong side of the road, once even on the wrong side of an oncoming lady in a Fiat who'd stopped to make a left turn. The police smiled and urged us on with their batons. School kids checked our numbers in their programs and shouted our names. Art director Larry Crane and photographer Jesse Alexander pursued us in an Alfa spyder and actually got it all on film. A.B. watched the whole thing through the viewfinder of his video camera, and why he never got carsick, I cannot say.

I'm going to write the whole lovely saga, but not now, not yet. It's all a blur. Verona, Florence, Siena, Viterbo, Padua, San Marino, Pesaro, Assisi, Mantua. Where were we when the pointer pup stole our sandwiches? Where was it that city fathers pushed the pretty blond girl forward to give me a plastic cup of lambrusco and a shy kiss under the overhanging gullwing door? When did we make that phenomenal avoidance as we passed the tank truck? Maybe it'll all come together when I see Jesse's photographs and A.B.'s videotape. As Brock Yates once said: "This is the greatest story I've ever done. I just have to sit down and write the sonuvabitch."

What kind of car is this?

❧

Bill Ruger happens to be a good friend of mine. In the late Sixties Mr. Ruger—aided and abetted by his son, William B. Ruger, Jr.—conceived and built a pair of full-fledged prototype cars bearing the family name, described as "one of those solidly eccentric events in automotive history," and one of those cars was on display at the New York automobile show in 1969. *Road & Track* magazine threw a cocktail party on that occasion, and it was there that I met the man himself. William B. Ruger, Sr., has the look of one who does not suffer fools gladly, so I introduced myself somewhat tentatively, saying that I owned several Ruger firearms and that I greatly admired his work as an engineer and a designer. He grinned and replied that he was familiar with my work, too, and we were thenceforth pals.

I visited Bill at his home in New Hampshire during the summer of 1970 and drove both of the Ruger Tourer prototypes. We fished for trout and bass, shot rifles and pistols and shotguns, celebrated dinner by firing a salute cannon from the front porch, and talked endlessly about cars. We've been doing all those things together ever since. The following spring I was in New York on business, and Bill suggested that I might enjoy taking one of the big Rugers home to Michigan for a few weeks. The car had to be delivered to Detroit for some additional development work anyway, so we could kill two birds with one stone.

I was in the advertising business at that time, and I was accompanied on that trip by an associate of mine, a writer named Dick Candor, who was helping me put the finishing touches on a feature-length promotional film I'd produced. Dick Candor was a kind and thoughtful man, enormously talented, but so painfully shy that he was nicknamed "Bambi." He had no experience of cars like the Ruger, and he had absolutely no idea what he was letting himself in for when he accepted my invitation to ride shotgun on the trip back to the Midwest.

The Ruger was, and is, immense. It looks like a Bentley Vanden

Plas tourer of the type that ran Le Mans so successfully in the Twenties
and Thirties. My favorite of the two cars is buttercup yellow with green
wire wheels and green leather—the other being black with red trim—
and that was the car Bill turned over to me on a May day in 1971. The
car has no side curtains, no heater. The top sort of protects the occupants
from the elements, but only if the car is standing still. At highway speeds,
the weather comes swirling around the corners of the flat windshield,
and the kidneys take a beating. I warned Mr. Candor that he would need
warm clothing, but he interpreted this to mean a light gabardine topcoat.
Before the night was over, Dick Candor was the coldest, most miserable
man I have ever known. I had planned to drive straight through, in my
down parka and warm gloves, but Candor's condition made me stop at
a motel near Elyria, Ohio, where he could thaw out and get a few hours'
sleep. Early the next morning we resumed our trip, and I delivered him
to the Chevrolet he had left parked at the Detroit airport. No one ever
crawled into a Chevelle with greater pleasure than did my friend Dick.
A curious thing: I truly loved that man, and I went out of my way to
draw him into the more entertaining aspects of my work and play, and
every single thing I ever did in his behalf wound up making him miserable. He's been dead for several years and probably counts himself fortunate to be beyond my reach.

The yellow Ruger and its black sibling are still around today.
Although they belong to Sturm, Ruger and Company, the yellow one is
regarded as Bill's car and the black one, as Bill Junior's. In practical terms
the cars are identical—massive trucklike frames, built for the purpose to
the specifications of Ruger *et fils*, with a solid axle at each end, eighteen-
inch wire wheels at each corner, and a 425-horsepower Ford 427 with
two four-barrel Holley carburetors providing motive force. The bodies
and fenders are fiberglass, and the old Vanden Plas tourers' patent leather
skin is neatly replicated in vinyl bonded to the fiberglass surface. "High,
wide, and handsome" is a term that accurately describes the driving experience. The cars go like hell, as you might imagine, and the steering and
roadholding are of exactly the same vintage as the appearance. Obi-wan
Kenobi would be right at home behind the wheel of a Ruger Tourer,
since the experience is as much psychic as physical. As you hurtle into a
corner and the Buick Riviera aluminum drum brakes are taking hold in
random three-one-four-two sequence and the steering is always a heart-
beat behind the tall car's feints and lunges, you deeply and sincerely hope
that the force will be with you. But despite the car's ability to cause your
life to pass before your eyes once or twice on a summer sprint through
the mountains, you'd never turn down a chance to repeat the experience.

Bill Ruger's intent was to build the cars for sale, but that was when the federal government was closing in on the automobile business and nobody knew what to expect. Someone in the Department of Transportation told him that he'd probably have to crash at least one car to be eligible for production, and that alone was enough to discourage him, so nobody ever got to plunk down his money and drive away in a Ruger Tourer. A tragedy.

In a recent conversation with Bill Sharfman, Ruger said: "There were some areas where I might do it a little differently if I were able to do it over. I was never fully satisfied with the steering. It was something of a problem to have that big wide V-8 Ford 427 engine in a relatively narrow automobile, given the complications of getting the steering and the exhaust pipes and all that stuff fitted properly, and in that sense an in-line engine would have been a lot more readily dealt with. It would have been interesting to engineer a car with an in-line engine and, ultimately, to do our own engine. But there were always questions about whether or not it was possible to run a business of that sort profitably. And I think, really, it wasn't."

Two years ago, I went back to Bill Ruger's home in the hills of New Hampshire with photographer Dougie Firth. We drove the Ruger Tourer again, prowled among the Bentleys and Stutzes and Packards, sat in the Mercer Raceabout (which Bill acquired from the family that had bought it new), smiled at the Kissel Gold Bug, and fell in love with the 1935 Miller-Ford Indy car. Then, on a lovely summer morning, we fired up the Ferrari 250GT long-wheelbase California spyder. This is one of Bill's fondest possessions, a car he bought new in 1959. He describes it as a transitional Ferrari, with an old-style chassis and engine but one of the first production Ferraris to be fitted with disc brakes. The manufacturer's plate on the cowl describes the car as *Tipo 508D 128F, Motore 1581 GT, Chassis 1581 GT*. The engine is the beloved three-liter V-12 with three two-barrel Weber carburetors. In this form it produced 260 horsepower at 7000 rpm. The car is, of course, red (the factory says that the proper red paint job adds at least a thousand dollars to the resale value of any Ferrari), and the seats are flat, erect, and close to the floor. The only possible driving position is all east-west knees and elbows, and, after a few minutes' struggle to adapt, one gets into the spirit of the thing.

Lyle Patterson maintains all of the cars in the Ruger collection, when he's not supervising the building of shotguns at the Ruger works in Newport, New Hampshire, and he suggested that the Ferrari might benefit from a little judicious full-throttle operation. Aiming to please, I gave the car a zealous squirt of power as soon as oil and water temperatures rose to the task. Lyle was right. The engine ran raggedly at first, blatted several great ugly balls of sooty smoke out of the pipes, then began to run like the Ferrari of my dreams. I was cruising at a hundred on the Interstate while Dougie stood next to me taking pictures over the front end, when I noticed that a fully tricked-out Nissan Maxima was tucked in right beside me. We both stood on it—not considering the effect this might have on my photographer friend—and the Nissan was soon disappearing in the fender mirror. Dougie didn't even bother to sit down.

Heading back up the mountain to Bill's house, the V-12 now running as crisply and melodiously as the day it left the factory, I was again reminded of the pure, unalloyed joy of going fast on a winding road in a powerful car with skinny tires. It troubles me to think that new generations of drivers are coming along in this fat-tire age who have no idea whatsoever of what it's like to deliberately slide a car through one fast corner after another. Bill's California spyder really could be steered with the accelerator—little jabs at the pedal and little flicks of the steering wheel serving to position it exactly where you wanted it, and at exactly the correct angle. Exuberant bliss.

Bill Ruger once told me a nice story about his honeymoon in 1938, when he did a long leisurely motor tour of England and the Continent in a rented Renault cabriolet "that looked like a Chrysler Airflow." He was in London, standing where Regent Street flows into Piccadilly Circus at rush hour, when he spotted in the sea of traffic a tiny blue open car. Without considering the risk, he stepped off the curb, waded through the traffic, and at last stood towering above the little blue sports car. He recalls that he asked its driver, "What kind of car is this?" and the man smiled tolerantly and replied, "It's a Bugatti." Fifty years later, lost in the memory, he says, "Sort of a special moment."

In the twelve years I've known Bill Ruger I've done hundreds of miles in the creamy-yellow Ruger Tourer; a couple of hundred or so in the aged Land Rover; and, once, after a weekend hunting trip in the White Mountains of New Hampshire, a spirited hour's dash through the pelting rain from Bill's home to the Manchester airport in the car I really want, the one Bill calls "the worst Ferrari in the world." It is a 330GT 2+2, the ugly one with dual headlights, built in 1966. I don't know if it has ever run well, but I do know that it has never run well when I was driving it. On that dash to the airport it was hitting on eleven cylinders and one of the exhaust manifolds was cracked. Today it sits in its New Hampshire garage, listing slightly, faded and blotchy, looking for all the world like some terrific girl with whom you went to high school, found 30 years later slumped on a barstool in Calumet City. Romantic fool that I am, I want to save that old harridan from further deterioration. I want to love her and fix her up and let her do honest work for me. I also want to buy her cheap.

The last time I suffered a fantasy as virulent as this, it involved another of the several Ruger Ferraris, the '59 California Spyder. It seemed that each time I visited Bill at the New Hampshire place, he'd be fuming and pesting about the California. It had a flat. It wouldn't start. The battery wouldn't hold a charge. It would start, but it wouldn't run on more than ten cylinders. Oh, pain. Wires would be wiggled. Dark recesses would be peered into. Tires would be kicked. Then the kid from the gas station in town would come out with a new battery or some other form of serum from the settlement and the Ferrari would come reluctantly to life. On my way back to Michigan I would reason that sooner or later Bill Ruger would tire of this silly game. A man with all that automotive wonderfulness at his beck and call doesn't need to clutter up his premises with a non-starting California Spyder. After about four years of this I knew in my bones that he was about to call and offer me the car for $3500, since I'd always shown such understanding when it wouldn't work. Wrong. After inviting me to go shooting one day, he idly mentioned that he'd had Luigi Chinetti send a truck up from New York to take it away for a complete restoration. The irony.

Now as I sit here with the sun going down outside my office window, I feel a faint emanation from the telephone next to my typewriter. William B. Ruger, Sr., must be about to call! We'll shoot the breeze about this and that, and then he'll casually ask me if I remember that ghastly old 2+2 rotting in his garage. Careful not to jar our conversation with a commercial note, he'll discreetly suggest that it could be had for about $5000. I'll harrumph and allow that that's a lot of money, but that I'll take it off his hands, if only to keep it from making his other cars look bad. Then I'll hang up and faint.

Some guys just look peculiar, that's all.

Mr. Dennis J. Walker writes from Vernon Hills, Illinois, to tell me that "many people" were laughing at me behind my back at the Monterey Historic Automobile Races because I was wearing a white suit with a black Cogito Ergo Zoom T-shirt, which, he suggested, made me "look like an aging cross between Raymond Loewy and Don Johnson." He says his letter was inspired by my December column, wherein I suggested that we all celebrate Christmas at the Pittsburgh Vintage Grand Prix, with the caveat that the cops would throw out anybody who didn't subscribe to my own "infuriatingly arbitrary dress code." He also suggested that I check out J. Crew, Eddie Bauer, and perhaps Brooks Brothers and Ralph Lauren as firms that might spruce up my wardrobe.

Well, first off, Mr. Walker, let me congratulate you on a finely tuned instinct for the jugular. Well-meant advice should always inflict a little pain on the recipient, and anyone who says that he writes "as a friend" to tell me about people who are laughing at me behind my back demonstrates sensitivity worthy of a career in TV journalism. I feel rather strongly that it is not fear of death that prevents most people from achieving everything they want in life, but rather fear of looking ridiculous. Anybody who's followed my adventures over the years knows beyond the shadow of a doubt that I'm not terribly concerned about looking ridiculous.

As to your suggestions about my wardrobe, a keen sartorial observer like yourself should have recognized that the white suit I was wearing at Laguna Seca was made for me by Brooks Brothers, and if you think people laughed at me in *that,* just imagine how they'd have reacted if I'd showed up in cutoffs and a tank top. I think Eddie Bauer does nice Ford trucks, and J. Crew—unless I am mistaken—sells bargain-priced Rugby shirts. As for Ralph Lauren, he has spent the past ten years creating a line of men's clothes that look just like the ones I wear all the time. I appreciate your friendly concern, but I must point out that people have been laughing at me for years, sometimes behind my back, but in the case of my friends, generally right in my face.

Example: Doug Mahoney. Doug Mahoney got me into the retail end of the imported-car business in 1953 and got me into sports car racing more or less simultaneously. A couple of years later, I'd crashed badly and wound up with the face I now wear. The car I was supposed to drive in an endurance race at Elkhart Lake didn't make it, and I'd flown all the way from California, so I went on to Michigan to see some old friends. When I went to Doug's house, his wife took one look at me, then fled, weeping, and locked herself in the bathroom. Doug went to the door and said, "Come on out, Joyce. It's just your pal David E. Same as he always was, but now he's got something that character actors would give a lot to have. In his case, it's one bedroom eye and one bathroom eye."

(Two years ago I was interviewed and photographed by the *New York Post*. The next day some guy from the editorial department called me and said, "Have you seen the photographs that we took of you yesterday? I wish you could take a look at them before we go to press. There's something wrong. In every one of them it looks like one of your eyes is bigger than the other." I replied, "One of my eyes *is* bigger than the other." The stricken voice at the other end said, "Oh, GOD, I'm sorry!")

Example: Frank Winchell. Frank has been a friend of mine since 1962, when he was running Chevrolet R&D. In those days he was just beginning an involvement with automobile racing—most particularly with the Jim Hall/Hap Sharp Chaparral racing team—that would make him one of the great engineer-innovators in that sport. Once, on a bear-hunting expedition on the White Mountain Apache Reservation in Arizona, I was criticizing Frank for hiding his light under a bushel. "Frank," I grumbled, "you're making a huge contribution to General Motors, but nobody knows your name. Every day they hire some new lightweight, make him a vice-president, and a week later he's being presented on television as the greatest thing since the four-stroke engine. You need to come out and let the world know what you do."

Frank said, "You may be right, but I'm not like you. You're so damn sure of yourself, and you can talk to anybody. We're down here for two hours, and you already know all these Indians by their first names. I can't do that. I walk into a room full of people, and I fully expect everybody to turn around and say, 'Who is that stupid sonuvabitch that just walked in?' I'll tell you the goddam truth. If I looked like you, *I wouldn't be able to leave my house!*"

It should be apparent, by now, that people laughing behind one's back are as child's play compared with the behavior of one's friends. But nonetheless, Mr. Walker, your thoughtfulness in bringing this to my attention is sincerely appreciated. I'm just not sure that I can do anything about it. I'm not even sure that I want to.

Black Label, black Ferrari.

here are worse things than a black Ferrari 328GTS. There are worse things than being picked up by your wife in a black Ferrari GTS at the West Palm Beach aerodrome for a drive to Ann Arbor, Michigan, by way of Lynchburg, Tennessee. Lynchburg is, after all, the home of the Jack Daniel distillery, the oldest registered distillery in the United States, made famous by an inspired low-key advertising campaign and decades of Joe Clark's black-and-white photographs. However, the whiskey itself deserves most of the credit for that fame. Jack Daniel's Black Label—a charcoal-filtered sour mash called "Tennessee whiskey"—is the libation of choice for an awful lot of drinkers around the globe. People who take sides in the Scotch versus Bourbon wars accord Jack Daniel's a special place, a sort of good-humored demilitarized zone where discussions are carried on at a more leisurely pace and in a more laid-back tone. A visit to the distillery explains why that is so. More to the point, a visit to the place where they make Jack Daniel's Black, in a black Ferrari GTS, helps one to appreciate that a world without great whiskey and great automobiles would be a sorry place indeed.

Having finished that paragraph, and now rereading it, I know beyond the shadow of a doubt that I will receive pious letters of outrage from blue-nosed Pecksnifs scourging me for mentioning whiskey and fast cars in the same space. They should not waste their paper. I will open their letters, snort with derision, and throw them away. I know that drunk driving is stupid. I know that it kills more people than all other automotive causes of death combined. I am an ardent supporter of the good works done by people like Mothers Against Drunk Driving. But I am also an enthusiast of good cars and good liquor, though I strive to keep them separated. I'm fortunate in this regard, because my wife doesn't drink much and is delighted to take the wheel whenever I determine that I may have surpassed the legal blood-alcohol limit. Nonetheless, I have no interest in being preached at. So save those cards and letters, Pecksniffs.

I came by the black Ferrari 328GTS in the usual way. Pure luck.

Dr. Emilio Anchisi—president of Ferrari North America, interviewed in last month's *Automobile Magazine*—called to discuss our shared passion for shotguns and shooting and, in passing, mentioned that he had a black 328GTS—one of his new ones with ABS—at Shelton Ferrari in Fort Lauderdale, Florida. Perhaps, he suggested, I might like to drive it for a while. "Do chickens have pointed yellow lips?" I asked. "When can I pick it up?"

A deal was struck. J.L.K. Davis would fly to Fort Lauderdale, collect the Ferrari, visit her sister in Boca Raton, and meet me at West Palm Beach the next morning. I would give a speech to the SEMA (Specialty Equipment Market Association, formerly Speed Equipment Manufacturers Association) management group at their annual meeting in Scottsdale, Arizona, then fly to Dallas and check into an airport hotel so that I might watch the Detroit Pistons humiliate the Boston Celtics on television while I lounged around in my underwear and gnawed on ribs from room service. Next morning I would rise at five and fly on to the rendezvous with my Ferrari and the woman who changed my life.

Coming out into the fetid midmorning air of West Palm Beach, I looked in vain for the Ferrari. I *heard* it, but I couldn't see it, fifty yards away behind an assortment of bucks-up civilian machinery. It accelerated smartly around Hertz buses and waiting Jaguars and rolled up to my feet. Top off. Very black. *Very* sleek. The driver, my wife, looking very pleased with herself. She popped the front and rear lids, and it was clear that the only way the nylon garment bag containing the navy suit and blue blazer was going to fit would be if I rolled it up. Done. My *Automobile Magazine* weekend bag and briefcase went into the little rectangular space behind the engine where they would be perfectly secure at a constant 150 or 200 degrees Fahrenheit. We headed north on the Florida Turnpike, where an astonishing percentage of the traffic seemed to be moving at speeds in excess of eighty miles per hour.

At seven-thirty that evening we were checking into the Hilton Hotel in Macon, Georgia, sunburned and happy. We'd done 550 miles in about nine hours and the car was our friend for life. We asked the doorman, the bell captain, the security guy, and the lady who checked us in to recommend a superior barbecue place. After washing up, we went to their unanimous choice, a couple of blocks away. The barbecue was okay, but not superior. Memphis and San Antonio put Macon on the trailer, barbecue-wise.

The scene back at our hotel was not conducive to late-night hell-raising. The main floor was thronged with lugubrious-looking people attending a regional convocation of Alcoholics Anonymous, drinking some unidentifiable soft drink from plastic glasses in grim silence. We rode up on the elevator with a guy who'd been drinking something more easily identified. He leaned precariously and stared at my wife as though he'd never seen one of those before. We hoped that he was not a fallen member of the AA flock.

We were in Lynchburg, Tennessee, by noon the next day. Departing Macon at dawn, we'd left the top panel in place. With its roof on, the GTS is not so terrific for tall guys. I am six feet two and rather long-waisted, so I must drive it as though I were balancing a basin of hot water on my pelvis, or maybe doing the limbo, the former being more likely than the latter. As soon as the sun was up, we stopped at Bob Evans restaurant for breakfast and removed the top. Ahhh. Much better. I could sit up like a normal person. I could see. My backache disappeared. The top of the windshield frame was almost touching my eyebrows, virtually guaranteeing that I'd be killed deader than Kelsey's nuts in the event of a collision, but did I care? I know that when I was born by the light of a kerosene lamp in Pulaski County, Kentucky, a prancing horse reared in Maranello. We're talking destiny here. Decapitation seems a small price to pay.

Jack Daniel was about five feet tall and wore a size four shoe. His statue stands welcoming visitors to the very spring that provides the water for the whiskey, and the statue's feet are too big. It was the only way they could securely anchor his graven image. Mr. Daniel bought the land at Lynchburg in 1866, and they've been turning out the magic elixir ever since, interrupted only by the Republic's irrational fling with prohibition, 1920 to 1933. The tour is a must. One sees everything, from the great barrel-houses—there are forty-three of them, each one holding over a million gallons of whiskey—to the tall ricks of locally grown maple waiting to be turned into the filtering charcoal. We stuck our fingers into the vats and tasted the rich, powerful beer which is distilled to become the essence of Old Number 7. (We couldn't get any whiskey because the surrounding county is dry. *Savages!*) My question: "How many people work here?" Their answer: "About half of us." Actually, there are 350 employees, none of whom seem to be particularly stressed. With the tour behind us we drove into town, to the Lynchburg General Store, where we bought some Jack Daniel's shot glasses and a country ham. I also bought a black Jack Daniel's Old Number 7 baseball cap—the first one of that style ever to look good on my head—which I wore to the Pepsi shop where I consumed two chili dogs and listened to the proprietress, an *Ausländer* from the suburbs of Detroit, bitch about the local citizenry. She must be very popular with her neighbors.

Central Tennessee is as beautiful as any place in North America, and we enjoyed a glorious drive north into Kentucky on the two-lanes, including some marked as scenic routes in our Rand McNally atlas. The best of the best was the drive from McMinnville to Mount Crest on route 30, and thence to Crossville on route 101, beautifully maintained roads that twist and dive over the Cumberland Plateau through incredible scenery. Even if the rest of the 1667 miles had been drudgery, which it most emphatically was not, this afternoon's drive would have made it an unforgettable day in a lifetime of unforgettable days.

The Ferrari never put a foot wrong. It may be the best-damped car of its type I've ever driven. It handled everything including some dirt road without a hint of harshness or crash-through. The clutch and shift linkages were perfect, and the combination of large vented disc brakes and Goodyear Eagle VR tires was so effective that I never got into the ABS, even though we worked the car very hard. I believe that this was the first time I've ever exceeded 140 miles per hour in an open car, save racing cars, and not only were wind and noise beautifully managed, but my Old Number 7 baseball cap stayed on. Even so, we averaged slightly more than twenty miles per gallon. I only wish I could have introduced Enzo Ferrari to Jack Daniel.

Jaguar.
What would Bill Lyons and Bill Heynes do?

———————

*B*ritish Airways Flight 0095, London-Detroit*—Bill Lyons and Bill Heynes were a great team. Bill Lyons had the hustle and the vision to turn a motorcycle sidecar business into a thriving car company called Jaguar, and Bill Heynes had the engineering skills and artistic sense to make sure that the cars called Jaguar were always exciting. Bill Lyons—Sir William, by then—died in 1985. Bill Heynes died this week, while I was in England driving the 1990 Jaguar XJ6. He was eighty-five years old, having retired in 1969.

I was fortunate enough to meet both of them during the Sixties. My encounter with Mr. Lyons was a sharp one. He criticized Jaguar's former U.S. distributor, Max Hoffman, and I suggested that without Max Hoffman Jaguar might never have been more than an interesting curiosity in this country, Jaguar's most important export market. One remark led to another, and we parted on that acrimonious note. I never saw him again. With Bill Heynes, I was inclined to be kind of reverent, first because of his role in the development of every Jaguar from the SS-100 to the XJ6, second because of the incredible record of his C and D-type racing cars at Le Mans, and third because of the profound effect that his original Jaguar XK120 roadster had upon me.

If any one car is responsible for my becoming who and what I am, that car would be the black Jaguar XK120 roadster that I saw in Birmingham, Michigan, in the spring of 1950. Deliveries of the XK120 had only begun in England in July of 1949, so the car that I glimpsed that afternoon must have been a very early model brought over by one of the Detroit manufacturers. Struck dumb by its beauty, I had trouble adjusting to the scale of it in American traffic. *It was so tiny!* We'd seen Austin A-40s and Ford Anglias and Prefects on local streets by then— we'd even seen a few MGs—but they didn't prepare me for this exquisitely sensuous two-seater. I had to know more about it, and I began buying car magazines. Any car magazines. *All* car magazines.

Had I been able to examine the inside of that black Jag's biscuit leather cockpit, I would have seen a brass dash plaque affixed to the passenger's side of the instrument panel. It was a feature of XK120 roadsters, and it said: *Certified that this Jaguar car is an EXACT REPLICA of the record-breaking car which achieved the speed of 132.6 m.p.h. at Jabbeke, Belgium, 30 May, 1949. Certified by [signed]] Wm. Heynes, Chief Engineer, Jaguar Cars Ltd., Coventry, England.* Stirring words, those. Some people bought the car just to get the dash plaque.

The Jaguar XK120 was the Ferrari of the early Fifties. That was where it stood in the automotive hierarchy when the great General Eisenhower became President Eisenhower in 1952. It was not seen on every street corner, its performance was outstanding for its time, and it looked like nothing else. Of course, there were Ferraris around in the early Fifties, but they were really quite rare, and *extremely* expensive. A Jaguar roadster could be bought for less than $4000 in 1952, while a Ferrari might have cost as much as $16,000! Until Porsches came along in significant numbers in 1953 and '54, an upwardly mobile car enthusiast started with an MG or two, then traded up to a Jaguar.

Bill Heynes and Bill Lyons were a lot like Ettore Bugatti and Harry Miller, as was Donald Healey, of Healey Silverstone, Austin-Healey, and Jensen-Healey fame. They believed that "what looks right must be right," and the cars they did together reflected that idea. The shape of Bill Lyons's XK120 was perfect, and when you opened the hood for the first time, you saw that Bill Heynes's 3442cc twin-cam six-cylinder engine was at least as beautiful as the car itself. You were greeted by a mass of gleaming aluminum cam covers and SU carburetors. Nothing in that breathtaking mechanical vista warned you that the engine would overheat again and again, or that you'd burn the back of your hand on the beautiful porcelainized exhaust manifold when you checked the oil, or that you weren't smart enough to ever balance those SU carburetors, or that your creator had not endowed you with sufficient patience to sort out the little shims of varying thicknesses that you needed to adjust the valves. Sooner than later, you'd also discover that the Jag's brakes were nowhere near capable of coping with the car's performance. One serious 90-mph stop was it, folks. After that, all you got was a bad smell and an awful sensation in the pit of your stomach whenever you hit the pedal. None of that mattered very much. Jaguar owners wore the characteristic burn scar on the back of their hands with pride, and complaints about bad brakes and overheated radiators sounded more like boasts than lamentations.

Like so many great cars, the Jaguar XK120 began as a sudden

inspiration and grew into a fully fledged prototype in a matter of weeks. No product-policy committees dragged that idea into a conference room month after month to trample the life out of it. No cost accountants were accorded veto power over things like voluptuous bodywork or an aluminum head with double overhead camshafts. There were no planners or strategists or market research guys, so they never got to vote on the XK120, either. Lyons and Heynes had long planned to create a twin-cam luxury sedan, but they were held up by a variety of postwar problems. The engine was ready, but the rest of the car was lagging far behind. For the 1948 Earls Court show they created a stopgap car, the Mark V, an elegant Bentley-ish sedan—also available as a drophead coupe with three-position top—powered by a 3.5-liter pushrod six that had been used in the SS-100 and the Mark IV. Then somebody said words to this effect: "Hey, you guys. We've got the new twin-cam engine, right? We've got the new frame for the Mark V. So why don't we modify that frame, drop the twin-cam engine into it, and turn it into a sports car?" And that's exactly what they did. Lyons personally supervised the creation of an aluminum body—as he did the bodies for all Jaguars through the original XJ6—while Heynes ramrodded the mechanical side. The project name for the engine was XK. They figured the car would do something on the order of 120 mph. So they called it XK120, and it blew the doors off everything at Earls Court in 1948.

That car was the foundation for everything that followed. The XK engine, first conceived in 1943, powered every Jaguar up to and including the first XJ6. There were some clunkers in that long parade of Jaguars. The Mark X was as ugly as a mud fence. The two-plus-two XK-E was the impossible—a clumsy E-type. The 3.8 Mark II was fast and beautiful, but began to rust as it rolled out of final assembly. All Jaguars had electrical problems, and no Jaguar was made truly reliable until John Egan—now Sir John Egan—joined the firm in 1980 and started the rebuilding of the company that led to the Series 3 XJ6, a car that (finally) delivered the level of day-in, day-out usefulness that the public expects from modern luxury cars. Messrs. Lyons and Heynes could make them beautiful and exciting, but it took John Egan to make them reliable.

Unfortunately, John Egan had a little trouble with the beautiful and exciting part when it came time to replace the Series 3 XJ6 with the XJ40—now also called the XJ6. (Figure *that* one out.) As a result, he's had to throw himself on the barbed wire—just as he did with the original XJ6—to upgrade a car that fell short of its public's expectations. It won't hurt to reveal that he succeeded and that the 1990 XJ6 will be a dramatically improved car.

What next? Well, some people think that the heavily hyped XJ220 show car should be Sir John's next step, if he doesn't sell the company first. I disagree. I think Jaguar's next breakthrough should be an XK120 for the millennium, a sort of British Mazda Miata with a heavily breathed-upon XJ6 engine and a ZF six-speed gearbox. They have a splendid relationship with Tom Walkinshaw's TWR racing team and its JaguarSport subsidiary. Why not utilize those extremely valuable resources to create a real Jaguar sports roadster for real car enthusiasts? Bill Lyons and Bill Heynes would have gone for it, in their prime, and they'd have priced it right, too.

Oh, to be in England, now that the Mazda Miata's here.

❧

I went to England last month, to drive the new Jaguar XJ6. It was, as always, an absolutely terrific place to be, and it occurred to me that I ought to write something about traveling in the British Isles. I go there a couple of times each year, at least, and I know that it's a favorite destination for American tourists, but there's an aspect of British travel that's especially enticing for car enthusiasts: i.e., the U.K. is car heaven. They may build wonderful cars in Italy, but you don't really see any more exotic or historic automobiles on the road there than you do here. In Great Britain, people are *driving* that stuff. England is like a giant automotive museum, and British country roads have defined the sports car experience for the rest of the world for seventy-five years.

My wife and I have been shooting driven birds in the U.K. for the past seven or eight years. Our birthdays are a few days apart in November and—autumn being a wonderful time to visit those sceptered isles—we've made that our preferred method of natal day commoration. Shooting trips have taken us to Wiltshire, Hampshire, Shropshire, Devon, the Lake District, Wales, the Scottish Highlands, and, last year, the Isle of Arran, off Scotland's west coast. Our purely automotive wanderings have taken us to many other British destinations, and, with experience, we've begun to refine a list of favorite spots.

On the recent Jaguar trip, we spent most of our time in the Cotswolds—a couple of hours from London, in Wiltshire and Gloucestershire—staying at a wonderful little hotel called Charingworth Manor, near Chipping Campden. Charingworth Manor is a converted country house with very comfortable rooms, a good dining room, a decent wine list, wonderful vistas from every window, a high-spirited springer spaniel named Pepper, and up-to-date plumbing. Plumbing is a big deal in Great Britain. No two buildings seem to be plumbed in the same way. Every toilet, every shower, every bathtub is different. It has been said that there's better plumbing in the Roman ruins at Bath than you'll find anywhere else in the country. Cultural note: The British run their water pipes up the outsides of their houses because, that way, it's easier to fix them when they freeze.

Driving on the other side of the road is not terribly difficult, but it does require constant vigilance. I protect myself by reciting a mantra I learned from Brock Yates, who says he got it from Phil Hill (Phil Hill says we're both crazy). It goes: "Keep left, look right. Keep left, look right." After thirty years I still find myself muttering it, especially in intersections, and _most_ especially when making right-hand turns. Americans seem to be at greatest risk of straying onto the wrong side of the road when exiting right turns and after turning around. Say the mantra aloud, if necessary. "Keep left, look right. Keep left, look right." It's also useful when you're a pedestrian. Urban traffic is quicker and more aggressive than in the States, and it's easy to get blind-sided when you step off the curb.

Motorway traffic is also faster and more aggressive than our local variety. The motorway speed limit is 70 mph, but there seems to be some kind of unspoken compact with the police, who will sit at the side of the road and comfortably watch traffic flowing past at 90 mph. The rule seems to be that you're in no danger of arrest if you're driving in a respectable manner. Lane discipline is less good in Britain than it is here, but nobody _ever_ passes on the left—which is the equivalent of passing on the right in this country. It simply isn't done, my dears.

Roundabouts—traffic circles—are a British institution that requires some getting used to, though once mastered they are the most rational form of highway interchange, skidpads for the poor. The vehicle in the circle has the right of way, so once in the circle you can do laps all afternoon, if that's your fancy. This is helpful when you're confused. If you didn't see the route number or the town name you were looking for, you just go around again. But getting lost is also nice. Some of our best discoveries have been made when we were blundering across the British countryside, and we've never been lost for long.

Where should you go? If I had two weeks, I'd begin and end my trip in London, capital of the civilized world. I'd stay at Brown's Hotel and ask for a room on the Albemarle Street side. Brown's is a longish block from Piccadilly in one direction, and a very short block (through one of London's many shopping arcades) from Bond Street in another. If you're a runner, Green Park is close by. Savile Row is only a couple of blocks. My favorite bookstore, Henry Sotheran, is five minutes away in Sackville Street, and Fortnum & Mason, in Piccadilly, is also a five-minute walk. Fortnum's sells everything from food and wine to furniture. Their food room is worthy of a trip to London all by itself. I buy picnics there, to be eaten along the roadside, or abroad the plane home when flying steerage. Their meat pies are the best, and their house-brand sherries and ports are as reliable as anvils. Buy your umbrellas at Swaine, Adney, Brigg, next door, your Havana cigars at Davidoff's in St. James's, your shirts and ties at Turnbull and Asser in Jermyn Street, and your hats at Herbert Johnson in Bond Street. I go to Herbert Johnson partly because they make great headware, but, more important, because they made those shellacked linen racing helmets worn by people like Juan Manuel Fangio, Stirling Moss, and Archie Scott-Brown in the early Fifties. Brown's Hotel serves London's most civilized tea, but you must book a table in advance.

You should drive to Wales, because it is uniquely beautiful, and you can stop at the Falkland Arms in Great Tew for a pint of pale and frothy and a Ploughman's Plate along the way. The Welsh are dour and cold, more so as you penetrate more deeply into their country. The English and the Scots are generally as glad to see you as the Welsh are not. I prefer the part of Wales around Powys Castle that adjoins the Shropshire border, not far from correspondent Phil Llewellin's home. I'd drive from there to Riber Hall at Matlock in Derbyshire, at the foot of the Pennines, for great food and lovely rooms. Northwest to the Lake District, then across Scotland to Crieff, where I'd stay at the Murraypark Hotel. If I were feeling rich, I'd go a few miles farther on, to stay at Gleneagles and take a lesson at the Jackie Stewart Shooting School. On the way back to London, I'd stop at the Duke of Roxburghe's Sunlaws House in Kelso, where I might try my hand at the local salmon. I'd visit pubs whenever I could, because pubs have done more to shape the British nation than the Magna Carta.

I've done all this in a variety of cars: Jaguars, Lotuses, once in a Bentley Turbo R, once in a Ford Escort, thrice in Ford Scorpio four-by-fours, and several times in Range Rovers and the British version of the Mitsubishi Montero four-by-four. The Range Rover and the Mitsubishi Montero are particularly nice because they enable you to see over the hedgerows. However, a car that I'd *really* like to drive over these roads is the Mazda Miata—the British sports car we always dreamed of, but never thought we'd see.

Some friends and I have already made reservations for a trip back to Shropshire and Powys Castle in January. If you need me for anything, look in at the Hare and Hounds, on route B4386 just southwest of Shrewsbury, during drinking hours.

Bad news, but a sensational journey.

᷎ᴖ᷎

Hail and farewell: The Porsche 911 Turbo has been with us in various forms since 1974. It was introduced by that name at the '74 Paris Automobile Show. Later, they called it the Carrera Turbo, and still later the 930 Turbo. Porsche stopped selling it here in 1979, but reintroduced it in 1985 as the 911 Turbo, in a successful attempt to stop the gray-market importation of European-spec 930 Turbos, and, at the same time, to shift those gray-market revenues to the pockets of Porsche's official U.S. dealers. Whatever the factory called it, in the United States it was always enough to say "Porsche Turbo," and everybody within earshot knew exactly what sort of car we were talking about. The Porsche Turbo was the fastest production car in the world: a driver's car in the purest and most urgent sense.

Now they've stopped selling it, again. In response to a phone call from us, president of Porsche Cars North America Brian Bowler said: "We decided to introduce the Carrera 4 before the Carrera 2, and the Turbo was not compatible with the Carrera 4's all-wheel-drive system. Therefore, the Turbo had to take a back seat. The Turbo will reappear on the Carrera 2 in another year's time. It will have all the Turbo hallmarks: whale tail, wide look, and so on."

The 911 Turbo has been around for a long time, and all cars—no matter how wonderful they may be—disappear sooner or later. The Mercedes 300SL Gullwing went. The Porsche Speedster went. The bug-eye Sprite went. Time marches on. But I, for one, will miss the Turbo. It wasn't just fast, it was *mean* and fast. It separated the men from the boys, the women from the girls. Anybody who ever drove one can tell you exactly how it felt the first time he or she stood on it in second gear. Two weeks ago, my wife and I drove a white 911 Turbo from San Francisco to Monterey (for the Monterey Historic Automobile Races), from there up the California coast to Arcata, through the gorge of the Klamath River to Ashland, Oregon, and from there back down to Reno, Nevada.

J.L.K. Davis had never driven one before, and shortly after taking the wheel for the first time on the scenic route north through the California redwoods, she changed down to second gear, pointed the nose out to the left of the Chevy station wagon she wanted to pass, and legged it. We shot by the Chevy, and one syllable escaped her lips in an uncharacteristically small voice. She said, "Wow." "Wow" is the operative word. I'll bet you a dinner at the Alte Post in Stuttgart that everybody who ever drove a Turbo said the same thing the first time he or she encouraged this greatest of all Porsche production cars to fully express itself.

I'd also be willing to hazard a small wager that the 911 Turbo's replacement won't be as exciting as the 911 Turbo. The Carrera 4 is a wonderful car, but it is a bit more "German generic" than Porsche 911. At dinner in Colorado a while back, a colleague remarked that all Carreras should bear a decal that says, "Sanitized for Your Protection." They have tamed the 911 at last. It runs straight and true. Neither crosswinds nor surface irregularities cause it to change course now. The Carrera's shift linkage is positive, mechanical, and direct, where the 911's linkage always felt vaguely hydraulic. There were no defined slots for gears one through five, there were zones. If you were an experienced Porsche driver, you tossed the shift knob in the general direction of the appropriate zone, and it always went there. They've sorted out the heater and air conditioning controls, too. You can now set the controls for amount and direction of airflow, and level of temperature, without first consulting the owner's manual. It is all too much. You'd think that with extremely civilized cars like the 928 and the 944 available, the Porsche people would have been willing to keep one *un*civilized car in the fold for old geezers like me. One suspects that the cars will become more and more genteel as the company moves farther and farther away from the control of the Porsche family. Such is progress, I guess.

On the road, again. We managed to cover only slightly less than 1700 miles in the 911 Turbo. It was a marvelous trip. The Monterey historic car races were bigger than ever. It was Aston Martin's year, this time, and on hand was probably the finest collection of Aston Martins ever convened in North America. The people from Newport Pagnell really pulled out all the stops. They actually re-created the facade of the Aston pits at Le Mans in 1959, the year Carroll Shelby and Roy Salvadori won the 24 Hours in a DBRI. The artists even peopled the gallery above the painted pits with recognizable faces from that day thirty years ago. One wag suggested that this year's Aston Martin effort was so spectacular that whoever is chosen to be marque of the year next year would be well advised to gracefully decline. The stakes are getting pretty high.

We left Pebble Beach halfway through the concours d'elegance. The drive from the Monterey Peninsula to the Golden Gate was drudgery, but beyond the bridge things opened up. Highway 1, north of Point Reyes Station, rapidly turns into one of the most beautiful stretches of pavement in the world, better even than its more famous southern segment between Pismo Beach and Carmel. Despite the fact that it was Sunday afternoon, traffic was minimal and decreased steadily as we sped toward Bodega Bay. North of Bodega, we picked up a white IROC Camaro whose driver wanted to race and, to his credit, kept us in sight all through the tight climbing stuff there, which included several first-gear hairpins. But when we topped out in the grazing land high above the Pacific and the turns changed from flat-out first gear to flat-out second or third, he lost his appetite for the game. That night we slept the sleep of the just in a nice little inn called the Old Milano, between Gualala and Anchor Bay. Dinner was good, the wine was a justly famous Napa Valley cabernet, and our room overlooked a small bay with its own castle rock (crowned with a watchful eagle) and its own cheerful mob of sea otters. On the road at dawn next morning, we raced the clock to Mendocino so that we might have an eight-o'clock breakfast at the Café Beaujolais. God, what a breakfast. And what a drive. Between Point Arena and Mendocino I passed a half-dozen logging trucks, a handful of locals in their pickups and Subarus, and saw a dozen or more places where I'd like to spend the rest of my life. The rolling, deep-cut countryside is so beautiful that the ocean views become sort of anticlimactic, a bit like having ice cream on your ice cream.

We should have stopped at Mendocino for a day or two. After the coastal highway, even the redwoods seemed to pale by comparison, and the city of Eureka was destructive to the soul. Evidently Eureka, California, was created to punish tourists for having such a nice time on the coastal road and in the redwoods. We ate lunch there, at the first new-wave Mexican restaurant in my experience, watching a scrawny white kid in a Bob Marley knit beret and lavender Converse All-Stars nuzzle his pregnant girlfriend. When they got up to leave, he was carrying a skateboard. Their child is not destined to become president, I fear.

North of Eureka is Arcata, and there we left the coast on Route 299 and entered the gorge of the Klamath River on Highway 9. The Klamath River Highway was designed with the Porsche Turbo's third gear in mind. A perfect, flawless, car enthusiast's road. Late that afternoon we arrived in Ashland, Oregon, home of the Oregon Shakespeare Festival, where my youngest son, Matthew, is an actor. We spent four nights with him, saw him perform in *Cyrano de Bergerac, Two Gentlemen of Verona,* and *Henry the Fourth, Part Two,* ate breakfasts, lunches, and dinners with him that all seemed to merge into one giant meal, fell in love with Oregon's Rogue Valley, and made a quick dash to Crater Lake so that he might experience the Porsche Turbo firsthand.

The final leg was a solo drive from Ashland to Reno, less than 400 miles by way of California's breathtaking Mount Shasta and Lassen Volcanic National Park, which is breathtaking in its own way due to the innumerable sulfurous springs that puncture the earth's surface there. Approaching Mount Shasta, I rolled out of a produce checkpoint on I-5 and the devil made me hurl the Turbo against the redline in the first three gears. In nothing flat I was doing 150 on the speedometer and feeling sort of weightless. The rest of the drive was conducted in a more gentlemanly fashion. In Reno I stayed at Harrah's, shot craps all weekend, and wound up with a net profit of seventy dollars. My purse was fattened by a mere four or five percent, but my soul had benefitted immeasurably from 1700 miles in the last of the Porsche 911 Turbos.

God is my unindicted co-conspirator.

❧

Adelaide, South Australia—Inspired by a prayer session and a midnight Bible reading, Ayrton Senna drove brilliantly to record the fastest lap ever over the Adelaide street circuit, for the pole position in the Australian Grand Prix. The Brazilian sizzled around the 2.35-mile course in one minute 16.665 seconds, an average speed of 110.293 mph. McLaren teammate and archrival Alain Prost, who has provisionally clinched the 1989 world title after a season-long duel with Senna that could still end up in the courts, was fastest in Friday's opening qualifying session, but was unable to improve his time of 1:17.403. From the Ann Arbor News.

Ann Arbor—One tries to imagine little Ayrton Senna on his knees beside the king-size bed in his hotel suite, praying like crazy. "Please, God, let me humiliate the entire field, but most especially that unspeakable Prost. If I have to run into him again, O Heavenly Father, in order to get by, please don't let me damage my own car whatever I may do to him and his. And please help me to remember that if I do have to run him off the road again, I must reenter the track at the same place where I left it, lest I get a load of procedural claptrap from the officials. And finally, God, if I can't win the championship on the track, please guide and inspire my attorneys so that I can win it with a lawsuit."

In the event, the Lord had the last laugh. He brought down a Biblical deluge and neither Senna nor Prost finished the race. Prost didn't even run, though we don't know whether or not he sought divine guidance before chickening out. So much for our heroes. The high point of the proceedings came when Martin Brundle was motoring along in his Brabham Judd BT58 in about eighteenth place when Senna appeared out of the mist and bunted him clear into the Australian Outback. This was fortuitously recorded by the victim's rear-facing in-car camera. Some American TV watchers wondered aloud if those guys should have been racing in such awful conditions, but a more jaundiced viewer suggested

that, as F1 drivers, they were being paid about $8 million apiece to per-
form for their public and their sponsors and one might assume that they
should have the common sense to do that without hitting each other.
There's nothing in their contracts that requires them to be stupid; being
stupid is apparently the one thing they'll do for nothing. Our Maker
must have howled with laughter at the outcome, if He was watching the
satellite feed from Adelaide.

God is playing an increasingly important role in sports these
days. Boxers, football players, baseball players, and stock-car drivers
invoke His name at the drop of a microphone. But Ayrton Senna's midnight seance in Australia is, to my knowledge, the first time the Almighty
has been brought into an intramural Formula 1 squabble. We have seen
any number of crooked government officials try to shift some of the
blame for their misdeeds His way, and God knows we've been treated to
an endless procession of crooked and/or corrupt preachers weeping their
way across our television screens. So, apparently, when it began to appear
that God might be prepared to involve Himself in some serious sleaze, it
was only natural that the world-class sleazebags of international Grand
Prix racing would try to bring Him aboard.

My mother was a religious woman in my childhood, and still is.
Hunting and fishing formed the backbone in my father's faith. I spent a
lot of Sundays fidgeting through sermons, until I became an usher at the
First Baptist Church of Royal Oak, Michigan. Being an usher at the First
Baptist Church of Royal Oak, Michigan, was a perfect occupation for an
adolescent like me, because once the collection was taken the adolescent
ushers could sneak out, skipping the sermon altogether, and dash next
door to the Chevrolet dealer's garage where several dozen hearty blue-
collar types would be racing tethered miniature Indy cars powered by
tympanic-membrane-shattering model airplane engines. The place
reeked of castor oil and two-stroke exhaust, and forty minutes there
would cause your head to ring for a week—that is, until you could get
back for another fix on the following Sunday morning. It has been said
that God exists in the details, and I was convinced that He'd be more apt
to turn up in the blue smoke of that Chevrolet dealership's service area
than in the labored syntax of our preacher's texts. I still think so.

A couple of years later, as a junior in high school, I was told by
my father that my overall performance—both as a student and, more
broadly, as a human being—was so utterly shoddy and substandard that
I would henceforth be allowed the use of the family's '46 Oldsmobile
only when I was going to church or to some church-affiliated activity.
This led me to join several different churches' youth groups—the

Baptists, the Presbyterians, the Episcopalians, the Congregationalists—because I had learned that girls in religious youth groups were just as apt to be promiscuous as their unaffiliated sisters. I had regular access to the '46 Oldsmobile and occasional access to the girls. How could I doubt God's existence, or that my life was regulated according to His great plan?

All of that—and a lot of things that have happened since—has sustained my belief in the Supreme Being, even though I doubt that He involves Himself overmuch in point spreads or lap times. I have even formed a picture of Him in my wandering mind. I see Him as a sort of Edwardian English squire, a ruddy-faced old gent with fluffy white sideburns who wears tweeds and doeskin waistcoats and has had His shoes made at Lobb since the dawn of time. He likes a little Armagnac, but only after the roast has been consumed and the empty bordeaux bottles cleared away. He drives one of the old fastback Bentley Continentals, and He drives it both vigorously and well. He also owns an army-surplus 1942 Willys Jeep, but He doesn't drive it much because it always requires push-starting.

This God, whom I trust implicitly, is of course infallible, but He isn't very organized. He forgets some things and overlooks others. His garage is a mess. His flower beds are always in need of attention. People wonder if He even knows that Ethiopia is part of His territory. He has given the Japanese the most advanced automotive sensibilities in the universe, but failed to provide them with any place to drive. He has given the Americans the best driving landscape on this planet, but saddled them with the world's silliest traffic laws. (He enjoys making Americans miserable because the place was founded by a bunch of religious fanatics, whom He has always found truly detestable. He prefers Australians, inasmuch as their country was founded by a better class of people.) He is not evenhanded in His charity, leading some people to wonder if He exists at all. For instance, poor old also-ran Ayrton Senna, sulking there on his vast pile of money, must feel singularly unblessed after Australia. Our Father who art in heaven may be erratic in His dealings with us, but He sure has a great sense of humor.

It turned out to be a great time to start a new automotive magazine.

~꒷꒦~

Today I flew to Dallas from Ann Arbor and got a shoeshine. I'll be flying home again in a couple of hours. Not even I am ordinarily that extravagant. I was supposed to fly on to Los Angeles, where I would have had lunch with Nissan's senior management and presented them with the unprecedented three awards that they garnered in our 1990 All-Stars competition, but my American Airlines DC-10 suffered a mechanical, and lunch in L.A. went on without me. I faxed some remarks suitable for the occasion and hoped that they'd get read, but except for that—and a very good shoeshine—I was in danger of blowing a whole day. Fortunately, the Dallas Admiral's Club provided me with a desk, and I had one of my trusty yellow legal pads in my briefcase, so I decided to write down my thoughts on the occasion of *Automobile Magazine*'s fourth birthday.

As Mr. Dickens said: It was the best of times, it was the worst of times. It was a difficult time for the automotive industry, but that made it a terrific time to launch a new automotive magazine. Never has there been so much going on in our automotive universe. There's real tragedy, real suspense. Real heroes, real goats. Imagine yourself coming to work tomorrow morning, knowing that you had to make the final decision as to whether your company would gamble a couple of billion dollars on a new product. Bet wrong, and your company will probably go out of business or be absorbed by another. Bet right, and your company will barely survive. Those are not great odds, and the automobile business in 1990 is no place for sissies.

Automobile Magazine has benefitted hugely from all that and from the fact that there have never been so many really good cars available to the public. Perhaps even more important, we seem to be living in a golden age for car enthusiasts. David Holls, of the General Motors Design Staff, brought that to my attention at the Pebble Beach Concours d'Elegance last year. It was first morning light, and we were standing together watching one extraordinary car after another roll across that beautiful lawn to its assigned place on the Pebble Beach golf course. An incredibly noisy, very low Scaglietti coupe came blatting in.

We marveled at its percussive progress, and David, a concours judge, said: "There's never been a better time to be a car nut. When you and I started out, we could look at pictures of great cars in the books and magazines, and that was about it. How many great Ferraris or Bugattis or Hispano-Suizas did anybody see in the Fifties or Sixties? Today—with concours like this one or Meadowbrook, and vintage-car races all over the country, and museums, and even the auctions—a guy can see cars that you and I never dreamed of. Half the great cars that were ever built are alive and well today and accessible to anybody who can afford an airplane ticket."

David Holls is right, of course. There was a period, last summer, when I was away from home on five weekends in succession, attending one automotive event or another. I missed the Pittsburgh Vintage Grand Prix, but I made it to the Meadowbrook Concours d'Elegance, the Rolls-Royce Owner's and Bentley Drivers' annual affair at Newport, Rhode Island, the Monterey Historic Automobile Races and the Pebble Beach Concours d'Elegance, a Porsche Owners' Club convention in Baltimore, and the national convention of the Mercedes-Benz Gullwing Group here in Michigan. During that same period I could have attended two dozen other events in various parts of the country and probably had the time of my life. North America is a beehive of automotive activity, and we seem to be right in the middle of it all.

The most important development in the four years we've been doing business at the corner of Liberty and Fourth is the steady decline of Detroit. The imports, especially the Japanese cars, are clearly dominating the public's automotive consciousness and coming ever closer to dominating the North American marketplace. Lest we forget, the Honda Accord was the best-selling car in the United States in 1989. How long will it be before a Japanese company takes a controlling interest in one of the American Big Three? What if Lee Iacocca succeeds in his dream of marrying Chrysler off to Fiat?

A disproportionate share of Ford and GM profits comes from their overseas operations, and as the bad news piles up month after month, their core business in Detroit finds its situation more and more perilous. Many have expressed the notion that Ford is immune just because it looks so strong right now. Don't believe it. Ford has to navigate the same American-market reefs and shoals as the other two, and it was only ten years ago that those same soothsayers were wondering if

Ford could survive at all.

In *Automobile Magazine*'s next four years, it will be essential that we see the dawn of the Great Car Era in Detroit. By the year 2000 Detroit has to be building *some* of the best cars in the world, and must be launched on an unalterable course to build *the* best cars in the world. Our government must take this fundamental fact into consideration when it considers further regulation of what is still the nation's largest industry. When Toyota's Lexus people had to announce that they were recalling the first few months' worth of LS400s for some minor fixes, they were sharply rebuked by the Japanese government. I wonder if President Bush shouldn't simply order up a couple of new official limousines, let's say a stretch Lexus and a stretch Infiniti. Maybe, while he's at it, he should announce that he intends to invite the Japanese truck manufacturers to bid on all military contracts from now on. Perhaps a little of that sort of presidential rebuke might be the burr under Detroit's saddle that would make some stuff happen.

In the meantime, of course, America has to keep the Japanese government's feet to the fair-trade fire. What's happened to the Detroit automobile industry is more Detroit's fault than Japan's, but nonetheless, our government must do what it can to help the home team, whether we're talking about cars or textiles or agriculture. South Korea ought to give some thought to its trade relationship with this country, as well. As Eastern Europe begins to get its act together in the next decade, our trade officials just might lose interest in putting up with any more South Korean posturing. Robert Eaton, GM's president in Europe, is dashing around like a dervish orchestrating pan-European arrangements. BMW's chairman, Eberhard von Kuenheim, suggests that in a few years BMWs will still be assembled in West Germany, but of parts manufactured almost entirely in the East. Germany has found its own Mexico, and everybody in the West has a new potential source of low-cost manufactured goods. If I were South Korea's trade minister, I'd be trying to find new ways to make America love me.

We have, for years, bitched about the fact that Ford and General Motors sold much better cars overseas than they sold here. We applauded Ford's attempt with the imported Merkur line, particularly with the Scorpio, which was without question the nicest sedan one could buy from Ford. We have to agree that the retail effort was no better than half-hearted, and now the Scorpio has gone away—just when we were about to get a four-by-four Scorpio with power by Cosworth. But all is not lost. General Motors has engineered a buy-in arrangement with Saab, and now the best sedan an American can buy from General Motors is a Saab

9000 Turbo. Saabs will not be for sale in Chevrolet, Pontiac, Oldsmobile, Buick, Cadillac, or GMC dealerships, but they will be, sort of, General Motors products. Now it is essential that the General resist any temptation to run Saab through the corporate blanderizer. Saab could teach General Motors a great deal about building cars with vivid character and personality, and it's a lesson that the General could use.

So, GM buys Lotus and half of Saab. Ford buys Jaguar and Aston Martin. Chrysler buys American Motors. The Corvette ZR-1 comes to market, as does the even more wonderful Mazda MX-5 Miata. Infiniti and Lexus go head-on against the traditional European and American makers of luxury cars. Japanese factories pop up like mushrooms on the American greensward, even as a Volkwagen factory closes its doors in Pennsylvania. The Evil Empire begins to self-destruct, the Iron Curtain is drawn back, and a vast new automotive market is revealed, probably changing the entire equation for the European Economic Community and its neatly laid plans for 1992. It has not been boring. All of this has occurred while *Automobile Magazine* was reaching the ripe old age of four. The alarums and diversions that beset Detroit have cut advertising budgets and delayed our march to profitability, but our circulation has reached 400,000 and continues to grow. You, and all the people, products, and corporations I've mentioned here, have combined to make us what we are. One should not wish one's life away, but I cannot *wait* to report all the things that will have taken place in our field in another four years.

To be read as it was written, while listening to the Beatles' "In My Life."

~ↄᛞᡕ~

One of the great roads in New York State is Route 97 from Port Jervis to Hancock, where it joins Route 17. It is a fast, winding asphalt two-lane that clings to the eastern bank of the Delaware River. We always used it when driving from New York City to Watkins Glen for the U.S. Grand Prix. Watkins Glen was—and is—the only suitable venue for a Formula 1 race in this country. Not Long Beach. Not Detroit. Not Las Vegas. Not Phoenix. Watkins Glen, hard by Seneca Lake in New York's Finger Lakes district, is the place. A racing car looks comfortable at Watkins Glen in a way that it will *never* look when running in a moat in downtown Phoenix. I was there when Jo Bonnier drove a Maserati to win a Formula Libre race in a snow shower in 1958, and I was there when Innes Ireland won his first world championship Grand Prix in 1961, and I'd be standing at the head of the line at the press gate if the people who preside over Formula 1 racing ever found enough soul to return there.

I learned about the goodness of Mercedes-Benz automobiles on Route 97. One year my former wife and I drove to the Glen in tandem with Pedro Rodriguez and his wife, Angelina. I drove a dark blue Ferrari 250GT two-plus-two, and he drove a dark blue Pontiac Grand Prix. It was raining—it seems as though it was always raining on those weekends—and my wife was a wreck. She was all white knuckles and sharp intakes of breath. The glorious madness of racing Pedro across the back roads of upstate New York was lost on her. The next year we did it again, only this time Pedro was in a Ferrari 330 two-plus-two and I was in a Mercedes 230SL. We went just as fast and it rained just as hard, but my wife knitted, never dropping a stitch, never looking up. We could have been motoring gently off to church, for all the strain she apparently felt. That marriage is history now, but I still harbor that day's special feelings for the cars from Untertürkheim.

About a third of the way up Route 97, in the town of Barryville, if memory serves me, there was a nice restaurant called Reber's that used to be saving a bottle of wine for me. We'd stop there for a late lunch on the way home from the Glen on the Monday after the race. In 1967 I was supposed to meet Jo Bonnier and Jo Siffert there, as had become traditional. But I was late, and when I came flying down the road, one glance told me that their car wasn't parked out front, so I kept going, not knowing that Bonnier had bought me a '61 Puligny-Montrachet and asked the bartender to hold it for me. I never got that bottle of wine. Jo Bonnier was killed, Jo Siffert was killed, Pedro Rodriguez was killed, and the Grand Prix at Watkins Glen was killed, and I had no reason to pass that way anymore.

Of all the guys who used to laugh and lie and linger over lunch with me at that nice place on Route 97, only Masten Gregory and I were still alive. Then, the year we launched this magazine, Masten Gregory died of a heart attack in Italy, leaving me. Masten jumped out of at least three racing cars when they were about to crash and survived every kind of mishap the racing driver is heir to, only to succumb to a bad heart.

Now I only look in on the sport occasionally, having walked away from it the day Bruce McLaren was killed. That was June 2, 1970, and I was sitting in my office at the advertising agency when our number one client called. It was John De Lorean, then general manager of Chevrolet, and he said: "I just got a call from England. Bruce McLaren was killed this morning. He was testing at Goodwood." I was upset by the news, certainly, but my friends had been dying in racing cars since I first got involved in the early Fifties, and I was getting used to it. By the time I got home from work that night, I'd made my peace with the idea that he was gone. It was in that frame of mind that I passed the news on to my three kids in the kitchen, and they were thunderstruck. They'd had a helicopter ride around the Elkhart Lake circuit with Bruce just months before. He'd invited them to sit in his big orange Can-Am car in the paddock. Their horror at the news of his death peeled away the business-as-usual protective veneer that I'd been wearing for fifteen years, and I, too, came face to face with the reality of Bruce McLaren's death.

The more I thought about it, the more my own insensitivity bothered me. I began to make lists of friends who'd died in racing cars, starting with Ira Garfunkel, who'd rolled his 1500cc HRG in a hill-climb the day I got married in 1955. The lists grew, until at last there were the names of more than fifty people who'd eaten dinner at my house, played with my kids, called me in the middle of the night, borrowed my cars, helped me close bars in towns from Riverside, California, to Caltavuturo, Sicily, and then suddenly died. I decided it was too much.

I announced to friends and family that I wouldn't attend another race until all of my friends were out of it. It didn't make any difference; they continued to die anyway. But time passed and everybody I'd known, save A.J. Foyt and Mario Andretti, had packed it in. And, I must confess, I found a wide range of uses for weekends, once I'd stopped spending them all at races.

Now, I feel a bit like somebody who can't get over an old girl-friend. I know that racing has changed completely in the years that I've been away, and I'm not crazy about any of the changes, but that's probably just the dry-in-the-mouth bitterness of an ex-lover. Two years ago I watched Jackie Stewart strap himself into a Benetton Formula 1 car and streak out of the pits at Oulton Park, and I felt exactly the same rush of excitement and admiration I'd felt the first time he raced in the United States, at Watkins Glen, in 1965. I felt like Humphrey Bogart in *Casablanca,* for Crissake. It's the oldest cliché in the world: Just when you think you've gotten over some woman, you meet her on the street and you go all warm and moist again.

I hadn't thought much about any of this until quite recently, when I received a letter from Pedro Rodriguez's stepson, Mr. Guy Zugasti. He enclosed a sheaf of photographs, including one I had taken of him at a party at Pedro and Angelina's home in Cuernavaca a couple of days after the Mexican Grand Prix of 1965. Graham Hill and Jackie Stewart were there, as were Ludovico Scarfiotti and Lorenzo Bandini. A riotous soccer game was part of the day's festivities, and, as usual, Graham Hill was more riotous than anybody. Mr. Zugasti's letter reminded me that next year will mark the twentieth anniversary of Pedro's death at Germany's Norisring, July 11, 1971.

Pedro Rodriguez was a very special individual. He began racing with his younger brother, Ricardo, when they were in their early teens. I remember that in 1956 a gaggle of well-known California drivers went down to Mexico for a local race and found themselves being eaten alive by a couple of Mexican teenagers in Porsche Spyders. Ricardo died practicing for the Mexican Grand Prix in 1962 when he was twenty years old, and his death became a heavy burden for Pedro. A lot of people in Mexico always believed that Ricardo was the better driver—Pedro's father was outspoken on this point—and I felt that a lot of the joy Pedro might have taken from his own successful racing career was blunted by the ongoing competition with a dead brother. He once asked me if I'd be his manager, and, as a journalist, I felt compelled to turn him down, but with sincere regret. He was as tough and brave as a whole company of marines, but he always struck me as a man who needed a friend.

Earlier in 1965, Pedro asked Mike Spence and me to help him promote a race at an airport in Guadalajara. It was a riot. Guadalajara was one of the most pleasant cities I'd ever visited, and there was a party somewhere every night. The race probably didn't make Pedro any money at all, but we sure had fun. Two years later, Pedro and Angelina invited me to dinner after the 1967 Monaco Grand Prix. Piero Taruffi was there, and I'd never met him. It should have been a gala dinner, but that was the day Lorenzo Bandini was fatally injured in an awful flaming crash, and we were all a little subdued. About a year would pass before Mr. Spence would be dead at Indianapolis, and Ludovico Scarfiotti would die in West Germany within a few weeks of Spence.

If there's a point to this, I guess I'm trying to say that I'd go back to racing again tomorrow if I thought the people and the camaraderie would be anything like the same. But I'm afraid all that's gone forever, banished by drivers who come and go by helicopter and sequester themselves away in air-conditioned motorhomes when they're not driving. It's the John McEnroe/Bob Dylan syndrome: They've become too important to waste time on their publics. I long for one, just one, Grand Prix driver who comports himself as Stirling Moss and Bruce McLaren and Jackie Stewart did—never too busy for the enthusiasts, always ready to go the extra mile, always appreciative of the sponsor's investment.

Grand Prix racing is a beautiful, even a noble, sport. All those friends who died knew the risks and accepted them because of that beauty and nobility and how it shaped their very lives. But Grand Prix racing has fallen into bad hands. The bean counters and the merchandisers are in control, and the market for heroes has gone soft. I just wish I'd drunk that bottle of wine.

When I win the Michigan lottery.

~ジピ~

O nce, when I was a boy, I heard a tale about millionaire Tommy Manville driving a brand-new yellow Packard convertible up to a group of young guys in front of a Pennsylvania pool hall and saying to one, 'Hey, kid, howdja like to have this car?' The kid came up with the right answer, the story goes, and Manville flipped him the keys, dismounted, and walked away. That story formed the foundation for all my (automotive) fantasies from that day to this.

Now the Michigan lottery is my Tommy Manville. The problem with Michigan's Lotto 47 drawing is that they pay your winnings in twenty annual installments. Thus, if I win, say, ten million big ones, I'll only get $500,000 (pretax) in that first check, and that severely limits my options. If I hit them for twenty million, it'd be better. I'd get a million a year and the bookkeeping would be a lot easier. It would also be a lot easier to purchase some of the things I'd be wanting to purchase with that money burning a hole in my pocket.

But I have no confidence in my ability to win twenty million. I think of myself as a ten-million kind of guy, I guess. Every time the pot gets up to ten I *know* somehow that I'm going to win it. I've always been blessed with extraordinary good luck, so there's no question in my mind that I'm destined to collect, one of these weeks. The other aspect is that I'd use the money so well, and the gods of fortune must surely appreciate that. If I win it, they'll be proud of me, except those hair-shirted whiners and bedwetters who fill the daily editorial pages with their lamentations about this being an age of greed. Greed? I just finished reading an excellent book about eleventh-century Spain, and those guys made greed into an art form! Ellen Goodman, I'd like you to meet Alfonso VI.

So I win the ten million and collect the first check, which will maybe amount to only $310,000, after tax. I set aside ten percent for hunting and fishing and gambling, and another ten percent for good causes. Right away I'm in trouble. I can't buy both the Ferrari Testarossa ($162,250), and the Bentley Turbo R ($167,400), total price $329,650. I have to pick one, then wait a year for the other. (Unless I finance them. Hmmm, ninety-nine dollars down and ninety-nine a month for…Can there be that many months left in my life? No. Surely part of the fun of being a malted millionaire is the ability to make people's eyes bug out when you pay cash. Cash it will be.) The problem is I need them both. I can't just drive the Ferrari for a year, while waiting for the next check, nor could I commit myself solely to the Bentley, knowing that other *nouveaux riches* were already cruising the drive-ins in their fly-yellow Testarossas. These cars are not interchangeable. I will drive one just as fast as the other, but I will drive them to different destinations, with different cargo requirements. The dogs wouldn't fit in the Testarossa, and the dogs are passengers on a large number of my automotive journeys, and I know how much the dogs would enjoy a Bentley.

I have chosen the Ferrari Testarossa and the Bentley Turbo R as target expenditures for my lottery winnings because they're a lot like me—large, flashy, and requiring a great deal of tender loving care. (There is also the fact that the first car I ever owned was a custom-built prewar Mercedes-Benz roadster purchased from an air force colonel who brought it home from Europe at the end of the war and couldn't maintain it. I have a certain standard to uphold.) They appeal to me in another way, as well: Although they are very large cars, they're very fast cars, and each has a magical ability to become smaller as you drive it faster. Standing next to a Testarossa or a Turbo R, you get the impression that it's enormous, but drive either one in traffic or on a country lane and it constantly amazes with its dancer's ability to nip through tiny holes and change direction as an extension of your optic nerve.

There's another problem. Neither the Bentley nor the Ferrari is instantly available as a new car, and that's the only way I want one. If I'm going to make an automotive purchase of that magnitude, I should get a new one. So in either case I'd face a wait of months, at least, before I could take delivery. Am I doomed to win all this money with absolutely no prospect of instant gratification?

When I think of it, I've really backed myself into a corner with my lust for the good stuff. When I was kicked out of college, the only job I could find in Detroit was with a mail-order custom tailoring firm. I was a sales trainee on the showroom floor, and I had to dress the part. The regular guys, all very successful senior salesmen, ordered me a couple of suits and I became an instant grown-up, to the casual onlooker. (In my heart I knew that I would never grow up, however well tailored I might be, and I have proved myself correct in that.) I also became addict-ed to custom-tailored suits.

Shotguns. When I was eleven years old, my father gave me a sin-gle-shot Stevens twenty-gauge with a hammer spring that required all the strength of my right hand to cock. On cold days, rainy days, the birds would flush, my father and his friends would kill them, and I'd still be struggling with the hammer on my Stevens. My father would shake his head sadly, and we'd follow the setter to the next point. As I trudged along, humiliated, I laid my plans for the upgrading of my shotgun inventory. Now I shoot Parker VHEs and Winchester Model 21s that are about as old as I am, with a whole lot more class, and I plot to place my order for an Abbiatico & Salvinelli twelve-bore that will cost more than any car I have ever owned and will take a team of Indian artisans a min-imum of a year to manufacture, if that's the word.

Still no instant gratification. I'm going to win all this money in the lottery, make deposits on all these things I feverishly dream of own-ing, and then nothing will happen for a year. I may have to order the stuff, then, my capital exhausted, borrow some money and go away for a year while I wait for delivery, lest I implode from anticipation.

I have a friend who managed these things better. I guess he understood quality when he graduated from high school. He must have gotten that intuitive appreciation as an extra chromosome, or something. When he graduated from art school, he owned nothing but his clothes, mainly Levis and white T-shirts. He didn't take any vows or anything, he simply resisted the temptation to buy second-rate merchandise, on the reasonable basis that he didn't have much money, so he couldn't afford to buy cheap stuff. He lived in a New York flat without furniture for a long time. When he could afford furniture, he bought an Eames chair, with foot rest. When he could afford a suit, he bought a navy blue one from the best tailor in Rome. He was unable to afford a car for years, but when he finally bought one, it was a used Aston Martin DB2 coupe. As a result, he never had any junk to throw away. There were never any old bell-bottomed trousers or Nehru jackets embarrassing him in his closet. He probably never had to introduce his friends to any girlfriends named Bambi, either. It is entirely possible that he had to push-start that old Aston Martin more than once, but push-starting an Aston Martin while wearing a $2000 suit and Lobb shoes, with the help of a tall, willowy divorcée named Deirdre, is not the same thing as push-starting your '66 Electra 225 with the help of your co-workers from the carwash.

If you are a young reader, seeking your way in life, my friend's is the better example. Follow me, and you will wander through a maze of let's-try-this-and-see-what-happens experimental adventures, a lifelong orienteering course with a compass that sometimes, without warning, decides to point south. Follow the example of my quality-seeking friend, and you will, in the deathless words of the father of one of Max Shulman's feckless heroes, be able to "Get rich. Get rich, then you can sleep till noon and screw 'em all." Words to live by. My friend is successfully employed somewhere in Manhattan right now, gazing out over the city-scape, probably, and wondering if he ought to buy a Testarossa or a Turbo R, and he won't have to win the lottery to do it.

If this is our fifteen minutes of fame, we'd like to ask for a postponement.

E| very now and again *The Wall Street Journal* stirs in its chair at the club, checks to make sure it didn't drool on its waistcoat during the old postprandial nap, and decides to do something about car magazines. The reporter assigned to this task is usually somebody who has trouble getting the coffee order right, and the results generally leave the readers wondering what that was all about. The most recent *WSJ* assault on our thinly defended bastions was a couple of months ago, mounted via a front-page story headlined "Comfy Ride: Car Magazine Writers Sometimes Moonlight for Firms They Review." The sub-sub-head read, "They Also Rake in 'Freebies' from Auto Companies and Double as Advertisers."

One can almost hear the reporter, someone called Joseph B. White, shouting, *"Stop the presses! Gimme rewrite! I've got a story that's going to rip this town wide open!"* Unfortunately for Mr. White's Pulitzer Prize aspirations, the story that followed barely struck *Car and Driver* a glancing blow, and wound up producing more heat than light where the rest of us car magazines were concerned. All the information he presented was stuff freely given by the journalists involved, including me, stuff that no one has ever attempted to conceal, to the best of my knowledge. If he were a regular reader of *Road & Track, Car and Driver,* or this magazine, he'd know that, year in, year out, we've been pretty independent in our editorial judgments, and that history has usually turned out to be on our side on the major automotive issues of years past. As for "raking in freebies," I will happily turn over to Mr. White every twelve-dollar nylon wind-breaker jacket, every T-shirt, every Taiwanese ballpoint pen offered me in years to come, and he can pass them along to Mother Teresa.

Mr. White managed to imply that we are all on the take, here in automotive journalism, and struggled to present evidence of some sort of quid pro quo, a smoking gun that might prove the existence of an unholy relationship between us and the industry we cover. He failed to do so, but he did defame us. Reading Mr. White's snarky little diatribe revealed him to me as that fat kid in everybody's Boy Scout troop, the one who can't start a fire, who can't chin himself, who never learns to tie a bowline, and the one who runs to the scoutmaster every night to tell him that the other guys are smoking or telling dirty jokes after lights out.

Mr. White interviewed me by phone in New York, just as I was about to moderate a panel discussion on automotive advertising that was held in connection with the New York automobile show. (What would he have made of that, I wonder.) He asked me if the readers of this magazine should be warned that I was once in the advertising business—that, in fact, I had been employed as the writer of Corvette advertising and, later in my career, as an executive vice-president of the advertising agency that handled the Chevrolet account. I told him it was no secret, that I had mentioned that part of my somewhat checkered career often and was actually quite proud of the years I'd spent in advertising. I'm equally proud of the years I spent selling cars, working in automobile factories, and messing around as an amateur racing driver.

He then said that his information indicated that I was sometimes paid for giving speeches. Sometimes paid by automotive companies. I told him that his information was correct. He asked me what my honorarium was for such speeches, and I told him. His story said that I gave twenty or twenty-five such speeches a year, but didn't mention that about half of them are given to car clubs and similar organizations around the country, on which occasions I waive my fee. Again, his implication was that my speaking honoraria indentured my editorial point of view. I have spoken to national conventions of automotive fleet operators, automotive glass installers, automotive market analysts, tire wholesalers, advertising executives, marketing executives, parking lot operators, speed equipment manufacturers, motorcycle dealers, and any number of foreign and domestic automotive dealer organizations. I have neither the imagination nor the wardrobe to change my colors for so many disparate communities of interest.

My speeches generally derive from these columns and contain the same mixture of automotive philosophy, automotive gossip, automotive and personal history, and smartass remarks that characterize this space in the magazine each month. The people who invite me to speak invariably ask for an overview of the current automotive scene, thinking—with a kind of blind faith that I find very touching—that I'll actually be able to deliver such a thing. I always try, and I never function as a company spokesman. I am usually presented as a change of pace, an outside point of view, or, in some cases, comic relief. I invite Mr. White to attend a couple of these events—especially in the next few months. He has made an invaluable contribution to my fund of material, and I'll pass up no opportunity to have a little fun at his expense.

As much as I resent this righteous jerk's innuendoes and insults, I am grateful to him and to *The Wall Street Journal* for advertising my availability as a public speaker—in the left-hand column of the first page, just below the fold, no less. It is seldom that a publication of such stature and respectability performs a charitable act of this kind, and I appreciate it. Unfortunately, my calendar is pretty full, so if demand for my flights of automotive oratory should actually increase as a result of all this attention, I guess I'll just have to raise the price. Supply and demand, and all that, you know.

Mr. Ralph Nader, that tireless self-promoter, has stoutly maintained throughout the grim eternity of his celebrity that the car magazines are the paid slaves of the evil automobile manufacturers, fettered by our reliance on their advertising dollars. Ace reporter White's thesis springs from the same bottomless well of paranoid "Committee of Public Safety" accusation. How can we possibly tell the truth about their cars if we let them buy our dinner? How can we negatively review a car that was introduced to us at a hotel in the heart of the Alps? Surely we are corrupted by our willingness to drive cars that we have neither purchased nor rented. Well, Mr. White, I guess some people are more easily bought than others. You and your ilk may be willing to roll over and play dead for a ride in someone else's car, or a shiny royal blue nylon jacket with your name embroidered on the chest, but some of us don't sell out so easily.

In the past twelve months, at least six advertisers have threatened to withdraw their advertising from our magazine based on things we either said or failed to say. Only a couple of weeks ago I spent an entertaining evening in a very nice little neighborhood Italian restaurant with the president of a large car company who was pulling his advertising, we were told, because there'd been no favorable mention of his firm's products in the past two years. If there really were a quid pro quo—if there really were an unholy alliance between us and the industry we cover—I could fill the pages of *Automobile Magazine* with paeans of praise for every boring car that came down the pike, and the money would come pouring in. But that's not the way it works.

I think the problem that exists between people like us and people like *WSJ*'s Mr. White is based on the fundamental difference in the kind of work we do. Special-interest magazines are nothing like newsmagazines or daily newspapers, and this applies to yachting magazines, flying magazines, photography magazines, and bee-keeping magazines, as well as car magazines. We love our subject. We spend every waking hour involved very specifically with a single industry and its products as well as its people. Most of us who write for the special-interest magazines have some experience in the industry covered. There's a great deal of cross-fertilization. Lots of automotive engineers, formerly with car companies, write for the car books—which Mr. White likes to call "buff books." (How could I not dislike the man?) I've already described the varied automotive experiences that led me to this chair. I honestly believe, wrong, I *know* that I serve you, my readers, better because of the forty years I've spent in and around the automobile business. A journalism degree and forty years in general news work could not serve me as well in my chosen field.

And another thing. Old Scoop White—we like to call him Scoop—described *Automobile Magazine* as trying to be "an *Esquire* for car connoisseurs." Good God, man, *Esquire* is a men's magazine for *women*. Why would we want to be one of those? We just want to be the best car magazine in the country.

Trundling cross-country in a 1968 Mercedes 220D with a million miles on the clock.

❧

The old Mercedes was waiting for us at our hotel in San Francisco. It looked amazingly good, for a twenty-two-year-old car with more than a million miles on its odometer. Having received a short-block overhaul when the crankshaft broke at 902,000 miles, but otherwise unrestored, this 220D, VIN 115.110-10-012812, was owned for almost all of those miles by Mr. Edward Donaldson of Springfield, Oregon, who bought it with the specific intention of doing a million miles and perhaps getting into the *Guinness Book of World Records.* A West German journalist had already made one transcontinental crossing with the old dear, and J.L.K. Davis and I would add another 4007 miles, taking the northern route between San Francisco and Montvale, New Jersey. For all the miles it had covered, for all the paint blasted off the front, for all the worn carpets, and despite the cracked steering wheel and the missing driver's side door pocket, it was a helluva car.

Mr. Donaldson had owned a used 1963 Mercedes diesel, which worked so well and seemed so bulletproof that he was inspired to buy this one, brand-new, in 1968. He immediately installed an Engler Hubodometer—the kind used by long-distance truckers—in its left rear hub for record-keeping purposes (and that faithful instrument would indicate 1,009,781.1 miles when I parked it for the last time, in the visitors' parking lot at Mercedes-Benz of North America). Mr. Donaldson, now in his seventies, was a machinist at Willamette Iron and Steel in Portland, Oregon, and had a 250-mile commute, six days a week. He also used the car for long vacation trips—he was entitled to thirty vacation days a year—and ventured as far from home as the Pan-American Highway. The 220D was traded for a new 300SD in 1979 and has been in storage virtually ever since. (At last report, the new SD only had 272,000 miles on it.)

The British racing green 200D—a color called dark olive by the

Stuttgarters—suffered a failed alternator warning light in the Oregon desert, which my wife repaired, and a starter failure in North Dakota, which necessitated a call to the Mercedes-Benz roadside service number, but the trip was otherwise unalloyed bliss. The elderly oil burner averaged almost 33 miles per gallon and used only two quarts of oil. We drove north from San Francisco to Ashland, Oregon, where my actor son disports himself with the Oregon Shakespeare Festival, and thence to Spokane, Washington, where we picked up U.S. 2, an old two-lane that parallels the Canadian border through Idaho, Montana, North Dakota, Minnesota, Wisconsin, and the Upper Peninsula of Michigan. If U.S. 2 has a flaw, it is that it's so isolated up there that the motels and restaurants are all mom-and-pop places and their quality is spotty indeed. But the road itself is a good one, well worth driving.

A night in San Francisco allowed us to take my other son's recommendation and eat incredibly fine burritos at La Cumbre, on Valencia Street. La Cumbre has what may well be the best burritos in the Republic, but the clientele, with its kandy-kolored hair, black leather, and pop-top earlobe décor, may discourage all but the most determined seekers of the ultimate tortilla-wrapped bundle from heaven.

At six-thirty the next morning, the valet parking maven at the Stanford Court said, hey, no problem, he knew how to start a diesel, and though it did take him a half-hour, he did get it started. We left San Francisco, not knowing what to expect from a car with a million miles to its credit. Would it keep up with traffic? Would it overheat? Would it explode? The answer turned out to be none of the above, and we quickly learned to treat it like any other car.

We cruised at sixty-five miles an hour, followed by a fragrant cloud of black smoke, getting passed on long uphill stretches, catching up on the downhill side. The summer heat was blazing, but the un-air-conditioned Merc was actually quite comfortable. Being more than two decades old, all of its glass surfaces were quite vertical, so that sun-load was minimized, and there were lots of vent outlets blowing fresh air at the front-seat occupants. It was also old enough to be equipped with vent windows—operated by serrated knobs with about 250 turns lock to lock. One forgets what life was like before air conditioning. It turns out that one can drive 4000 miles with the windows open and survive. At seven forty-five, passing the Napa exit, a ghastly-boring little Chevette threw up a stone that starred the windshield just about level with the driver's brow. A Chevette. To think that this noble old steed, having been through so much, would get gored by one of history's truly stupid cars. We were mortified, but we managed about 350 miles, with stops for breakfast and lunch, by midafternoon.

On Day Two, 512 miles, we were admiring a big antelope buck and failed to avoid a large hole in U.S. 395 at about mile fifty. The impact was severe, and the alternator light came on and stayed on. We were fifty miles from the nearest gas station, and I was distraught. There is an entry in the log-book in my wife's hand: *I fixed the alternator light and changed my spouse's despair to rosy optimism—on to Burns, Oregon.*

On Day Three, 621 miles, we discovered that there is no Pendleton store in Pendleton, Oregon. The Pendleton store is in Portland, Oregon. Go figure. The shirt I meant to buy, and the blanket that would have dressed up a couch in the TV room, remain unbought.

The second great meal of the trip came at the end of Day Three, after thirteen hours on the road, at the Sports Club in Shelby, Montana. The starter had refused to crank in Kalispell, coming to life only when Mrs. Davis wiggled a wire. I am feeling stressed. The only people in the restaurant are two enormously fat young Indian guys (Sioux sumo wrestlers?) who have lost all of their money at the casino next door. One orders the six-ounce club steak and the other has a salad. Custer and the Seventh Cavalry are probably in no immediate danger from these guys. Our waitress is a very sweet Indian lady about my age who looks like Buddy Hackett in drag. My dinner is a T-bone steak that overlaps the plate by three inches in every direction. We drink cheap wine and chat with the proprietor, who is justifiably proud of his beef. The malfunctioning starter seems like less of a problem now.

Day Four, 763 miles: People who concern themselves with events like the recent collapse of all the Socialist utopias need not fly to Poland or Bulgaria to see what went wrong. A visit to an American Indian reservation will provide all the discouragement anybody could ask for. Saw a red fox and a huge flight of swans today.

Day Five, 472 miles: Late-ish start from Grand Forks, North Dakota. Had to call the Mercedes-Benz 800 number for a roadside service last night. Starter wouldn't respond to wiggled wire anymore. Paul Boese called back in fifteen minutes, arrived at 7:15 a.m. from Valley Imports in Fargo, eighty-five miles away. Thoroughly nice guy. Offered to replace the starter. I said no, hoping to keep the car original. Paul rigs very elegant hot-wire. Magic. Works every time. Local M-B roadside service deal is this: Time and a half door to door. For less than fifty miles, a flat fee of fifty dollars. One of the great bargains of all time when something's not working and you don't know how to fix it. Credit cards accepted. Crossed the headwaters of the Mighty Mississippi this afternoon—a little too wide to step across.

Day Six, 534 miles: With white-tailed does and fawns watching
as we smoked across Michigan's beautiful Upper Peninsula, I found that
I had fallen in love with this old Mercedes-Benz. I loved the noise. I
loved the way the four-speed manual box worked. I didn't mind that the
clutch was kind of unpredictable, and I was crazy about the hot-wire. We
were thrilled that we'd get to break the trip with a week-long stopover at
home—it gave us another seven days with that doughty old diesel. In the
meantime, if the Mercedes people would like this one returned to the
West Coast, Mrs. Davis and I are available. A week later, after we'd visited GM's Saturn plant, I finished the journey to New Jersey. I wonder:
Will some other Edward Donaldson put a million miles on a new Saturn
over the *next* eleven years?

September song.

~~~❧~~~

S unday afternoon. The white Range Rover showed up two days ago. It's one of the new Great Divide limited-edition models, and we'll be driving it to Colorado midweek. When we drove Range Rover's Great Divide expedition last year [March 1990], Charlie Hughes (president of Range Rover), Malcolm Smith (everybody's motorcycle champion and off-road racing driver), and I vowed that we'd return to do it again, this time with wives. Now the day of departure is nigh. When I left the house an hour ago, J.L.K. Davis was on her hands and knees muttering vile oaths as she tried to roll up our tent, which she'd been airing out in the yard. She'd also discovered a tear in the tent fly, and she was grumpy because she didn't know how to do a waterproof patch on nylon. I thought it best to come to the office.

November marks my sixtieth birthday. Six decades of decadence, some would say, and this little rerun of the Great Divide extravaganza sort of opens the festivities. It will be followed by a shooting trip to South Africa and Botswana, then a couple of days at Cader Cox's Riverview Plantation in Georgia, and then we'll come home and really get into it. We spent a couple of months commemorating my fiftieth, and surely we can do no less, now that my sixtieth year is winding to a close. I've only had one bad birthday, my twenty-fifth, and I spent that one mostly unconscious in Sacramento's Mercy Hospital. Otherwise, my birthdays have always been occasions for celebrations—no regrets, no angst, no forebodings about the encroachments of age. (Even the twenty-fifth was a celebration of sorts: I was alive, and I had no right to be.)

I was always touched by Walter Huston's rendition of "September Song." He's the only guy I ever heard sing it who sounded as though he knew whereof he sang. I'm sure somebody like Mabel Mercer (the interior voice says, "There *was* nobody like Mabel Mercer") might have done it justice, or Ray Charles, but I've never heard either of them sing it. Somehow, though, September seems like the wrong month for the sense of winding-down conveyed by "September Song." September is still a summer month in the temperature zone, and those lyrics really seem to be talking about November.

At my age, I'm developing some perspective about these things. Sixty, it seems to me, corresponds pretty accurately to the month of September in the song, which means that I still have glorious October to enjoy, followed by November—when the days really *do* begin to dwindle down—with December still to follow, which will be time enough and then some for speculations about mortality.

Being camped out in the tops of the Rocky Mountains next week means that I'll miss John R. Bond's memorial service aboard the Reuben E. Lee in Newport Beach, California. John Bond, and his second wife, Elaine, were the people who turned *Road & Track* into a real magazine, taking over in 1953. They were also the people who gave me my start in this business, in April of 1957, before my new face was even fully broken in. They'd paid off their predecessors' debts a year before and became sole owners of the enterprise. The magazine had actually been started by Oliver Billingsley and Bill Brehaut in New York, in 1947, but Billingsley and Brehaut between them couldn't muster the skills necessary to run a magazine, and it foundered, to be raised from the dead by the Bonds.

Their vision for the *Road & Track* of the Fifties was shaped like this: America has no magazines like *Autocar* or *Motor*. America's car enthusiasts need a magazine of that kind, a magazine that even covers the same basic portfolio of cars as *Autocar* and *Motor.* However, English magazines are really boring—remember, there was no *Car* in those days—and we must give our version of *Autocar* and *Motor* a distinctly American flavor. Elaine admired *The New Yorker* magazine immensely, and *The New Yorker* became their model. Their *Road & Track* combined the subject matter of English car magazines with the sly wit and understated elegance of *The New Yorker.* It was a brilliant plan, and it resulted in a brilliantly successful magazine.

Elaine Bond—dead, now, since 1984—was the ramrod that turned *R&T* into the magazine it was in the Sixties and Seventies. John was the voice. He was eccentric, suspicious, and generally out of touch with what was going on in the wider world of automobiles, but it didn't matter. He projected an aura of calm and good sense in public and in print. People loved him, and loved what he wrote, even when he proposed that a Ford flathead V-8 was the way to win Le Mans, or expressed the concern that the Alfa Giulietta Veloce engine had such radical valve timing that it would never run for any length of time, or announced that the Chevrolet Vega was the best-handling car in the world. He lived mainly on booze and cigarettes in the years that I was close to him, and spent most of every night at his drawing board, worrying over designs for front-steer sailboats, or oddball bicycles. He usually looked like he was about to die, and we were all certain that he'd outlive every one of us.

I loved Elaine Bond and admired John, and eagerly sopped up every drop of wisdom they let fall. In three years they taught me what I needed to know to make a better-than-average living as an automotive magazine person. When they fired me, in April of 1960, it was as though Dad had sold my dog. They canned me because another employee who wanted my job took them to dinner and fed them a lie about me. They never asked for my side of the story. We shouted at one another for thirty minutes or so, then I left and drove home. I slammed the car door, stalked out of the garage, and suddenly burst into wracking sobs. I stood crying with my face pressed into the stucco wall of that garage for five minutes before I could regain my composure and go into the house to tell my family what had happened to me.

In the twenty-fifth-anniversary issue of *Road & Track,* John wrote: "I suppose that my most famous faux pas was firing David E. Davis [*sic*]. I met DED at one of the monthly SCCA meetings in Los Angeles back around 1955. We hired him to work for us as advertising director. His oft-related story of his dismissal was that he was charged with being incompetent and insubordinate. Our story was that he was lazy. Neither is correct." I took some grim satisfaction from that quote, but I never completely got over the injustice of my dismissal. It has been an important motivator in all of my work since.

Even so, we did make up, and I can say without any caveat whatsoever that every success I've enjoyed—in the advertising business, at *Car and Driver,* and now with *Automobile Magazine*—can be traced back to my three years with John and Elaine Bond. I owe them both a great deal.

At the time of his death, John had remarried his first wife, Mercedes, who had brought him a measure of peace of mind and happiness that I doubt he'd felt in many years. Everyone should be so fortunate. As it happens, I am.

I wonder how John R. Bond felt on the eve of *his* sixtieth birthday.

Attitude adjustment: Take one Viper ride, just before sundown.

B

ob Lutz is a take-no-prisoners car enthusiast. He's also the president of Chrysler. He owns an MG TC and a two-liter MG Magna, a gorgeous Citroën 15, an even more gorgeous Riley MPH, a Brian Angliss Cobra, and a couple of high-mileage yet concours-clean BMW motorcycles. By the time you read this he'll have his commercial helicopter license. Last night he gave me a cigar from his limitless supply—stored in an antique bank vault—a Romeo y Julieta the size of a small salami. As it happens, he also gave me a rip-roaring ride in his baby, the Dodge Viper prototype.

Bob Lutz is unique among car-company presidents. He's Swiss-American for a start, a former marine jet pilot whose childhood memories include an uncle who used to visit in a Talbot-Lago 150S. When he was chairman of Ford of Europe, colleagues sometimes speculated darkly that his extravagant love of cars would get him into trouble some day, and it probably did. When the roundheads started to take the Ford Motor Company back from the cavaliers a couple of years ago, the word went out that Lutz would not fit in the new order of things. He was the best production man in the company, but he was always out on the end of one limb or another, and too many of his colleagues carried saws.

Lee Iacocca is unique in his own right, as the world knows. Mr. Iacocca watched Lutz losing his battle at Ford, and decided to make him an offer. A series of meetings took place at the Iacocca breakfast table and finally Bob Lutz joined Chrysler, just like a host of other Ford executives before him. Now he's the president, and he and Lee Iacocca seem to have worked out a mutually satisfactory arrangement for steering Chrysler away from the edge of the abyss. Lutz and his product team, led by engineer François Castaing (formerly with the Renault Formula 1 effort), seem to have instilled a lot of confidence and a clearer sense of mission in the corporation's car guys. The neat little Spirit R/T, as quick as or quicker than Ford's SHO Taurus, is rolling proof that they're on the right track. So is the winner-and-still-champion Chrysler/Plymouth/Dodge minivan.

Then there's the Dodge Viper. A number of my fellow automotive journalists have written stories about the Viper in which they claim they've driven it, or fudge the issue sufficiently to leave that impression. I am assured by Mr. Lutz and his minions that none of them have. Neither have I. But boy, howdy, have I had a ride in that sucker! The occasion was an annual gathering of Chrysler's top 150 suppliers at the Chrysler proving ground. There was a tent for the dinner meeting, and a display area for a full portfolio of Chrysler products, present and future. The Viper was one of these. A short ride-and-drive course had been laid out on the grounds, marked with orange cones at intersections, and we were sternly directed not to deviate from the official route.

Faced with a choice between the barbecue and the test fleet, I was sort of gravitating toward the cars when President Lutz intercepted me, offered me the Romeo y Julieta mentioned above, and asked if I wanted to go for a ride in the Viper. Inasmuch as he was already aimed at the driver's side, I flopped into the passenger's seat and groped for the various pieces of the five-point racing harness. The cockpit is very comfortable, partly because the seat is both large and supportive, and partly because there's lots of space. The instrument panel is strictly temporary, a flat panel to hold the instruments, no more. The big red beast is a test mule, and a thoroughly used test mule at that.

As he addressed the controls and twisted the key, he said: "I would be severely punished if I let you drive. So far no one has driven this car outside the family." The engine came to life with a very un-thoroughbred rasp. The eight-liter (487 cubic inch) cast iron V-10 didn't sound like a vee-configured engine at all. If anything, it sounded like a straight-eight with a leaking intake manifold. The sucking noise from the induction system drowned out the exhaust noise, at least for the passenger. It sounded like, well, a *truck* engine—pushrods, two valves per cylinder—which is exactly what it is. Ing. Mauro Forghieri of Lamborghini has been charged with the development of the sportier all-aluminum version of the V-10, and the word is that it will be more powerful and more carlike when his work is done.

Halfway through the first left-hand corner, Lutz stood on the loud pedal and all hell broke loose, as did the rear end (450 pounds-feet of torque will do that). In an instant we were at a 45-degree angle to the center line, and in another instant we were pointed off the other side of the road but still traveling in more or less the hoped-for direction. I silently prayed that he'd lift before the huge rear tires hooked up and fired us off into the bushes, and, sure enough, he did. When the whole car was pointing in the same direction again, he nailed it and wound it out toward 5000 in the first five of six gears. It was a good thing the cigar was in my pocket and not in my mouth. The engine is a torque generator—it isn't peaky, nor does it want to rev like a small-block Chevy or a Ferrari Testarossa. The torque curve is essentially flat from 2000 to 4800 rpm, and the cast iron engine is redlined at 5500 (Ing. Forghieri's all-aluminum version will probably rev to 6000). Sixth gear is an overdrive, so we didn't use it much. Besides, 5000 rpm in fifth gear is about 140 mph, and I was already beginning to feel a bit like Colonel Stapp on his rocket sled.

At the first cone-marked intersection, my president-chauffeur deviated from the official route by driving between the cones. A female security guard attempted to wave us down and restate the prohibition on detours, but Lutz yelled over his shoulder, "It's okay. I'll authorize it!" He then nailed the throttle again, and we roared off onto the long, winding durability road, I guess it was. Two lanes, bumpy, with two or three very long, fast sweepers. We ran one-forty-plus on the rough straights and the car really wanted to fly off into the woods. In the long sweepers, it suffered some kind of diagonal roll problem that caused violent corkscrewing. On a particularly rough stretch, panels flapped and banged as we bottomed violently coming off the thank-you-ma'ams. The president, his white hair plastered straight back from his forehead by the wind, shouted over the glorious din, "This is pretty extreme punishment." I knew that. Words cannot describe how wonderful it was. The car seemed to be full of fairly course grit, and when we really got to motoring, all this *schmutz* got sucked out of the carpet and into our eyes, ears, and mouths. When we returned, after a half hour, he stopped and the car was immediately enveloped in a cloud of acrid gray smoke—there was a clearance problem between the sill shrouds and the exhaust pipes and the plastic body material was trying to combust. Viper chief engineer Roy Sjoberg and one of his guys dashed into the tent and came back with cut-glass pitchers of ice water, which they poured over the door sills. No boring cars for *this* magazine, boy.

One wonders how many times that poor old beat-up prototype gets subjected to that sort of treatment in a typical work week. A couple of writers, after their rides in the Viper, wrote that it was already at the same stage of development as the current Corvette. Not so. I haven't the slightest doubt that it will be, perhaps even more so, but right now it's a mean old mule, not quite ready for prime time. Chief engineer Sjoberg—who happens to be the kid brother of a lovely girl I dated in

1954—allowed that most of the instability I'd witnessed was due to an overlarge front stabilizer bar, and apologized for all the smoke. (We would discover later that the steering rack had broken loose from the chassis.) There was a little tsk-tsking from the engineers, but the president just grinned like a kid whose home-run ball has busted a window.

I thought I wanted a Viper *before* Bob Lutz took me for that ride. Now I *know* I want a Viper. The Porsche 959 started a trend toward what we might call "super-performance cars a thirteen-year-old girl could drive." Honda's Acura NSX is the latest of these. Guys keep coming back from their first NSX rides saying, "Wow, it's *much* easier to drive than a Ferrari!" Well, I for one hope that Ferraris will always be a challenge to drive. Whenever I feel I've driven a Ferrari well, I know I've done something that thousands of people raised on automatic gearboxes and power everything will never be able to duplicate. Bob Lutz obviously felt that way when we climbed out of the Viper. He'd wrestled a ragged prototype around a difficult circuit at a very high rate of knots and had boundless fun doing it. When I finally get to drive a Viper it'll be much closer to production and a lot of the *Sturm und Drang* will have been refined out, but that'll be okay, and if I ever meet a thirteen-year-old girl who can drive one, I'm going to adopt her.

I was in the Chrysler lobby the day they killed De Soto. This was worse.

Well, Detroit's old London Chop House has finally exhaled its last gasp, turned up its toes, and expired. If any further proof is needed that the domestic automobile industry is in really serious trouble, I cannot imagine what it might be. Ever since 1938, the London Chop House was the place where Detroit's movers and shakers went for dinner. Lunch was salesmen and clients, but dinner was heavy hitters fueling up. Sometimes there was so much power in that room that you could feel it shake, like a well-tweaked Chrysler Hemi at idle.

Lester Gruber's London Chop House was New York's 21 and L.A.'s Chasen's in downtown Detroit. It was as good a restaurant as you could find in North America. An elegant steak, chop, and fish joint with a great wine list and a bar that was a *bar*. I can't imagine how many meals I bought there, for how many people, or how much my various employers must have spent over the years covering the resulting bills. I was not the champion, though, not even close.

Arne Gittleman was the advertising director of *Sports Cars Illustrated* when he began frequenting the Chop House in the Fifties. Later, Gittleman became *The New Yorker*'s man in the automotive industry, and established himself as a legendary figure on his frequent visits to the Motor City. One night in the early Seventies, Arne read the menu, which he now knew by heart, and waved the waiter away. Going to the phone booth at the end of the bar, he ordered a pizza to be delivered to his banquette. When the pizza arrived, the restaurant came to a halt. Everyone watched as the delivery guy threaded his way among the tables and put the pizza down in front of Gittleman. Lester Gruber, the proprietor, left his brother Sam on guard at the bar, strolled over to Gittleman's booth, sat down, and had a slice of pizza and a glass of wine. Lester Gruber was one of history's great saloonkeepers. (Gittleman enjoyed similar fame in New York. One night, when the waiters at The Palm seemed determined to ignore him, he gradually became more and more agitated and finally hopped onto the bar and tap-danced there among the martini glasses and ashtrays until he had their attention.)

Robert E. Brown, who has been selling *Motor Trend, Hot Rod,* and all of the other Petersen Publishing magazines for as long as anyone can remember, was practically a shareholder in the Chop House. You gave your car to the valet parking guy, went down the stairs, checked your coat with one of a succession of gorgeous hatcheck girls, turned left, and there was Brownie, camped at the corner of the bar. No one will ever know how many Cars of the Year were negotiated in Lester Gruber's joint by Brownie and his colleagues, and his bar bill alone must have run into the millions.

We all entertained John Z. De Lorean there, in his heyday. John liked to sit in Booth Number Two, right up front, where he couldn't be missed. When he was running Chevrolet, De Lorean tried to re-create himself as Engelbert Humperdinck—he truly wanted to be the first pop-star automotive executive, and he was not a man to sit for long in a room, unnoticed. He dropped names, gave company cars away to golf pros and starlets and third-rate movie executives, wore three-piece suits with the waist-coats left unbuttoned, fancy white shirts with collar points that came down to his nipples, and winkle-picker boots, just like Keith Richards and Paul McCartney. None of us were surprised when he turned up on the TV news bouncing a bag of cocaine in his hand and marveling at its value. *Automotive pop star meets Miami Vice!* John stopped having dinner with me after I called him Detroit's answer to Margaret Trudeau.

God, what a place! Tony Lapine, now retired as Porsche's chief designer, likes to celebrate his occasional arrival on our shores with a hamburger. The ground sirloin at the Chop House, accompanied by a $55 bottle of Nuits-Saint-Georges, always seemed to capture his fancy.

Some time back, when the late Gene Bordinat was in charge of Ford Styling, he asked me to look after his wife, Edelgard, while he was in Europe with Henry Ford II. I didn't know at the time that Edelgard was as wild as a deer, indiscreet, neurotic, and unable to handle her alcohol. I organized a dinner party at the Chop House. My old partner, Doug Mahoney, and one of his several wives. Former *Automobile Magazine* columnist Trant Jarman and his then-wife, Peg. Jarman was as crazy as Mrs. Bordinat, and they developed a crush on each other instantly. Mrs. Bordinat was pretty squiffed when she started feeding her dinner to Mr. Jarman. Mrs. Jarman was not amused. She waited a decent interval, then punched Mrs. Bordinat right in the schnoz. Blood flew in all directions. Tears were shed. My career was on the brink.

After Edelgard's nose was repaired in the ladies' room, I was driving her home in her husband's Lincoln, berating her for her irresponsible conduct, when she abruptly said, "Well, if you think I'm a drunk and you're embarrassed to be seen with me, I'll leave." That said, she simply opened her door and rolled off the seat. I managed to grab her arm and hang on for dear life as I slowed her husband's company car from seventy-five and headed for the shoulder. When she was back on her seat, seatbelt fastened, and we were under way again, I recognized my own handprint becoming an ever-deeper blue on her upper left arm. I spent the next two years waiting for the phone call that would finish me off as an automotive journalist and send me back to the assembly lines of my youth. Edelgard has gone to that big model agency in the sky, and I, for one, don't miss her a bit.

The London Chop House was the first place I ever saw with a pay phone in the men's room (absolutely indispensable for errant husbands), ice cubes in the urinals, and the day's sports pages hung where you could peruse them while melting those ice cubes, one by one.

I had a friend who loved the London Chop House and worked almost single-handedly all through the Fifties to elevate Detroit's consciousness where exotic cars and motorcycles were concerned. He raced Allards. His own Allard J2X was one of the most lovely machines ever seen, and he would take it to a gas station, when visiting some bar, and give the attendant twenty bucks to run it up on the hoist, to protect it from inquisitive fingers. He and I were working together on New Year's Eve when he asked me to entertain his girlfriend, Marge, that night while he fidgeted around the family hearth, out of action. I did my best to help him out, and Marge sent me home at noon the following day.

My friend's gratitude took the form of a dinner at the London Chop House, with his wife and very young son. The child was not having a nice time. He was grumpy and tended to squirm. When the meal was over and our waiter asked if we wanted coffee, the kid ordered a cup. "You're too young for coffee," his father snapped. The kid was adamant, so my friend ordered him a *café au lait*. When it came, the kid snarled, "If I'da wanted milk I woulda asked for milk." Dad took the little boy's hand in his, and said, "Drink your coffee, before I cut out your spine and nail it on the garage roof to bleach in the sun." The kid replied, "I'll drink it, but I won't like it."

When my friend died, not so long ago, that same mean little kid complied with his dead father's instructions by renting a Stearman biplane and scattering the old man's ashes over the Gulf of Mexico.

The London Chop House died when Lester Gruber died, in 1982. It continued to operate, but it was dead. One of his best customers bought the place, but then he died, too. His wife, a tall, slender blonde, trendy as all get-out, decided that red meat and red wine and a bar that stocked special glasses for Negroni cocktails were simply not up to her standards. She turned it into a dance club with a grazing menu for rich suburbanites who never showed up. Neither did the rest of us. When her attempt failed, another group took over and tried to rebuild something that they'd only vaguely understood in the first place. So yesterday the London Chop House closed up. Too bad. Several large chunks of my life are in there somewhere among the stacked chairs.

Like finding a bird's nest right there on the ground...

I was first introduced to Ferraris at a Sports Car Club of America road race in the early Fifties. There were several on hand that weekend, but I particularly remember cars driven by Jim Kimberly, Bill Spear, and Ebby Lunken. I got my first ride in a Ferrari—probably a 2.6 or 2.9 Vignale coupe—a year later. I was so excited that I neglected to find out exactly what kind of Ferrari it was. The cars dazzled me then, and they dazzle me now. I have long dreamed of owning a Ferrari. I've often used this space to muse about various Ferraris, and to speculate about the one I'd buy if I ever won the Michigan lottery.

In the years since my first brush with the red cars from Maranello, I've managed to drive quite a few, and have done several good long journeys wrapped in one Ferrari or another. Luigi Chinetti and Bob Grossman provided several test cars over the years. Friends lent me theirs. One friend—too busy to drive it perhaps—used to ask me to exercise his 250 Tour de France coupe. Bill Ruger handed over his 330GT two-plus-two, rusty, running on eleven cylinders, one header leaking, for a pre-dawn dash through the rain to an airport 100 miles away. (After that, I always nurtured the fantasy that he was going to sell it to me for $5000, but it now sits among the cars in his collection, an immaculate running chassis.) Some were old, some were indifferently maintained, but every one of them was a joyous experience that left me scheming and fantasizing about how I might possibly buy one of my own. In the year that we started this magazine I sold my minty little red-and-black Fiat Topolino to raise money for the down payment on a yet-to-be-found 250 two-plus-two—then the last affordable twelve-cylinder Ferrari—but blew the money on three automotive posters at a shop in Aspen. That was typical of my not-so-near-misses with Ferrari ownership until today.

Today the lightning struck. By several extraordinary strokes of good fortune and a coincidence or two, I was able to say, less than an hour ago, "I'll take it." "It" is a 1987 Ferrari 328GTS, red with tan interior, serial number 60199. The car has 11,947 miles on its odometer, and it has been beautifully maintained by a single owner. It is in the custody of my friend and occasional hunting companion, Dr. Emilio Anchisi—formerly president of Ferrari in North America, now chief executive officer of Miller Motorcars in Greenwich, Connecticut. I have not yet seen it, but my wife, who is an enthusiastic co-conspirator in this deal and happens to be in Connecticut, examined it this morning, we conferred by telephone, and an agreement was reached. The check, as they say, is in the mail.

It has taken almost forty years, and it happens on the eve of my sixty-first birthday, but it was well worth the wait. I can hardly wait to start it, feel my way through the gate into first gear, then engage the clutch—knowing that when I do it this time, it'll be my own Ferrari that's causing my pulse rate to rise and my breath to shorten.

Palm Beach to Ann Arbor. Ferrari 512TR. Nice ride.

~·~

Ferrari dealers saw the new 512TR (the Testarossa's replacement) for the first time at Moroso Motorsports Park in Florida, less than a month before the car was introduced to its public at the Los Angeles Auto Show. They were able to drive it on the track and, as far as we know, loved it. As well they should. It is a car to love. I blew into Palm Beach with a handful of other press folk the day the dealers left. We, too, stayed at the Ritz-Carlton and drove the cars at Moroso. I, however, had the secret ingredient. I got to drive a new 512TR back from Palm Beach to Ann Arbor.

I don't know for sure how the dealers behaved at Moroso, but I can tell you that there were buzzards perched in the grandstands and lining the fence around the track, and I can only assume that the driving conduct of Ferrari's North American retailers had led those big black birds to believe that we journalists might provide them with brunch. There were also two very tall sandhill cranes hanging around the start/finish area, and we were told that they regarded the racetrack as their turf. They hollered at us from time to time, but they were gracious enough to let us use their track.

Truth to tell, we do know that one dealer did a 360 and flat-spotted all four tires on one of the three cars present. We also know that a visiting Ferrari executive who shall remain nameless burned the clutch out of one by doing a full drag-race burnout leaving the pits. The clutch would almost certainly have survived this under normal circumstances, but unfortunately, he had left the hand brake on. One day later, toward the end of our morning at the track, this same Italian gentleman hopped into the car that I was to drive home, revved the engine to about 5000 rpm, and dumped the clutch. You should have seen the pained expressions on all the faces he left behind as he lurched out onto the circuit.

That, however, was nothing compared to the looks that were exchanged when a young man from *Motor Trend* got it all wrong with that very same car and went straight where he should have made a hard left. The front spoiler was broken and the front tires flat-spotted, and there were tufts of grass in various seams and orifices. He had the braking point right, he said, but he hadn't used enough brake. Ahem. Well, yes. Of course. Seeing the corner approaching at rather more miles per hour than he'd had in mind, I guess, he elected to take the road less traveled. The buzzards shrugged. The hard-working mechanics put things right again, and I was on my way north by early afternoon.

Before I left, I asked former Ferrari test driver, now service manager, Roberto Vaglietti if the broken spoiler meant that my car would be unstable on I-75 at 192 miles per hour. I was kidding, right? He thought for a moment, then said, very seriously, "You should be perfectly all right up to 250 kilometers per hour." That works out to 155 mph, folks, and I thanked him for his advice. I don't know whether he took me seriously or not, but I felt complimented. Roberto was doing demonstrations on the track, and like all Ferrari test drivers he was absolutely spectacular to watch. One corner worker exclaimed, "Boy, that guy really knows this track!" Wrong. "That guy" had never seen the track before. My own performance on the track is best forgotten. Insurance considerations forced us to wear full-face helmets, and there was simply no room in the cockpit for me and the helmet. I did a half-dozen tentative laps with the seatback reclined as far as it would go and my head jammed sideways against the Ferrari's overhead console, and gave it up. Try driving fast someday with one eye above the other.

Things were much better on the open road without a helmet. I could sit up straight, for one thing. The car seems smaller, rounder, and more manageable than its predecessor, much more like a 348, perhaps even a little like an F40 for grown-ups. The styling changes are subtle, but not minor. It is a struggle to get into, but once inside the visibility is quite good, and I found myself much more able to judge the location of all four corners than in years gone by. Revised shift linkage is also helpful. Missed or botched shifts have been an ongoing part of my experience with Testarossas, but I never even came close to missing one with the 512. The traditional Ferrari control relationship—wheel sharply canted away from the driver, shift lever at arm's length, seat very close to the floor—is still with us, forcing the driver to hold the wheel rim at eight and four and shuffle it through his hands in a sort of push-pull motion, but this quickly becomes routine with maneuvering in and out of parking places and dicing through heavy traffic.

On the Florida State Turnpike, running at a steady eighty, the big twelve-cylinder sounded less like an old Ferrari V-12 than two seriously sweet six-cylinder sports cars running along side by side—or perhaps a high-quality motorboat with a pair of sixes just slightly out of sync. People tended to stare, and every now and again some keen type would carve his way through traffic to get a closer look. One of these caught up, then fell back, then caught up again. On his second pass he was holding up a piece of ruled note paper on which he had printed, "Cogito?" I nodded yes, he responded with a grin and a thumbs-up, and we parted.

First gas stop was at Ocala, and it was nice to crawl out of the car and find that the temperature had fallen enough to allow me to shut off the air conditioning and go to fresh air. It was in Ocala, buying Fig Newtons and Diet Coke, that I discovered I'd left home with about sixty dollars. The toll at the intersection of the turnpike and I-75 alone was almost ten bucks. Then I stopped for a second tank of fuel at a station in Macon, Georgia, where large numbers of black people were filling shopping bags with cartons of cigarettes. I figured they were running a scam on some neighboring state's tax authorities, but I lacked the courage to ask them. When I made it to the cash register, I handed the lady my credit card, and she said: "We don't take no credit cards. Cash only." And there went another twenty-five grickles.

The guy who checked me in at the Quality Inn in Acworth, Georgia, reads our magazine, and was, of course, blown away by the 512TR. When I checked out at 5:45 the next morning, the lady on the desk told me that the police had come by every hour to make sure it was okay. I had no idea. I guess the night man/reader had alerted them. I'd no more than shifted into fifth on I-75 when a Honda Accord swept pass at about 100. I pulled into his slipstream, and we ran that way for almost forty miles. It was apparent that he had a strategy for going fast. He kept to the right lane as much as possible, winnowing through traffic like a salmon. Very impressive to watch, and it helped my average dramatically. I hated to see him turn off before Chattanooga. Third gas stop was in Knoxville, where they had the Lifestyles Stimula condoms ("For Her Pleasure") right next to the "I ❤ Jesus" air fresheners. Forgive them, Father, they know not what they do.

Breakfast at a Bob Evans north of Knoxville. (Credit cards accepted.) My waitress is cute as hell and, pausing for a moment at the order window, tells one of her fellow waitresses: "I left my car at that motel last night. He offered to drive me to work, so I go, 'Okay.' I can't believe I did that." Her compatriot replied: "It must have been a full moon, Ellie. A full moon will do you thataway." (It wasn't.) Bob Evans would be America's number one breakfast place if they'd learn how to make biscuits. The Bob Evans biscuit is too fluffy, too tall. My mother could help them. (Mrs. Margaret Davis, New Pittsburg, Ohio.) She'll want a million for the recipe (cheap), and her consulting rate would be something on the order of five grand a day. Better biscuits at Bob Evans are just a phone call away.

The trip was 1264 miles. Driving time, nineteen hours. The Ferrari averaged about fourteen miles per gallon. Yes, I broke the law. Yes, I squandered natural resources. It was wonderful. Like Edith Piaf, I regret nothing. I made it home with twenty-six bucks.

Real Americans buy what they like.

⚬✥⚬

President Bush and his Hole-in-the-Market Gang sped back from their impromptu arm-twisting tour of Japan with absolutely nothing to show for their efforts but some videotape of Mr. Bush doing a liquid laugh into the well-tailored lap of the Japanese prime minister. Golden moments in economic diplomacy. Mr. Bush said it was a great trip, but then Mr. Bush does love to travel. Mr. Robert Stempel, chairman of General Motors, announced that the Detroiters were not in Japan to ask for concessions and suggested that hostile media were at least partially responsible for Detroit's troubles. Mr. Red Poling, chairman of Ford and a man known for prudence and caution, said hardly anything at all.

Thus they all left it to that splendid old warhorse, Mr. Lee Iacocca, chairman of Chrysler, to sound the alarm and reacquaint America with the concept of the Yellow Peril, and he did this with a rousing diatribe to the Detroit Economic Club. It was Lee Iacocca at his best and worst. He blamed Japan for everything from the kidnapping of the Lindbergh baby to the suppression of the Fish carburetor. Mr. Iacocca is Italian and is thus both a good hater and a great operatic actor, and his histrionics were right out of Rossini. (This last sentence is an example of ethnic stereotyping of the very worst kind, but Mr. Iacocca's speech has made this sort of thing fashionable again.)

He suggested that to blame the U.S. auto industry for the success of the Japanese would be like blaming the U.S. Army and Navy for the success of the Japanese sneak attack on Pearl Harbor in 1941. Here, he hit the nail right on the head. We not only blamed our army and navy for the success of the Japanese attack, we sacked the two commanders involved. They had been warned of an impending attack. They knew that war was imminent. Their radar picked up the Japanese aircraft on the final leg of the attack. But they didn't do anything! Does this sound familiar?

Perhaps twenty-five years ago, the late Bobby Darin recorded a
song that accurately described anti-Japanese sentiments recently
expressed by various Democratic presidential candidates as well as Mr.
Iacocca. It was one of those instances where art uncannily predicts life.
I'm doing this from memory, so bear with me:

> There was a white mouse consultation
> Down at the county fair.
> All the church mice, field mice,
> And not so nice mice,
> Everybody gathered there.

> You see, the Muckidy Muck he was speakin',
> Tellin' them where it was at.
> He said, "Here, here, there ain't nothin' to fear,
> Except a three-eyed Siamese cat."
> And the crowd was stunned,
> You see, no single mouse had ever seen one.
> He said, "Don't be scared.
> We're prepared.

> "Two times two is forty-five,"
> The Muckidy Muck explained,
> "And the flat side of the moon is green,
> And the farmer don't need no rain."
> …They sang, "This land is mice land,
> Mice country 'tis of thee.
> My father stole it from the beaver-rat,
> And nobody's gonna steal it from me."

> And the crowd went wild,
> And every mouse began to fear for his child.
> He said, "Don't be scared.
> We're prepared.

> "We've got a million of our best young mice
> To go out and volunteer.
> To give up what they're livin' for,
> To make the cat disappear.
> Let's give 'em a hand."
> (Ya-a-a-a-y!)
> "We don't want that cat invading our land."
> (No way!)
> He said, "Don't be scared. We're prepared."

The immediate result of all this anti-Japanese invective was that most of the Japanese automotive executives left the Detroit automobile show for California. Next, the slimebags who always rise to these occasions felt empowered to deface some of the Japanese cars at the show. And then, of course, the daily press and the morning chat shows went into a dither about "the spread of anti-Japanese feeling."

I am a member of a generation that grew up morbidly fascinated by photographs of young Japanese officers practicing their swordsmanship on bound and blindfolded prisoners of war. I was chosen to recite Douglas MacArthur's "I Shall Return" speech to a large patriotic gathering at my school early in the war. (My triumph was marred only by my mother's insistence that I wear a white shirt with a Little Lord Fauntleroy collar, a gift from my doting Aunt Elizabeth in Cincinnati.) I can recite in chronological order the events of the naval battles at Coral Sea and Midway. I bitterly resent the people in Japan who want to be perceived as victims of their own aggression. I feel like a fish out of water when I'm in Japan, and I can barely wait to get home.

Nonetheless, Japan builds the best cars in the world, and because this magazine is about cars—good cars, particularly—I cannot allow prejudices I acquired in junior high school to blind me to the excellence of Japanese products. Neither should Mr. Iacocca.

Americans buy Japanese cars because they like them and because they perceive them to represent good value. Bashing the Japanese, or pretending that our economic problems are caused by Japanese unwillingness to accept vast shipments of American cars, is first of all dishonest, and is exactly the kind of behavior Americans have traditionally abhorred in other people. Fifty years ago, the Nazis blamed their problems on the Jews and insisted that Germans couldn't compete on an equal basis with Jews in business, in school, or in daily life, because the playing field wasn't level. The Jews, it was said, didn't understand the meaning of fair play.

In the years following World War II, the domestic automobile business was a relatively easy business. People were so starved for cars that they formed waiting lines for anything with wheels. The generation of executives who joined the car companies in those years learned a lot of bad habits. They became lazy and complacent, and every complaint about their narrow provincialism was met with the patronizing suggestion that the complainer simply take a look at the sales figures. Sales were excellent, profits were plentiful, and continued growth appeared to be automatic. Labor and management enjoyed a comfortable symbiotic relationship. When labor wanted more money, management gave it to them and passed the increased cost along to the consumer, who didn't seem to mind. There was a neat, de facto arrangement among the Big Three. With no real competition, Detroit operated like a single corporation, of which the three major car companies were divisions. There was no management committee, no chairman. It worked this way: No company would undertake any major innovation or institute any important change in strategy unless it knew that one of the other companies was going to do it first. It worked like a charm. Everything stayed in balance. Everybody made money. Nobody had to work too hard.

Then the Japanese came along. The Europeans had always been minority players with no intention of upsetting the established order of things in Detroit. The Japanese didn't see it that way. They came to compete, and if the former established order became a casualty of their competition, tough. Now we hear Americans complaining that the Japanese are too aggressive, that they're unwilling to limit the level of firepower they bring to the battle. Too aggressive? The disastrous presidential trip to Japan brings us back to the Japanese attack on Pearl Harbor. I don't know everything that President Roosevelt did in the days following the declaration of war, but I'm pretty sure that he didn't invite the disgraced General Short and Admiral Kimmel to fly to Japan with him and ask the Japanese warlords to back off a little during the war's early months. One struggles to sympathize, but sympathy comes hard. I don't think the Buffalo Bills asked the Washington Redskins to take it easy on them before the Super Bowl, and I haven't heard the Bills complaining since that the Redskins played too hard. One plays to win.

There are those who'd like to see the return of the good old days, when Detroit talked about dog-eat-dog competition without ever experiencing all that much. But an awful lot of Americans like their Japanese cars and trucks just fine, and there are a lot of others earning their livings in places like Marysville, Ohio, and Georgetown, Kentucky, and Fremont, California, building Japanese cars and trucks, who aren't very interested in seeing any artificial limits placed on their freedom of opportunity.

For twenty years I have doggedly held to the belief that Japanese competition would result in better products from Detroit, and to a large degree, it has. Unfortunately, as David Power of the J.D. Power organization has said more than once, the domestic manufacturers have closed the quality gap, but the product gap has actually widened. Be that as it may, Detroit has not lost the battle. Nearly 70 percent of the cars sold here are from here. At the recent International Automobile Show held in Detroit, the stars were Chrysler products—the new LH sedans and the Jeep (ZJ) Grand Cherokee. The styling of the new LH products looks to be one full generation ahead of the competition. The show was a real tour de force for Chrysler president Bob Lutz, chief engineer François Castaing, and chief designer Tom Gale. Cadillac's new Seville and STS have created waiting lists at dealerships. The Olds Eighty Eight and Ninety Eight, the Pontiac Bonneville, the Buick LeSabre and Park Avenue, the brilliant new Chevrolet/GMC Suburban are all healthy vital signs. Ford's Taurus, Sable, and Explorer, plus the very strong Mazda-based Escort and Tracer, may explain why Chairman Poling didn't complain too much while he was in Japan.

All of these point the way out of the nightmare for Detroit. Not protectionism. Not name-calling. Just first-rate cars—great cars—built one at a time. Cars that are merely good enough won't be good enough.

A thundering broadside from an automobile enthusiast splinter group. Ours.

꙳

Last Sunday night the Infiniti people sponsored a concert by the Detroit Symphony Orchestra as part of the launch of the new J30. During the intermission the car was on display in a big tent adjacent to Detroit's historic Orchestra Hall, but there were so many people around it that one could only glimpse a headlight or a door handle. Not a problem, inasmuch as we already have a perfectly good J30 in our test fleet, and I've even managed to drive it a couple of times. One more very nice car in that corner of the market. We admired the little snatches of car we *could* see, grabbed a bunch of grapes from the hors d'oeuvre table, and returned to our seats.

After intermission, the orchestra played Antonin Dvořák's ninth symphony, *From the New World,* the second movement of which I'd like played at my funeral, but not in the near future. The *New World,* as you might imagine, was written right at the end of the nineteenth century as a sort of celebration of the then-young United States, with all its ethnic diversity and awesome energy that Dvořák so admired. I really got caught up in the music and in the exciting image of the Republic that it conveyed. On the way home I wondered what sort of symphony some latter-day Dvořák might write if he came to the United States here at the end of the twentieth century, and it made me feel terrible.

The United States of America is in danger of becoming terminally trivial. Even as the mania for physical fitness sweeps the formerly young and upwardly mobile, mental fitness seems to be on the wane. The national literacy rate, of paramount importance to a guy who puts out a magazine for a living, is falling, even as the school dropout rate rises. The nation issues postage stamps honoring an obese drug addict named Elvis Aron Presley. Its citizens whine, seek scapegoats, sue one another at the drop of an attaché case, and seriously consider presidential candidates unfit to run township landfills. The few things that don't frighten them, they find offensive. Gay Talese, writing in *The New York*

Times, describes our country as "constipated with caution," and anyone who spends a disproportionate amount of his time enjoying automobiles could only say "amen" to that.

It is increasingly apparent that no presidential candidate has given much thought to the automobile, to the people who drive it, or to the infrastructure upon which it operates. When automobiles are mentioned at all, they are a cipher for something called "fair trade"—the definition of which varied with the occasion and the speaker. I have put myself forward as an automotive candidate in the past—just kidding, folks—but my life would not stand the scrutiny now given to people running for president, which means I'd have to run for king, or emperor, or some other category not currently included on our federal ballots. My chances are between slim and none, but unlike those other guys, I can at least tell you where I stand.

The cornerstone of my appeal to the electorate is a $1 increase in the gasoline tax. This would get us closer to the other major automotive nations of the West. The equivalent price per U.S. gallon in Great Britain is $2.98 with tax and $1.02 without. Germany is $3.33 per gallon with tax and $0.98 without. Italy must take the prize at the pump with a price of $4.28 per gallon with tax and $1.16 without. Even Japan, which has no petroleum of its own—or any other natural resources, for that matter—is only $3.62 per gallon with tax and $2.15 without. These were the prices in effect in February of this year. We don't pay enough for our fuel, and that leads us to improvident behavior where the use of that fuel is concerned.

An additional $1 tax on every gallon of gasoline sold in this country would raise $110,268,690,000 per year. For the first five years of my new energy tax, all of that money would be used to help defray the federal deficit, but only on condition that any pre-existing highway tax revenues be released and allocated to appropriate projects. (No holding back to fudge estimates of the deficit, or any of the other underhanded stuff that happens with currently available highway funds.) At the end of those five years, one-half of the Davis Energy Tax revenues would go into a transportation fund, to be used in the development of a balanced portfolio of public transportation that would include automobiles, trucks, trains, ships, aircraft, spacecraft, and urban mass transit.

(My friend Cader Cox, of Riverview Plantation in Georgia, recently told me that the Lord's Prayer has fifty-four words, the Ten Commandments have 296, the Bill of Rights has 462, and the U.S. Government's regulation for the price of cabbage has 26,911. Bearing that in mind, all federal regulations, existing and proposed, will be subject to the scrutiny of a plain-English committee made up of seventy-five-year-old retired fifth-grade English teachers. Final approval will be in the hands of *Automobile Magazine*'s copy editor, the scowling, no-nonsense Laura Sky Brown.)

P.J. O'Rourke's Perennially Indignant will blast my energy tax, pointing out that it will deny poor people the pleasures and benefits of driving around in twenty-two-year-old Chrysler Newports without shock absorbers or mufflers or tread on the tires. To this I say, "Good." If we get those people and their rolling wrecks off the roads, along with the drunks, the dim, the badly coordinated, and all the other habitual offenders who threaten our lives every day, we will have created a constituency for mass transit at last. Mass transit is inevitable, as is a comprehensive national health care program, if only because nobody will be able to afford the alternatives by New Years Eve, 2000.

Another important benefit of my energy tax will be the reestablishment of a good reason to drive smaller, more efficient cars. The people at the Insurance Institute for Highway Safety will deplore this, because they have staked their future on eternal life for large, inefficient cars. They keep telling us that greater reliance on smaller cars will certainly result in higher highway death rates, but they also predicted higher death rates from the 65-mph limit when it took effect in 1988, and they were wrong about that, too. Nothing warms the cockles of an old enthusiast's heart like disappointment and confusion among the Safety Nazis.

Which brings me to the next plank in my platform. Inasmuch as the highway death rate has actually declined since the federal speed limit was raised from 55 to 65 miles per hour, I say we should save a whole bunch more lives and raise it again, from 65 to 80. Large numbers of tax-paying citizens are already driving that fast every day, but always with the fear that a policeman—who ought to be doing something of greater value to society—is waiting around the next bend or over the next hill to arrest them. Our European cousins drive that fast all the time, and none of them have become sterile or vaporized their corneas because of it. It goes without saying that emptying our streets and highways of the pathologically inept and replacing or repairing those streets and highways, as described in the paragraphs above, will make driving even safer. The accelerating downward trend in the highway death rate—based on safer roads, draconian culling of driver's licensees, and higher speed limits—will probably be *creating* people by the arrival of the millennium.

Finally, my *pièce de résistance:* a billion-dollar quinquennial competition for the American Car That Knocks the World's Socks Off. We would set aside a portion of my $110,268,690,000 so that every five years the government could hold a competition for a truly great piece of automotive transportation—an innovative, exciting automobile conceived by an American company to be sold in competition with the world's best. The winning organization could be anything from the Boeing Company to Frog Design, including the existing domestic car companies, but the billion-dollar prize would only go to a firm that backed its concept with a fully worked-out scheme for development, manufacturing, marketing, and distribution, either in-house or as part of a joint venture. The billion would be paid out in increments of $100,000,000 (up to $800,000,000) as the new car progressed, and would be stopped instantly if at any time it was determined that we were dealing with another John De Lorean or Preston Tucker. The final payment of $200,000,000 would only be made when it was determined that the car was meeting its marketing objectives in worldwide competition.

The selection committee would be chaired by me, for life, and would consist of Jean Lindamood.

Los Amigos Americanos
del Museo Juan Manuel Fangio.

uenos Aires, Argentina—This is our second visit to Argentina. We were here in 1980 and loved the place so much that we swore we'd return. It took us twelve years, but these past two weeks have proved well worth the wait. In 1980, on our first night in Buenos Aires, we were collected at the Plaza Hotel by Juan Manual Fangio—still, in my estimation, the greatest man and the best racing driver in the history of motorsport—and taken to a wonderful restaurant in a parklike setting in the Recoleta district. As we came down a flight of stairs into the dining room, a diner at a nearby table noticed Fangio and quietly rose to his feet. Others noticing him rising, looked around, spotted Fangio, and rose to their feet. As we passed through the crowd to our table, the entire restaurant was standing. No one made a sound. They just stood, smiling. As we found our seats, Fangio directed a smile around the room, nodded, and everyone sat down and resumed their dinners. It's a moment I'll savor until my dying day, and a powerful motivator in getting me back to Argentina again.

Now we're down to the last day of our second visit. We fly back to the States tonight. Say this out loud: *"I'm catching the night plane from Buenos Aires."* Does that have a nice ring to it, or what? It could only be better if the plane were one of those big Sikorsky or Dornier flying boats from the Thirties. We spent ten days slogging around various parts of this large, hospitable country (eighth largest in the world) with shotguns and fly rods, and the last two days visiting Juan Manual Fangio in his hometown of Balcarce. Balcarce is also the home of the Autodromo Juan Manuel Fangio, and—more importantly—the Museo del Automovilismo Juan Manuel Fangio. Fangio is not involved with the racetrack that bears his name, but the museum has become his vocation as he approaches his eighty-second birthday. His whole career is in this beautiful, purpose-built, six-story building—all of the trophies and medals, many of the cars, and hundreds of the unforgettable photographs from his thirty-year career in automobile racing.

Fangio is a dedicated Argentine patriot, and had his first season of European racing in 1949 (where he won the first four races he entered) with the sponsorship of the Perón government. It was he who pressed the demand that his early European racing cars—Gordinis, Maseratis, one Ferrari—be painted the blue and yellow Argentine colors. His love of country is easily understood. Argentina has natural and human resources to rival those of any nation in the world. It is a beautiful country, with more gorgeous women relative to its total population than any place I've ever been. Its natural beauty is like that of the western United States, even to the crops grown and the livestock raised. Buenos Aires is a very large, cosmopolitan city that looks like a cross between Geneva and Chicago, but a little down at the heel. Argentina has had everything, in the years since it was first colonized in the 1500s, except good government. Though even that seems to be changing now, with the administration of President Carlos Saúl Menem. The country's frightful inflation rate has been reined in, and most of the people we spoke to were cautiously optimistic about the future.

We flew from Buenos Aires to the resort city of Mar del Plata on Aerolineas Argentinas, and were collected there by Mr. Luis Barragan, president of the Fangio Museum, and one of his associates, Mr. Carlos Alvarez. They drove us to Balcarce in Mr. Alvarez's Peugeot 505 diesel. These locally built Peugeot 505s are hot stuff in Argentina. The country's inadequate automobile industry is so rigorously protected that there are not enough domestic cars available to begin with, and imported goods of any kind are so overwhelmingly expensive that only a tiny handful of imported cars are in consumer hands. The automotive consumer gets no say in Argentina. He or she can buy from the limited range of makes and (mostly obsolete) models that the government deems appropriate, and that's it. The ancient Ford Falcon was state of the art in Argentina until quite recently, but at least Ford is now offering Escorts and Sierras. Across the border, in Chile, people drive a much broader assortment of up-to-date, more reasonably priced automobiles. New rules are afloat in the Menem administration that would ease this politically devised automotive poverty and liberalize choice in the marketplace, but the bureaucrats have blocked them so far. Anyone who thinks Detroit would benefit from increased protection should visit Argentina.

Arriving in Balcarce, we went straight to the museum, which is absolutely terrific. Having visited various automotive museums and collections around the world, an American is not sure what to expect from the Museo Juan Manuel Fangio. But the façade is enormously reassuring. It is the front shell of the former Balcarce municipal building, and it is handsome indeed. Inside, two extremely talented young architects, Eduardo Mandiola and Jorge Trivigno—both members of the museum board—have wrought a bright, contemporary construction wherein all the levels are tied together by a spiral ramp designed and painted to resemble a two-lane road. The museum is airy and light and filled with wonderful evocations of the automotive and racing worlds that Fangio has inhabited.

The great man arrived while we were wandering through the collection. We'd been warned that he was suffering from a kidney ailment, that he might not even be able to join us, but here he was, having just driven 400 kilometers from a doctor's appointment in Buenos Aires. He wore a navy blazer, gray flannel slacks, a plaid shirt with an ascot, and elegant jodhpurlike black boots. There was a soft wool shawl draped around his neck over the blazer, which I thought might have something to do with his ailment but was evidently a matter of style, because he wore it throughout our two-day visit. He looked tired, and his color was none too good, but he led us to the dinner table in the museum boardroom and sat us down. His chauffeur—who never gets to drive—is an older man named Juan Gimeno, who hovers around Fangio and heads off the red wine bottle when it comes around the third or fourth time, makes sure that he maintains the schedule and doesn't overdo. The board members, the local businessmen who run the museum, are all pals, and they're fixing the dinner tonight, a very successful chicken barbecue, served at about ten o'clock in the Argentine fashion. As the evening wore on, his color improved.

I've seen Fangio thirty or forty times, and it's always been a bit like seeing the pope, even that evening in 1980 when he brought the whole restaurant to its feet. He enters a great hall somewhere, accompanied by a mayor or a governor or a chairman of the board, acknowledges the applause of the crowd, greets a few old friends, and sits down at the head table. To sit next to him at a private dinner table in his home town, surrounded by his friends, is to see an entirely different person. He was fun, he was inquisitive, he laughed and kidded with everybody in the room. J.L.K. Davis exhausted herself translating the two or three conversations that seemed to be going on simultaneously all evening. He says he can't imagine why he's so popular in the United States. "I only won there once, Sebring, in 1957. But you'd think I'd driven there all my life the way they treat me." I tried to explain it, but I was quite tongue-tied sitting at the same table with him.

He says he gave up racing in 1958 because it wasn't fun anymore. It was becoming too commercial. ("I wasn't going to go out like

Nuvolari, still driving past his prime, an uncompetitive driver in uncompetitive cars—an embarrassment to himself and the sport.") The centerpiece of the museum is currently a gleaming silver Mercedes-Benz W196, like the ones he drove in pursuit of his second and third world championships. But on one of the upper floors is a beautiful red Maserati 250F, the car in which he won his fifth and final championship in 1957. "I saved the best car for the end," he says. "This was the easiest, most enjoyable racing car of my life."

The next morning, we met for coffee at the museum and he led a two-hour tour, explaining a wide variety of engines, front suspension designs, and carburetion systems, as though he'd just watched his brother, Toto, assemble them before breakfast. (Toto, an inspired mechanic, is the father of Juan Manuel Fangio II, currently running for Dan Gurney's Toyota team in IMSA racing.) He was constantly accosted by adoring fans during our tour, never refusing to sign a museum catalog or a fresh peso note.

He drove us to lunch in his Mercedes 300D (he's chairman of the Mercedes-Benz distributorship in Buenos Aires), showing us his own home, Toto's home, the little house where his grandfather first settled on arrival from Italy, and then taking us to the Autodromo Juan Manuel Fangio. We drove up to the ticket kiosk, and the functionary didn't even look up from his magazine. Picking up a book of tickets, he walked to the driver's window. Fangio, in that soft, high-pitched voice, said, "I have no money." The guy finally looked in the window, saw Fangio, and whacked the heel of his hand against his forehead, thunderstruck. We drove in.

On the track, he drove quickly but easily, his left hand at seven o'clock on the steering wheel rim, his right resting on his thigh, moving only to make neat gearchanges or to help when a sharp turn demanded both hands. I was delighted to see that he cocked his head entering corners exactly as we've seen him do in countless films and still photographs. As we hauled around the track, he said: "Nürburgring—the old Nürburgring—and Spa were my favorite circuits. They were quite dangerous, and were therefore places where the driver could really make a difference, even if he was driving a somewhat inferior car. Today's circuits are less challenging, and there's less opportunity for the driver to demonstrate that extra bit of skill." And a moment later: "My favorite adversaries were Ascari and Moss. They were both very strong, very fast, and they could beat you on a given day." You knew that he's said these things hundreds of times, to hundreds of journalists, but it didn't matter, because this was the first time he'd ever said them to you.

After lunch—another great barbecue—at a ranch-house guest facility that's being developed as part of the museum, Fangio had to return to Buenos Aires. Gimeno had been looking significantly at his watch for a half-hour, and as my all-time hero walked toward the driver's side of the Mercedes, I again noticed the athlete's bowed legs and the jaunty stride that earned him the nickname El Chueco ("Bandy Legs") early in his career. When he'd driven away, the board members invited us to join them under a huge shade tree and drink champagne, something we were more than delighted to do. None of these men ever saw him race. All of them are at least a couple of decades junior to him. But they worship him, and they're determined to make the museum they've built in his honor a lasting success.

I'm determined to help. To that end, I'm going to ask a small group of American friends—*Los Amigos Americanos del Museo Juan Manuel Fangio*—to join me in an effort to help keep the Juan Manuel Fangio Museum racing into the next century. I want to go back to Balcarce in the future, and I'd love to take some of you with me. I want everyone to see it. I intend to ask Tom Bryant at *Road & Track* to join in, and I'm going to speak to our mutual friend John Weitz and the great French racing driver and restaurateur René Dreyfus—eighty-seven years old himself—to give me the benefit of their ideas, too. Juan Manuel Fangio has given me so much, since I first saw him race in 1957, that I'd now like to return the favor.

"If I should love you, what business is it of yours?"

—Goethe

⁓⋅∽⋅⁓

Trant Jarman was present at the creation of *Automobile Magazine*. He did a wonderful column for us—T.J. Technoid—a column that many people, including me, still remember fondly. Unfortunately, Trant was a verbal stunt flier, a story-teller and all-around colorful talker, not a writer, and several staff members had to perform work above and beyond the call to turn his stories into finished columns. This, and some unexplained damage to test cars, led me to fire him in 1988. He was terribly hurt, because he and I had been friends for almost forty years, although it wasn't the first time we'd disagreed.

About a year ago we learned that Trant had a brain tumor, and that it was malignant. He and I talked about the fix he was in, and I urged him to keep a journal, a record of the experience of his own death, if you will. Jarman was such a colorful teller of tales that I knew his slant on his own impending doom would be worth having. Many of his best stories involved impending doom, either in racing cars, or on motorcycles, or at the hands of outraged cuckolds. I asked him if the doctors knew how long he'd had the tumor, and suggested that if it had been in there for a while it could explain a lot about his behavior over the years. We laughed immoderately, as we always did.

He died a few weeks ago. He didn't get around to doing the journal. But it's okay because he left such a vivid trail that nobody who knew him will ever forget him. Nobody could ever forget his maniacal giggle, just for a start.

When I finally reached Denise McCluggage, she had already written a lovely piece about T.J. for *AutoWeek*. On the phone, she suggested that Trant changed the way we all talk. Denise and Trant and I were part of a Chevrolet Corvair rally team in the very early Sixties, and she and Trant had continued to be telephone correspondents for more than thirty years. She feels that he saw things differently—from a uniquely funny point of view—and thus described them in eccentric and hilarious ways that none of us had ever heard before we met him. She says that sometimes she'll get off a great line, and everybody will laugh, and she'll remember that it was Jarman who used that line the first time. I'm reminded of the same thing every day.

The simple declarative sentence was usually beyond Jarman's grasp. Conversations with him were elliptical. He embroidered. He stopped. He started. He always ran through a half-dozen words and phrases while he sought the right one. He did the same thing with entire thoughts. He'd blurt out snatches of everything that went through his mind, while we, his listeners, tried to collate the information and prepare it for use when we finally understood what he was talking about.

Trant Jarman came sailing into my life in 1955. He was not at the wheel of anything spectacular, although he did own a racing car, or I guess I should say "most of a racing car." It was an anonymous special, powered by a BMW 328 engine, and I don't believe I ever saw it in a race. I heard it run a couple of times, and I towed it to one race where it ran a couple of practice laps, but that was the extent of it.

It sort of prepared the ground for a series of oddly conceived specials that Trant would drive over the next twenty years. There was the Lotus Valiant, a Lotus Eleven with a race-tuned Valiant slant-six installed. It was an odd marriage, but Trant won several club races with it. There was also a front-engined, mid-engineered, Chrysler powered special that was sponsored by a crooked police inspector. This car had its moments, but nothing it ever accomplished managed to be as exciting as the source of the money.

Jarman was driving it in Ontario, at Green Acres, I believe, halfway through a fast bend when a keeper let go in the rear end and the whole wheel and half-shaft assembly began to come out from under the back of the car. The rear track just kept getting wider and wider until the whole thing fell off.

Trant finally got it stopped, and a Canadian driver who'd been running right behind him slid to a stop and leaped out of his own racing car. He yelled, "God damn! I knew you were some kind of hotshot suspension engineer from Detroit, and when I saw your rear wheels getting farther and farther apart, I said, 'That sonuvabitch has really got something!'"

His racing experience was extensive, and it all began in 1937. As a teen-age car fanatic, he had helped a friend rebuild an old Bentley, and his reward was a trip to the Bonneville Salt Flats. At Bonneville, he met the great Rex Mays, who invited Trant to come to Indianapolis—an invitation that he wasn't able to accept until 1946, due to time spent as a lieutenant in the Canadian armored forces in World War II.

After that, he worked as an apprentice engineer at BRM, which was headquartered at Raymond Mays's home at Bourne, in England. He told me that they never allowed him to work on the BRMs—which at that time were the fantastic supercharged sixteen-cylinder cars—but he was allowed to work on the ERAs, both the road racing and the hill-climb cars. It was during this period that he raced motorcycles on both grass and speedways, whenever there was time.

According to Trant, the BRM team of those days tended to be non-gender-specific, and the place was always thronged with friends and hangers-on from the exotic world of the London stage, making it difficult indeed to get the work done between races. He gleefully told tales of Raymond Mays's aged mother, who was in her dotage, and who would show up a couple of times a week in her underwear to chat with the mechanics and tend her flower garden.

Human behavior fascinated Jarman at least as much as motor vehicles, and he spent all of his own life pushing the edges of the envelope. He saw parallels in racing, boxing, and ballet, and most admired those people who were willing to risk their lives to do something beautiful. For T.J., running a good race wasn't a metaphor for life, it was life itself.

In the thirty-seven years that Trant and I were comrades in arms, we came to love each other in the ways that guys sometimes do, if they're lucky, and we shared the highs and lows of each other's lives and careers. We were friends during most of that time, though not all of it. The pressure was too great, and we were actually very different people. We may not have been good for each other—because each of us was a cheerleader and coach for the other during the most irresponsible periods of our lives—but it was a great race.

In the last few years of his life, Trant was very happily married to a woman who could not have been more right for him. Only weeks before the discovery of the tumor, they had moved to her former home in Virginia Beach, Virginia. Only days before, he'd ridden an old-timers' motocross (and had come off, pranging his knees). His wife, Lynn, told us that last spring he was out on the terrace with her while she gardened, and he said: "I don't understand all these people coming down to see me with long faces. Nobody's ticket is good forever, and I've had a wonderful life. I got my turn in the arena, and I did okay. You and I have had each other, and now you're back home, and you'll be okay. I'm very happy with the way things have worked out."

Something wonderfully appropriate happened on the Sunday afternoon that we were holding the memorial service here in Michigan. ESPN was covering the Des Moines SCCA Trans-Am race. Early in the race, they cut to the in-car camera in Ron Fellows's AER/Mackenzie Ford Mustang. On the dash among the sponsor decals was a hand-lettered sticker that read "R.I.P. T.J." in large block letters. The announcers noticed it and explained that it referred to Trant Jarman, an engineer who'd been a fixture on the Trans-Am circuit, who'd been involved with Tom Kendall's championship Beretta Trans-Am team, and who had passed away recently and would be sorely missed. During all this, Fellows was ramming the Mustang through the streets of Des Moines right on someone's tail, going up and down through the gears, the engine note ringing in the background. Our friend could not have had a better eulogy.

Corvette.

❦

A new General Motors is in the works, and nobody knows what it's going to look like, or what kind of cars it will build. There've been several GMs, the most recent one created in 1920, when the board of directors dumped William Crapo Durant and elevated Alfred P. Sloan, who'd come along with Hyatt Roller Bearing in 1918. Durant subsequently tried several schemes, all in vain, worked in a restaurant in later life, and died penniless. He was my kind of guy, a genuine high flier, and I'm sorry that a bear market and his own incurable optimism conspired to undo him. Chevrolet was one of Durant's best ideas. We suspect that racing driver Louis Chevrolet was induced to lend his name to the enterprise with promises of great wealth and power—promises that were never kept. Had Louis Chevrolet actually run Chevrolet, the Corvette might have happened in the Roaring Twenties instead of the Fifties—the last decade of Detroit's rulership of the automotive world, and a time of great automotive change.

I saw the original Corvette show car at the old GM Motorama in 1953. I saw my first Corvette on the road when a guy named Ed Glowacke, a GM executive, entered one in the 1954 Press On Regardless Rally, of which I was rallymaster.

I first saw a Corvette race at Pebble Beach in 1956. My friends Barney Clark and Frank Burrell were both part of that team. Barney was the Corvette copywriter at Chevrolet's advertising agency, and a tireless and articulate cheerleader for the Corvette racing program. Frank had been a mechanic with the Cadillac-Allard teams at Le Mans and worked at Chevrolet engineering. Dr. Dick Thompson was driving. He was a well-known production Porsche driver from the Washington, D.C., area, but Barney Clark, a Californian, had no confidence in any driver from the East Coast, and besides, his first choice had been Fred Warner, another GM employee and sometime Allard driver. Dick Thompson put the Corvette on the map that day. He led for the first part of the race—

against the very best of the West Coast's cars and drivers—but fell back when the Corvette's brakes began to fail. Nonetheless, the Corvette's potential was clearly recognized by everybody at Pebble Beach, and Thompson went on the become famous as a conductor of Corvettes.

In 1960, that same Barney Clark called me from Detroit. How would I like to come back to my old home town and work for him at Campbell-Ewald? Exploring his offer got me fired at *Road & Track,* so my bridges were burned, and I hastily put my house on the market, put my meager goods and chattels in storage, borrowed a thousand dollars from Bill Tritt (builder of the Glasspar sports car), and raced across the country with my then wife and two babies in a Peugeot 403. In the meantime Barney had left *his* job, and a month later I was working at Campbell-Ewald, not as Barney's assistant, but as his replacement. They simply pushed me off the dock and made me the Corvette copywriter. My office was cheek by jowl with that of a guy named Elmore Leonard, who got up before dawn every morning, wrote a very disciplined few pages of his latest western novel, went to mass, then came to work and wrote testimonial ads for Chevrolet trucks. Elmore Leonard taught me to read my stuff aloud before turning it in. He also read all of my Corvette copy, shaking his head in bemused wonder at the out-of-control ornateness of my prose. He believed in a world without exclamation marks, and he had a huge blown-up photograph of Ernest Hemingway above the desk where he wrote his novels, with a line of type on Papa's lower lip saying, "It's up to you now, boy."

Chevrolet was a powerhouse in those days, apparently unable to do anything wrong. We were like an annoying Greek chorus, droning away in the background about the importance of imported cars, the dangers of provincialism, the need for a vision that ran deeper and broader than ten-day sales reports. Nobody at Chevrolet took us seriously. They'd smile tolerantly and say, "We only build what the people want." To them, the Volkswagen was a bad joke.

We once put together a radical new proposition for selling Corvairs. We worked for a long time and sent our ideas off to a meeting we weren't allowed to attend. One of our bosses, Jim Hastings, came back an hour later and stood in my office doorway. I asked, "What happened?" He answered, "You know how they give a horse medicine?" No, I didn't. "Well," he said, "they stick a great big pill in the end of a tube and they stuff it down the horse's throat and then they blow hard." Okay, I understood. "This time, the horse blew first."

Barney Clark had told me that he always wrote the Corvette ads by summoning up the most glorious automotive fantasy he could imagine, writing it down, then going through the copy and substituting the word "Corvette" for "Ferrari." I had a different view. By 1960, the Corvette was a real automobile, winning a lot more races than it lost, and I wanted to talk specifically about that car. Thus, my ads were quite different from Barney's, and that fact aroused the suspicions of people like Zora Arkus-Duntov, Corvette chief engineer, and Joe Pike, Corvette sales promotion manager. This was the beginning of a love/hate relationship with Zora that has continued to this moment. Joe Pike was a zealot who passed up promotions so he could continue to pilot his beloved Corvette through the shoals of Chevrolet sales department indifference and cynicism. He would have happily walked over live coals or thrown himself on the barbed wire for that car. We understood each other. I would write every word of Corvette advertising up to and including the introduction of the 1963 Sting Ray, and drive a bunch of miles in any number of Corvettes during those years. The things I learned working with all those gifted writers and art directors at the advertising agency were the things that made *Car and Driver* sing when I took it over in 1962. They taught me how to write, and they taught me that having fun in my work was the next best thing to being independently wealthy.

I was reminded of all of this by an invitation to attend a celebration in honor of the one-millionth Corvette, held in the street outside the General Motors Building in Detroit. Zora Arkus-Duntov is finally beginning to show his age, but he hasn't lost the spark that made him one of the greatest characters ever to appear on the American automotive scene. At the microphone on the stage, standing in front of the dopey band that seems to show up for all such automotive affairs, Zora was the only one who didn't have much to say, and said so. The then-chairman and president of General Motors and the general manager of the Chevrolet Motor Division gave the sort of speeches corporate executives always give on such occasions. Joe Pike has suffered a stroke, and he watched the proceedings from his wheelchair.

I spoke to Larry Shinoda and Tony DeLorenzo and was introduced to the great Ed Cole's widow, Dolly (who looked terrific), by Jerry Burton, who used to be with *AutoWeek* and now works on *Corvette Quarterly.* Then I found Dick Guldstrand, another guy who has given a large chunk of his adult life to making Corvettes do things no other American car has ever done. That's not quite right, because Guldstrand stoutly maintains that he never grew up, and cites his years of tweaking Corvettes for the ultimate rush as proof. We sipped our free Cokes together and watched the proceedings, wishing that people like Ed Cole and Harley Earl and Bill Mitchell and Bob McLean and Betty Skelton and Frank Burrell and Barney Clark and Dr. Dick Thompson and Bob D'Olivo and Racer Brown and Bill Pollack and Jim Jeffords and Dave MacDonald and Briggs Cunningham and Don Yenko and Delmo Johnson and Bob Clift and Bob Bondurant and Jim Rathmann and Walter Mackenzie had made an appearance.

The millionth Corvette is a white LT1 with a red interior and a black top. You can't buy an LT1 equipped that way, but they wanted it to be exactly like that first 1953 Corvette. It was even lumbered with an automatic transmission, just like the original. Chevrolet commemorated the millionth Corvette with a ten-inch metal and plastic model of the '53. Mine arrived a few days after the street show looking exactly as though it had been rolled. The windshield frame was busted, along with the driveshaft and the right rear spring. The whole rear axle assembly had fallen off. The shift lever was bent flat on the tunnel, and the left front wheel cover had disappeared. It was all sort of sad in its insubstantial tackiness. A decal on the back wall of the display box said "Greatness Endures." I'm not so sure.

President Clinton: Welcome to Detroit, where the weak are killed and eaten.

Well. We have a new president who drives a 1966 Mustang, smokes very large cigars, and is widely rumored to chase women. This is not a bad prescription for winning the hearts and minds of us disaffected Americans. I share his love affair with old cars and long cigars, and I guess if I were married to Missus Clinton, I'd chase women, too. In addition to the redoubtable Hils, however, President Clinton has lumbered us with Vice President Gore, who is an avowed enemy of the automobile. Let us hope that his breast-beating environmental tract, *Earth in the Balance: Ecology and the Human Spirit*, was simply a cynical attempt to line up support among the eco-weenies, and not something he really cares about.

I wonder if we could get our new president out to Michigan to join us for three or four days of car testing. He was a little squishy in his positions on protectionism during the campaign, and I'd like him to drive some cars that show how well collaboration between the Americans and the Japanese can work. We'd drive the Toyota Corolla and the Geo Prizm, the Ford Escort and the Mercury Tracer, the Ford Probe and the Mazda MX-6, the Ford Explorer and the Mazda Navajo, and the Mercury Villager and the Nissan Quest. Then we'd drive the Toyota Camry, the Nissan Altima and Sentra, the Honda Accord, and the Subaru Legacy as examples of sensational cars built in America by Americans employed in Japanese-owned factories. Finally, as the *pièce de résistance,* we'd drive the Chrysler minivans; the Jeep Grand Cherokee; and the Chrysler Concorde, the Dodge Intrepid, and the Eagle Vision as examples of what an American car company can do when it stops whining and starts building competitive products. Had Mr. Iacocca gotten the kind of protection he used to demand for Detroit, we might never have seen such wonderful cars from Chrysler.

While we flogged these most excellent automobiles around the roads of Michigan, I'd point out the fact that traffic on our Interstates habitually flows at about 75 miles per hour and doesn't seem to be slaughtering the populace by doing so. At the same time, I'd keep asking him to focus on how well these various automotive prodigies handled the humps and craters and ledges of our national highway system, suggesting that maybe it isn't fair to expect the cars to do all the work of delivering a smooth ride to American taxpayers and their well-heeled overseas visitors. The French, the British, the Belgians, the Dutch, and especially the Germans seem to be able to build super-highways that hold up better than ours. I don't think it's because they have better highway engineers than we have, but I do believe that their governments have a more sensible view of how highways should be built and how long they should be expected to last. I might also suggest, at every fuel stop, that Mr. Perot was probably on to something when he proposed a fifty-cent-per-gallon gasoline tax. President Clinton wants to launch some public works programs to put people back to work. Well, a fifty-cent gasoline tax would pay for a lot of highway and bridge repairs, and a dollar-a-gallon tax would pay for a whole lot more.

On one of our test days, I'd take him to meet Al Papazian, proprietor of the Hunter House restaurant in Birmingham, Michigan, right on the Woodward Avenue bypass where the action was in the muscle-car era. Al makes a heart-rendingly accurate reproduction of the prewar White Castle and White Tower hamburger, wherein a ball of ground beef is smashed on the grill with a crown of shredded onions. Nothing about the place has changed very much in several decades—this helps to explain the great taste of the burgers and other things that come off the prehistoric grill. There are always four or five cheery, efficient women behind the counter at Hunter House, and Al is generally bustling around the joint greeting friends, picking up dirty dishes, and yelling instructions to the cooks. Al Papazian should probably be on our new president's Council of Economic Advisers. Al knows a whole bunch of good stuff that may have gotten past guys like John Kenneth Galbraith. I walked in there this morning to reward myself with two double hamburgers with everything (they aren't very big), to celebrate a successful visit to the dentist, and Al was just visible in the back room, peeling onions for the hundreds of burgers that his staff would dispense as the day wore on.

There's little danger of a revolt by the board of directors at the Hunter House. Al will remain in charge, holding his own against the fast food giants, because Al is taking care of business. The Al Papazians are the linchpins of the free enterprise system. They work hard and they know, in the final analysis, that their job is to create happy customers. If there was ever a society that needed to create happy customers, it's this one. An hour at Al's counter during the lunch rush would teach anyone who aspires to lead us a great deal about this Republic, but the most important thing would be the unforgettable taste of a genuine 1941 model hamburger.

Before President Clinton left town, I'd want to take him to the Acapulco, which is Detroit's best Mexican restaurant and the place where *Automobile Magazine* traditionally holds its office Christmas party. In order to get there, we'd have to drive through the ruins of one of North America's prettiest cities—which Detroit was until it was blighted by the good intentions of urban renewal in the Fifties, the riots of 1967, and the virtual abandonment of the place ever since. Twenty years ago I wrote that, while a lot of people then believed that Los Angeles was the city of the American future, the real city of the future was Detroit, with all its dreadful problems. For once I was right, and Los Angeles has now fallen into line behind Detroit, and New York, and Washington, D.C. In that same essay I wrote that no country can exist without cities, and that nobody remembers the suburbs of Athens and Rome. The man from Little Rock really needs to get Detroit right in his face.

Just across Jefferson Avenue from the naval armory where I enlisted at the beginning of the Korean War, the Acapulco looks boarded up from the outside. Some people avoid the place because they think it has gone out of business. Not so. Inside, it's a warm, friendly haven. Phil Llewellin, his wife, and I once drove all the way from West Virginia for dinner at the Acapulco, and last Saturday night the Davises raced 275 miles through the dark to get there before they closed the kitchen. The proprietor is a tall, cheerful man named Armando Apess, who came here from Mexico, from the area around Tampico, in 1956. Armando handed me a snapshot the other night. Taken in the late Forties, it shows a young Armando on a burro hauling a very large barrel of water into town. The Acapulco is a helluva fine Mexican restaurant, but it's been on the verge of going out of business for a while now. It's the Detroit disease. People from the suburbs aren't willing to risk their cars or their lives driving into Detroit anymore, and there aren't enough customers for carne asada à la Tampiqueña or huevos con chorizo in the immediate neighborhood.

I, on the other hand, have risked my life for much sillier things than a plate of beans and rice and tortillas, and I think that our new president ought to meet someone who came here, started a business that consistently delivered superior quality, and is still in danger of losing it all because a great American city has rotted away around him. There's a message for our leader in the Acapulco, and I'll pay for dinner if he'll try to see our urban problems through Armando's eyes. Besides, none of those guys in Washington who claim to have the answers for our cities has ever cooked an order of shrimp à la Jorge.

A breathtaking lady lawyer in a black leather dress swished into my office a few days ago and asked me—sort of snarkily, to my mind— if I thought that the domestic automobile industry would come back to life with Mr. Clinton's help. I replied that I was unaware that he had offered any help. She said, "Well, he's going to set up a government group that will plan and coordinate industrial activities, just as they do in Japan." My thought was that I'd like to see our new president, and the Congress, try to sort out the fundamental structural ills of the federal government and the country it governs before they try to save the automobile business.

Good luck, Bill.

Seven years, and no trace of any septennial itch.

❧

I t is now seven years since we launched this magazine. I wonder how many miles I've driven, in how many cars; how many airplanes I've been on; how many words I've written; how many phone calls I've made; how many corks I've pulled; how many business lunches and dinners I've hosted; how many times Greg Dawson has cut my hair; how many tubes of moustache wax I've used; how many cigars I've smoked; how many cases of shotgun shells I've shot; how many hotel and motel rooms I've slept in, in how many cities and towns; and how many times I've lain awake at three in the morning pondering my own failures and shortcomings, since we set out to create *Automobile Magazine.* It is a regular source of amusement, now, when friends ruefully admit that they didn't give us a Chinaman's chance in 1985, however much they wished us well. Some didn't wish us well at all. Mr. Don Hufford, senior vice-president and group publisher of *Car and Driver* and *Road & Track,* has made it his life's work to exterminate us, yet here we are, unexterminated—another source of amusement for those of us who work upstairs from where the Pretzel Bell used to be.

Fortunately, most people wished us well and many were extremely helpful. The first person to learn of my plans to launch a new automotive magazine in 1985, beyond my wife and the insiders involved, was my pal of three decades, Moon Mullins. Moon Mullins was the head of the Dodge News Bureau for years and now—semiretired—works for Toyota. He'd asked me to speak at a Carroll Shelby tribute in Las Vegas, and I took advantage of the opportunity to ask if I could borrow a Dodge minivan, which then served as the magazine's basic unit of transportation for several months. That Dodge Caravan was later augmented by a Mitsubishi Montero, and those two cars saw us all the way from speculation about what kind of magazine this would be, to the frantic last-minute scramble of printing Volume One, Number One, the April 1986 issue of *Automobile Magazine.*

Several companies wanted to be our first national advertiser, and we assured several that they were. First to sign on the dotted line, however—no kidding, folks—was actually Mercedes-Benz, followed by B.F. Goodrich, Dodge, and Lincoln-Mercury. We received a great deal of our early support from Detroit. I think there was some pleasure taken from the fact that a new magazine was being launched, not in New York or Los Angeles, but right here in Ann Arbor, only forty miles away from the Motor City. Chevrolet was among the first, and Chevrolet was also the first to cancel its advertising because of something I said. It is ironic that, as I write this, Chevrolet is once again refusing to advertise with us because of something I said. Like the guy said, "The only thing we learn from history is that we never learn anything from history."

In that first issue my column was entitled "Where the Good Life Gets Rolling." In part, it said, "*Automobile Magazine* is a celebration of quality—quality in automobiles, quality in life, and quality in magazines. We seek adventure and the good life, and we seek them in cars that are fun to drive. We'll drive exciting cars to unforgettable places. We'll go wherever the roads go, and sometimes beyond. We'll wring out and review some of the finest, fastest, and most interesting cars in the world each month, and we'll bring them to life with the most evocative photography and illustration money can buy. We won't waste your time with tiresome tales of boring cars."

That still sums up my feelings about this magazine and its mission. We drive interesting cars to interesting places and we talk to interesting people when we get there. I wanted to create a magazine that would reflect my own forty years of car enthusiasm, not some marketing committee's notion of what a "buff book" should be. I wanted to reach out to a few kindred spirits and share the excitement that I feel behind the wheel of some great new car, or in the paddock at the Monterey Historic Automobile Races, or coming through the doors into a great automobile show in Frankfurt, Tokyo, or Detroit. As it turned out, I seriously underestimated the number of kindred spirits who would respond. Our circulation now stands at 550,000 and continues to grow, despite the fact that I originally predicted a total audience somewhere in the range of 440,000 to 475,000.

There's a trend among this country's automotive magazines to move away from the dedicated car enthusiast and the subjects that interest him, to become new-car buyers' guides—sort of automotive news monthlies—and to concentrate more on the average citizen who may be considering a new-car purchase. This is an ill-considered attempt to curry favor with advertising agencies who don't understand special-interest magazines, and an equally ill-considered attempt to compete with television for advertising dollars. I have no interest in producing a car magazine for people who aren't particularly interested in cars. I love cars too much. I love obsessive behavior too much. I don't want to be the editor of some pallid television substitute. This is a car magazine for and by car nuts, and it will remain that until I'm carried out of here.

A magazine, any magazine, is a unique media form. Every issue is a portfolio of events and encounters and experiences you can hold in your hand. A magazine, properly done, is like a hand-held computer that converts raw information to useful knowledge. Part newspaper, part book, part personal letter, it is current without being superficial or time-limited. Timeless, yet brisk and on-the-spot. Unlike its electronic competition it can be easily saved, and often is.

A special-interest magazine, like this one—or *Wooden Boat* or *Gourmet* or *Cigar Aficionado* or *Double Gun Journal*—takes the idea a step further, refines it. A special-interest magazine serves as a catalyst for thousands of far-flung and disparate individuals like yourself, putting you in touch with one another and welding you to a sharply defined community of interest. Through your participation in a magazine like ours, you become a cohesive audience with a personality and a will of its own. Linking you individuals, broadening and deepening your knowledge and understanding of the subject that is your special interest, then produces a synergistic effect. You guys become an active and dynamic force, a sharply defined group of highly motivated and well-informed car buyers. You have clout. We're very proud to be in the same community of interest with you, and we appreciate the fact that you always seem to get the jokes.

These seven years have seen the arrival of Acura, Lexus, and Infiniti, and the North American luxury-car market knocked on its ear as a result. It was a seven-year period when a dozen manufacturers, or would-be manufacturers, strove with one another to bring us ridiculously expensive sports cars that would carry Mom and Pop to church at speeds approaching 200 miles per hour. Yet it was the little Mazda Miata that people lined up to buy, while the Corvette ZR-1 lay dead in the water. The 200-mile-per-hour sports car turned out to be the answer to a question that nobody had asked. We saw Chrysler fall again, and rise again. We saw General Motors fall, and now—like a crowd of 250 million football fans—we're all pulling for him to get back up on his feet.

We saw Sterling and Yugo go out of business here, and Fiat and Renault and Peugeot and Daihatsu pick up their remaining marbles and go home. We saw Richard Petty retire from stock-car racing, and we may finally see A.J. Foyt and Mario Andretti opt out of IndyCar racing and get some richly deserved rest. We always knew that if the state-of-the-art European rally cars ever showed up at the Pikes Peak Hill-Climb they'd dominate it, just as European mid-engined single-seaters took over at Indy thirty years ago—and they did come and they did dominate. Mr. Lee Iacocca rumbled off into retirement—at least for the time being—and the executive team he left behind at Chrysler heaved a huge sigh of relief. We saw automobiles gradually become larger and heavier and more expensive, all bad things, but we also saw them become more reliable and better than anyone could have predicted, a very good thing indeed.

It was the best time, ever, to be a car enthusiast.

Springtime in New York:
Another opening, another show.

~~∿❦~~

The New York International Automobile Show is a little like the annual Geneva salon—not one of the world's leading automobile shows, but a wonderful and rewarding place to go nonetheless. Spring comes earlier in New York, and the New York show has always been a perfect venue for car enthusiasts to celebrate its arrival. New York's Jacob Javits Center is a nice facility, much nicer for the purpose than the crowded old multilevel Coliseum on Columbus Circle, and press days are a chance to renew acquaintances with a lot of old friends and to sample the good life as it is lived in the Big Apple.

The main topic of conversation at the show this year was the remarkable behavior of General Motors' purchasing agent from hell, Mr. J. Ignacio Lopez de Arriortua, who had just performed a dance of incredible complexity and agility lasting several days, which reached its climax when he sneaked aboard an airplane heading for Germany and a new life with Volkswagen. His abrupt departure came just as his mentor and champion, GM president Jack Smith, was convening a press conference to announce that the extremely eccentric Basque was going to stay put. Instead of holding on to the Basque, Mr. Smith was left holding the bag.

In a few short months, "Iñaki," as Mr. Lopez was called by his tiny group of fanatical admirers, broke agreements, ignored contracts, busted heads, created a whole category of new enemies for GM among the supplier community, and then fled to the arms of Ferdinand Piëch, the new chairman at Volkswagen. It was some performance. He may actually have done some good at GM, but it's hard to tell. His boss, Mr. Smith, evidently thought so, because he was prepared to give away most of the store to keep Mr. Lopez—even offering him all of GM's North American operations, a position absolutely no one else believed him qualified to handle. Mr. Lopez's claim to fame was his ability to beat price concessions out of suppliers, and he had raised this form of corporate extortion to an art form. There's no doubt that GM's purchasing operation had been the most inefficient in the entire automotive industry, and no doubt that the purchasing operation was paying far too much for an awful lot of parts, but it seems unfair that the suppliers were the only ones forced to pay for all those decades of laxity and maladministration.

It will be fascinating to watch things develop at Volkswagen. Chairman Piëch is the gifted engineer who rebuilt Audi and brought us one great Audi product after another, but he is at least as eccentric as his new lieutenant, Mr. Lopez, and the fur should fly. As this is being written, GM is trying to prevent Volkswagen's dynamic duo from luring a whole bunch of Lopez loyalists away from GM purchasing operations in Europe. Go figure. GM is in the middle of massive white-collar cutbacks, so why not let Messrs. Piëch and Lopez have all of those people they want? Gee, I remember when General Motors was like a bank that had stumbled into the automobile business, and the automobile business as a whole was a fairly dull affair. This is highly entertaining stuff, and, if nothing else, it proves just how inextricably multinational the business has become.

The first New York show I ever attended was the International Motor Sports Show at the old Grand Central Palace in 1953, organized by TV star Herb Shriner. I was on active duty with the U.S. Naval Reserve, and my ship was tied up in Newport, Rhode Island, so it was easy to hop the train and spend a weekend in Manhattan. I saw the American introduction of the Healey 100—later the Austin-Healey 100—at that show, and was knocked out by its beauty. (A year later, my friend Barry Wayburn had the first one in the Detroit area, and before I could get over to his house to admire it he had completely dismantled it in an attempt to cure the unbearable cockpit heat.) Donald Healey himself was in New York for the unveiling, and I got close enough to speak to him, although I lacked the courage to actually do so. No one could have convinced me that within five years I'd be on a first-name basis with the man. On Sunday, I toured the Italian liner *Andrea Doria,* which was on her maiden voyage to New York, and which sank (with some Chrysler Ghia show cars in her hold) in 1956.

The New York show was one of the annual rituals when I worked at *Road & Track*. We flew in from Los Angeles overnight on a DC-7C, holed up in coach with a picnic basket full of Scotch and edible delights, arguing about cars and magazines all night and thoroughly annoying our fellow passengers. On arrival in New York, we were immediately summoned to John and Elaine Bond's hotel room for Ramos fizzes and picking up the arguments where we'd left off. We'd always do at least one dinner *en famille* at René Dreyfus's Le Chanteclair, where we'd see nearly everybody else who'd come to town for the show. Le Chanteclair closed in 1979, and no restaurant, here or abroad, had ever filled the void it left in the lives of a small army of car enthusiasts. I miss it every time I go to New York, which is currently about once a month.

This week I walked over to Forty-ninth, between Madison and Fifth, and stood for five minutes on the sidewalk where Le Chanteclair used to be, remembering how much fun it was. René Dreyfus, the great prewar French racing champion, ran a very nice French restaurant that catered specifically to the automotive crowd. His colleagues were his brother, Maurice, who acted as greeter and captain, and his sister, Suzanne, who ran the cash register at the end of the bar and kept an eye on things from there. The place reeked of motor racing history, with dozens of framed photos and drawings around the bar, and a steady stream of past and present heroes coming by for lunch or dinner throughout the year.

René set aside a round table in the dining room for several years, where a handful of regular customers could lunch together on an impromptu daily basis. (If they filled all the seats, René bought the wine.) I was not part of that group—I never seemed to be part of *any* group—but René would occasionally offer me an empty seat at that table, and I'd find myself lunching with people like Walter Cronkite, or Peter Donald, the radio personality and raconteur who had done so many of the famous voices on the Fred Allen show, and who was sort of an enthusiast-at-a-distance. René asked me to join him for lunch a couple of times after everyone else had left—at his table, right at Suzanne's elbow. He was also kind enough to buy my lunch—eaten alone and in a daze—the day my first son was born. He was a very generous host, and we'll never know how many of the regulars we saw there all the time were actually beneficiaries of René's own personal welfare program.

I ate dinner in a nearly empty Chanteclair the night of November 22, 1963, after Jack Kennedy was assassinated. I was in the room at the French consulate in New York in 1959 when René received the Legion of Honor, and I'm enormously proud to be able to call a man of his many achievements my friend. But René and I did suffer a major falling out once, after Ford celebrated its 1966 Le Mans victory in Le Chanteclair. The Ford guys were all as drunk as lords and the evening was a debacle. In their endless round of garrulous speeches, they forgot to acknowledge the race winners, Bruce McLaren and Chris Amon, and as the evening wound down, I coerced a shellshocked PR man into yelling, "What about the winners?" Bruce was hastily introduced, and as he started his characteristically graceful remarks the Ford victory banner came unstuck from the wall and fell over him and everybody else at the speakers' table. I complained to René that I thought his waiters had kind of taken advantage of the disorder to shed their usual calm professionalism, and René replied, "If you don't like the behavior of my waiters, you don't have to eat in my restaurant." And, for almost ten years, I didn't. It was Brock Yates who brought us together and got us to bury the hatchet in 1976. Now somebody needs to do the same thing for me and Yates.

So, a couple of days ago, I stood on the sidewalk at 18 East Forty-ninth Street where Le Chanteclair used to be, and reran all those old movies on the insides of my eyelids, wishing I could step through that long-closed door, shrug off my raincoat with the hatcheck lady, then turn and shake hands with Maurice Dreyfus, and see René—trim, fit, immaculately double breasted—hovering over some mutual friend's table in the dining room. Should some good fairy ever offer me three wishes, I might ask for one last evening at Le Chanteclair during the New York International Automobile Show.

Death of a genuine hero.

❧

F rom *The New York Times*, Sunday, 22 August:
DREYFUS-René. The Vintage Sports Car Club of America records with sorrow the death, on August 17, 1993, of our revered and beloved member. Racing Champion, Sportsman, Soldier, Restaurateur, Enthusiast, Gentleman. We will remember René always with affection and respect. We offer our profound sympathy to his family.

Gilbert L. Steward, Jr., President

M. Jacques Grelly called from Dallas on Monday to tell me that René Dreyfus had gone into the hospital for open-heart surgery. The doctors said it was dicey for an eighty-eight-year-old man, no more than a 60/40 chance, but René was in excellent spirits. According to M. Grelly, René allowed that those were better odds than he'd had in most of his adventures, and he was looking forward to being the oldest Grand Prix driver ever to experience successful open-heart surgery. He was calling me, he said, because René wanted me to know that he wasn't trying to get out of the reconciliation lunch he'd promised to host for me and Brock Yates, only postponing it two or three months. We continued to chat for a few minutes, about René's bravery and good humor, and about M. Grelly's collections of historic Deutsch Bonnet racing cars and vintage racing posters (going back to the Paris-Madrid race of 1903). When we signed off, he was going to New York to be with René, and I was going to Las Vegas to judge a national walkaround (sales pitch) contest among Subaru salesmen.

When I arrived in Las Vegas the next day, I made the obligatory call to my office as soon as I was inside the McCarran International airport terminal, and Kelly told me that René hadn't made it. The operation was successful, but they'd been unable to restart his heart. I wished that I'd gone to New York. That's probably a dumb idea, because I wouldn't have been able to do anything anyway. His brother, Maurice, was at the hospital with René's friend and biographer, Beverly Rae

Kimes, and New York was home to many friends closer than I, but he'd always been so thoughtful and decent with me that I felt I'd owed him one. He and I had spoken on the phone several times since my July column where I wrote of him and his wonderful New York restaurant, Le Chanteclair. He had decided that it was his responsibility to get Brock Yates and me back together again and was doing a telephone shuttle between us trying to set that up.

René and Maurice attended the first party we threw for our then brand-new *Automobile Magazine* at Rockefeller Center in New York. I vividly remember how pleased I was when I looked up and spotted them coming through the door. For the past three years I'd offered to fly René out to be with us at Pebble Beach, for the concours and for Steve Earle's Monterey Historic Automobile Races, but he always maintained that he was too old and frail for such arduous travel. Nonetheless, he was always busy, always on top of things, always available to his friends and admirers.

I have a wonderful woman friend in France—Mme. Yvonne Korda, my wife's former mother-in-law—who was honeymooning in Monaco the week that René won the Grand Prix there in 1930. We were able to take her to Le Chanteclair in 1977 and introduce her to René, and the dinner that ensued was one of those jolly multilingual affairs that crop up in my mind whenever I think back on all the great times I've enjoyed through my involvement with automobiles and automotive people.

René Dreyfus was everything Gil Steward said he was in that elegant little tribute in the *Times*. He was our link to a time when Grand Prix drivers were larger than life, heroic, risking their lives *pour le sport* and not merely for vast sums of money. A lot of us are going to miss René as a man, and the whole world will miss the qualities he represented.

Travels with P.J.: Or, how I went all the way to Bologna and barely got to drive the Bugatti at all.

I had hustled down to Bologna from Turin on Wednesday to drive the Bugatti EB110 with my friend and sometime colleague P.J. O'Rourke. The Fiat people had provided me with a willing but sober Lancia Dedra for the occasion. The trip went without mishap until I got rattled and blew past a ticket-dispensing machine on the autostrada, which forced me to dismount at the next tollbooth and show the officers there exactly what one so stupid looked like. They helped me fill out several forms, all of us speaking, none of us understanding, then I paid them several thousand lire and departed. I can still see their eyebrows raised in question marks.

What we now call Bologna was not built with the automobile in mind, and grumpy Communist city administrations in the years since World War II have not helped. Barbarians, even worse than automotive journalists, controlled the place for about a thousand years, and it wasn't until the twelfth century that things got rolling. Europe's oldest university is there, and the city is often referred to as "Bologna the Fat" because Bolognese food is so uniformly seductive. The city is a warren of arcaded boulevards and narrow streets that periodically change name or stop short of the place you're looking for. The people at the Grand Hotel Baglioni had faxed me a little map that was only partly legible, but it did say that the street upon which their hostelry was located had been turned into a pedestrians-only thoroughfare, so guests would have to approach from the back. I got to know several piazzas and traffic circles quite well before blundering into the street that would lead me to the hotel's side door.

The Grand Hotel Baglioni was indeed grand. My room was right out of a Bertolucci movie, and the chair-height bar downstairs was tendered by a slender man with heavily brilliantined hair who made great drinks, had all the moves, and lost points only because of a tendency to carry on interminable personal phone calls while the customers were trying to hold conversations of their own. In the hotel dining room I asked the maitre d' why, in the country that created a large portion of the greatest music ever heard, did feckless Italian rock 'n' roll tinkle out of every speaker. He rolled his eyes, agreed fervently, and strode toward the kitchen. A moment later, the speaker over my head squawked and buzzed as he twirled the radio dial to a local classical music station. Then he brought me my tagliatelle alla Bolognese.

Next morning I was collected by Dr. Stefano Pasini, public relations director of Bugatti and a practicing ophthalmologist, in his Sterling—perhaps the only Sterling ever seen on the streets of Bologna. Sterlings in Italy, it turns out, are every bit as discouraging as Sterlings in North America, and as we drove out to the airport to collect P.J., Pasini recited his litany of engine replacements and other horrors. He also spoke reverently of his enthusiasm for the works of P.J. O'Rourke, which he has collected almost in their entirety. He even quoted at length from stories P.J. wrote for me at *Car and Driver,* i.e., "I don't know anything about cars except that they aren't as good as they used to be, and before that they weren't even as good as they are now." He confided that he had every one of O'Rourke's books stacked in his office, ready to autograph.

O'Rourke, the Grim Nineties' answer to the Gay Nineties' Richard Harding Davis, came off the plane looking like a senior from a good eastern prep school—perhaps a senior who was redshirted for about twenty years before completing his degree. Guys who grew up in Toledo don't naturally look like this. Personal-appearance-wise, P.J. owes a great debt to Holden Caulfield. His luggage is that dark green canvas stuff from Orvis, and every piece looks as though it has been buried for a while in a landfill. When one thinks of P.J. O'Rourke and his travels— as in *Holidays in Hell*—one wonders how his luggage has survived at all.

The good *dottore* and I toured Bologna on foot while P.J. unpacked, showered, and changed. Everybody in Bologna seemed to be talking to everybody else on a cellular phone. Later, at the Tennis Club, where the three of us had lunch, women of all ages in string bikinis were murmuring into black handsets. At the table next to us, a man and his wife both spoke on phones while eating their lunches. In a park, I saw a guy talking on the phone while necking with a blond woman who would make your eyes bug out. Bologna is a wonderful city, a beautiful city, with brilliant restaurants and shops, but I came away with the feeling that it was covered by a dome of electronically suspended nouns, verbs, adjectives, salutations, and terms of endearment. *What do they all have to talk about all the time?*

By the time lunch was over, photographer Martyn Goddard had arrived from London, and we all raced north, past Modena, to the Bugatti works at Campogalliano. P.J. and I wandered through the plant while Martyn got ready for the obligatory sunset photo shoot. We ran into chief engineer Mauro Forghieri, who was escorting a group of FIA technical people through the factory. He grinned at me and said: "I remember you from before! We are both still alive!" A lot of cars have been around the track since Henry N. Manney III introduced me to Forghieri about a thousand years ago.

Dr. Pasini's assistant in the PR department is Alessia Regazzoni, daughter of the great Clay Regazzoni and a racing driver in her own right. She found us some coffee and acted as Martyn's assistant, moving the blue Bugatti around as required. This last gave me hope. The idea of a car so fast and so expensive and bearing such an awe-inspiring name tended to intimidate me, and I kept having to repress dark fears about screwing up when the time would come to actually drive it. But watching Ms. Regazzoni whip our photo car around the factory grounds as though it were a Mazda Miata, I began to think that I might be able to operate it successfully after all.

When we did get to drive the car the following morning, we were accompanied by Giuseppe Montorsi, a factory test driver. Mr. Montorsi had been working for Bugatti for eighteen months; before that, he spent thirteen years as a test driver at Ferrari. He asked where we wanted to take the car, and I showed him the route book from our magazine's Italian Grand Tour of the previous May, turning the map that traced our readers' route over the Apennines and back. He whistled and said: *"Madonna! Fiorano due!"* ("Holy Mother of God! Fiorano two!") and then explained that those roads were regularly used as an extension of the Fiorano test track by Ferrari's test drivers. And it was absolutely true. All day, as we shrieked up and down the two-lane hill roads, we saw everything from F40s to Mondials with the little white *prova* plates hung on them, shrieking along on missions of their own. The drivers all knew our Mr. Montorsi, and everybody grinned and waved, or occasionally stopped to chat for a moment before getting on with it.

I drove the car first. It is every bit as fast as you thought it might be. The dynamic combination of all that power, four-wheel drive, and great big superomigod Michelin tires is absolutely unforgettable. It comes off a corner like a naval fighter coming off a carrier catapult. What I wasn't prepared for was the ease of driving the thing. It is just a car, it turns out, but a car that just happens to go 342 kph [213 mph]. It is much easier to drive than Ferrari's 512TR. As one might expect from an

Italian carmaker, though, the air conditioning is hopelessly inadequate, even on a 70-degree day in the foothills of the Apennines. The wrath of the customer in Houston or Phoenix who spends $249,000 for one of these magnificent animals, only to find that the A/C is a limp jet of humid air trying to sneak out of the center duct on the dash, is beyond imagination.

That was the last time I drove the Bugatti EB110. O'Rourke planted his buns in that driver's seat and only grudgingly got out for lunch and a visit to the gents'. *I* arranged the trip. *I* paid for his ticket and his fancy hotel room. *I* begged Pasini's permission for him to drive the Bugatti, this dog in the manger who puts the clutch in when he goes around corners, and this was the thanks I got: standing at the side of the road with the photographer, listening to my pal P.J. howl through the mountains. His story about the experience appears on page 80. I'm not even going to look at it.

The drive of my life,
in the 1994 California Mille.

orte Madera, California—One of the best things you can do with a pre-1958 sports car is to run Italy's Mille Miglia *storica*. A large number of American drivers, including this one, have made the pilgrimage to Brescia to drive the thousand miles in company with some of the greatest cars and best people who ever hurtled down a mountain road in the middle of the night with weak headlights and fading brakes. I'll never forget the thrill of the start from Brescia, or the floodlit arrival in one little town or another where pretty girls kissed me and handed me bottles of wine or olive oil, loaves of bread, boxes of candy, key fobs, lapel pins, or amusingly translated screeds about the touristic wonders of their region. This one event is reason enough to take the money you were saving for the kids' college education and buy yourself a Lancia B20 or a Le Mans Replica Frazer Nash. If your kids are worth a damn, they'll be able to scam government grants.

Since several thousand Americans would like to run the Mille Miglia *storica* and only a couple of hundred will ever make it, Mille Miglia-like events have begun to pop up like mushrooms around our country: the Copperstate 1000 in Arizona, the Colorado Grand, the New England Tour 1000, and the one I just finished, the California Mille. Martin Swig, the innovative San Francisco car dealer who was interviewed in the May 1989 issue of our magazine, must bear the blame for most of this Mille Miglia-inspired activity. Martin is an Alfa enthusiast to the very marrow of his bones. It is he who founded the *Amici Americani della Mille Miglia* (American Friends of the Mille Miglia), and it is he who has helped a bunch of Americans enter the event in Italy. Four years ago, he founded the California Mille.

It came about when Martin Swig and Gil Nickel and vintage racer Dr. Lou Sellyei were running in the Colorado Grand. In Steamboat Springs one night, they slipped away from the crowd to go off on their own for a little serious food-and-wine activity. Gil Nickel, who is the proprietor of Far Niente—the great Napa Valley winemaker—and owner of a very tasty little car collection, said, "Somebody's going to do a California Grand one of these days, and when they do, we probably won't like it." Therefore, they designated Martin Swig point man to organize a 1000-mile historic-car rally along Mille Miglia *storica* lines in California.

Martin, wondering how he got volunteered for this duty, created an event in which he would be sure to have fun. It would be like the Italian original in spirit. The roads would be challenging, the food good, the entries accepted on the basis of their historical appropriateness (and whether Martin and a shadowy six-person committee liked them or not). That is to say, Italian rules. The California Highway Patrol cooperates to the degree that it assigns a couple of officers to follow the route and watch out for really egregious violations of good sense and good manners. Martin wants everybody to have fun—and that means that there will be some spirited driving—but he doesn't want anybody hurt or killed. Hence the presence of these affable officers of the law.

We gathered in Corte Madera, just north of San Francisco. Fifty-seven cars showed up: seventeen Alfas, six Porsches, five Ferraris, four Jaguars, four ACs, three Chryslers, three Lancias, and, as they say, a host of others. My favorites included two 1957 Ferrari 250 Testa Rossas, one 1932 Alfa Romeo 8C2300, one 1955 Chrysler 300, John Lamm's 1955 Lancia B20 coupe (previously owned by Lawrence C. Crane, our art director), and one 1952 Siata 208S. The event was sponsored by Il Fornaio restaurant in Corte Madera, Gil Nicke's Far Niente Winery, Motochron (a maker of snazzy wristwatches with automotive-instrument faces), and Chrysler Corporation. This meant that we would enjoy two excellent Italian suppers and one breakfast at Il Fornaio, that there would be Far Niente chardonnay (my favorite) and cabernet sauvignon poured each evening at our overnight stops, and that there would be several prototype twin-cam Neons and two Vipers for us to drive whenever we felt like it. Motochron gave each official entrant a watch with a Porsche 356 speedometer face, but we press types didn't make the cut.

The first day's route took us from Corte Madera to Lake Tahoe by way of the Napa Valley, and included a major rainstorm and three inches of snow at Tahoe. On the second day, we drove from Lake Tahoe to Willows, California. On the third, from Willows to Eureka. Each day was better than the day before. The fourth and final day was the best for me—from Eureka back to Corte Madera by way of Mendocino and the coastal highway. On that last day, Martyn Goddard and I had to get out ahead of the field so that he might take some scenic action photos along the coast above Fort Bragg. We arrived at the two-lane road that would take us there—through the redwoods, over the mountains—before anyone else was up. I drove the little iris gray twin-cam Neon coupe as fast as I could make it go for the best part of an hour, up and down through the gears, sailing through the corners. It was wonderful! The Neon coupe is a very nice car to begin with, but when you add a 150-horsepower twin-cam engine, a nicely staged five-speed manual transmission, and a shorter final-drive ratio, it becomes a really cheerful little giant killer. The wise guys are saying that this breathed-upon Neon is going to lay waste to its class in Showroom Stock racing, and I shouldn't be surprised.

On the last afternoon, I enjoyed, perhaps, the best drive of my life—which has featured a lot of very nice drives indeed. A small group of us abandoned the official route and took another road south. Highway 1 was clogged with motorhomes and other obstacles, so we took Route 128 from Albion out to Highway 101, leaving the rally behind. I was driving a red Viper. Martyn Goddard was my passenger, loaded down with Nikons. With about twenty-five miles remaining before we reached the freeway, something chemical and emotional happened between my Viper and Lou Sellyei's Ferrari 250TR, and we were off through the redwoods. The Viper is so magnificently fast, its tires so wide, its brakes so good, that I could stay twenty-five feet behind Lou's Ferrari with minimum fuss. I later told Martyn that I've been listening to those Ferraris yowl past on racing circuits ever since they were first introduced. On this day I sat behind one in an open car for almost a half-hour, looking straight into those four megaphones, hearing every percussive exclamation as Lou hammered it through its rev range. Martyn shot all of it, every corner.

The Viper I drove was just outstanding. With so much torque available, I shifted far less than Lou, sometimes leaving it in third gear for whole series of corners. I only wish it made a better noise. Somebody said it sounded like a very fast United Parcel Service truck. I think it sounds like a huge vacuum cleaner. Lou's passenger was Chris Jensen of the *Cleveland Plain Dealer*, who'd leaped into the Ferrari's passenger seat on an earlier roadside stop. Somebody pointed out that Lou had no passenger, and Chris went for it, saying, "I'm not *entirely* stupid." As we tore through the dips and esses and off-camber corners, Chris would occasionally wrench his eyes off the road ahead to see if Martyn and I were still on station astern in the red Viper. I'm proud to say we were.

When we reached the end of the road, Lou pulled around the corner and stopped in front of a country beer joint. Looking across at me, he pulled off his sunglasses, grinned, and said: "We must be two of the oldest guys on this trip. Nobody would believe what we just did. It would be like the tree falling in the forest that nobody hears. You need to have another car along when you do something like this, just to be sure it really happened." At the finish line in Corte Madera, Martin Swig's executive assistant, Kate Nyland—who, truth to tell, does most of the work organizing the California Mille—greeted us with bottles of Miller Genuine Draft. Nothing ever tasted so good. Overcome, I told Kate I wanted her to bear my child. She was amused. I climbed out of the Viper one last time, shook the kinks out of my legs, and walked across to Lou Sellyei's Testa Rossa. He was still planted behind the steering wheel. Taking a pull on his Miller, he said, "I'm just going to sit here for about an hour."

Warren Weith called him
"the man who invented Ferrari."

arroll Shelby called me at home, after work. "We're about to lose Luigi," he said. "I love that old man." That last part is what Shelby says every time Luigi Chinetti's name comes up. Luigi Chinetti was in the hospital, having suffered a heart attack, and hospitals and tubes up the nose and patronizing residents who have no idea who this ninety-three-year-old man with the heavily accented English really is can kill just as readily as viruses and worn-out organs. Sure enough, he was dead within a few days.

Tom Burnside had called to tell me about Luigi's cardiac event the day it happened, just as he'd called me a couple of weeks before to remind me to call Luigi on his birthday. Tom said that Luigi was alert and responsive when he was awake, but that he slept a lot, and that he had a lot of stuff sticking in him. When I'd called the house in Connecticut to wish Luigi a happy birthday, somebody yelled him to the phone and he was bitchy because they were making too much noise celebrating his birthday and he couldn't hear me.

Most of my early memories of Luigi Chinetti involve that grumpy demeanor. In the Fifties and earliest Sixties, he always stood between me and the Ferrari pits. He was the guy who wouldn't let me drive the latest Whatever from Maranello. He did not suffer fools or lightweight automotive journalists gladly, and he evidently had me relegated to both of those categories.

Then, one day in 1963, I had suddenly and miraculously slipped past the barrier. I don't know what happened. Maybe I'd just been around long enough. Maybe he'd actually read something I wrote. (Naaaaah!) Maybe it was because I was a friend of his friends. But suddenly I was invited to dinner when Amerigo Manicardi—Ferrari's commercial director in those days—came to the United States with his wife. He took me to lunch at the Casa Rex on west Fiftieth Street in Manhattan. He loaned me cars on a fairly regular basis. I could hang out at the shop on West 54th Street at the corner of Eleventh Avenue. I was a made man!

Warren Weith, in his column in *Car and Driver,* once called Luigi Chinetti "the man who invented Ferrari." It is quite likely that Luigi Chinetti and his wife, Marion, made it possible for Ferrari to become Ferrari. Enzo Ferrari was single-minded in his approach to racing. He built cars to race, and everything else came second. Non-racing cars, even Ferraris, bored him. He treated non-racing customers with the disgust he might show for something moving in his wastebasket. He was not destined for success in the commercial world.

But Luigi Chinetti was his friend. Luigi had known him for years, was accustomed to the abuse, and knew how to handle the old bastard. At enormous personal cost and effort, Luigi and Marion Chinetti made Ferrari a commercial proposition in North America. Enzo Ferrari wasn't much help, but he did build the wonderful cars that Luigi raced and sold, and that was enough for Luigi.

Contributor Ken Gross and I visited Luigi at his home in Greenwich, Connecticut, not long after I launched *Automobile Magazine.* The resulting story appeared in the August '86 issue and is—by my lights—one of the nicest pieces we've yet run in these pages. I reread it after Larry Crane stuck his head in my office door and told me Luigi had died. I should simply reprint the entire story, but there's only time and space for a sampling.

"Luigi Chinetti—with his wife, Marion—brought the first Ferraris to America. Luigi Chinetti helped launch the international racing careers of Phil Hill, Carroll Shelby, Dan Gurney, Richie Ginther, Masten Gregory, and the Rodriguez brothers. He sold Ferraris with the same spirit that he brought to racing: first, love; then dogged determination, a worldly willingness to take life as it came, and an utter absence of the doubts and fears that assailed lesser men when the situation seemed to be in doubt.

"Example: 'One day I asked my wife, 'Can I have money for two cars I want from Ferrari?' She says, 'Yes, you can have it.' I send the money to Ferrari, and that night I wake up at three o'clock. I go to the checkbook and I look. A negative balance of $365. Marion is very good with money, very careful, but she never says no to me'."

On another subject: "We ask him to describe his favorite Le Mans race, thinking he'll zero in on his victory in the 1949 race, when he drove twenty-three hours and forty-three minutes..."

He responded: "My favorite race at Le Mans I did not win. I won in 1932, with Raymond Sommer, but 1933 is my favorite. I finished second, behind Nuvolari. In the last lap, after twenty-four hours, I was first three times. At the Maison Blanche...I had at least 500 rpm more, and I was set to pass. Not because I was a better driver. After twenty-four hours, even a champion cannot do better than the next competitor if he's in good health. There's a limit, you know. So here it was at the end of the race, and I pretended I was as good as he was.

"I passed him after the bridge, and, going down, I remembered that the Shell Oil Company had promised me 60,000 francs if I won the race using a special fuel. Can you imagine? I couldn't even pay for the car. Nuvolari was already rich. So he looked me in the eye—I was so determined—and he understood that he *had* to let me pass. In the esses after the bridge, I touched his car with my rear wheel a little, like this [he gestures]. I got by, but he passed me again in the straight. He was running benzole, getting at least twenty horsepower more than me.

"Can you imagine? All I can think of is the 60,000 francs. So I passed him at Maison Blanche, and he passed me again at the esses. I thought I'd have an advantage in second, but when I tried to shift down, there was a tremendous noise (he imitates a long, drawn-out *graaaauuu-uuunch!*), and nothing happened. I got back in third, Nuvolari passed me, and it was goodbye. I finished about 100 yards behind him. In my mind, while it was no disgrace to finish closely behind Nuvolari, I could only see the prize going away.

"I catch Nuvolari after the finish, and he shouts to me, 'You drove a good race, but I am driving to the cashier!'" Fortunately, Shell awarded the special fuel money to Chinetti after all.

What would you give to have been there that Sunday afternoon? Or on that night in 1946, when he and Marion arrived in Modena from Paris in a Citroën they'd borrowed from Amédée Gordini and went straight to see Enzo Ferrari?

"We arrived in Modena very late. Ferrari was waiting in his office—on the left side, the old one. It was snowing, and I got lost, but finally we got there. He was freezing in his office. It was past eleven p.m. Imagine!

"After we said hello to each other, I told him: Stop making machine tools. The French, the Americans, the Germans will make better ones. You should make automobiles, a new breed. If you will build five cars for me, I'll sell them."

In our 1986 story, René Dreyfus said: "Ferrari owes Luigi Chinetti a lot. Certainly they might eventually have established themselves in America, but Luigi did it beautifully for them—with his racing and his understanding of the car and the clients—in a way that no one else could. He always knew what he wanted. Once he'd made up his mind, there was no changing him—not even Mr. Ferrari could do that."

I didn't know Luigi Chinetti when he won Le Mans in 1932, and I didn't know him in 1940 when he came to this country with René Dreyfus and René Le Bègue as chief mechanic of Lucy O'Reilly Schell's Écurie Bleue Indianapolis effort. But I knew him for thirty years, and I doubt if he ever changed very much. Thank God for that.

Great Drives.

M y first transcontinental drive was in June of 1955, my honeymoon. In October of 1954, I'd been jailed for reckless driving with a revoked operator's permit—a mandatory seventy-two hours in the slammer under Michigan law at that time. (A couple of years ago, I applied for a permit to purchase a Ruger target pistol, and the sergeant on duty brought me up on the computer to see if I was a wanted serial killer. "Aha!" he chuckled. "You've been a guest of ours.") Since I was a short-timer, they didn't take me out to the country farm the next morning with all my roommates, and I had some time to reflect on my misdeeds. I decided that the cure for my troubles was marriage to a strong, sensible woman, and that woman was Norma J. Wohlfiel, a high-school classmate and co-star in several theatrical productions. By the time I was out of jail, I'd written my marriage proposal and mailed it to Norma in California. Her letter of reply said, "I'll be home in December to see if you've lost your mind." We were married in June, and although Norma was too strong and sensible to stay married to me, the marriage actually lasted twenty years.

We drove cross-country in my MG TF 1500, with the side curtains in and the top down. We both got terrific tans, and it was a wonderful way to see the Republic. We stopped for service at a British-car dealership in Denver and met a young racing driver named Dabney Collins who was delighted to talk cars with me. They had a beautiful aluminum-bodied competition XK120 Jaguar (we called it the "Silverstone Jag") on the showroom floor, and I could tell that I was getting closer to the fulfillment of all my dreams. We crossed the desert at night, so that the MG wouldn't overheat, and were almost hypnotized by the hundreds of jack rabbits crisscrossing the road in our headlights. We wound down out of the mountains into northern California on a Saturday morning, and even Highway 99 seemed beautiful to a wide-eyed car enthusiast from the Midwest. We slept that night in the house Norma had rented in Manhattan Beach and I had already seen all manner of interesting cars, as well as my first open-air California automotive repair shop. It really was the promised land!

I've lost track of my cross-country trips since then—in an Austin-Healey, a Chevy van, a Saab, a couple of Suburbans, a V-8 Plymouth Barracuda, a Peugeot 404, a couple of Volvos, Mercedes old and new, a Studebaker Hawk, a couple of Ferraris, and a dozen others—but two stand out.

In 1959, I took delivery of my new Triumph TR3A at the New York Auto Show. It was black, with a black interior and a black hard top. It was, by my reckoning, the prettiest TR ever constructed. I drove it from New York to California, breaking it in, and from Chicago west I followed famous Route 66. Around Gallup, New Mexico, the wind came up, and before long the air was full of sand. Being equipped with side curtains, the Triumph was also full of sand. I made it to Flagstaff that night, utterly parched and exhausted. I checked into a motel, went to the fanciest restaurant in the neighborhood, and ordered—God knows why—a dry Rob Roy. This soaked into the tissues of my mouth before I could swallow it. I ordered another, and then I lost track. I woke at 3:30 in the morning lying face down, fully dressed, on the bed in my motel room. The door was open, and my Triumph was sitting outside the door with its engine running and its headlights on. I had no memory of the evening, nor did I know when I'd returned. I got up, washed my face, and left town, thoroughly ashamed of myself and terminally hung over. The Triumph, it turned out, was very badly sandblasted. Everything that faced forward had to be repainted, replated, or replaced. This was not an unmitigated disaster, however, because it offered me the opportunity to customize the little dear and remove some unwanted trim.

In January 1967, I was visiting the General Motors Desert Proving Grounds in Mesa, Arizona. One thing led to another, and some Chevrolet engineers offered to let me drive a prototype Camaro Z28 back to Michigan. I left late in the afternoon and followed U.S. 60 out across the high country—over the Salt River Canyon, across the San Carlos Apache reservation and the White Mountain Apache reservation, through Show Low and across to Socorro, New Mexico. That car's 302 engine was as good a Chevy V-8 as I'd ever driven, and I'd driven about 100 that were really strong. After sundown, I burned a six-hour hole through the darkness along U.S. 60. Headlights would appear in the distance and I'd slow down, only to discover that they were *miles* away in the desert night. I turned on the dreadful little AM radio and picked up radio stations thousands of miles away, all gabbing nonstop pseudo-reverence about the astronauts—Roger Chaffee, Virgil Gissom, and Edward White II—who'd burned to death that day. But I was safe under a great black glass dome. I was a time traveler. I had found my element, and the Z28 was the perfect tool to exploit it.

Last month, J.L.K. Davis and I drove a new Range Rover 2400 miles in less than a week—Ann Arbor to Montgomery, Alabama, for some concentrated automotive immersion time (and hunting) with Knox Kershaw (owner of the Duesenberg Special Phil Llewellin wrote about in "The World's Finest Motor Car," November 1991); Montgomery to Washington, D.C., to present the All-Stars award for the Land Rover Discovery to the entire staff of that company; then back to Ann Arbor by way of Maryland, Pennsylvania, West Virginia, and Ohio. Next week, we'll take our Four Seasons (long term) Mazda Millenia to New York and return. That car is about to leave our fleet, and it's just too good to let it get away without one last long drive. Next month, we'll take our new long-term Chevrolet Tahoe to Baja California, and after that we'll run our own '55 Chrysler 300 in the California Mille. This is shaping up to be another great year, great drive-wise.

Egomaniacs at the gate:
the battle for Chrysler.

~ひひ~

T|he big news at the New York Auto Show was the announcement by Mr. Kirk Kerkorian that he—and his treasured associate and automotive advisor Mr. Lee Iacocca—intended to make an offer for the 90 percent of Chrysler Corporation stock they didn't already own. This raid, reminiscent of the Eighties, was painted in the most pious colors possible—lots of stuff about Chrysler shareholders deserving a better deal, ad nauseam. More likely, these two aged multimillionaires felt mortality pressing in upon them and decided there was still time for one more big score. Chrysler has been in the tank for a generation or more, but there's the smell of money about the place now, and Messrs. Kerkorian and Iacocca wanted their big payoff. Rape Chrysler, sell Jeep to some unnamed overseas automaker, and run with the money.

Kirk Kerkorian has to be the last heavy hitter in the world who still believes that Lee Iacocca could actually do something positive if he again had his say within Chrysler's management councils. Lee Iacocca did get Chrysler out of the ditch a decade ago, but then he put it right back into the ditch on the other side of the road. While running Chrysler, Mr. Iacocca worked every angle in the book of corporate governance to line his own pockets and to plump his already stretched-to-the-limit ego, and he just can't stand the idea that old age and failing powers finally forced him off the gravy train.

If this scam had worked, Chrysler would have returned to its former status as "beleaguered Chrysler Corporation," walking wounded, and Chrysler shareholders and dealers would have been left holding the bag.

I have known and liked Chrysler chairman Robert Eaton since he was a youthful project engineer at Chevrolet in the Sixties. (We were reminiscing at lunch, a couple of years ago, about where we were when Jack Kennedy was assassinated, and he said: "I remember exactly where I was. I was in a dynamometer cell at the [GM] Tech Center, putting the finishing touches on an engine that Roger Penske was going to run in a Corvette Gran Sport at Nassau.") I have known Lee Iacocca for about as long, since he was an up-and-comer in Ford Division, but I've never been able to feel much warmth for the man. He is too tempting a target, I guess, with his bluster, and his hovering sycophants, and his questionable taste in friends and women and cars. Lee is a Bill Blass Designer Series Continental Mark V kind of guy.

Bob Eaton is quick to point out that he has had relatively little to do with the recent success of Chrysler, preferring to give credit to the management team already in place at the time of his hiring, a management team led by multinational car enthusiast Bob Lutz. Further, he's had a lot of help from a very robust automotive market. Nonetheless, he has been a more than competent chairman of that perennially troubled car builder. Not so long ago, investors eagerly shopped for companies run the way Bob Eaton and his team have run Chrysler. Now, Wall Street is in it for the short run. What happens to a company after a raid like the one proposed by Kirk Kerkorian is not their problem.

But no good deed ever goes unpunished. Having done most everything right, Eaton has been forced to fight off an attack that—no matter how it finally comes out—will leave Chrysler damaged. In *USA Today,* Lee Iacocca took time out from his new career as the Johnny Appleseed of Indian gambling casinos to do a little character assassination, saying that *he'd* hired Eaton to straighten out Chrysler's quality problems, and Eaton wasn't moving fast enough. This was clearly a case of the pot calling the kettle Italian, because Mr. Iacocca was famously bored by quality concerns throughout his automotive career. Nor was safety ever very high on Lee's list until he belatedly became Mr. Air Bag in Chrysler's television commercials. He really can't take credit for hiring Bob Eaton, either—if he'd had his way, he'd have continued at the helm of Chrysler, and there'd have been no place for Eaton. Ah, well.

When I am old, I will wear purple...*

ed's Bog—I got a purple Porsche 968 cabrio last fall, with a six-speed manual gearbox and a gray leather interior. I have long believed that purple would be a great modern car color. It certainly worked on coach-built cars in earlier times, when car designers were less inhibited and car colors more venturesome, and sometimes in the middle Fifties I began to ask my friends in the automobile business why they didn't include purple as a regular choice, along with colors like burgundy, dark blue, and British racing green, but I was never taken seriously. Most manufacturers now offer purple, in one shade or another, and I'm overjoyed, but I can take no credit for this. They did it without my advice. Alas, I am a prophet without honor in my own business.

The Porsche 968 is the final iteration of Tony Lapine's 924 and 944 designs, and I ordered it because of my affection for him as much as for its many charms—dynamic and cosmetic. The 924, a sort of upmarket Karmann-Ghia coupe, was never much of a car. Tony Lapine himself once told me that the design would have worked better on a two-liter Maserati. But then they created the 944 and gave it some serious help in the engine room, and suddenly it was a great car in its own right. I once wrote that every automotive enthusiast magazine ought to have a 944 on permanent duty in its fleet, to be used as a baseline for evaluations of vehicle dynamics, particularly handling. Mainstream Porsche buyers, being permanently locked into Hans Ledwinka's seventy-five-year-old notions of rear-engined cars with swing axles, never warmed up to the 944. Its engine was at the wrong end, and it was too easy to drive, too directionally stable, and too comfortable for people who thought the 911 was the only Porsche ever built. As the decades passed and Porsche engineers made the 911 more and more like a real car, I too loved it, but I could never get over my prejudice in favor of front-engined cars with adequate luggage space and a certain willingness to go down the road in a straight line.

---

*Lifted, in modified form, from Jenny Joseph's poem *Warning* ("When I am an old woman I shall wear purple"). I apologize for the liberty taken.

Thus, I ordered my new 968, and had it equipped with Porsche's optional cellular telephone, a very snazzy Fujitsu Ten flip-phone that mounts face up on the console in a hard-wired bracket, so that it's usable either as a hard-wired car phone or as a battery-operated portable phone. On the first day that I set out to carry it as a pocket phone—the first press day at the New York Auto Show—I slipped it into my black nylon *Automobile Magazine* briefcase, went out the front door of the St. Regis Hotel, and hopped into a cab. When I got out of the cab, paid the driver, and dodged through traffic to reach the other side of the street, I patted the bag just because I liked the feel of the phone in there, but the phone wasn't there. And the cab was gone, carrying the phone which I had neglected to lock. I went to a pay phone, called our business manager, Harriet Stemberger, and asked her to start the process of canceling my relationship with that particular handset before some third-world dope dealer found it in the cab and placed ninety-bazillion dollars' worth of calls. An hour later she informed me that it was handled, and that she would order me a replacement from the Porsche folks in Reno.

But the plot thickens. The next passenger in that cab was a young man named Jimmy Marsicano, who works in the mailroom of a firm called MacAndrews & Forbes. MacAndrews & Forbes is the holding company (Revlon, New World Entertainment, Marvel Comics) controlled by Mr. Ronald Perelman, who is only marginally less powerful than Ming the Merciless. Jimmy Marsicano was handling some errand for Mr. Perelman when he followed me into the cab. He found my phone. He did not call his relatives in Italy. He took it back to the office and turned it over to Ms. Jennifer Meyer, director of facilities at MacAndrews & Forbes. Ms. Meyer called Porsche, and they traced the phone to me. My snazzy cellular phone is now back in its bracket and all's right with the world, thanks to the nice people at MacAndrews & Forbes.

We ran the 968 through the winter with Bridgestone Blizzak tires on the original-equipment wheels, and, with the arrival of spring, installed state-of-the-art Dunlop SP Sport 8000s on Momo R3 (three-piece) wheels. It was a good snow-and-ice car with the Blizzaks, but they seemed to make it just the tiniest bit squirmy on dry pavement. Conventional wisdom regarding snow tires—and the seat of my pants—told me that I shouldn't commit the car completely to any of my favorite test curves and corners, thus equipped, and I didn't. Came summer, and the new Dunlops are working well, definitely living up to their promise of better traction, better high-speed stability, and better handling than the OE tires. But even if they were only a set of convenience-store rim protectors, they'd be pretty wonderful on those gorgeous Momo wheels. The R3s look as though they'd been designed with my car in mind. Now I have to pull them and paint the brake calipers red, like those on the Porsche 911 Turbo. When that's done, it'll be perfect. (In addition to being purple.)

It's interesting to compare my Porsche 968 with my wife's Ferrari 328GTS (which is now for sale). The Porsche is the better car, but the Ferrari is a better experience. If my Porsche were a 911 Turbo, the experience thing could be a tie, but the nine-year-old Ferrari 328 is simply more exciting than the new Porsche 968. Having said that, I must confess that I prefer the Porsche and find it a much more satisfactory car for daily use. It's more comfortable, more user-friendly, and almost as fast. It's silly, but for me there's an undeniable spiritual lift in the knowledge that I'm driving the largest four-cylinder engine (three liters) currently available in a passenger car. The Lotus Esprit's turbo four-banger may be more powerful, and the Saab turbos may be more exhilarating, but I make it up on volume.

Our government, long may it waver. So, the Clinton/Kantor International Trade SWAT team decided to wage war against your next-door neighbor, the ophthalmologist who was planning to buy a new Lexus LS400. Our government has demonstrated so little skill in its attempts to sort out our enemies that it apparently decided it would be more productive to beat up on our friends. We celebrated the fiftieth anniversary of the end of World War II in Europe with the Russians—who connived with the Germans to start the whole thing—and simultaneously snubbed our British allies. The Somalis think we're the biggest wussies in the world. The Bosnian Serbs have decided that we're more fun to watch than Comedy Central, and moon our aircraft as they leave contrails over the former Yugoslav skies. Given our sagging reputation for international leadership, why *not* renew the war with Japan as the fiftieth anniversary of V-J Day drew near?

There is one huge and overriding reason for the dramatic improvement in American-car quality in the past decade: The great superiority of Japanese cars, stealing market share from the domestics and thus goading them to do better. The argument between our bureaucrats and theirs was really about automotive parts, not automobiles, but it was Japanese luxury automobiles that our government set out to punish. In reality it's always the American consumer who gets hurt by this sort of brinkmanship over trade. The net-net of the Clinton/Kantor tariffs on Japanese luxury cars would be to curtail the automotive choices available to American car buyers, shut down a bunch of very expensive dealerships, and raise the prices of American cars. Thanks a lot.

Mr. Clinton may have hoped to regain some ground with organized labor by looking resolute against our Japanese friends and allies. But his administration's recent assault on free trade has alienated most of our friends and made us a number of enemies, and he'll probably *still* lose the support of that ophthalmologist who was about to buy an LS400. One wonders if the automobile owners and drivers of the United States have any friends at all inside the beltway.

God rest ye merry.

❧

hristmas is upon us, and it is safe to assume that my stocking will not contain the immaculate Lancia Aurelia coupe or the Churchill XXV shotgun that I have longed for so enthusiastically. Therefore, I have rigged the deal by arranging with Mr. Rob Robbins of Crestwood Dodge in Garden City, Michigan, to accept my wife's 1986 Ferrari 328GTS in trade on a new Dodge Viper RT/10. That way, even if my stocking contains the lump of coal so often threatened by my parents when my behavior went off the scope, I'll have a ridiculously merry Christmas. Mrs. Davis has not weighed in on this transaction, beyond barely audible grunts and imperceptible head shakes, but the deal is on track, and Mr. Robbins has suggested that I might even visit the Viper works to see my car being built. Too cool.

My Viper will be a white one with a blue racing stripe down its middle. It will have white wheels and a removable (hard) top panel. I ordered it with air conditioning for resale reasons, and because there have been enough 100-degree, 100 percent humidity days in my life that I know there'll be summer afternoons when I'll prefer to leave the roof in place. Amazingly, the Viper has enough headroom for me. I say "amazingly" because the car's windshield and top look so low, and because the only way I was ever truly comfortable in the Ferrari was with its top panel removed. I have now accumulated enough Viper miles to know that I love the car and know that we'll be very happy together. I've always believed that the faster car is the safer car, and I love having bags of torque at my disposal. There's huge gratification in having enough engine flexibility to be able to use the shift lever as a sort of final-drive pre-select, especially on long twisty sections of mountain road. How it behaves in the snow will be another matter, I guess.

I chose the white and blue color scheme, first, because I love the way it looks, and, second, because of the American tradition. The original rules for our national racing colors said that the bodywork should be white and the frame rails blue. When Briggs Cunningham arrived at Le Mans the first time in the early Fifties, his cars had no exposed frame rails, and he elected to go with the blue stripe as an acceptable substitute. I saw those great cars race several times, and the impression they left on my automotive sensibilities was as though graven in steel. I seriously considered ordering the Viper in red with yellow wheels, because that's exactly the way I painted my 1994 Ford pickup, and because both of the '96 Vipers I've driven have worn that paint scheme. I guess both Chrysler and I were inspired by the old Ferrari racing cars that were done that way. Those were years when I stood close to a lot of Ferrari racing cars and got to know a number of Ferrari drivers. I hope that none of them—alive or dead—takes offence at my memorializing those wonderful days with my F-150 four-by-four.

It's a very nice truck, even though I ordered it without all the bells and whistles. It has vinyl seats and rubber mats and hand-crank windows and no air conditioning. I replaced the original-equipment tires with some more aggressive Goodyear Wrangler GS-As, and they're terrific. We installed a Reese trailer hitch, then installed a special Warn grille guard that includes a bracket for a pair of Warn auxiliary lights and a two-inch trailer-hitch/receiver for a portable Warn Pull Pak 3500 winch. My last Warn winch was permanently installed inside the front bumper of my Toyota Land Cruiser (which now belongs to our art director, Larry Crane, winch and all) and Michigan's salty roads caused some corrosion around the terminals, rendering it *hors de combat*, and, of course, you never discover something like that until you need the winch. Now the winch stays dry and clean in the toolbox until I'm ready to use it. We powder-painted the grille, the grille guard, the Reese trailer hitch, and the bumpers in red to match the body color, using powder because those pieces will suffer a lot of wear and tear around the farm.

We drove a new Jaguar Vanden Plas (long wheelbase) to P.J. O'Rourke's wedding in Westport, Connecticut. The bride is Tina Mallon, a Washington, D.C., PR executive and surely one of the most courageous women in the world. P.J., in black tie, with a Montecristo No. 3 in his fist, greeted the guests on the terrace of the Cobb's Mill Inn. (P.J. had told a dozen or so randomly chosen invitees that the affair was black tie but neglected to tell the rest of us, so the male dress was, shall we say, eclectic.) Some of us, being of a serious turn of mind, had already spent some time in the bar. When the bride appeared she was radiant, as brides are supposed to be, and the short ceremony at the edge of the pond was accompanied by a raucous chorus of ducks—undoubtedly left-wing ducks blaming P.J. for the recent Contract with America.

Postnuptial conversation with the bride and groom was out of the question as they were too much in demand. I shouted my best wishes over the heads of a number of their admirers, the bride bobbed her head and smiled, and we legged it back to the bar. We saw no one with burning underpants on his or her head, so we can assume that the bride's parents had things pretty much under control.

On the way to Connecticut, we stopped at Bill Ruger's home in New Hampshire for a visit. He has built a new barn for the eastern half of his car collection, and they looked magnificent as Lyle Patterson drove them into place: a 1913-14 Rolls-Royce Alpine Tourer, a 1913 Mercer raceabout, a 1919 Stutz Model G, a 1922 Stutz KLDH, a 1928-29 Stutz four-passenger Fishtail Speedster, a 1933 Stutz Monte Carlo, a 1927 short-wheelbase Bentley Speed Six, a 1923 Kissel Gold Bug, 1923 and 1926 Wills Sainte Claires, a 1927 Type 43 Bugatti, a 1969 Ruger special, and a 1989 Ferrari Testarossa. Of these, the car that I most fancied was the Stutz four-passenger Speedster, red with black cycle fenders, probably much like the Stutz cars that ran at Le Mans in the late Twenties. I guess I'd rather have the Stutz than something like the Bentley, if only because I could drive it. My experience with Bentleys and Bugattis has been mostly uncomfortable and self-conscious. They're hard to drive, and I don't drive them very well, especially the Bentleys with their awkwardly placed shift levers. Larry Crane argues that I shouldn't take it personally, that everybody has trouble shifting the old Bentleys, but I remain doubtful.

On the second day of our stay, the Bugatti Owners Club arrived for lunch—about 180 members, with almost fifty cars—on their annual tour. The tour was winding down, and several members had left their Bugattis behind at the hotel and driven their support vehicles (including one Bentley Turbo R). As one lady put it, "My husband just couldn't steer anymore." However, there were still more than enough to go around. Type 35s, Type 43s, Type 57s, and a whole covey of spindly little Brescias filled the new-mown hayfield behind the house. Bill Ruger, directing the activity from a sort of industrial golf cart, said: "You'd better walk up there. They'll all be taking their engines apart." It was not the first time I'd heard about the tendency of truly *pur sang* Bugattistes to dismantle their engines and gearboxes on the spur of the moment (photographer Martyn Goddard says, "You can recognize them by the oil covering their shoes"), but this time it didn't happen. They were all in the tent attacking the hors d'oeuvres.

A few years ago we worried that all the great cars were being bought and hidden away by nouveau riche guys wearing gold chains and noisy after-shave lotion, but that crisis passed. Here were four dozen hugely expensive and well nigh irreplaceable thoroughbreds being driven as though they were late-model Porsches. A couple of years ago, David Holls, now the chief honorary judge at the Pebble Beach concours, said, "There's never been a better time than this to be a car enthusiast," and I'm inclined to agree.

Merry Christmas!

The Twenty-Four Most Important Automobiles of the Century

Two dozen cars that made a difference, and, in so doing, made history.

⚬⚬⚬

A designers' group asked me to think about the most important cars of the automobile's first century. I canvassed our staff and contributors for their opinions, and with a great deal of advice and sound critical judgment from art director Larry Crane and technical editor Kevin Clemens, winnowed the list down to two dozen. They are not simply cars that sold well or went fast. They are cars that we believe made a difference—cars that significantly influenced automotive history.

1908 Cadillac

By 1908, American car builders were well-versed in interchangeable manufacturing, a lesson they'd learned from the firearm manufacturers. European cars were still made one at a time, and replacement parts had to be carefully hand-fitted by skilled mechanics. A test was devised by Great Britain's Royal Automobile Club challenging manufacturers to prove the feasibility of interchangeability. Cadillac rose to the challenge. Three 1908 two-seater runabouts were completely disassembled. The parts, more than 2000 of them, were mixed together and randomly separated into three car-sets. Eighty-nine parts were then chosen to be replaced by standard replacement parts. By the end of the second day, the first reassembled car was up and running. Five days later all three cars were driven around the Brooklands track for 500 miles at full throttle. For this feat Cadillac became the first non-British manufacturer to win the Sir Thomas Dewar Trophy, awarded annually to the company that had made the most important advancement in the automotive field.

1908 Ford Model T

The Model T Ford began its remarkable nineteen-year, fifteen-million-unit production run in 1908. In 1909 production reached nearly 11,000 vehicles. In 1913 Ford produced more than 168,000 Model Ts, and America was suddenly on wheels. By 1918, half of the cars on the entire planet were Ford Motel Ts. As productivity improved through Henry Ford's creation of the first moving automotive assembly line, the price was cut repeatedly, making his simple, reliable car available to literally everyone. Ford loved his Model T so much that he stubbornly allowed it to overstay its welcome, nearly breaking the company before the advent of the Model A.

1912 Cadillac

In 1913, just five years after Cadillac won that first Dewar trophy, they captured another. Charles F. Kettering invented an electric starter for automobiles around the time a friend of Cadillac boss H.M. Leland was killed trying to crank-start a Cadillac. Kettering's solution was a combination motor and generator meshing with the fly-wheel. It was straightforward, it worked, and it made it possible for people with less than stellar upper-body development to drive. Cadillac introduced the Delco electric self-starter in 1912, and by 1916, 98 percent of American models in production featured electric start.

1914 Stutz Bearcat

If you say "sports car" to anyone my age or older, their immediate reaction is apt to be "Stutz Bearcat." Created by the flamboyant Harry C. Stutz and minimal in the extreme—consisting of little more than an engine, four wheels, a gas tank, and two seats—the Bearcat's purposeful appearance seems sports car even today. The Bearcat had a rear-mounted transaxle and was available with either a six- or a four-cylinder engine, and 1915 racing versions boasted sixteen valves and a single overhead camshaft. In 1915 Cannonball Baker drove a four-cylinder from San Diego to New York in a record eleven days, seven hours. I've driven one of these, and it is an astonishingly modern car.

1922 Lancia Lambda

Vincenzo Lancia's revolutionary Lambda of 1922 reads in specification much like today's cars: unit-body construction, independent front suspension, and a 2.1-liter four-cylinder engine with an overhead camshaft. Lancia developed the innovative monocoque chassis by noting the rigidity of a ship's hull and applying the concept to an all-steel body at a time when most car bodies were coachbuilt on wooden frames. Though the superb handling offered by the Lambda chassis left many with the impression that the car was meant to be a sports car, Vincenzo Lancia never intended it as such, and his comfortable touring car stayed in production until the end of 1931.

1926 Bugatti Type 35

When Ettore Bugatti introduced his Type 35 racing car in 1924, it began a period of more than seven years during which evolutions of that single model would dominate racing in Europe. More than that, it opened up racing by providing a car that allowed any talented driver a fair shot at winning. The Type 35 changed racing, taking it out of the hands of factory engineers and putting it into the hands of the drivers. In 1926 the Type 35 won twelve Grand Prix races, clinching the world championship. But the Type 35 wasn't just successful as a Grand Prix car. Simply by adding fenders and lights, the lightweight two-seater became one of the most successful of the era's sports cars.

1932 Duesenberg SJ

This was a car for a new kind of royalty, the stars of the Saturday matinee: Gary Cooper, James Cagney, Mae West, Clark Gable. Nothing was standard, everything could be changed and built to the needs of the customer. It was perhaps the last time that the best of American quality and refinement could and did compete with the best from Europe. Duesenberg's peak, in 1932, was the supercharged SJ model. The engine produced 320 bhp. Zero to 100 mph was possible in seventeen seconds, and the top speed was close to 130 mph, depending on the body style chosen. Duesenberg actually survived the Depression, only to collapse, along with other concepts of elegance and grace, in 1937.

1932 Ford V-8

The '32 Ford V-8 was the first car to uncouple performance from price. John Dillinger loved it. It was nothing short of a bombshell dropped on Ford's unsuspecting competition. A V-8 engine, at an affordable price (about $50 more than the four-cylinder engine), and in a car that almost anyone could afford. Almost 200,000 Ford V-8s were sold that first year, all that Henry's factory could build. The V-8 developed 65 bhp at 3400 rpm and could maintain 75 mph. It was offered in fourteen different body styles, and it featured one of the most beautiful radiator shells ever put on an automobile.

1934 Citroën Traction Avant

André Citroën envisioned a car that would combine most of the features seen on today's cars: unit-body construction, four-wheel independent suspension and torsion bars, front-wheel drive, and an automatic transmission (which didn't make it into production). The development costs were astronomical and eventually overwhelmed the company, which was sold to Michelin in 1934. André Citroën died a few months later, allegedly of a broken heart. Engineer André Lefebvre made Citroën's vision into brilliant reality, and the resulting Traction Avant remained in production until 1957.

1936 BMW 328

The 1936 BMW 328 established the benchmark for almost every sports car that would appear after the war and well into the mid-Sixties. The 328 ushered in a whole new era of sports cars with streamlined bodies and headlights integrated into the front fenders, hydraulic brakes acting on all four wheels, and high-rpm overhead-valve engines. Highly tuned versions raced in the Mille Miglia and at Le Mans, but like the Type 35 Bugatti of a decade earlier, the BMW 328 was most at home in the hands of a host of private owners. Ten years later, after World War II, BMW 328 components were used to create cars like the Frazer Nash, the Cooper-Bristol that launched Mike Hawthorn's racing career, the Tojeiro-Bristol that inspired the AC-Bristol, and the German Veritas. It was a truly seminal car.

1936 Cord 810

In 1936 the name Cord reappeared after being swallowed in 1932, a victim of the Depression. The new Cord 810 was an advanced aerodynamic concept from designer Gorden Buehrig and featured a 4.7-liter V-8 Lycoming engine that powered the front wheels. The shape was very aerodynamic with a wraparound grille and retractable headlamps. In spite of the aerodynamic shape, front-wheel drive, and the addition of the supercharged model 812, fewer than 2500 810 and 812 Cords were built before the company folded again in 1937. The body panels lived on in the Hupp Skylark and the Graham Hollywood, but its sales performance never lived up to the magic of its appearance.

1936 Fiat 500A Topolino

Dante Giacosa gave Italy its own people's car in 1936—the elegant little Fiat Topolino, perhaps the first truly modern economy car. Featuring a 570-cc four-cylinder engine, hydraulic brakes, independent front suspension with transverse springs, and a convertible (sliding roof) or coupe body, the aerodynamically streamlined car stayed in production largely unchanged until 1948. The high quality, light weight, and small size of the components used in the Topolino made them suitable for use in racing cars from specialists such as Abarth, Cisitalia, Gordini, Moretti, Siata, and Stanguellini, but the Topolino itself—the sum of those parts—was a truly beautiful little car that got the job done.

1945 Volkswagen Beetle

In 1924, Adolf Hitler envisioned a "small economical car that the little man could afford." By the time he was *Reichsführer* in the 1930s he was in a position to direct Ferdinand Porsche to design such a car, and the Volkswagen Beetle was the result. The Beetle was so successful that more than 20 million were made, and the car continues in production today in Mexico and Brazil. But the Volkswagen was more than just an inexpensive small car. The quality of the components not only ensured reliability, perhaps creating the mystique that still surrounds German craftsmanship, but also spawned several generations of racing cars, dune buggies—exemplified by the brilliant Meyers Manx—and ultimately the legendary sports cars that Porsche built bearing his own name.

1945 Willys Jeep CJ2A

The Jeep must surely be the most recognizable automobile in the world. Enzo Ferrari called it "America's only real sports car." Following its role in World War II, Willys sensed the workhorse capabilities for its rugged little vehicle and introduced the CJ2A civilian version in 1945, ten days after the victory in the Pacific. Farms, ranches, and oil fields replaced the battlefield as Jeeps evolved into practical go-anywhere vehicles through the Fifties. Ultimately, work led to play and Jeeps became the forerunners of what has become the huge sport-utility-vehicle market—the name Jeep at the pinnacle.

1948 Ferrari 166MM

Of all the significant Ferraris that have been built, the Touring-bodied 166MM is probably the most important. The V-12-engined roadster served to establish Enzo Ferrari as a manufacturer of racing cars, and its phenomenal success led to a larger-than-life aura that still surrounds the man and the company. The 166 used a steel tube frame with an aluminum body. In 1948, major victories included the Mille Miglia and the Targa Florio. In 1949, the little cars won again at the Targa Florio and the Mille Miglia, and Luigi Chinetti won the twenty-four-hour races at Le Mans and Spa. But more important, the shape of the 166MM Barchetta (little boat) influenced the way sports cars looked for another decade.

1949 Citroën 2CV

In the 1930s, Pierre Boulanger recognized the need for cheap, rugged, basic transportation for a new and much broader-based generation of car buyers. His specifications were simple: he asked for "an umbrella on four wheels" that could carry two peasants in their working clothes with 110 pounds of potatoes. If Boulanger's peasants were to put a box of eggs in it and drive it over a plowed field, not a single egg should be broken. André Lefebvre, the father of the Citroën Traction Avant, set about in 1936 building a car that would meet Boulanger's specifications.

The war intervened and the production of Boulanger's lightweight car had to wait until 1948. Eleven different variations of the 2CV were built over more than forty years of production.

1949 Jaguar XK120

I saw my first Jaguar XK120 in 1950, and it changed the course of my life. I never dreamed that an automobile could be so tiny or so exquisitely realized. When Williams Lyons launched his XK120 at the 1948 London Motor Show, he planned only a limited production of 200, but the XK120 was a huge success. Its sensuous curves created an instant car lust—like none before or since—and its racing and rallying successes, along with the success at Le Mans of the derivative C-Type racing car, saved Lyons's company. I was fortunate enough to race one in the middle Fifties, and I feel honored to have done so. Going back for a moment to the BMW 328, it is clear in hindsight that the aerodynamic 328 that won the 1940 Mille Miglia had a profound effect on the shape of Mr. Lyons's XK120. A total of 12,078 XK120s were made before the similar but less elegant XK140 replaced it in 1954.

1949 Oldsmobile Rocket 88

If ever an engine made a car, it was the Rocket V-8. The overhead-valve V-8 engine had been under development since World War II by General Motors chief of research Charles "Boss" Kettering, who we remember from the first electric self-starter in his Delco days. The architecture of the Rocket V-8, complete with overhead valves operated by hydraulic valve lifters, is only just now being replaced in America by V-8 engines with overhead camshafts. The Rocket V-8 was installed in the smaller, lighter 88 body shell to produce a very fast car—the first muscle car?—and pave the way for every lightweight V-8 that followed, including the small-block Chevy.

1953 Ford F-100

Until the appearance of the restyled Ford F-100 pickup in 1953, trucks were thought suitable only for commercial uses. But Ford's 1953 F-100 was the first truck planned, styled, and engineered by a corporate management team, and suddenly pickup trucks became an alternative for personal transportation. An all-new "driverized" cab had a large curved windshield, "armrest height" side windows, a wraparound instrument panel, and wider seats. Every comfortable, driver-friendly pickup on the road today owes its existence to the original Ford F-100.

1955 Citroën DS19

All of the innovations that made up the Citroën DS19 have found their way into modern cars. Advanced aerodynamics have become a feature of even the least expensive models, front-wheel drive is the propulsion of choice, and even the advanced hydropneumatic suspension system that was such a sensation in 1955 has been developed into the adaptive and active suspensions found on everything from Grand Prix cars to the late lamented Infiniti Q45a. What was remarkable about the DS19 and the subsequent ID19 and DS21 versions is that such sophistication was created for high-volume family cars and not for limited-production ultra-high-performance sports cars. The DS19 could cruise all day at high speeds, absorbing poor pavement surfaces with its sophisticated suspension and using very little fuel because of its slippery aerodynamics and frugal four-cylinder engine.

1959 Morris Mini

When Sir Alec Issigonis created the Mini, he designed in very broad margins of dynamic performance to guarantee, as nearly as possible, a very safe little car that would excel in accident avoidance. When the Mini was introduced, he was horrified to learn that people were driving it right to those limits every day, just for the pure joy of it. Its compact transverse front-engine front-wheel-drive powertrain allowed plenty of interior space for four people in an incredibly small package. The Mini used a rubber-based four-wheel independent suspension and tiny ten-inch wheels and tires. The handling was so good that in stock trim the little car could and did beat larger, more powerful cars on the racetrack. But the Mini was much more than a good racing car. It was a world better than any small car that had come before, and it set the pattern for many of the cars we now drive. The Mini remains in production today, with more than five million produced since 1959. In 1961, GM's great engineer Frank Winchell tried to convince his bosses that the Mini should be the blueprint for their new small car. They refused to take him seriously, and created the Chevrolet Vega instead.

1984 Chrysler Minivan

Chrysler was saved by the revolutionary minivan. Assembled from existing K-car components and Mitsubishi engines by the great Hal Sperlich, the concept created the cash flow that Chrysler Corporation needed to survive its early-1980s financial horrors. Volkswagen and Dodge had created boxy people movers before, but Chrysler's Dodge and Plymouth seven-passenger boxes created a whole new segment and all but killed the market for station wagons. The key to the Chrysler mini-

van was its carlike drivability. That feature, and the even more fundamental concept of a van that would fit in any suburban garage, made it
the logical choice for millions of American families. Whether called a
Plymouth Voyager, a Dodge Caravan, or a Chrysler Town & Country,
this is probably the most important car in the last quarter of the automotive century.

1986 Mercedes-Benz 300E

The 1970s left the automotive industry in a shambles. The evil
effects of Energy Crisis I, emissions control requirements, the beginnings
of legislated fuel economy, and newly awakened public interest in safety
had resulted in some truly terrible cars, especially in the United States.
The Mercedes-Benz 300E was a breakthrough, a car designed from the
ground up with these new priorities in mind. Its use of an ultra-stiff
body/chassis provided the perfect platform for exceptional comfort and
high-performance handling. Decades of Mercedes-Benz crash testing
created a progressively deformable structure that would sacrifice itself to
protect its occupants. But equally important, its power output, combined with excellent aerodynamics and low rolling resistance, made it
one of the first truly quick cars of the fuel-efficiency age. It still feels as
modern and fresh as when it was first introduced.

1990 Lexus LS400

After the huge Japanese success of the Seventies and Eighties,
there was only one automotive world left to conquer. The Lexus LS400
introduced a new luxury franchise for Toyota and revolutionized that
end of the business. The car was everything it needed to be: fast, luxuri-
ous, extraordinarily comfortable, and priced lower than its primarily
European competition. Its quality set new standards that have only
recently been reached by some of the competition. The appearance of the
LS400 has caused even old-line luxury makers like Mercedes to rethink
and revamp their product and pricing strategies worldwide.

That's the list. Highly personal, and subjective to a fare-thee-
well. Should the 1965 Ford Mustang have been included? Should there
be a Porsche on the list? Was the '55 Chevy small-block more important
than the 1949 Olds Rocket 88? If a tree falls in the forest, how many
angels can dance on the head of a pin?

The roadster legend.

~•~

My first car was a 1935 Mercedes-Benz roadster, purchased for one thousand dollars in 1951. An American colonel had brought it home from Germany, only to be defeated by its service needs. That car was my friend and constant companion for more than a year, until I decided to become a racing driver and sold it to raise money for a competitive entry-level sports car. I was living in a very small town, a hundred miles from my parents and my childhood. I worked at a variety of jobs during the days, and drove to see friends and farmland and forests (and life) in the nights. The car ran like a train. It had a six-cylinder engine and an overdrive transmission. We were a team, that car and I. I accelerated through its gears, pushed the lever to the overdrive fourth gear, waited a moment for it to engage, then droned across high-crowned two-lane country roads in the gathering dark. The top was stowed behind the seats. The warm wind wrapped the back of my neck like a scarf and the moon lit the backs of my hands on the steering wheel. The instruments glowed softly, barely legible in their faint yellow light. Sometimes I drove for miles without lights, just following the road by its contour and by the march of the utility poles stretching away toward the ends of the earth in the moonlight.

Going where? Going to see women who were sleepy and tousled and warm when I parked beneath their windows and walked quietly across the grass to their doors. Going to see old friends, who wanted to drink and talk about women whom they used to visit in the night. Going to a Gypsy restaurant where the owner played the violin and his wife accompanied him on the accordion and the hatcheck girl loved me. Going to the right, because that road led to a secluded lake. Going to the left, because the road seemed to promise more curves. Going to the end of the road, because I'd never been there before. Going to…I don't know where. Perhaps going to the future, to the rest of my life.

Then there was the MG. White, with black-edged yellow stripes over the louvered hood and front fenders. The grille painted checker-board. The engine was tuned to its limit. The exhaust pipe was a copper tube, one and a half inches in diameter. The sound was much greater than the performance, but to drive it fast was pure unbridled joy. The headlights were the best Marchals available at the time. On the badge bar stood a pair of Lucas flamethrowers that made the scenery of the night all flat white foreground, two-dimensional, pierced by the reflected light of deer's eyes in the forest that lined the road. My windscreen was fold-ed down and bugs stung my cheeks and forehead as I tore across the agri-cultural heartland.

We drive cars because they make us free. With cars, we need not wait in airline terminals, or travel only where the railway tracks go. Governments detest our cars: They give us too much freedom. How do you control people who can climb into a car at any hour of the day or night and drive to who knows where? An open car gives us another dimension of freedom. In an open car we enjoy the heightened freedom of the coursing hound, racing across the land with only the wind for clothing. It is the freedom of wild ducks, shining in their colorful plumage, flying at impossible speeds through the treetops to impress the duck-women they love. In a closed car, the world is a horizontal place, seen through windows that are too much like television screens. In an open car, the world becomes properly round above us, a vast dome of pure possibility, limited only by what we know of the universe. In an open car on an open road, we can feel what that man felt eons ago, when he first managed to grab a horse's mane, throw himself on its back, and feel himself transported at unthinkable speed into mankind's next stage of development.

In the beginning, all cars were sports cars. Only the most ven-turesome travelers chose the automobile over the more reliable trains and horses of that era. When the internal combustion engine at last became useful, it was simply bolted into the front ends of wagons and carriages, where the horses used to be. Those wagons and carriages suddenly found themselves being propelled at greater rates of speed than those for which they were designed, and it was all pretty exciting for their drivers and passengers. Over the years, as speeds increased, the vehicles became more comfortable and secure, offering better weather protection to their occu-pants, but the real sports, the true believers, still wanted to feel the wind and sun on their faces, and the cars that made it possible for them to do this were called roadsters, spyders, cabriolets, phaetons, touring cars, and—sometimes—sports cars.

A sports car is one which offers more sport than utility. One in which fun is a more important design goal than practicality. In the early days, sports cars were simply racing cars that had been modified sufficiently to make them legal, or appropriate, for use on the public roads. Today's sports car is more apt to be a fully tamed production model offering all the amenities, but still spiced with the zesty flavor of those great bellowing crudenesses that smoked across the country roads of our grandfathers. To quote a dear friend and mentor of mine, Barney Clark: The modern sports car is a "child of the magnificent ghosts." One puts down the top, sets off down a country road, and relives years and miles of automotive legends.

Once, years ago, I was involved in an imported car dealership in a university town. Our service manager was something of a loner, a man who kept to himself and told us little of his life beyond the hydraulic lifts and Craftsman tools. From what I knew of this guy, he loved four things: Three were tattered BMW 328 sports cars and the fourth was any woman who would go home with him. "Home" was a tiny rented house full of BMW 328 parts. One speculates as to why any woman would have gone home with him in the first place, but the mind boggles at what she must have felt when he unlocked the door and she saw that they would be sharing the single bed with a cylinder head and a bouquet of pushrods. Nonetheless, his enthusiasm for the 328 communicated itself to me, and I grew particularly fond of its lovely two-liter engine. I drove Arnolt-Bristols powered by that engine, and to this day I long to own a 328-powered LeMans Replica Frazer-Nash, surely one of the most delicious sports cars of the automotive century.

I still drive open cars with great enthusiasm. I recently fulfilled two of my automotive dreams: One, by actually owning a beautiful Kougar-Jaguar, a modern replicar that looks a bit like my beloved Frazer-Nash; and, two, by finally getting rid of it. I had begun to believe that I was the last man in North America to want a Kougar-Jaguar. It was a car without a top, without doors, without windshield wipers, and it taught me a great deal about the proper clothing for open car motoring. Sheepskin coats and trousers like those worn by air crews in World War II are very nice, and very popular, but they're bulky and restrictive and they are not waterproof. I prefer the Barbour line of outdoor clothing, made in Great Britain. It is absolutely waterproof—being constructed of oiled cotton—and when worn in combination with wool, silk, cashmere, polyfleece, or quilted down, it will protect one from anything the weather gods have to offer. For headgear, nothing beats the old leather or cloth flying helmet that buckles under the chin. This is absolutely secure, will not blow off, and keeps the ears warm. It is hard on the coiffure, but it works. A full coverage racing helmet is also warm and relatively comfortable, but it does make you look ridiculous backing out of your suburban driveway. English flat caps look wonderful, especially on women, but they tend to blow off at high speeds. Never, ever, wear the sort of baseball caps with advertising messages so favored by the more feckless Americans.

Is an open car the answer to all of your transportation needs? Probably not, at least not entirely. But, will a fast drive on an open road in an open car lift your heart and light your dreams? Of course it will, unless you have no heart and no dreams. Open cars transport us, not just in the sense of getting from home to work, but by showing us a side to life we might otherwise have missed. They put the fun back into driving, and they remind us of a time when automobiles represented the sum of human progress, and the people who designed, built, and drove them were heroes.

Coda.

~⚜~

There you have it. I was thirty-two years old when I joined *Car and Driver* magazine in 1962, and sixty-six years old when I wrote the final column selected to be included here from the pages of *Automobile Magazine.* I'm sorry that I have nothing to show for the time I spent earlier at *Road & Track* magazine, 1957 to 1960, but I was, after all, an advertising salesman, and the ad salesman's paper trail is not a very interesting one. I did write an ad for a nice couple who were selling chamois cloths in the pages of *R&T.* The headline was "I Wish I Could Chamois Like My Sister Kate." I even wrote a road test or two, but my real mission was to learn everything I could about this wonderful corner of the publishing business. My years at *Road & Track* were very, very important in everything that followed. My bosses at Campbell-Ewald Advertising later told me that silly chamois ad was the item in my scanty portfolio that tweaked their interest and got me hired. Whatever it takes, right?

The experience gained at *Road & Track* and Campbell-Ewald made it possible for me to hit the ground running at *Car and Driver.* I had watched Chevrolet and General Motors interact with their advertising agency, and learned a great deal about what a major automotive client expects from the advertising media, particularly magazines. I had been plunged into the middle of a vast creative department full of talented writers, art directors, and broadcast producers who were without doubt the funniest, most stimulating, off-the-wall personalities I'd ever encountered. After three years among them I knew that I wanted to do a magazine that would capture their attention. I had listened to them joke and discuss the events of the day. I had learned what tickled their fancy and what bored them. I believed that if I could produce a car enthusiast's magazine that they'd discuss over coffee in the morning, I'd be on my way to a commercial success.

When I was offered the editor's chair at *Car and Driver* in 1962, I was ready. I would strive to create the best written and best edited magazine in the automotive field—a magazine with editorial standards fully as high as those of the best magazines on American newsstands, in any category. If the critics were prepared to take fashion magazines seriously, if they could respect magazines about food or film or art then, by God, they could be seduced by a properly done magazine about automobiles. My plan was that simple, and it worked. When the writers and graphic artists in the field learned what I was trying to do, I suddenly had my pick of talented, highly motivated people who loved cars. With their help, most of my dreams came true.

Through it all, I knuckled my brow, stared at the walls, and told my stories to various typewriters, yellow legal pads, and, now, computers. In 1960, my friend and co-worker Elmore Leonard admonished me to write the way I talked, and I worked hard to do that. He also taught me to read my stuff aloud to some real or imaginary audience, as a test. Was it conversational? Was it logical in its flow? Could it have been read aloud by a complete stranger and still say what I'd set out to say? Later, as that process refined itself, it became a closed loop, and I worked as hard to speak like I wrote as I did to write like I spoke. I still read everything aloud—as my unfortunate wife will attest—and I still think of Dutch Leonard every time I do so. I see myself as a guest in the homes of several hundred thousand avid car enthusiasts each month, talking about what I've driven, where I've been, and who I've met. I strive to be entertaining as well as informative, because I want to be liked, to be remembered, to be invited back. It usually works.

David E. Davis, Jr.
Ann Arbor, Michigan
June 1999

Index